Gihan Adam Abdalla

The Influence of Financial Relations on Sustaining Rural Livelihood in Sudan

AF827990

Spektrum

Berlin Series on Society, Economy and Politics in Developing Countries

edited by

Prof. Dr. Dr. Dr. Ulrich van der Heyden
Prof. Dr. Volker Lühr
PD Dr. Ulrike Schultz
Prof. Dr. Manfred Schulz

Volume 108

LIT

Gihan Adam Abdalla

The Influence of Financial Relations on Sustaining Rural Livelihood in Sudan

Reflecting the Significance of Social Capital in the Village Al Dagag, North Kordofan State

LIT

Cover Photo: Giahn Adam Abdalla

Thanks to Günter Lorenzl and Margret Otto for financing
the publication of the book

Bibliographic information published by the Deutsche Nationalbibliothek
The Deutsche Nationalbibliothek lists this publication in the Deutsche Nationalbibliografie; detailed bibliographic data are available in the Internet at http://dnb.d-nb.de.

ISBN 978-3-643-90403-4
Zugl.: Berlin, Freie Universität, Diss., 2012

A catalogue record for this book is available from the British Library

©LIT VERLAG GmbH & Co. KG Wien,
Zweigniederlassung Zürich 2013
Klosbachstr. 107
CH-8032 Zürich
Tel. +41 (0) 44-251 75 05
Fax +41 (0) 44-251 75 06
E-Mail: zuerich@lit-verlag.ch
http://www.lit-verlag.ch

LIT VERLAG Dr. W. Hopf
Berlin 2013
Fresnostr. 2
D-48159 Münster
Tel. +49 (0) 2 51-62 03 20
Fax +49 (0) 2 51-23 19 72
E-Mail: lit@lit-verlag.de
http://www.lit-verlag.de

Distribution:
In Germany: LIT Verlag Fresnostr. 2, D-48159 Münster
Tel. +49 (0) 2 51-620 32 22, Fax +49 (0) 2 51-922 60 99, E-mail: vertrieb@lit-verlag.de

In Austria: Medienlogistik Pichler-ÖBZ, e-mail: mlo@medien-logistik.at
In the UK: Global Book Marketing, e-mail: mo@centralbooks.com
In North America: International Specialized Book Services, e-mail: orders@isbs.com
e-books are available at www.litwebshop.de

To my son Mohamed and my daughter Ayat who missed me the most during the different stages of this research. I cannot forget what Mohamed said one day. That evening I returned from the library, it was raining heavily and I had forgotten my jacket. When I reached home Mohamed met me at the door and said:
"Mama, when it started raining I was thinking and worried about you because you forgot to take your jacket in the morning".

and

To those who gave me their unconditional love and care.

"In Al Dagag we are one big family, we help each other, and if I know someone does not have food for his kids I take my food and go to eat with them."

In-depth Interview with Abdulrahman, 2010

Table of Contents

List of Tables and Figures

Abstract

Finance has been realized as an imperative aspect of economic development. Economists have usually linked the financial development to the economic development of a country and to the alleviation of poverty as well. It would be easier to understand, explain and assess the effects of finance if it was linked to more specific and related approaches like the livelihood one. This research started with a vision to portray the Sudanese rural livelihood and the question whether microfinance is able to sustain rural livelihood. Al Dagag village in North Kordofan State, Sudan is chosen to be the research case study. However many further questions arose due to using the inductive methodology of Grounded Theory. Throughout the entire research process different categories emerged from the data, which conceptualize the perspective of the rural people on livelihood and microfinance. This perspective suggested integrating the discussion of poverty and vulnerability within the livelihood thinking. The path to remodel the livelihood approach by use of the constructivist Grounded Theory methodology led to including the determinants of the rural livelihood such as the household composition and the decision making process and household livelihood strategies. Moreover, the analysis of interviews prompted the focus on two types of capital, the economic including the financial and the social capital that both seem to have a significant impact on rural livelihood. The significance of the social capital was revealed to be essential. It emerged from the data to shift the question of the research from the concept of microfinance to the concept of financial relations, which seems to include various types of financial institutions and practices that go beyond the concept of microfinance in its institutionalized or formalized way, which are part of the current microfinance revolution in Sudan. Thus, indigenous financial mechanisms such as *Shail* and *Sandouqs* were examined in detail as their importance to the people's livelihood was suggested and also the mechanisms of the social capital type like *Wajib* and *Nafeer*, which were revealed to be the first choice of the respondents to deal with poverty and vulnerability and have tremendous effects on people's livelihood. It has been revealed from the interviews that the microfinance in its institutionalized form (in the case of Al Dagag village provided by International Fund for Agriculture Development, IFAD, and the Agriculture Bank of Sudan, ABS) has left minimal impacts on the livelihood of the rural people. Due to several problems presented in this research, from the perspectives of the rural people themselves even after receiving microfinance from these institutions the majority of respondents fares the same like before or is even worse off. The main result of this research shows that microcredit with weak savings component and with no insurance mechanisms is not sustainable in such poor and vulnerable situations.

Der Einfluss finanzieller Beziehungen auf die Sicherung ländlicher Livelihoods im Sudan: Die Bedeutung von Sozialkapital im Dorf Al Dagag im Bundesstaat Nord Kordofan

Das Finanzwesen ist als ein bedeutender Aspekt ökonomischer Entwicklung erkannt worden. Ökonomen haben finanzielle Entwicklung meistens mit der ökonomischen Entwicklung eines Landes in Verbindung gebracht und ebenso mit Armutsminderung. Es wäre einfacher, die Auswirkungen des Finanzwesens zu verstehen, zu erklären und zu erfassen, wenn sie mit spezifischeren, verwandten Ansätzen zusammengebracht würden, wie dem Livelihood Ansatz. Dieses Forschungsprojekt begann mit einer Vision, Lebensunterhaltssicherung und Livelihood im ländlichen Sudan zu portraitieren, und mit der Frage, ob Mikrofinanzierung den Lebensunterhalt auf dem Lande sichern kann. Das Dorf Al Dagag im Bundesstaat Nord Kordofan wurde als Fallstudie ausgesucht. Viele Fragen kamen jedoch hinzu, da die induktive Forschungsmethodologie der Grounded Theory verwendet wurde. Im gesamten Verlauf der Forschung entstanden verschiedene Kategorien aus den Daten, die die Perspektive der Menschen auf dem Land auf Lebensunterhalt und Minkrofinanzierung konzeptualisieren. Diese legte nahe, die Diskussion um Armut und Vulnerabilität in die Diskussion des Livelihood Ansatzes zu integrieren. Der Weg zur Remodellierung des Livelihood Ansatzes mittels der konstruktivistischen Grounded Theory Methodologie führte dahin, die bestimmenden Faktoren des ländlichen Lebens einzuschließen, etwa die Haushaltzusammensetzung und den Entscheidungsfindungsprozess und Überlebensstrategien der Haushalte. Außerdem ergab sich aus der Analyse der Interviews die Anregung, sich genauer mit zwei Kapitalsorten zu befassen, dem ökonomischen einschließlich finanziellen Kapital und dem Sozialkapital, die beide eine bedeutende Wirkung auf den ländlichen Lebensunterhalt aufzuweisen scheinen. Die Bedeutung des Sozialkapitals wurde als wesentlich offengelegt. So ergab es sich aus den Daten, die Forschungsfrage vom Mikrofinanzkonzept zum Konzept der finanziellen Beziehungen zu verschieben, die verschiedene Typen finanzieller Institutionen und Praxen zu beinhalten scheinen, die über das Konzept der Mikrofinanzierung in seiner institutionalisierten oder formalisierten Form hinausgehen, was Teil der gegenwärtigen Mikrofinanzierungs-Umwälzung im Sudan ist. Deshalb wurden indigene Finanzmechanismen wie *Shail* und *Sandouqs* detailliert untersucht, deren Wichtigkeit für das Überleben der Leute angedeutet wurde, und auch die sozialkapitalseitigen Mechanismen wie *Wajib* und *Nafeer*, die sich als die erste Wahl der Befragten herausstellten, um mit Armut und Vulnerabilität umzugehen, und eine gewaltige Wirkung auf den Lebensunterhalt der Menschen haben. Es hat sich aus den Interviews offenbart, dass Mikrofinanzierung in institutionalisierter Form (im Fall Al Dagags bereitgestellt durch den International Fund for Agriculture Development, IFAD, und die Landwirtschaftsbank Sudan, ABS) minimale Wirkung auf die Lebenssicherung der Landbevölkerung hatte. Aufgrund mehrerer in dieser Arbeit dargestellter Probleme, geht es aus der Perspektive der Landbevölkerung selbst der Mehrheit der Befragten nach Inanspruchnahme von Mikrofinanzierung von diesen Institutionen genauso wie vorher oder sogar schlechter. Das Hauptergebnis dieser Forschung zeigt, dass Mikrokredit mit einer geringen Sparkomponente und ohne Versicherungsmechanismen in solch armen und verwundbaren Umständen nicht nachhaltig ist.

Acknowledgements

For me this research was more an intensive learning process than conducting a PhD research project. During all stages, I have learnt so much about the topic, conducting qualitative research and grounded theory and many other things in both the academic and the social life in Berlin, Germany as well as in Al Dagag, Sudan. Thus, many people and institutions deserve my deepest heartfelt thanks and gratefulness.

First of all, I'm very very very thankful to my supervisor Ulrike Schultz who was always and deeply involved during all phases of this research including the field work; this was helpful because for me it was the first time to conduct a qualitative research and to use grounded theory. She visited the village Al Dagag in Sudan with me and she attended parts of the data collection procedures. Also from her, I have learnt many issues about grounded theory and I appreciate that she introduced me and trained me personally how to use the atlas.ti computer software. I am extremely thankful for the time she spent reading my simple ideas; moreover without her advice, suggestions, directing me to the reading materials, and of course critique, this research would never have gone initial stages. Her presence in both the academic and the social life spheres in Berlin was very supportive and has provided me with a sense of security.

I am also thankful for my second supervisor Cjlia Harders for her knowledge, help and support thoroughout the period of the study. She is the one who helped in finding funds for proofreading, without her efforts, this assignment could not have been done.

I am extremely grateful for the people in the village Al Dagag who were so friendly and patient during my long stay in their houses and fields, interviewing them for hours. Their contributions brought tremendous insights to the general knowledge about the topic. Many thanks to those of them who have been calling me and caring about the results until the time these words are put on paper.

Special thanks are extended to the DAAD, the prosperous German institution for funding the first two years of this research. I would also like to extend many thanks to Ahfad University for Women in Sudan, the institution for the financial support provided during the three stages of field work and the staff and friends for their help and support. I am also grateful to the experts and staff of institutions, mainly IFAD, ABS, and the microfinance experts I interviewed in Sudan for their time and appreciated knowledge. Many thanks also to the colleagues in the two colloquiums of Ulrike Schultz and Cjlia Harders at the Free University Berlin for their comments and contributions and to the staff of libraries in Germany and in Sudan. And thanks to Daniel Kumitz, the proof reader.

Finally yet importantly, I would like to thank all my family members, Magdi, the field work assistant Walla Nogdalla, and the many friends in Germany or in Sudan for their truly wonderful support and being there for me at any time.

List of Acronyms

ABS:	Agricultural Bank of Sudan
ACORD:	Agency for Cooperation and Research Development
ADB:	African Development Bank
ADS:	Area Development Schemes
BAAC	Bank of Agriculture and Agricultural Cooperatives Thailand
CBC:	Commercial Banks Consortium
CBS:	Central Bank of Sudan
CBOs:	Community Based Organizations
CC:	Credit Co-Operative
CGAP:	Conductive Group to Assist the Poor
CPA:	Comprehensive Peace Agreement
DFID	Department of International Development
DUGAP:	Dutch University Gadaref Assistance Program
etc.	et cetera
FAO	Food and Agriculture Organization
FDI	Foreign Direct Investment
GDP	Gross Domestic Product
GT	Grounded Theory
GTZ	Deutsche Gesellschaft für Internationale Zusammenarbeiten
IFAD	International Fund for Agriculture Development
IMF	International Monetary Fund
KORAG	Kordofan Rain-fed Agricultural Project
INGOs	International Non-governmental Organizations
MDG	Millennium Development Goals
MDF	Microfinance Development Facility
MFU	Microfinance Unit
MFIs	Microfinance Institutions
MOF	Ministry of Finance and National Economy
NCF	National Consultative Forum
NELM	New Economics of Labour Migration
NESP	National Economics Salvation Program
NGOs	Non-governmental Organizations
NKRDP	North Kordofan Rural Development Project
NKS	North Kordofan State
PASED	Port-Sudan Association for Small Enterprises Development
PRA	Participatory Rural Appraisal
ROSCAs	Rotating Savings and Credit Association
SDA	Sudanese Development Association
SDF	Social Development Foundation
SDD	Sudan Dinar (old Sudanese currency)
SMEs	Small and Micro Enterprises
S£	Sudanese Pound
SSDB	Savings and Social Development Bank
UN	United Nations
UNDP	United Nations Development Program
UNICEF	United Nation's Children's Fund
USAID	United States Agency for International Development
VDCL	Village Development Committees Law
WB	World Bank
WCED	World Commission on Environment and Development
WHO	World Health Organization
WCED	World Commission on Environment and Development

Glossary of Arabic Words and Measurements

Al gafaf al kabeer	The big drought
Al gafaf al sager	The small drought
Al Khala	Open space, which is not inhabited by people
Al Maeesha	The livelihood
Allah Kareem	God is the greatest
Ameer	The head of the native system
Asida	Porridge
Bait	House
Berak	Small surface water reservoirs
Dahwa	Working shifts that starts early in the morning and ends afternoons
Doom	Type of tree (scientific name Hyphaene Thebaica (Thaita))
Durdur	Rooms in shape of huts; mud is used to construct the lower part and thatch for the top part
Eid	Muslim festival
Elkifaya	Self- sufficiency
Gameea	Non-rotating indigenous associations for sugar contributions
Gharar	Ambiguity
Guntar	(measurement) One Guntar = 143.8 kilogram
Guran	Contribution of people in cash or in-kind on sad occasions like death
Hafeer	Small man-made surface water reservoir
Hail	Something to support or pillar
Haya Kareema	The decent life
Hila/Halal	Village or part of the village
Ijara	Equivalent to the leasing and installment-loan, hire-purchase, practices that put millions of drivers on the road each year. These techniques as applied by Islamic banks include the requirement that the leased items be used productively and in ways permitted by Islamic law.
Jubraka	Small gardens near or inside the house used to grow certain crops
Karama	Money shared to buy some goods to be distributed between the contributors
Khalowa	Schools for teaching the holy book of Islam, Quranic school
Khour	Small seasonal river
Khulud	A small vessel filled with crops or sugar or coffee brought to the women who have an occasion like birth giving by the people with whom she has social connections
Mafrag al habatain	The small space between two parts of one seed, e. g. groundnuts
Maisir	Gambling
Mal al tanmeea	Money for development

Mehjar	A common place in the village for keeping livestock
Mid	(measurement) One Mid = 508.75 gram
Miskeen	Poor person but not destitute.
Modam	Destitute
Mudaraba	This implies a contract between two parties whereby one party, the rabb al-mal (beneficial owner or the lender), entrusts money to the other party called the mudarib (managing trustee or the labour partner).
Mukhamas	One Muchamus = 3.75 feddan and One feddan = 0.42 hectare
Mulah	Sauces
Muqarada	This technique allows a bank to float what are effectively Islamic bonds to finance a specific project. Investors who buy muqaradah bonds take a share of the profits of the project being financed, but also share the risk of unexpectedly low profits, or even losses. They have no say in the management of the project, but act as non-voting shareholders.
Murabaha	Islamic mode of finance; based on sales
Musana	A contract in which a party orders another to manufacture and provide a commodity, the description of which delivery date, price and payment date are all set in the contract.
Musharaka	Islamic mode of finance of partnership
Muzara	Islamic mode of finance specialized for agriculture
Nafeer	Group work done for free to help someone in need
Nasee	A rope made of *Doom* tree leaves, used for building houses and roofs out of grass
Neem	Type of tree (scientific name Azaderechta Indica)
Quard Hassan	Loans without interest
Qur'an	The holy book of Islam
Rahad	Large water reservoirs
Ratul	(measurement) One Ratul = 450 gram
Riba	Usury
Sack	(measurement) one sack = 105.7 liters based on the U.S. bushel, or 109.1 liters based on the British Imperial bushel
Sahra	Working shift starts with sunset and ends at or after midnight
Salam	A buyer pays in advance for a specified quantity and quality of a commodity, deliverable on a specific date, at an agreed price. This financing technique, similar to a futures or forward-purchase contract, is particularly applicable to seasonal agricultural purchases, but it can also be used to buy other goods in cases where the seller needs working capital before he can deliver.
Samin	Butter
Sandouq or *Khata*	Rotating saving and credit association
Santa	Crop disease
Sarba	Working shift starts in the afternoon and ends with sunset
Sewal	Contribution of people on happy occasions like weddings

Shaikh	Local chief of the native system at village level
Shail	Indigenous money lending system
Sharia	Islamic Law
Sharoopa	Crop disease
Tablia	Table used for selling things in small amounts in front of the house or in the communal places
Takaful	Helping each other (social insurance)
Tawaree	Emergencies/shocks
Turdah	Medium water reservoirs
Tyjara Sabat	Basket trade that is used in petty trading by door–to–door vendors
Umda	Local chief of a group of Shaikhs of the native system
Usra	Family
Wadi	Valley
Wajib	Contribution paid in cash or in-kind to persons who have an occasion
Zakat	Islamic taxes
Zalabeea	Cakes that are commonly cooked in Al Dagag especially for group gatherings like in case of Nafeer
Zareeba	Place for keeping livestock in the house

1 The Context of the Research

1.1 Introduction of the Research

In Sudan as in other "developing countries"[1], people living in rural and remote areas are considered chronically poor. They are identified with their poor situations and lack of access to livelihood capital, i. e. economic, financial, human, and physical capital. Rural livelihood is also characterized by high risk, stress and natural disasters that endanger people's lives and capital and contribute to worsening poverty and vulnerability among other dimensions of deprivation.

Dependency on agriculture, especially rain-fed, which is the main rural livelihood pattern, is considered one factor that renders the livelihood of rural people vulnerable to threats like seasonality of rains. The situation of rural poor deteriorates due to many challenges in the rural environment; developmental efforts until now have not yet enhanced people's livelihoods in Sudan as well as in most other developing countries (Ellis, 2000).

Among all this deprivation the main finding of this research shows a distinctive advantage in rural Sudan, the social capital. I have intentionally omitted it from the set of forms of capital mentioned above when describing poverty, for social capital is what the rural poor rely on and use to compensate lack of other forms of capital; they keep it functioning from one generation to another. The main reason is simple, in the absence or existence of inappropriate developmental efforts of external organizations, social capital, social networks and indigenous institutions and arrangements play a significant role in sustaining people's wellbeing and security. They constitute the cultural institutions of the Sudanese community, where traditions, norms and beliefs shape the social structure of the society, reflecting concepts like solidarity and mutual help. This distinctive feature is clear in the village studied in this research, Al Dagag, in the North Korfodan State. It is typical for Sudan in aspects like the social structure of the rural village where the family and households are still considered a unit of social institution and social relationships. Families and households are further connected to a wider set of relationships that reflect the tribal settings, which play a significant role in Al Dagag. The family structure I found in Al Dagag is embedded in the concept of the "peasant household" found in the literature (e. g., Bernstein et al., 1992; Evers and Schrader, 1994; Grawert, 1998) where social and economic activities are considered shared and influenced by social capital. Moreover, the nature of livelihood of rural people, the production systems and types of division of labor are all shaped by the social capital. Another issue also unique in Al Dagag is related to the gradual transformation of rural livelihood, which is obvious in the many changes that are taking place over time.

Inevitably, a vision to portray how people live in villages in rural Sudan developed through time when I participated in implementing rural development activities in different rural areas of Sudan. I realized also from interviews that it is impossible to study rural livelihood without elucidating poverty and vulnerability[2] themes; these are the topics rural people talk about. Nevertheless, I understand that rural life cannot be reduced to these concepts. I found out that it is not only remarkable to picture how people suffer and live in miserable situations in many rural areas but more importantly, how they survive and deal with such situations. Thus, the scope to study rural villages explicitly includes the analysis of livelihood activities, strategies and capital that enhance people to build sustainable livelihoods.

The vision of portraying rural livelihood including poverty and vulnerability is initially linked to a question that recently arose in Sudan whether microfinance is an appropriate tool to alleviate poverty

---

[1] I use the terms development and poor considering the audience in Sudan, where they are used by academics and politicians, simply because they include many aspects like economic political disadvantages. However I'm aware of the fact that these concepts are criticized in the international thinking for discrediting countries of the South and positioning them in degradation to the developed countries. I'm also aware of the debate over aid provided from the "North "to the "South" and whether this aid leads to any sort of improvement and if it is aid at all given the global trade relations. This issue is also debated within the discussion about the provision of microfinance in this research.

[2] In the context of this research, the concept of poverty is going to be elaborated later within the livelihood approach. That is to say, poverty in this research is not only the income poverty alone or basic needs or capabilities but also to include all types of livelihood capital, capabilities, and resources (that do not include the social capital which found to be rich and supportive for sustaining rural livelihood).

in general and how this could be achieved specifically in the remote rural areas where there is no access to formal finance. This takes place within the existing discussion about the role of finance to help the poor. Finance is then seen as one of the solutions to alleviate poverty. During my research, the question gradually transformed to include other financial relations that might exist between borrowers, lenders and savers. This transformation is suggested and grounded in the data to reveal that the poor resort to indigenous financial and social relations as a source of finance. This might take place even in the existence of formal opportunities, especially when the latter show a degree of inappropriateness to deal with the poor and their situation. Hence, elaborating the financial demand of the rural poor seemed important and the main argumentation was thus broadened to discuss informal financial arrangements amongst the other relations that were crucial to shaping rural livelihood.

Providing microfinance is believed to be significant in alleviating poverty in Sudan (UNICONS, 2006). Huge efforts are taking place to reform the financial sector in the urban areas in addition to attempts to reach the poor especially in rural areas. This takes place through shifting polices from managing conflicts including the war between the South and North that lasted for two decades, to pursuing pro-poor development efforts to reduce escalating poverty[3]. The Central Bank of Sudan (CBS) has allocated huge amounts of funds to the sector of microfinance (Central Bank of Sudan, 2008). The CBS aims at supporting the microfinance sector by establishing different and specialized institutions, offering capacity building, downscaling banks and providing a regulatory framework that enhances rules and regulations for all institutions working in the sector. (UNICONS, 2006; CBS, 2007) The main motivation behind these efforts is the debate in the international development sector that has taken place since the 1980s and1990s and identifies microfinance as a significant contribution to reduce the number of poor around the world based on the successful Grameen Bank experience in Bangladesh[4].

Looking at the financial landscape in Sudan and the efforts of the CBS since 2002 and comparing this to the advances of the microfinance thinking raises various debatable issues. Keeping in mind the national efforts to liberalize and Islamize the financial sector in Sudan, what is revealed form this comparison is the fact that recently the microfinance sector around the world has been commercializing rapidly, which leads to regard microfinance as a poverty trap (Lont and Hospes, 2004; Bateman, 2010; Roy 2010). It is clear that the efforts of developing the financial sector to serve "the poor" in Sudan lags behind and does not benefit from previous and other experiences around the world. Moreover, the effects of liberalization are not fully realized and the efforts to Islamize the whole financial sector do not incorporate the exact meaning of the Islamic finance that emphasizes the partnership between lenders and borrowers of profits or loss (*Musharaka*) (Rahman, 1995; Imady and Seibel, 2006).

In addition to that, in the efforts to enhance the microfinance sector in Sudan, the informal and community based financial relations are ignored, even though they have been embedded in the society and trusted by the people for a long time. The indigenous institutions constitute the only resort for the poor, even in the existence of the formal financial services that undertake much regulated and aggressive lending procedures. It is obvious that the money lending system of *Shail* and the role of Rotating Savings and Credit Associations (ROSCAs) which are called *Sandouqs* in Sudan are completely ignored. Meanwhile, around the world, the role and importance of indigenous institutions in providing finance for the poor is recognized and efforts are increased to link them with the formal financial system (Krahnen and Schmit, 1994; Nagarajan and Meyer, 2005) whereas in Sudan they are either resisted or ignored. The effectiveness of these informal indigenous financial arrangements is revealed and elaborated in the findings of this research.

It is also revealed that the main reason for the effectiveness of indigenous financial arrangements stems from the fact that they are linked with the social capital. One of the aims of this research is to elaborate on the social relations and networks that are based on reciprocity, in which much of the rural financial capital is exchanged. This follows Bourdieu's (1986) explanation of social capital and the whole idea of capital types and their conversion. Thus, going beyond the classic approach in development theory and practice that favors formal finance and formal institutions, my research puts a focus

---

[3] Most of the information and references used in this research are referring to the one Sudan before the separation of the two countries

[4] However the experience of Grameen bank is also debatable and recent critiques show many weaknesses and view it as inappropriate for poverty alleviation, for the percentage of poverty is still increasing in Bangladesh (Compassion Politics, 2009; Kalajian, 2007).

on the question of what about the local arrangements of people? Are they valuable? Which are more appropriate and why? This is conducted in comparison between the formal and the informal financial opportunities and institutions rural people have access to.

The case of the village Al Dagag in NKS allows for this because it shows a diversified range of financial institutions, and a combination of informal rural indigenous arrangements and formal institutions. The latter are represented in the work of the International Fund for Agriculture Development (IFAD) that works in collaboration with the Agriculture Bank of Sudan (ABS) in the town Al Rahad. The IFAD project was implemented in NKS in the period between 2001 and 2007 and aimed at poverty alleviation and the enhancement of local and natural resources generally and included a component of rural finance. NKS is considered one of the poorest states in Sudan (IFAD, 2004; IFAD, 2007b), which makes the case of Al Dagag distinctive to represent the debate about the role of the financial relations in sustaining rural livelihood.

In the research a qualitative methodology is employed, mainly to deal with the urgent need for empirical and recent data about Sudan that reflects the perspective of the rural poor. For the same reason Grounded Theory (GT) is used, because it allows a significant contribution in constructing theories grounded in data (Glaser and Strauss, 1967; Strauss and Corbin 1990, 1997; Charmaz, 2006). A theory constructed by using this methodology draws from how financial relations influence rural livelihood and social capital, in terms of social networks and relationships that are believed to be strong in the context of Sudan. Social capital is not only very important in providing credit and savings facilities but also as a sort of insurance and safety net for the poor in Al Dagag. I have realized that this discussion constitutes a real addition to the knowledge about social capital.

Specifically and purposively, I have selected the individual cases of households and families and used in-depth qualitative methodology for data collection and analysis, detailed in chapter 5. Varied qualitative research instruments like in-depth interviews, focused elites interviews, group interviews and Participatory Rural Appraisal (PRA) are employed. Moreover, the GT was complemented by the application of the atlas.ti software to analyze interviews.

Using GT advocates the fact that the theoretical framework developed in this research was constructed to mirror the empirical findings of the research since GT reflects a qualitative methodology of induction. I would like here to stress the fact that the use of previous literature and theories within the GT was done in a way that makes the findings of the research understandable and only theories explaining the findings of the analysis, concerning categories and concepts emerged from the empirical data are discussed in the next three chapters.

1.2 Specific Intentions of the Research

When I began this research I did not have strong presumptions; however, I did start with the vision and the question explained above. The vision was to create substantial analysis and knowledge about rural livelihood of villages in the Sudanese context and how microfinance can positively affect rural livelihoods. In other words, what I wanted to do was to draw the general portrait of rural livelihoods and to locate microfinance in this big picture and see if it fits. However, along the research process, a set of objectives and questions was developed gradually, their development enhanced throughout data collection and analysis.

Generally drawing this portrait of rural livelihood in Sudan was in itself an attempt to construct a meaningful analysis of rural livelihoods. The only way to achieve that was through analyzing the main features of rural livelihoods in Sudan including poverty and vulnerability. The importance of social capital emerged from the data itself where one comes to realize that social relations are the key in shaping livelihoods in rural Sudan. They provide means for credit, savings and most of all insurance against shocks and risks that frequently happens in rural villages. This also highlights the linkages, which exist between social and financial relations. Social capital became later one of the main objectives of this research, where it was found necessary to elaborate the networks and exchanged of resources and benefits that help the poor in rural Sudan. The category of "helping each other", which reflects how social capital can be a mechanism for insurance, became one of the main research categories and consequently one of the main contributions to constructing the theory about processes shaping rural livelihood in Sudan. Other forms of capital are also dealt with to illustrate the main features of rural livelihood. Looking at rural livelihood in the context of poverty and vulnerability and the people's perspectives necessitates the incorporation of the discussion of social capital, specifically in fighting poverty and vulnerability. Social networks and relations create a considerable mobility of recourses in and between households, particularly financial resources. Thus in this research the topic of social capital is elaborated and linked to financial capital. Likewise, analyzing the main determinants of the rural livelihood in the Sudanese villages complements the discussion. Thus, livelihood activities and the composition of households and the intra-household decision-making lines as well as the critical processes that include migration, diversification and coping strategies have been found crucial.

Looking at the financial landscape of Sudan and comparing it to other experiences of pro-poor finance was revealed to be important and hence constituted another objective in this study. This was realized by scrutinizing the financial sector with regard to the implementation of both the liberalization and Islamization and how they have affected the extension of finance to the rural poor. This research not only provides a critique of the financial sector in Sudan but also presents advances and experiences around the world in both the microfinance industry and the financial institutions to learn from in the field of pro-poor finance.

The focus on the general financial landscape has revealed the importance of studying formal and informal financial institutions and relations that exist between savers, lenders and borrowers at rural level. Financial institutions, both formal and informal including varied opportunities of microfinance were studied in detail in Al Dagag. These comprise of the IFAD credit project and its linkages with the ABS, different ROSCAs, called *Sandouqs*, the money lending money system of *Shail* and other informal financial transactions. Thus, both the demand and the supply sides are considered crucial; however, the focus is more on the demand side or on the perspectives of rural people. Comparison of these institutions proved important. Consequently, one objective of this research is to describe and compare institutions from the perspective of the rural people themselves. Ranking and comparing formal and informal institutions aims to investigate which institutions are more appropriate to meet the demand of financial resources in rural areas.

1.3 Focus and the Rationale behind the Research

Chronic poverty and vulnerability are studied at different levels, individual, household or family, socio-economic group or entire region; however, in this research for the importance of households and families for the rural context of Sudan these two are in the focus. I believe that rural households are important elements when thinking about rural development since they reflect units of social and economic structures and relations.

One of the main starting points of many livelihoods studies is that, if one wants to understand poverty and vulnerability, it is not enough to look at employment and income but needs to also address other aspects. The works of Chambers and Conway (1992), Chambers (1995, 1997), Ellis (2000), Ellis and Freeman (2005), and Lont and Hospes (2004) emphasize the need to focus more on people's capital, capabilities, strategies, activities and access to resources mediated by institutions and social relations. All of these combined together determine the resources gained by individuals or households; thus it is not only the narrow definition of income or employment that matters. The theoretical debates and analysis reframe and shift the balance of objectives of development: from reducing income-poverty to diminishing deprivation and enhancing wellbeing and security; and from increasing employment to sustaining livelihood. Development then demands and generates diversity, as deprivation is so much more than lack of income, livelihood is so multifarious, and wellbeing and security as people experience and desire have many dimensions (Chambers, 1995). The concept of capabilities introduced by Amartya Sen (1980, 1984, 2005, 2006) is also relevant since it represents one of the essences of the livelihood concept. For Sen, poverty is not about lack of income but rather about lack of capabilities of people that determine what people are able to do or to be.

Based on the above and supported by the findings, this research focuses on describing poverty and vulnerability within the livelihood perspective to emphasize the notion of resources, capital and assets that people have and that are supposed to enhance their security and wellbeing. As it is quoted by many respondents, poverty and vulnerability are connected to the concept of "decent life" and security and wellbeing to the concept of "having something". These phrases are supposed to include not only income put also people's capabilities, tangible assets, like agriculture production and livestock in form of savings and intangible assets including social networks and relations.

It is obvious that poverty and vulnerability are severe in rural areas of Sudan even though not much information is available about Sudan. Different symptoms and causes of poverty and vulnerability are not available and when they are found they seem to be general, quantitative, not recent, or mentioned repeatedly by many institutions and writers. This suggests a need for contemporary information and more importantly, qualitative studies to describe poverty and vulnerability.

Moreover, if most of the poor and vulnerable people live in rural areas as suggested in the literature, then rural areas should be central to this discussion. This issue is especially relevant in Sudan where the available literature points to the huge gap between regions and mainly between the center and the periphery (IFAD, 2004, 2007b). Much of the development efforts of the government are concentrated in Khartoum and its surrounding area while remote areas are left outside and most of the developmental work relies on few NGOs providing different types of help and assistance for the poor. The rural poor themselves build their own strategies to cope with their situations. Chambers (1989) has argued that in the absence of appropriate help and assistance the poor resort to their own coping strategies. It is evident from literature and also in the case of Al Dagag how creative these coping strategies are. Thus, the question is within the scope of this research how the poor themselves act to survive in such situations in rural areas of Sudan, as household livelihood strategies often involve different members in diverse activities and sources of support, at different times of the year. It is the role of social capital that is revealed to support most household strategies. The poor prove to build diversified portfolios of activities and capital in order to survive and to improve their standard of living. Within the boundaries of this discussion emerged the importance of discussing the process of diversification and the main coping strategies found to be essential.

In most literature of livelihood as well as about finance (presented in chapter 2 and 3) the existence of adequate financial services, especially microfinance is considered effective to fight poverty and vulnerability by building assets for the poor. Moreover, it is argued that in agrarian and peasant economies, there is increasing need for credit (Adams and Fitchett, 1992). The demand or the need for microfinance comes from the disadvantaged sectors of any community, this refers to those who are without access to financial services from the formal sector and/or formal financial intermediaries, those who are excluded from the formal banking system either due to lack of collaterals or high risks and costs of services.

This discussion brings me to highlight the focus of the research with regard to the concept of finance. It worth starting this discussion by pointing out that the most relevant theory to discuss finance at local or rural level focusing on the household is the finance for the poor theory. This is a general theory that extends over a long period of time to back up the practice of providing finance for the poor. Different concepts and practices are involved like agriculture finance, microfinance, informal finance, as well as the discussion about proper financial products and institutions that can take the responsibility of serving the poor as well as the role of the state. When presenting their perspective about the microfinance efforts in Al Dagag, respondents discuss much of these concepts. Besides, after looking at the works of many scholars (Adams et al., 1984; Christen, 1992; Bouman, 1989, 1994; Bouman and Hospes, 1994; Krahnen and Schmidt, 1994; Mayer, 2001; Zeller and Meyer, 2002; Lont and Hospes, 2004; Nagarajan and Meyer, 2005) one can establish connections between theory, practice and people's perspectives. In most of these literature the question how to put more emphasis on the interests of rural savers, informal lenders and borrowers, on both farm and nonfarm rural firms and households finds much attention. In other words, there is a need to focus on the demand side of finance. This research tries to provide analytical and empirical information about this issue in rural Sudan.

Finance for the poor to be effective, credit and other financial services need to be recognized as situated within a framework of "financial relations" that allow looking for what rural people demand and actually use to satisfy their demand for finance. One of the pioneers to acknowledge the importance of the concept of financial relations, Crow (1994), argues that finance is defined as financial relations that bring the rise and fall of relations between groups of lenders and borrowers. As illustrated by him (1994: 271f.), the concept of financial relations is illuminated in sociology and economic anthropology, which have clarified the diversity of the relations through which access to credit is obtained. Economics has been the dominant discipline in the theorization of financial landscapes (ibid.), which may prove insufficient, for the many ways financial relations are embedded in social structures, thus linking both financial and social capital and locate the discussion within the livelihood thinking. That is why there is a need to study financial relations in connection with other relations and forms of capital such as social networks. This approach also allows including different types of financial institutions and arrangements.

From the literature mentioned above one can further observe that most of the research since the last decade has concentrated on the role of formal financial institutions providing rural finance services. It is since the 1980s when the significance and the persistence of the informal finance began to be focused on within the finance thinking (Lont and Hospes, 2004: 4)[5]. Some writers argue that in some places informal institutions are much more important than formal ones (Vogel, 1984; Bouman, 1994; Lont and Hospes, 2004: 4). These comprise traditional money lending systems, self-help groups like ROSCAs and other financial transactions that take place between kinship relatives, neighbors and friends. Bouman (1994) points out that informal arrangements provide very valuable services to many rural people and policy makers and formal lenders should take a positive view of informal finance. Bouman concludes that with appropriate conditions, informal lending should be expanded in line with the growth of the overall economy and formal finance. The importance of the informal arrangements in the context of rural areas has also emerged in the findings of this research. Thus, this research tries to shed light on different types of institutions from the perspective of the poor. Therefore, beside the comparison between formal and informal institutions in serving the poor, this research puts more focus on the indigenous financial arrangements as emphasized by the villagers in Al Dagag and tries to explore any direct or indirect links between formal and informal financial services in rural Sudan.

The theoretical debate about the practice of the microfinance is relevant to the case of Sudan. The contradiction between what financial services rural people demand in the case of the village Al Dagag on the one hand and the microfinance revolution initiated in Khartoum on the other hand reveals the need to elaborate on this issue. Discussing the efforts of IFAD in Al Dagag and exploring the financial landscapes in Sudan forces the need to explore whether the microfinance efforts are successful in enhancing the rural livelihood. Does the microfinance revolution deal with the evidence and the current debate that the recent commercialized provision of microfinance might not help the poor? Keeping in mind that microfinance is now often viewed as a poverty trap and poverty capital, which among other reasons results from its commercialization, its role in making significant changes in the wellbeing of the poor, specifically in remote rural areas, has been questioned, and thus, more research is required to investigate this issue (Bateman, 2010; Roy, 2010). This research looks deep into the case of IFAD providing microfinance in Al Dagag and tries to study the effects of this effort in sustaining rural livelihood and to compare it to the impact of the indigenous financial arrangements.

This discussion brought out another set of questions with regard to the microfinance, about the microfinance clients or who are the "poor" who are supposed to be helped by providing microfinance, and what financial products suit their demand? Helms (2006: 17) addresses the need to understand actual and potential clients of microfinance, and argues that recognizing the diversity of people who are excluded from the formal financial services has enormous implications on building inclusive financial systems. Moreover Thankom et al. (2009: 9) state that conceptualizing the poor as a heterogeneous group of vulnerable households and complex livelihoods reveals the need for microfinancial, client-oriented services. This argument urges the need for more studies that focus on understanding the microfinance clients and their demand and the need to for these studies prior the provision of microfinance.

Helms (2006: 29) also addresses the issue of financial products and institutions and asserts that most research focuses on credit in measuring the impact of financial services to the poor, but what about the role of institutions like ROSCAs in providing savings, and the social capital in providing insurance (Helms 2006: 29)? Thankom et al. highlight the gap in understanding microfinance clearly:

> "*After two decades of experiences a better understanding of the preferences of financial service and behavior of the poor and poorest, we still needed to expand the scope of microfinance initiatives in addressing the concerns about welfare implications of the microfinance institutions*" (Thankom et al., 2009: 9).

It is clear that the lack of empirical studies on the demand side of microfinance has limited the understanding of ways to improve the sector. Moreover, microfinance documents are highly promotional, designed to disseminate the idea and to seek increasing funds. Likewise, some publications that at-

[5] The start of this discussion was highlighted in the work of Geertz (1962) and Ardener (1964).

tempt to quantitatively evaluate the strongest claims made by its advocates have a weak empirical basis (Zeller and Mayer, 2002: 2). This research seeks to contribute empirical knowledge and research methods for explaining households demand and access to financial services. Zeller and Mayer (2002) also argue that since microfinance has been mainly explored in quantitative measures, studies are mostly limited to the main concepts of profitability and outreach. I also believe that deeper understanding can be gained by studying this phenomenon using a qualitative research design. Such a type of analysis can provide answers to questions like what do the poor want, how do they use loans, how profits from using loans are used and what impacts microfinance have in accumulating households assets?

Finally, because this research is directed to audiences in and outside Sudan, I realize that it is important to stress the recent advances in the microfinance practices that are taking place around the world. Presenting these current advances reflects gaps in the implementation of the microfinance in Sudan and helps shape any future vision to develop the sector.

1.4 Structure of the Research

The first chapter of the research provides a general introduction to the topic and a general framework for the study that includes intentions, questions, and the scope of the research.

Part I: Theoretical Considerations

Chapter 2 provides a theorization and conceptualization of concepts concerning poverty, vulnerability, livelihood capital, and livelihood activities. Moreover, theories that support different categories that emerged from the data concerning the concept of livelihood are presented in this chapter. Chapter 3 constitutes the theorization and conceptualization platform for the concepts emerged from data analysis regarding financial relations and the provision of finance for the poor. The main theoretical perspectives and backgrounds are illustrated in this chapter starting from the provision of excessive and cheap credit viewed to undermine rural development, to the commencement of the microfinance revolution to recent developments when microfinance has been considered a poverty trap and poverty capital. Chapter 4 constitutes the part of the research that focuses on theorizing financial institutions. The main theoretical argumentation and explanation of formal and informal institutions will be provided. The chapter describes the main advances with regard to the microfinance practices, for example, the performance of banks in providing finance for the poor, which shows disappointments with their performances and goes further to present the recent advances in the field of formal financial institutions when providing microfinance.

Part II: Methodology

Chapter 5 elaborates the use of the constructivist, qualitative Grounded Theory (GT) methodology in this research. GT is not just a research method; it is a full methodology that I have followed throughout the research. Its main aim is to construct a grounded theory about the research topic. Chapter 5 first provides a general overview of the development of GT since the beginning of its application. Second, the detailed description of the research process from the beginning to the end is offered and issues and debates about the GT process of coding and categorization presented. Third, it details examples and illustrations for the steps of data collection and analysis, something rather unusual in the literature, a gap I seek to fill.

Part III: Discussion and Results: Theory Construction

In the third part of the dissertation the main results of data analysis in terms of codes and categories and as the result of constant comparison of categories are presented. The part starts with a chapter that critically describes the main features of livelihood and the financial landscapes in Sudan based on interviews and a literature review. This is followed by four chapters that describe the research findings in detail.

Chapter 6 contains the contextual main analysis where the Sudanese livelihood will be described generally emphasizing poverty and vulnerability. The financial landscape is investigated in detail to show some of the effects of the liberalization and Islamization processes. Generally, the main financial institutions in Sudan are presented. Chapter 7 portrays livelihood in the village Al Dagag. At the beginning of this chapter, a general overview about NKS and Al Dagag is provided, and most of the categories related to the concept of rural livelihood are described and explained. This includes the main livelihood patterns and the role of women in securing livelihood. Besides this, the description of the intra-household economic arrangements, needs and expenses, patterns of income allocation are discussed.

The debate about how people in Al Dagag perceive poverty and vulnerability is presented in chapter 8. The role of the social capital as insurance mechanism is also discussed in this chapter. Chapter 9 deals with the microfinance experience of IFAD in Al Dagag. In this chapter, not only a detailed analysis of both formal and informal institutions is provided but also a comparison of these institutions from the perspective of rural people. In chapter 10, the importance of the informal finance in Al Dagag is revealed in discussing the indigenous financial arrangements like *Sandouqs* and loans from shops, relatives and friends. The chapter also deals with the discussion about the money lending system of *Shail*. The last chapter 11 encompasses concluding remarks for the theory constructed and grounded in data and concludes the overall research discussion.

Part I: Theoretical Considerations

2 Theoretical Perspective on Rural Livelihood

Living on the edge: "*this phrase evokes the sense of a small push sending a person or people over the edge and it is just this knife edge between ability to survive and thrive and sudden loss of ability to do so*" (Ellis and Freeman, 2005: 6).

Social capital: "*membership in a group which provides each of its members with the backing of the collectivity-owned capital, a 'credential' which entitles them to credit, in the various sense of the word*" (Bourdieu, 1986: 249).

2.1 Introduction

For a long time, the conceptualization of poverty and the solutions provided have shifted along with the transformation of development goals, policy thinking, political relations and social sciences as expressed in changing paradigms of poverty alleviation. This ranges from the income poverty paradigm of the 1950s and 1960s to the basic needs [1] approach, Amartya Sen's 'capabilities' approach, both of which established in the 1970s and 80s, and Robert Chamber's sustainable livelihood approach in the 1990s (Green, 2007; Sen, 2006; Chambers, 1997: Chambers and Conway, 1992; Chambers, 1989; Stewart, 1985; Stewart et al., 2007). And yet, poverty remains a serious problem in developing countries; and poverty alleviation has become the main concern of interest in development; and in the provision of significant means for promoting economic growth. The main two questions guiding thoughts about poverty are: Why are the poor poor in general? Why do most of the poor live in rural areas specifically? And finally, what should be done to reduce the extent and gravity of poverty?[2] The above mentioned developmental approaches and theories provide different explanations for these questions.

It is clear when reading about the livelihood approach that it comprises a comprehensive vision of people's lives including the discussion of poverty and further the discussion about vulnerability. Moreover, what I have found from analyzing the interviews and present in chapter 7 and 8 is that what respondents are talking about to a great extent matches the livelihood approach. It is revealed that the livelihood approach is mingling various aspects of people lives; these include people's capital, resources, capabilities, strategies, activities. Considering the focus of rural livelihood in most developing countries among them Sudan, all these issues are explained within the framework of poverty and vulnerability. Thus, poverty within the livelihood approach is the context where these factors of capital, strategies, etc. might play different roles. The answers from respondents and reading the livelihood literature both have convinced me that the livelihood approach could be a combination of the income poverty approach, the capabilities approach and limited aspects of the basic needs approach. Therefore, I may say that income is only one aspect among many others,[3] like the different types of livelihood capital, strategies, and capabilities, all of which constitute the livelihood approach. That is mainly why I want to discuss the livelihood approach in combination with the concept of poverty and vulnerability and include different approaches that I have found relevant. Thus, the discussion in this chapter starts with the income paradigm, the capabilities approach, the basic needs approach and then I will start to focus on the livelihood approach.

The idea of livelihood capital in terms of social, economic, human, physical and natural capital (Chambers, 1998; Ellis, 2000; Ellis and Freeman, 2005) is central to the livelihood analysis. The livelihood theory supposes that investments in these types of capital enhance people's wellbeing and security, and, further, make the livelihood sustainable when people are enabled to cope with risks and disasters they face in their vulnerable environment; thus, suggesting equality between these types of capi-

[1] In fact the capabilities approach does not really come after the basic needs approach; however, it became accepted by the development institutions only after the basic needs approach already was the leading paradigm for these organizations.

[2] The first question will be discussed in this chapter while the second is presented in the discussion of finance for the poor in the following chapter.

[3] Other approaches also include different aspects but I could argue here that livelihood is more encompassing and basic, focusing on people's immediate lives.

tal and their weight to sustain rural livelihood. The empirical results of the research found the financial and the social capital[4] have been found most significant for this and constitute the scope of this discussion, which is not to say that other types of capital are ignored.

Rural livelihood activities are also discussed in this research in order to include activities related to agriculture or others. In this chapter, the theoretical debate about these activities within the livelihood approach is presented. Seasonal migration is considered an activity of rural livelihood in Al Dagag. Thus, the most relative theoretical discussion to this type of migration is the New Economics of Labour Migration (NELM) theory which is the most relevant theory for the prevailing type of migration found in Al Dagag. The main theoretical assumption of this theory suggests that first, the main aim of migration is economic; and second it comes as a combined household decision, not as an individual decision. It basically assumes that the individuals in a household act collectively not only to maximize household income but also to minimize risk and to loosen constraints associated with different types of risks, shocks and disasters (Stark, 1991; Haas, 2008; Rabby et al., 2010).

The livelihood approach allows investigating not only poverty but also other dimensions of deprivation such as vulnerability (Chambers, 1995: 18; Ellis and Freeman, 2005; Naudé et al., 2008). The vulnerability analysis includes the discussion of risks, shocks and disasters people face in rural areas.

The main determinants of rural livelihood, which represent people's strategies, are discussed in this chapter below. This includes *first* the theoretical debate about households' strategies, intra-household decision-making and financial behavior. The latter has been found connected to the sustainability of people's livelihood in Al Dagag. The concept of household is too complex to just be defined by setting its boundaries; the literature points to the importance of discussing intra-household relations and decision-making. This was also revealed from the empirical data that households are important because they are considered as units of social and financial relations.

Diversification and coping strategies are the *second* determinant of livelihood in Al Dagag. That shows how in the complex system of livelihood strategies and institutions work together to lessen different types of risks and shocks that rural people face. This forces the discussion toward explaining how diversification in rural areas takes place and to what extent helps the poor. However, diversification in this research does not only include income diversification but the results of analyzing the empirical data also suggests digging deeper to explore other specific coping strategies that are employed by the poor in rural areas to cope with specific risks, shocks and disasters.

In the conclusion of this chapter I explore the implication that if poverty and vulnerability do not exist, people live in a world of security and wellbeing—and ask, what do these concepts actually mean? Ellis' expression of "living on the edge" which is used to describe the life of vulnerable people is reversed in the conclusion to "living far from the edge" and used to explain how the life of people within a context of wellbeing and security might be like.

This chapter is designed generally to provide theoretical understanding of the main categories and concepts that have emerged from interview analysis. This is also considered the purpose of all the theoretical chapters in this research, which is to mirror the research findings and make the research categories understandable.

2.2 Poverty and Development Paradigms: From Income Poverty Paradigm to Chamber's "Sustainable Livelihoods"

2.2.1 Income Poverty Paradigm

The vision of the 1950s and 1960s for economic growth; of a better world with full employment, decent incomes, universal primary education, health for all, safe water supplies, a demographic transition to stable populations and fair terms of trade between rich and poor countries in the 1970s has not been realized (Chambers, 1997: 1). Since that time, a lot of the economic literature on poverty was governed by

[4] In this research the terms capital and relations are used interchangeably when discussing financial and social capital and relations.

the "income poverty paradigm". According to this paradigm, the poor are identified according to their standard of living, which is expressed in a monetary metric. These are typically income or consumption expenditure per capita, falling short of a subjective fixed level that is the "poverty line". The extent of poverty is measured by the proportion of people in the population below this line, possibly combined with the average distance they are from it. The goal of development policy is therefore to reduce the extent of poverty by increasing income of the people below the poverty line (Bourguignon, 2006: 76). Poverty then is seen as any shortage in income, which can reduce a person to serious deprivation.

This income paradigm dominated the development thinking for a long time. It proved useful to some extent; yet, as it was developed over time, limitations of the basic concepts behind the paradigm have been observed. As a result, many critics have challenged the income poverty paradigm. No one can deny that income is an important measurement of poverty; however, it is not the only metric since income poverty reflects only the economic dimension of poverty. Definitely, poverty is more than that. Many writers like Chambers (1997), Bourguignon (2006) and Sen (2006) support this argument; it is also necessary to ask whether income, despite its relevance, can really be the appropriate informational basis for assessing poverty and vulnerability. This question relates to the understanding of what the underlying goals of development are and how, in particular, the quality of human life can be best assessed (Sen, 2006: 34).

For Chambers (1997: 1), the beliefs of earlier times in linear and convergent development through stages of income for growth, in central planning, in unlimited growth, in industrialization as the key to development, and in the feasibility of a continuous improvement in levels of living have proved inappropriate. Hundreds of millions of people are worse off now than twenty years ago. Over the years, the indicators of wellbeing have improved in some areas and declined in others (Chambers 1997: 1). The latter means lower incomes, fewer children in schools, deteriorating services in health, mounting civil disorder, lower expectation of life and greater vulnerability (ibid.). In the same line of reasoning, Stewart (1985: 8f.) and Stewart et al. (2007) in their recent book "Defining Poverty In the Developing World" argue that during the 1950s, growth maximization and industrialization were taken as the main objectives of development, and resulted in marked acceleration in growth rates. However, various aspects of the development process proved unsatisfactory, for instance while economic growth accelerated in most countries, levels of unemployment, underemployment, social exclusion and other problems remained consistently high.

Bourguignon (2006: 76f.) provides an analytical view about the transformation of poverty thinking from income to endowments and asserts that the main critique of the poverty income paradigm comes from the social justice theory. It questions the use of current income or expenditure as the only basis to define poverty; rather decisions regarding expenditure for individuals and households are governed by many social factors not only by income. In Green's (2007: 40) point of view, although the quantification of poverty permits the homogenization of poverty across time and space and allows the construction of poverty rankings that aim to compare the amount and depth of poverty, it is not useful for exploring its causes and consequences. So many important issues have been absent in the approach, which defines poverty as income and consumption poverty.

I would like to argue here that in addition to what has been said about income as an indicator of poverty, what I have observed in Al Dagag is that increasing income alone in a very vulnerable situation cannot be the appropriate aim of developmental initiatives. Since the income will vanish in a short time due to the regular shocks and disasters in the environment. Moreover, income or its extent might not be as important as the way the income is used. This touches on the debate about the unit of analysis, is it the individual or the household? Is income used to maximize the wellbeing and security of members of households or for other purposes? In addition to that, within one community, people might have different levels of income but still spend it on the same social services. For instance, all people with no regard to their levels of income need to use the same education facilities available to them, which might be provided in poor quality. What is clear from this is income alone is not complete measurement, but also what are people capable of doing with it, it is more about the capability to use income in a way to satisfy the desirable wellbeing level. For instance, in the literature, the income is often measured by the food expenditure of the family; in Al Dagag almost all the people with no regard to whether they are poor or better off are eating almost the same type of food. It was also not easy for me to detect obvious differences between the households of the poor and the well off just using indicators like the building materials, the household furniture, and the services they are using. Almost all people live in the same way; use the local resources in the same way and the same facilities and social services available to them.

Several other critiques arise to the income poverty paradigm such as the lack of different instruments that actually permit efficient measurement of poverty and the practice of using individuals as the unit of analysis. All these critiques of the income poverty paradigm revolve around the same basic idea. The analysis of poverty should concentrate not only on income and expenditure but also on multiple attributes including different kinds of capital, which determine the wellbeing of individuals and households. Therefore, other approaches emerged to deal with the shortcomings of the income paradigm, specifically the basic needs approach.

2.2.2 Basic Needs Approach

The basic needs approach emerged in the development thinking to concentrate more on people and their lives rather than their incomes and consumption of goods and services. It emerged parallel to the capabilities approach, but captured the development thinking earlier. It was initiated by the International Labour Organization (ILO) during the subsequent World Bank program launched in 1978 to investigate the operational implications of meeting basic needs of the whole population, by national development efforts. As well as to list indicators for measuring the basic needs to assess the satisfaction of the basic needs of a group of individuals or population within a specific geographical area (Saith, 2007: 61). Meeting of certain fundamental human needs became a development priority, deduced from the simple view that development should be concerned with removing the deprivation of people (Stewart, 1985: 1). Later on, a study by Hopkins and Hoeven (1983) prepared for the ILO to locate the basic needs approach in development planning and Stewart's book (1985) "Planning to Meet Basic Needs" were the starting initiatives to integrate the basic needs approach into the international development discourse.

The list of basic needs discussed recently by Saith (2007) includes health, food, water supply, sanitation, education, and freedom of expression and religion (Saith, 2007: 62**)**. According to Saith (2007: 63f.), Doyal and Gough's theory of human needs, which was developed in 1991, contributed the understanding to the discussion that poverty within the basic needs approach is linked to the avoidance of serious harm. In trying to identify this idea, Doyal and Gough define serious harm "*as dramatically impaired participation in a form life*". Furthermore they identify physical survival (physical health) and personal autonomy as constituting the most basic human needs "*those which must be satisfied to some degree before actors can effectively participate in their form of life to achieve any other valued goals*" (Saith, 2007: 46). Doyal and Gough also developed a classification between what they call basic needs and another set, the intermediate needs, which contain physical health, mental health, understanding and having opportunities while food, water, protective housing, appropriate education, etc. make up the as main basic needs.

I would like to argue here that this approach considers the individual the center of measurement and ignores the relationship within and across households, family, society and nation or even between nations. In addition, the idea of dividing basic needs into basic and intermediate is not clear concerning the basis and the reasoning of such a classification; it ignores how diverse each community is with regard to this classification, and there are many overlapping areas between the basic needs stated in the list. The question arises here also if the local people themselves classify their needs in the same way.

Critics of the basic needs approach in the literature focus on three issues; *first* the inaccuracy of measurements of indicators; for example, literacy standards may differ between countries (Stewart, 1985: 55). *Second*, there is a problem that measures and indicators do not fully reflect the objectives of the basic needs approach; for example, people may have long life expectancy but suffer from debilitating diseases. *Third* is the problem of distribution of basic needs. A fundamental aspect of a basic needs approach is that everyone should have access to health and education but how could this be ensured with the existence of urban bias, centralization, and other similar problems (Stewart, 1985: 55).

For Hopkins and Hoeven (1983) the major problem of the basic needs approach lies in the definition and the listing of basic needs themselves. There are several listings of basic needs presenting different opinions starting from the early works of Booth, Marx and Maslow to more recent works of Khan, Sen, Ghai, and Carr-Hill (Hopkins and Hoeven, 1983) and even many more lists of basic needs indicators by various writers and organizations. That there are several lists offered reflects the disagreement about meaning and indicators of basic needs; still there are basic needs consented to be universal and included in most of these lists such as food and nutrition, shelter, clothing, health and education and others like social security.

In the view of Saith (2007: 63), the interpersonal variations in the conversion of goods into benefits and the absence of the concept of "freedom of choice" in the basic needs approach is the main critique. Later on, the achievement of the translation of the basic needs approach into reality, action plans, policies, and projects became more complex both in terms of identifying the appropriate measures and in terms of mobilizing the required political will (Stewart, 1985: 1).

The link between the basic needs approach and the livelihood approach lies in the fact that the livelihood at the beginning was defined as adequate stocks and flows of food and cash to meet basic needs; depending on the list and discussion of the basic needs approach as I will explain later. However, the recent working definion of the livelihood approach is different since the concept of the basic needs has being modified, as will also be presented later in this chapter.

To sum up, after all these efforts the meaning of poverty has remained ambiguous. A consistent definition and indicators of poverty are still lacking as well as a satisfactory explanation of poverty that allows answering the question why people are still poor. What is also or even more relevant than income, and what basic needs should be added to the poverty view? What could be more inclusive to reflect people's situation? The capabilities approach tried to offer answers to these questions.

2.2.3 Amartya Sen's Capabilities' Approach

Sen (2006: 34) explains that whereas income is merely one means of good living, we have reason enough to look directly as the quality of life that people are able to lead and the freedom they enjoy to live the way they would like. If life consists of various things that people are able to do or be (such as being able to be in a good health or to be able to read and write, and so on) then it is the capability that has to be put at the center stage of assessment. Sen (2006: 34) clarifies that it is precisely the distinction between income on the one hand and wellbeing and the freedom of a person on the other, that matters here. So poverty for him should be seen as a failure of certain basic capabilities rather than of income; and development as enhancement of human living and the freedom to live the kind of life that we have reason to value (Sen, 2006: 34). The capabilities of relevance are not only those that relate to avoiding premature mortality, being in good health, being schooled and educated, and other basic needs: but also various social achievements including being able to appear in public without shame and being able to take part in the life of the community (Sen, 2006: 35).

Saith (2007: 55f.) claims that, in the end of the 1970s Amartya Sen provided the central critique of the income poverty approach in his essay "Equality of what?", delivered as Tanner Lecture on Human Values in 1979. Sen criticized the primary goods approach and supported "the theory of justice" to measure inequality developed by John Rawls in 1971. Rawls' theory focuses on acquiring equality in the space of primary social goods (2007: 55f.). Sen's criticism of the primary goods approach is directed towards the emphasis on the goods and their equal distribution rather than the relationship between goods and persons. Sen argues that the possession of commodities may not always be translated into wellbeing given the large interpersonal differences of personal characteristics or the differences in the natural and social environments that affect the conversion of goods to a particular ends (Saith, 2007: 56). So, the acquisition of goods does not only matter but rather what the person actually succeeds in doing with these goods. From here, Sen develops the concept of capabilities, which is explained as the main achievements, which are the "functionings" that a person can accomplish; this implies the notion of freedom of choices, where any person has the right to choose the type of life or the set of achievements that he/she wants to have (Saith, 2007: 57).

Amartya Sen's capabilities approach explicitly articulates that what matters is not the income but rather is the set of "capabilities" or the "choice set" an individual faces, not the choice he or she actually makes (Bourguignon, 2006). Sen (1982) provides an explanation of the concept of capabilities. It is to be able to perform certain basic activities, i. e. what people are capable of doing and being. This includes "*being adequately nourished, to be comfortably clothed, to avoid mortality and morbidity, to have live without shame, to be able to have friends and visit them, to keep track of what is surrounding you, what is going on and what are the other people know and talking about*" (Sen 1987). Obviously this list includes many other things than the ability to work and gain income. Chambers and Conway (1992: 5) claim that

Sen focuses on the quality of live which is recognized in terms of activities and the ability to choose among and perform these activities.

However, Sen does not give a concrete definition of capabilities; instead he suggests some examples like being well-nourished, or avoiding preventable morbidity. One can argue here that still the concept of capabilities is ambiguous in the sense that this could include many aspects and could be different from one person to another depending on many conditions and situations. This lack of definition is the main critique of Sen's capabilities approach as expressed by Dejong (2007: 79). Rather Sen suggests that "*if we want a properly satisfactory measures of inequality or poverty we cannot define it over the income space alone and have to supplement the income data by information about social relations between people and about comparison groups in a particular social context*" (Sen, 2006: 45)

Indeed, what has been repeatedly discussed with regard to the capabilities approach is the need for a list of capabilities. However, I would like to argue here that a universal list like the one of the basic needs approach should not be used for all communities, unless the list could be flexible enough and adjusted to suit each community. Surprising as it may have been to other writers, that Sen never came with a list of capabilities, he answers the critics by saying:

> "*What I'm against is the fixing to a cemented list of capabilities, which is absolutely complete (nothing could be added to it) and totally fixed (it could not respond to public reasoning and to the formation of social values). I'm a great believer in theory... But pure theory cannot 'freeze' a list of capabilities for all societies for all the time to come, irrespective of what the citizens come to understand and value... There is also the problem of determining the relative weights and importance of the different capabilities included in the relative list. Even with a given list the question of valuation cannot be avoided*" (Sen, 2005: 336).

As contribution to this debate, Martha Nussbaum developed a basic human functional capabilities list in 1995 (Nussbaum, 2005: 35). She argues that the list of capabilities she developed is to explicitly express what Sen has mentioned implicitly (Nussbaum 2005: 39). Her list encompasses basic capabilities with a threshold below which a life will be so impoverished that it is not human at all. She describes her list as open-ended which includes life, bodily health (nourishment and shelter), bodily integrity, senses, imagination and thought, emotions, practical reasons, affiliation, living with other species, play and control over one's environment (Nussbaum, 2005: 44). The last one includes two further aspects, which are the political participation and the material capability to hold property. Her main argumentation is that these capabilities are closely related to human rights. She argues that the idea of rights is by no means crystal-clear but also people differ about them in many aspects: "*Regarding fundamental rights, I would argue that the best way of thinking about what it is to secure them to people is to think in terms of capabilities*" (Nussbaum, 2005: 44).

While I agree with Sen that a universal, fixed list of capabilities is not useful for all societies and all the time to come, I would still like to argue here that the existence of a list that is flexible to include what people themselves consider crucial in explaining their standard of wellbeing. What people want to accomplish and how they can accomplish it in their lifetime should be clear, measurable and respectable by policy makers and development practitioner in every community or country. This list could be altered over time to cope with changes in the community.

Evidently many writers have followed and adopted and added to Sen's capabilities approach, such as Chambers and Conway (1992), Scoones (1998), Ellis (2000), and most recently Bourguignon (2006), Saith (2007) and Stewart (2007). Based on the work of these writers I argue that the livelihood approach is an extension to the capabilities approach.

Capabilities are present as a concern in the livelihood approach. Ellis (2000: 7) explains Sen's ideas and tries to produce a general definition of capabilities. He argues that capability "*refers to the ability of individuals to realize their potential as human beings in the sense both of being (i.e. to be adequately nourished, free of illness and so on) and doing (i.e. exercise choices, develop skills and experience, participate socially and so on)*". For Ellis such use of capabilities in this context might be confusing and overlaps with the concepts of activities and capital. Nevertheless, this is not fully agreeable, for any person requires certain capabilities to perform activities and own or control capital. In other words, the activities any person performs and the capital he/she has, depends on his/her capabilities.

Yet the concept of capabilities is vague and has a "wide span" as Chamber and Conway (1992) describe it. To them, what is important about people's capabilities, is "*the dynamic competence, the ability to perceive, predict, adapt to and exploit changes in the physical, social and economic environments*" (Chambers and Conway, 1992: 16).

2.2.4 Robert Chamber's Sustainable Livelihood Approach

According to Chambers (1997: 9) near the millennium, accelerating changes had taken place, more people than ever before are wealthy beyond any reasonable need for a good life, and more are poor and vulnerable below any conceivable definition of decency. The acceleration of change in many aspects like political, social, economic and environmental issues sharpens the challenges for development. As well, ideas for development policy and practice have continuously changed, not least in response to the conditions from which they drive and on which they act (Chambers, 1997: 9).

A massive shift in priorities and thinking from things and infrastructure to people and capabilities has taken place in the 1980s and 1990s. Consistent with this shift, five concepts came to the fore, which are wellbeing, livelihood, capability, equity and sustainability (Chambers, 1997: 9). The relationship that combines these concepts is clear, in the way that the overarching end is wellbeing, with capabilities and livelihood as means. This in my view supports the link between the capabilities approach and the livelihood approach mentioned above and keeps the livelihood approach at distance from the basic needs approach.

But what is livelihood? At the beginning of the debate about livelihood, the concept was defined by the World Commission on Environment and Development (WCED) (1987, quoted in Chambers and Conway, 1992: 7) as "*adequate stocks and flows of food and cash to meet basic needs. Security refers to secure ownership of, or access to, resources and income-earning activities, including reserves and assets to offset risk*". Chambers and Conway modify this definition to be:

> "*a livelihood comprises the capabilities, assets (stores, resources, claims and access) and activities required for a means of living: a livelihood is sustainable which can cope with and recover from stress and shocks, maintain or enhance its capabilities and assets, and provide sustainable livelihood opportunities for the next generation: and which contributes net benefits to other livelihoods at local and global levels and in the short and long term*" (Chambers and Conway1992: 7)

Since this work of Chambers and Conway (1992), livelihood as a concept has been interpreted by many writers and organizations (Chambers and Conway, 1992: Chambers, 1997; Scoones, 1998; Brock, 1999; DFID, 1999; Shankland, 2000; Ellis, 2000; Ellis and Freeman 2005; IFAD 2007 and UNDP and CARE experiences indicated in Krantz, 2001). Most of the literature about livelihood is centered on studying the poor and their situations, other studies have treated the concept neutrally (Lont and Hospes, 2004: 6). For Lont and Hospes (2004) the focus on the poor originated in the work of Robert Chambers who proposed the use of the term in his criticism to the prevailing poverty alleviation programs which position the poor as passive victims. I can detect two groups of writers who have enlightened the steam of livelihood thinking. One group focuses on the situation of the poor, their capital, options and strategies: These are Chambers (1992, 1997, 1998), Chambers and Conway (1992), Ellis (2000), and Ellis and Freeman (2005). Other writers stress the vulnerability side of the livelihood concept, how people react in cases of shocks, risks and disasters; these are Scoones (1998), Wisner et al. (2004), and Dercon (2005). The importance of livelihood evolves when livelihood security is considered basic to wellbeing.

Some writers like Ellis (2000) argue that the crucial point of Chambers' definition is to give direct attention to the links between capital and the options people possess in practice to pursue alternative activities and opportunities that can generate the income level necessary for survival. Furthermore, Ellis (2000: 7) has raised a crucial question about the concept of capital in Chambers' definion, which is what type of capital or stocks can legitimately be included under the overarching description of capital that comprises the concept of livelihood?

Ellis (2000) comes up with a specific definition by adding some modifications to Chambers' and Conway's (1992) definition of livelihood. In his well-known book "Rural Livelihoods and Diversity in Developing countries", Ellis describes livelihood as "*a livelihood comprises the capital (natural, physical, human, financial and social capital), the activities, and the access to these (mediated by institutions and social relations) that together determine the living gained by individual or household*" (Ellis, 2000: 10). In general, Ellis' definition is more extensive and inclusive than the other definitions provided above, for he gives more attention to the types of capital livelihood can comprise, and categorizes them as natural, physical, human, financial and social capital. Also, he brings out the concept of access more strongly. Moreover, Ellis (2000: 10) adds institutions to the definition of livelihoods as ones regulating behavior that could have an impact on people's life. He not only includes institutions but also goes on to raise the issue of social relations, which is of a great importance for the scope of the research. Moreover, he focuses on the rural livelihood unlike other writers.

Regarding livelihood in rural areas, the discussion is more specific and focused on the features of rural areas in developing countries. The context of the rural livelihood is described by the concept "rural life" as discussed by Haan and Long (1997: x)[5]. They see rural life as multidimensional life where different social actors conceptualize and respond to this diversity; it is shaped and reshaped by actors' perspectives and actors' orientation toward their life, people's response to the state, the rural society, nature, the history and cultural construction of rural life. This rural life is constructed in networks of other actors like traders, policy makers and the political construct; "rurality" thus for Haan and Long (1997) is best illustrated by the concept of "co-operation" in the broadest possible sense of the word. Co-operation refers to the interaction between man and living nature; this is the process of production in which nature is converted into goods and services for human consumption. Agriculture is one basic component of such co-operation, but also involves the reproduction of specific social relations.

In describing the term 'rural livelihood', a set of interesting questions emerges; such as what differentiates rural areas and rural livelihoods? What makes rural livelihood unique and important to be described, researched and analyzed? Nevertheless, the comparison of urban and rural livelihood is beyond the scope of this research and an interesting topic for future research.

Rural livelihood in developing countries is viewed to struggle with both poverty and vulnerability. Most of the poor and vulnerable people live in rural areas. Even if a detailed description of rural livelihood in Sudan will be provided later in the empirical chapters about Al Dagag, there are some general statistics, which are important to keep in mind that justify the focus on rural areas. According to the United Nations Rural Poverty Report 2010 (UN, 2010), in the developing countries 59.5 % of the total population live in rural areas (UN, 2010: 11), and even 70 % of the poor (UN, 2010: 60). This clearly shows why much of the developmental effort should be focused on rural areas. Moreover, a lot of evidence and studies show that most of the rural people are more poor, deprived and vulnerable than their urban counterparts. Chambers (1997: 162) describes the realities of the rural poor as local, complex, diverse, dynamic and unpredictable. He explains that most rural livelihood activities involve vulnerable farming; forest-based and pastoral livelihoods often seek security by complicating and diversifying activities and multiplying linkages and supports to exploit varied and varying local resources and opportunities. In Sudan it is obvious that despite the accelerating urbanization and migration from rural to urban areas still most of the population, and specifically the poor, live in rural areas (IFAD, 2004).

Coming back to the definition of livelihood it is obvious that livelihood is seen in terms of capital, activities and strategies; next, I would like to present the theoretical debate about types of livelihood capital. A general description and classification of all forms of capital is presented first, and then the two types, which are seen as important by the people of Al Dagag, are explained further.

2.3 Livelihood Resources: Mingling Different Forms of Capital

Bourdieu (1986) was one of the first writers to differentiate between economic, cultural and social capital. He explains capital as "*accumulated labour which when appropriate on a private, i.e. exclusive, basis by agents or groups of agents, enables them to appropriate social energy in the form of reified or living labour*" (Bourdieu, 1986: 242). Bourdieu continues that the distribution of different types of capital reflects the immanent structure of the social world. He argues that the picture of the social world is not complete until different forms of capital are reintroduced. Thereby he challenges main-

[5] In their 1997 study, Haan and Long celebrate the study of rural life from a sociological point of view that seldom exists in the contemporary literature. Their book constitutes an important input to the description of rural life in what they call Western and non-Western societies.

stream economists who look at capital only as economic capital, since the economic capital is oriented toward exchange and the maximization of profit. Although Bourdieu's work is original in emphasizing the concept of capital into the sociology discussion, his work is still expressed in a philosophical way, which sometimes makes it hard to understand. What is interesting in Bourdieu's work is the notion of conversion between different types of capital and his explanation of social capital, which will be provided later in this dissertation.

Bourdieu (1986: 243) argues that the real logic of the functioning of capital is the conversion or transmission from one type to another. Capital can present itself in three forms as economic capital, cultural capital or social capital. The economic capital is immediately and directly convertible into money and may be institutionalized in the form of property rights. The cultural capital is convertible in certain conditions into economic capital and may be institutionalized in the form of educational qualifications and social capital is made up of social obligations, of 'connections', which under certain conditions are convertible into economic capital. The case of Al Dagag suggests that the benefits or resources circulated within the social capital are mainly economic or financial. Moreover, most of the financial relations are based mainly on and created within the social networks crucial for sustaining people's livelihood and providing them with security and insurance.

Other classifications of capital are offered by Swift (1989: 11) and modified by Chambers and Conway (1992: 9ff.) who differentiate between two types of capital in the livelihood thinking: tangible and intangible capital. The former is described in terms of resources and stores and the latter encompasses claims and access. Stores include such things as food stock, stores of value such as crops, gold or cash savings in banks and credit schemes, while resources comprise land, water, trees and livestock and farm equipment, tools and domestic utensils. Claims are demands and appeals for material, moral or other necessary support. For instance, food, loans, gifts, or labor assistance can be considered types of support. Chambers and Conway (1992) think that these claims are often needed at times of stress or shocks. They take place with relatives and neighbors or organizations like informal institutions or self help groups or NGOs, government or even on international institutions. However, these claims could be also made in times when there is no acute risk, for example gifts given at birth. Chambers and Conway (1992) see them as opportunities to get resources, stores or services or to gain information, material, technology, employment, food or income.

Swift (1989: 11) classifies investments as one form of capital to include human investment in such issues like education and health, individual productive capital including animals, farming equipments, houses and domestic equipment, land, trees wells and so on and collective capital as the other form, including soil conservation or water harvesting works, irrigation systems and access to common property resources.

The separation of capital into stores and resources on the one side, and claims and access on the other side by Chambers and Conway (1992) is rather confusing since they do not point to the areas where these forms of capital overlap. For instance, considering a loan taken from a relative or an organization, this loan could be transformed into a store if it is used for buying crops to keep until a time of higher prices, or could be transformed into a resource by buying different farm inputs or equipments. At the same time it is a financial claim which should be paid back and which an individual can only get if it has access to it. In addition to that, I could not locate aspects like people's skills, knowledge, social relations and networks to fit into this classification.

The aspect of access is also recognized by Scoones (1998) and Ellis (2000) but they extend it to include other issues. Ellis (2000: 9) explains access as rules and social norms that verify the differential ability of people in rural areas to own control or make use of resources such as land and common property. For Scoones (1998: 8), different people have different access to different livelihoods resources, and that depend on the institutional arrangements, power relations and political relationships. In addition to that, such factors as gender, wealth, and age can affect the allocation or control over resources. Another imperative point added by Ellis (2000: 9) is that access refers to the ability to get and drive benefits from social and public services offered by the state like education, health services, roads, water supply, and so on.

Two more issues should be mentioned within the discussion about forms of capital, for they have an effect on rural livelihoods. These issues are policies and institutions that exist in rural areas and have an impact on people's life. Brock (1999) argues for the inclusion of these two aspects to make the livelihood approach more comprehensive. He argues that institutions are crucial for people's livelihood and they range from the local institutions that mediate people's access to resources, to the macro institutions of state, markets and civil society (Brock, 1999: 15).

The categorization of Ellis (2000) is up to today the most comprehensive in the classification of forms of capital; natural, physical, human, financial and social capital:

> "*Natural capital refers to natural resources base (land, water, trees) that yields products utilized by human populations for their survival. Physical capital refers to assets brought into existence by economic production processes, for example, tools, machines and land improvements like terraces or irrigation canals. Human capital refers to educational level and health status of individuals and populations. Financial capital refers to stocks of cash that can be accessed in order to purchase either production or consumption foods and access to credit might be included in this category. Social Capital refers to the social networks and associations in which people participate and from which they can drive support that contributes to their livelihoods*"(Ellis, 2000: 8).

In the general debate about capital in the livelihood approach all types of capital are seen as significant for describing people livelihood. However, this research does not focus equally on all types of capital, as the scope and the case of the Al Dagag village require stressing two main types of capital, the economic capital that includes the financial resources, and the social capital, which plays a major role in sustaining people's livelihood. Nevertheless, the natural, physical, and human capital will also be highlighted when introducing the rural livelihood in the Al Dagag village in chapter 7.

2.3.1 Economic Capital Emphasizes Financial Relations

Ellis (2000: 8) explains economic capital as stocks of cash that can be accessed in order to procure goods and services that might be used for consumption or production. However, for Ellis the economic capital also includes the access to credit that constitutes financial capital[6]. Thus, economic capital does not only consist of cash but also of claims of credit that evolve from the need for finance. By defining economic capital, Scoones (1998: 8) focuses explicitly on including financial capital. Scoones believes that financial capital includes cash, credit/debt, and savings.

Based on the work of DFID (1999: 15), economic capital is defined as the "financial resources" that people use to achieve their livelihood objectives and these resources including:

- **Available stocks:** Savings are the preferred type of financial capital because there are no liabilities attached and they usually do not entail reliance on others. They can be held in several forms: cash, bank deposits or liquid capital such as livestock and jewelry. Financial resources can also be obtained through credit-providing institutions in which case liabilities are attached.
- **Regular inflow of money:** Excluding earned income, the most common types of inflow are pensions, or other transfers from the state, and remittances. In order to make a positive contribution to financial capital these inflows must be reliable—while complete reliability can never be guaranteed there is a difference between a one-off payment and a regular transfer with which people can plan investments.

This definition of DFID is broader and more practical than the two definitions stated above by Ellis (2000) and Scoones (1998), since it includes such factors as non-cash resources like gold and livestock, claims and transfers people have. Furthermore, it introduces the notion that not only the stock of cash is important but also the inflow and movement of cash flows.

In the large literature about economic development, it is obvious that little attention has been given to financial aspects; much concentration focuses on economic capital formation. Consequently, this literature provides only a narrow definition for finance as public finance, i. e. government revenue and expenditure. In their book "Money, Finance and Development" Drake and Robertson (1980) significantly contribute to developing the attention given to finance recently. This book has been a starting point of many contributions to the debate about finance; each from different points of view, resulting in different notions of what the concept of finance means.

Drake and Robertson (1980: 8) define finance as "*a process involving the creation, sale or transfer of financial assets including money*". Furthermore, Drake and Robertson (1980: 9), followed later by

[6] Financial capital and financial resources are used interchangeably in this research.

Schmidt and Kropp (1987: 5), differentiate between direct and indirect finance. Direct finance occurs when an actual saver (person, firm or government) lends to an actual spender (for investment or consumption). Finance is then considered a financial asset for the lender and a financial obligation for the borrower. Indirect finance involves intermediaries or middlemen, so savers lend to intermediaries who in turn lend to spenders. The intermediaries may be individuals or institutions and simultaneously engage in borrowing and lending. In progressive economies, banks and other financial institutions mainly play the role of intermediaries. However, in the developing countries, individual traders and moneylenders are very important intermediaries (ibid.). The classification of Drake and Robertson has also drawn attention to self-finance, in which spenders finance their own spending; however the question arises here whether this should be considered as finance, investment, or capital formation.

In spite of the fact that economists agree on defining finance as a process of channeling funds between surplus and deficit spending units, different writers focus on different aspects. For McLeod (1994: 88) finance is finding the best ways of transferring funds between surplus and deficit spending units and generate the greatest welfare gains to lenders and borrowers alike. However, Zander (1994: 193) focuses more on the demand side of finance, he describes finance as borrowers' preferences for specific savings and credit systems and that depends on their purchasing power or the price they should pay for that. Emery and Finnerty (1991: 1) reason that finance is also concerned with decision making about sources of funds. As other writers they also consider finance to be used only in production and investment. Most economists ignore that finance also plays a role in smoothing consumption. The distinction between production and consumption credits is crucial at macro level of finance, but at micro level of finance this could be misleading, a fact that will be explained in the next chapter.

More development oriented writers and economic anthropologists argue differently. For instance, Adams et al. (1984) and Krahnen and Schmidt (1994: 3) give a broad definition of finance as it encompasses the financial side, i. e. the monetary aspects and the inter-temporal decision aspects of all economic processes. This includes all activities, which involve savings, financing and insuring against (financial) risks. The work of Krahnen and Schmidt (1994: 9) has enlightened the discussion of what is finance by focusing on the financial system or the process of providing finance and the institutions involved.

Finance is also seen in a wider sense of "relationships". Crow (1994: 271) is one of the writers who pioneered the concept of financial relations in the definition of finance. Finance is here explained as the financial relations that have brought the rise and fall of relations between groups of lenders and borrowers. As illustrated by Crow, the concept of financial relations originates in the work of writers in the fields of economic anthropology and sociology, which have illuminated the diversity of the relations through which access to credits is obtained. Financial relations are embedded in the social structure. Political scientists and sociologists have shown how the outcome of policies directed at credit provision may depend on the power structure with special focus on the agrarian society and the ways that financial and other exchange relations reflect that power (Crow, 1994: 271).

Along the same line of argumentation, Bouman and Hospes (1994) argue that finance, financial relations and financial intermediation are all parts of what is called "financial landscapes". This includes "*the physical features of finance such as the offices of financial institutions and so on but also relations, norms, actions and processes influence, directly or indirectly the transactions of savers, borrowers and lenders*" (ibid.: 3). Financial landscapes also consist of the connections and disconnections between different kinds of savers, borrowers and lenders which constitute finance. Furthermore, the networks of money lending traders, money guards, banks and saving clubs and also the deliberate non-use of financial services and short-circuits between financial intermediaries are important in building up a financial landscape.

For simplicity, Seibel explains:

> "*If production is the motor of the economy, finance is its fuel. Unless there is a functioning fuel injection system, the motor will not run. The faster the motor is to run, the more fuel it needs. It is the financial system which has to pump the money into the economy: it has to mobilize savings, provide credit and assure an adequate growth of the money supply. An undersupply of money will stall the engine, thus halting the economy; an oversupply will lead to inflation, thus chocking the engine*" (Seibel, 1994: 23).

With these definitions and argumentations as a background and in the context of this research, I would argue that a definition related to financing the poor could be a combination of the definitions of finance by Crow (1994), Blake (2000) and Bouman and Hospes (1994). In such a combined definition, finance encompasses all financial relations and financial networks within the financial landscape that bring together borrowers (typically households), savers and lenders (institutions and individuals) to exchange different types of financial assets between the present and the future (including contingent inter-temporal transfers and insurance), with special emphasis on how this takes place in rural areas. Financial relations include concepts and practices of microfinance, agriculture finance, informal finance and others where they exist.

This further suggests that finance includes all financial relations and financial networks that directly and/or indirectly influence all financial transactions between borrowers (deficit spending households), savers (with surplus) and lenders (individuals and institutions) in rural areas. This includes not only credit relations but also mobilizing savings, and providing insurance and risk sharing mechanisms, to ensure general welfare gains to all parties involved alike.

2.3.2 Social Capital

The concept of social capital is broad, has been tackled from different points of views and applied to different areas of studies and places. I would like to argue here that the case of Al Dagag suggests focusing on the definition and explanation of Bourdieu (1986). However, I would like to highlight the philosophical roots of the social capital theory in brief before I give the theoretical explanation of the concept that matches the case of the research.

The main idea of social capital challenges the theoretical thinking of the methodological individualism, which insists on the individuals and their purposive behavior within a socio-economic context (Hodgson, 2007: 1f.). It assumes that individuals could live and succeed alone (Baker, 2000: 2). Baker also states that individualism confronts the thinking that social capital is an essential part of achieving personal success, business success and even a happy and satisfying life. Individualism also argues that society consists of a set of independent individuals each of whom acts to achieve goals that are independently achieved (Baker, 2000: 4; Groot et al., 2007).

The discussion about social capital emphasized in the work of Bourdieu (1986) was followed by the work of James S. Coleman (Bartkus and Davis, 2009: 17). In the 1990s more and more scholars started to focus on the social capital and to realize its importance for all social sciences. However, the work of Robert Putnam et al. (1993) places more attention on the concept of social capital (Bartkus and Davis, 2009: 17). For Quibria (2003), the concept of social capital has been recently applied to explain different social and economic phenomena such as growth in Africa, mortality crises in Russia, successful group lending in Peru and the flourishing township village enterprise in China (Quibria, 2003: 1).

Bartkus and Davis (2009: 3) collected and discussed a group of what they have called "accepted" definitions of the concept of social capital in a table. It is obvious that some of the scholars focus on the structure of the social relations like Tocqueville (1945), Hanifan (1920) and recently Adler and Kwon (2002). Others focus on defining it in terms of benefits or resources embedded within, available through and derived from a network of relationship (Bourdieu, 1986; Bourdieu and Wacquant, 1992; Loury, 1992; Putnam, 1993) and I add here the recent and relevant work by Scoones (1998: 8), Ellis (2000: 8); Hulme and Toye (2007) and Bartkus and Davis (2009) themselves. The structure is viewed in terms of the network size, configuration and density. Meanwhile the content includes resources, norms and values prevailing in the social network. The case of Al Dagag suggests focusing on the relationship aspect of benefits as this shows how social capital is used to deal with poverty and vulnerability within the development thinking. However, the aspect of structure is not completely ignored. I would argue here that the resources gained by members of a network also depend on the structure and content of the network.

The question arises when scrutinizing the case of Al Dagag what does the concept of social capital mean in the context of poverty and vulnerability? It is worth mentioning here that there is a gap in the literature regarding studying social capital in the context of rural poverty and vulnerability in the Third World[7], how social capital works in the day-to-day life of rural people in the village, and how

[7] The most relevant work done to link social capital with financial development is the working paper prepared by Guiso et al. (2000) that research the role of social capital in financial development. However, it focuses on the Italian society and considers social capital as national characteristic as it compares between the Northern and Southern regions of Italy. The focus on this paper is the work of Putman (1993) and Fukuyama (1995) that is noticed to be

people surviving in the world of poverty and vulnerability have made use of it. Thus, this research aims to provide the practical or day-to-day meaning of social capital in the context of rural poverty and vulnerability using the case of Sudan.

Thus, to understand the social capital in Al Dagag Bourdieu's definition is illustrative; he argues that social capital is

> "*the aggregate of the actual or potential resources which are linked to possession of a durable network of more or less institutionalized relationships of mutual acquaintance and recognition or in other words to membership in a group which provides each of its members with the backing of the collectivity-owned capital, a 'credential' which entitles them to credit, in the various sense of the word*" (Bourdieu, 1986: 249).

This definition is far-reaching and thorough for putting social networks of people and their mutual relationships in the center of social capital, and also sheds light on the importance of the benefits (or as he calls it, "profits") that could be gained by each member of these social networks. These profits, which accumulate from membership in a group or a network, are the basis of the solidarity that exists between the group members. Thus, the volume of the social capital achieved by a given member depends on the size of the network of connections he or she can effectively be involved in and on the volume of the capital (economic, cultural or symbolic) possessed in his or her own right by each of those to whom he or she is connected. Bartkus and Davis (2009: 2) add to this discussion that the benefits of joining any social relationship vary to great extent and they might include learning enhanced skills, gaining new information or accessing opportunities.

Furthermore, Bourdieu (1986: 249) emphasizes that the network of relations is the product of investment strategies, individual or collective, consciously or unconsciously intended to establish or reproduce social relationships that are directly exploitable in the short or long term. That is to mean the transforming of relations, such as those of neighborhood, the work place, or even kinship into relations that are vital and not obligatory but at the same time imply strong responsibilities subjectively felt (feelings of appreciation, respect, friendship and so on) or institutionally guaranteed. Glaeser et al. (2000: 29) support this view and argue that individuals accumulate social capital when the private incentives for such accumulations are high.

Because analyzing interviews of respondents has revealed the effect of social capital in Al Dagag, I started asking myself why it is so successful and sustainable over long period of time. I found a theoretical answer in the work of Baker (2000) who argues that social capital is based on the two concepts reciprocity and trust. He suggests the phrase of "help others helps you" to be the real meaning of reciprocity (Baker, 2000: 128) that can build long-term social relationships that focus on what you get out of the relationship. The same phrase has been used repeatedly by respondents as will be demonstrated in chapter 8. Baker (2000) argues that reciprocity is one of the most powerful principles in the world of relations, local or in everyday life, national and even internationally. The reciprocity principle works because it is universal, sociologists have called it a "principal component" of all moral codes or rules that governs all human relations (Baker, 2000: 134). Baker suggests that the principle of reciprocity explains why building social capital works. The main principle is that when you use your networks to contribute to others, others contribute to you. Reciprocity enforces uninvited debts and triggers unfair exchange (Baker, 2000: 135). Indeed, whether or not you think it through to its logical end—when you help someone—you implicitly expect help in return and you would be miffed if you did not get it. Thus, the paradox is that the less we worry about reciprocity the more we get out; the more we contribute to others without expectation of repayment the more we are paid in the future (Baker, 2000: 170).[8] The same idea is provided in the work of Bartkus and Davis (2009) who argue that the focus on social capital reveals that relations are build every day with family, friends and others. The relationships we enjoy in their own right, but they also serve to help us through tough times or enable us to achieve our goals. I have found this also applicable to the case of Al Dagag since the social networks play a major role as insurance mechanism used to deal with shock or disaster.

---

the point of capturing the attention of several economists (Guiso et al., 2000: 1). This paper also is looking at the institutional and economic consequences of social capital and trust.

[8] In most of literature about social capital the concept of trust has been highlighted as the basis of forming networks and associations (Groot et al., 2007: 3).

2.3.3 Social Capital in Business and Trade[9]

Tackling the concept of social capital within the context of poverty and vulnerability suggest that different aspects of people might be affected by their involvement in such relations. In Al Dagag, I can argue that as the social capital affects people generally in a positive way, however, it might have positive and negative effects on trade and businesses. This is mainly explained in theories of moral economy, embeddedness of the economic activities within the social structure, and the trader's dilemma.

I find the work of Granovetter (1985) that elaborates the concept of embeddedness of the economic action in the social structure relevant to describe the link between social capital and business and trade in Al Dagag. In his famous paper "Economic action and social structure: The problem of embeddedness" (1985) he challenges the presumption of economists that market processes are not suitable objects of sociological study because social relations play only a fractioned and disruptive role in premodern and no actual role at all in modern societies.

Granovetter (1985) addresses the question of how institutions are affected by the social relations. He argues that it is misleading to understand insinuations in separation of the social relations in any community. Moreover, he stresses the point that the embeddedness of the economy in social relations is something that has been taking place for a long time before the emergence of the modernization when the transactions in the market became more autonomous. He tries to bring together both ideas of the modern market that undersocialize behavior and the sociological perspective that oversocializes behavior. In the space between the two spheres comes the concept of embeddedness.

The concepts of trust and malfeasance illustrate Granovetter's argument. He argues that the economists, or as he calls their viewpoint, the "undersocialized thinking" assumes that institutions and agents in the market might behave with guile and deception carrying out the market transactions. They assume that the competitive market perfectly treats such behavior; and by doing so, they portray the picture of the "gentlemanly fashion" of agents. The embeddedness theory challenges this idea by asking the question, how such behavior could be eliminated in the imperfect market. In contrast the oversocialized thinking assumes a generalized morality that corrects and guides behavior. In the middle rung of these two views, the embeddedness theory argues for the existence of the social networks norms that discourage malfeasance. What guides agents and people behavior is the set of choices built on the pervious relations between people in the society, Granovetter positions trust as one of these choices. To him embeddedness theory is at the core of the moral economy, which Booth (1994) explains as follows:

> "*Pre-modern economies are moral because they are an integral part of social relations and non-economic institutions. Of course, how economic and social relations work together will differ depending on various contexts but the common thread running through an understanding of a pre-modern moral economy is that aims, objectives and processes are informed and directed by the non-economic*" (Booth, 1994: 1).

However, the effects of social capital are not always positive for both parties in trade especially in the peasant society where the main determinant of individuals and households behavior is their social connections. The traders' dilemma is the best explanation of this issue and related to the case of Al Dagag. The traders' dilemma was originally discussed in the famous book of Evers and Schrader "The moral economy of trade" in 1994. Evers and Schrader explain that "*a dilemma is a situation in which an actor has to choose between two courses of action, both deemed to be equally unfavourable, undesirable or at best neutral*" (Evers and Schrader, 1994: 7). Moreover, there is no clear-cut solution or guidance to direct this actor toward the right choice. In the traders' dilemma, the actor is a trader who lives in a peasant society that is described by a high degree of solidarity and by the existence of a value system that emphasizes mutual help, the sharing of resources and subsistence security in a reciprocal manner. In this society, the social pressure on the traders in the village to be open-handed toward their less fortunate neighbors, relatives and friends (ibid.) makes it difficult to impose a system of market trade. Thus, considering these features of society, traders find themselves faced with many problems in dealing with the members of their society with whom they are well socially connected. These traders face a problem

[9] I have selected this title to reflect on the specific case of Al Dagag since the theory of embeddedness takes the economic actions and behavior more into account.

that "*arises out of their moral obligation to share proceeds with kinfolks and neighbors on the one hand and the necessity to make profits and accumulate trading capital on the other*" (Evers and Schrader, 1994: 5)[10].

The next part shifts the discussion from capital to livelihood activities in rural areas.

2.4 Rural Livelihood Activities

Rural livelihood activities highlight the distinctive features of rural areas. Chambers and Conway (1992: 11) point out that rural livelihood comprises one or frequently several activities in any rural household. According to Ellis (2000: 10), activities are sources of income, reflecting different features of the resources required to generate them, their seasonality and accessibility to them depending on capital and skills and their nearby or remote location. Within rural communities, different individuals possess differing potential access to different activities and therefore different income sources convey varying impacts on poverty and income distribution.

These livelihood activities can incorporate cultivation, herding, hunting, gathering reciprocal or wage labor, trading and hawking, artisanal work such as weaving and carving, processing, providing services in transport, fetching and carrying and the like, begging, and theft. That is to mean, rural livelihoods are not of homogeneous nature or stereotyped forms of activities. What is important about livelihood activities is that they variously provide food, cash, and other goods to satisfy a wide variety of human needs. These are called by Ellis and Freeman (2005: 5) the "material welfare". However, rural people do not consume all these outputs immediately; some of these outputs will be stored for short or long periods of time or to be reinvested in acquiring other capital (Chambers and Conway, 1992: 11).

Evidence from many studies like Bernstein et al. (1992: 3), Chambers and Conway (1992) and Ellis (2000) shows that farming is central to rural economies almost everywhere in the Third World. Farming is important as a direct source of employment and income and as an indirect source through a range of activities connected with farming like supply of inputs, equipments, seeds, fertilizers and services like credit, technical assistance and construction and maintenance of infrastructure such as irrigation work and roads.

The assumption that rural livelihood only depends on agriculture is not completely true since livelihood in rural areas can be generated from other sources; some of these other sources are related to agriculture but others are not, like petty trading or small scale entrepreneurship and enterprises. This is specifically true concerning the climatic changes that are taking place recently and leaving serious affects on rural livelihood activities, mainly agriculture. Many environmental changes have led to a shift in rural activities from focusing only on agriculture to other means of living. Agriculture in a very vulnerable situation is not a reliable source of income, especially for those rural poor who do not own any land, or whose land is not sufficient for adequate production to sustain their livelihood. Others lack the essential facilities and equipments or finance crucial to agriculture and farming. Rural poor characterized by landlessness or marginalization as farmers must pursue livelihood through a range of means.

In the literature, general classifications made with regard to activities people usually pursue in rural areas, often divide them into farm and non-farm activities and income (Ellis, 2000: 11f.). Dolan (2005: 82) provides a different and more detailed classification of livelihoods activities, ranging within agriculture (crop or farm based activities), from agriculture (livestock rearing), over non-farm income activities, self employment and trade, wage employment, to income acquired from remittances and other transfers. This detailed classification allows for more activities to be included and described like income gained from remittances and transfers which are of great relevance for rural people.

Livelihood activities are also found to be different between women and men in rural areas. Thereby, the work of Moser and particularly her Gender Planning Framework (Moser, 1993; UNDP, 2001: 43) that refers to women's triple roles (productive, reproductive, and community involvement) and maps them over a 24-hour period is important when discussing the role of women in securing rural livelihood. According to Moser, productive roles are work done for remuneration, in cash or kind like wage labor, farming, or craft. Reproductive roles are those associated with child rearing/raising and caretaking of the home and domestic

---

[10] Evers and Schrader further discus different theoretical solutions to the traders' dilemma and discuss action strategies open to traders in pursuit of solving their dilemma (1994).

tasks that guarantee the maintenance and reproduction of the current and future work force like cooking and cleaning. Community involvement highlights those tasks related to collective support and community gains that support collective consumption and maintenance of community resources. Women are perceived as main contributors to the wellbeing of all members of society in most of the literature about livelihood activities. Women in developing countries contribute majorly to the wellbeing of members of society. Seebens (2009) provides a comparative description of both male-headed and female-headed households in theory and its application in Kenya. Seebens' main argumentation is that even with their major contribution in the household's wellbeing, the status of women in developing countries is often precarious as women are deprived in many aspects.

For most of the rural population, livelihood activities include distant and nearby, cash as well as non-cash income generating activities. Migration and remittances are considered part of these activities (Dolan, 2005: 82). Other writers like Chambers and Conway (1992) and Scoones (1998) look at migration as a coping strategy rather than an activity normally carried out by rural people. In the case of Al Dagag, the prevailing type of migration is seasonal migration in summer and considered a livelihood activity by the respondents themselves for it is used to generate income to complement agriculture income. Other types of migration like migration in case of drought are considered a coping strategy.

Commonly most literature about livelihood locates migration as a central process of social transformation, especially rural urban migration. Migration is considered a dynamic process that shapes rural livelihood. This also applies to the case of Al Dagag as will be demonstrated in the empirical chapters. Interview analysis revealed that the seasonal migration in Al Dagag fits the attributes of the theoretical perspective of the New Economics of Labor Migration (NELM) approach, for the main aim behind migration is economic as described by Rabby et al. (2010: 279). Seasonal migration is a source of income diversification of households to find work in summer when there is not farming work available, as soon as the autumn starts men who migrated in summer return back to cultivate their land. Even those few men who migrated to cities and stay there permanently usually come back and cultivate their land in autumn.[11] Moreover, the decision to migrate is taken by a collective of household members and not by individuals (Stark, 1991; Sander and Maimbo, 2003; Deshingkar and Start, 2003; Konseiga, 2005; Haas, 2008; Rabby et al., 2010).

Stark shifts the emphasis on households rather than on individuals as units of analysis with regard to migration:

> "*Migration decisions are often made jointly by the migrant and by some group of nonmigrants. Cost and returns are shared, with the rule governing the distribution of both spelled out in an implicit contractual arrangement between the two parties.*" (Stark, 1991: 25)

Rabby et al. (2010) consider this shift the main contribution of the NELM approach to the theory of migration. He argues that it conceptualizes the decision to migrate as a combined decision of many household members rather than any isolated individual. To explain further, the individuals in a household act collectively not only to maximize household income but also to minimize risk and to loosen constrains associated with different types of market failure for instance crop insurance and imperfect capital markets, and future markets (Stark, 1991; Rabby et al., 2010; Haas, 2008). Haas adds that migration can be a household strategy to enable households to invest in productive activities and to improve their livelihood. Thus, migration is a part of a broader household livelihood strategy to diversify income sources and overcome social, economic, and institutional development constraints in the place of origin. Sander and Maimbo (2003: 11) explain how the decision is made within the household; when a farm household is in need, they might choose to place a family member in a migrant labor market; such a household can create a new financial intermediary in the form of the migrant. In turn, migrants provide their households with liquidity (in the form of remittances) and with insurance.

While remittances do not play a role in neo-classical migration theory, within the NELM model they are perceived as one of the most essential motives for migrating (Haas, 2008: 36; Deshingkar and Start, 2003: 3; Stark,1991). Konseiga (2005: 4) studied the household migration decisions as survival strategy in Burkina Faso, and argues that remittances could play a major role in improving the agriculture technology. Konseiga explains that migration and remittances could raise production output of the

---

[11] Alhadi and Alnaeem who work in Khartoum but still have their wives and kids in Al Daggag are good examples to illustrate this phenomenon.

migrant household when they are used to resolve the constraints that limit the growth of their activity. The resulting benefits are expected to be stronger in the case of seasonal migration as opposed to geographically distant and permanent migration. This approach is supported by the findings of this research about the issue of remittances in Al Dagag.

2.5 Vulnerability Analysis: "Living on the Edge"

Diverse scientific disciplines define vulnerability in varying ways since they focus on different components of risk (Naudé et al., 2008: 1). In economics, main interest has been on vulnerability to poverty and income shortages, which is frequently defined as the risk of households falling into or remaining in poverty. Meanwhile, other researchers have been concerned with vulnerability to natural hazards and macro-level shocks. For example, Sen (1980, 1982) mainly focuses on linking vulnerability to food shortages and hunger. Chambers (1989) therefore considers vulnerability as one among other dimensions of deprivation, which are poverty, isolation, physical weakness and powerlessness. Nevertheless, unlike the other dimensions, vulnerability has remained neglected in analysis and policy actions as pointed out by Ellis and Freeman (2005: 6).

Vulnerability is not identical with poverty. For Chambers (1989: 1) and Naudé et al. (2008), vulnerability can be seen as the risk that a "system" would undergo a negative change due to a "perturbation". Therefore, vulnerability is not a lack or want, but defenselessness, insecurity and exposure to risks, shocks and stress (Chambers, 1989: 1). It also refers to exposure to contingencies and stress. Not only that, it also denotes any difficulties in coping with such stress. Ellis and Freeman (2005: 6) argue that vulnerability refers to proneness to a sudden, catastrophic fall in the level of a variable, which is usually access to enough food for survival but could also be capital in general. Ellis and Freeman portray a very interesting physical picture of the concept vulnerability when introducing the phrase "living on the edge". As they explain, this phrase provides a graphic image of the livelihood condition that vulnerability addresses. In their words, "*this phrase evokes the sense of a small push sending a person or people over the edge and it is just this knife edge between ability to survive and thrive and sudden loss of ability to do so*" (Ellis and Freeman, 2005: 6). Vulnerability then is "*the proneness of a household or family to acute food insecurity when confronted by a calamitous event like drought or flood*" (ibid.).

I would like to stick to Chambers' explanation of vulnerability provided above more than Ellis' and Sen's meaning of vulnerability. It is true that even in the case of Al Dagag food shortage is one of the people's concerns but vulnerability is more than that, requires a wider view. I find the work of Adams et al. (1998: 262) matches what I have found in the case of Al Dagag. According to them, the narrow focus on famine and food insecurity has limited the analysis of vulnerability and reduced the attention to other aspects. There is a variety of other household crises that also deserve analysis, such as conflicts, droughts, illness or death of a productive worker. For instance, rural people could be vulnerable to rainfall, seasonality, drought, instability of income sources, animal or plant diseases, market failures, trade failures and others. This idea is clearly discussed by Swift (1989: 8) when he gives examples of other types of vulnerability of people in rural areas. Landless laborers and people in the informal sector are vulnerable to disruption of the rural economy. Also small pastoralists may have a reasonable cash income and high nutritional standards most of the time, but are especially vulnerable to disruptions of the livestock market or to epidemic disease.

Analyzing the respondents' perspective in Al Dagag reveals that assets are at the core of analyzing and measuring vulnerability. This is also identified in the work of both Chambers (1989: 1) and Swift (1989). I would argue here that vulnerability can be measured with respect to the assets to which rural people have access to or control over and can be used to cope with shocks and disasters. This argument is also supported by Swift (1989) in his critique of Sen's entitlement approach; he develops a new analysis of vulnerability and security and argues that any analysis of vulnerability should be focused on assets. According to him, in order to improve our understanding of vulnerability and its measurement, a detailed analysis of assets should be carried out. These assets are created when production leads to a surplus beyond immediate consumption requirements and households use this surplus willingly or unwillingly to invest, to build up physical stores of all kinds and to invest in claims by putting more resources into the community government. Much of this capital brings cash when a household is in crisis, production capital is sold, granaries are emptied, gold is cashed in, bank accounts emptied, loaned animals recalled, labor debts called in and community support mechanisms activated (Swift, 1989: 11).

Many factors can dispose rural people to vulnerability such as shocks and risks, seasonality, which causes what is known as the consumption smoothing problem in many rural households (Morduch, 1995). Since poor rural households in low-income countries build their livelihood in a risky environment, they are subjected to many types of risks and shocks such as personal shocks of sickness, accidents and death or natural disasters. Seasonality is another type of risk that the poor face in rural areas as well as fluctuating and failure of markets and prices. Seasonality refers to seasonal changes in weather, capital, activities, prices, production, health, employment opportunities, etc. Vulnerability arising from seasonality is often caused by seasonal changes in the value and productivity of natural capital and human capital (through sickness, hunger, etc.). However, the effects of these shocks and risks may differ between the poor and non-poor. In other words, it varies between those with fewer assets and those who have more entitlement to assets, according to the measurement of vulnerability mentioned above. It has been argued that the poor are often more vulnerable to these shocks and risks than wealthier groups (DFID, 1999).

Some of these shocks and risks are predictable others are not. The household might become more affected and with less ability to cope in the case of unpredicted shocks and risks. Fafchamps (1999) emphasizes the notion that risks and shocks dramatically affect rural people's livelihood because of their unpredictable nature. Predictable risks are like the absence of rain in the dry season. Other risks occur in a hazard fashion that cannot be predicted, at least not precisely, and have a serious and always negative impact on people's life. These risks affect both health and wellbeing on the one side and income and utility of rural people on the other side (1999: 2).

Some risks have less impact than others do. Some are devastating in nature while others are minor. Chambers and Conway (1992: 14) and Fafchamps (1999) argue that there are types of shock and disasters accumulative in nature. They give examples for livelihood stress, which accumulates over time and leaves a devastating impact on individuals and households. Such stress is for instance a combination or succession of declining labor work availability, declining real wages, declining yields on soil, declining common property resources. In addition to having to work longer for less, thus gaining less access to fuel, fodder, grazing or water, declining rainfall, population pressure on resources leading to declining returns, indebtedness, physical disabilities, and the effects of these gradually affect the whole household.

Another view examines another dimension of shocks and risks by focusing on whether stress affects individuals or the whole community. Examples of shocks that affect whole communities are wars, persecutions and civil violence, droughts, storms, floods, fires, famines, landslides, epidemics, and the collapse of a market. This kind of focus on vulnerability is, for example, found in "At risk" by Wisner et al. (2004). Examples of shocks that affect both individuals and households are accidents, sudden sickness, the death of a family member or of a valued animal, loss of capital through theft, fire or other disaster and loss of a job; examples as stressed in the work of Chambers and Conway (1992), Morduch (1995) Fafchamps (1999), Ellis (2000) and Ellis and Freeman (2005).

Fafchamps (1999) points to yet another set of risks: "*ritual risks which emerge from expected or unexpected customary expenditures for example the expenditure for a funeral*" (1999: 4). Another category are business risks that emerge from the fact that a large majority of households living in poor rural economies have businesses, such as a farm, an artisanal workshop, a trading activity or a service operation. Most of these businesses are related to agriculture and offer little protection against natural events. In addition, most of the non-farm businesses found in rural areas are small, undercapitalized and underequipped and this makes them very vulnerable to shocks. Even wage employment when available in rural areas is typically casual or not permanent (Fafchamps, 1999: 5).

I would like to conclude this discussion by arguing that any developmental efforts cannot be successful as long as they ignore vulnerability in terms of shocks and disasters that affect the assets and capital people have control over. As it is clear from the case of Al Dagag, vulnerability is linked to great degree to poverty. It is further considered one of the causes of poverty and it plays a major role in deepening the degree of poverty. In Al Dagag where there are no developmental efforts from the government to enhance the livelihood of the poor and but few NGOs provide a limited scope of help a set of questions arises. How do the poor and vulnerable survive and thrive? What are the livelihood strategies and activities they conduct and what coping strategies are used in situations of shocks and risks? Do they present appropriate solutions? These questions are the basis of the next sub-chapter that provides the theoretical background to what people might do in rural areas and provides a better understanding of what actually happens in Al Dagag.

2.6 Determinants of Rural Livelihood

In the livelihood literature many determinants have been discussed (Ellis, 2000), however, in the context of Al Dagag I found two determinants of livelihood more significant. These are, rural household strategies, composition of households, intra-household decision making and financial responsibilities on the one hand and the diversification of coping strategies that are taken by household to react to poverty and vulnerability on the other hand.

2.6.1 Rural Household Strategies

In the beginning of this section, I will briefly reflect on the concept of the household. Then I will discuss the general theoretical debate on household strategies. Within the discussion about household decision-making, the bargaining model explaining the relationships between members of a household is relevant to the case of Al Dagag, thus the focus of the analysis of household will be concentrated on this model. Later in this section, I discuss income allocation systems in Sudan in the literature, even though the work of Schultz et al. 2008 and Schultz 2005 focuses on semi urban areas in Sudan. Nevertheless, some models of household decision making and allocation of resources discussed in this literature I found to be applicable to the case of Al Dagag.

2.6.1.1 Questioning the Concept of the Household

Kabeer (1994: 113) discusses the concept of the household from an anthropological point of view. Some anthropologists have started to challenge the very validity of the concept of household, because it views households as monolithic, clearly bounded units. Therefore, anthropologists have provided an alternative view of the household's flexible structures in which boundaries are difficult to determine (Kabeer, 1994: 113f.). The main argumentation is that the composition of households and relations of members within households are diverse and mostly mediated through marriage or kinship, but can create a variety of marital and residential arrangements. Anthropologists also doubt the idea that only familial rules guide the composition of households and refer to different other rules like adoption and temporary residential sharing (Kabeer, 1994: 114). They also reject the notion that familial ties necessarily imply purely voluntary and altruistic interactions, pointing to the contractual nature of household relations (ibid.).

The findings of this research confirm the argument that households are difficult to define and set their boundaries, as will be explained later in chapter 7 in the case of Al Dagag. Moreover, what is going on within and between households is found to be shaping the social and financial relations in the community.

Consequently how household are going to be classified in this research will depend on Kabeer's (1994: 113) definition of household: "*the term household refers to the bundle of relationships in a society through which its primary reproductive activities are organized, recognizing that these frequently involve principles of kinship and residence.*" Kabeer's definition falls in line with the research findings suggesting that it is not so important to define the concept of household but to explain the intra household relationships and the household economy which "*refers to the rules, relations and distribution of the valued resources essential for meeting the needs of its members*" (Kabeer, 1994: 115). In addition to that, Agarwal (1997: 3) points to the importance of analyzing the main actors in the household who have different interests and different abilities to pursue these interests.

In her study of one village in the Darfur region, "Making a living in rural Sudan" (1998), Grawert points to the concept of "peasant households" in rural Sudan. I find her descriptions could in certain aspects also be applicable to the case of Al Dagag. She identifies peasants in rural "*Sudan as women and men who live in farm households, have access to land which they use as a means of livelihood and utilize mainly labour in farming. Peasants are socially differentiated and cannot be categorized in one single social class. They share adherence to the land, even if they are active in diverse livelihood-securing activities*" (Grawert, 1998: 24). She highlights the importance of agriculture to the peasant household in rural Sudan and links much household behavior to that. She locates peasant as the main actors in their life, they are responsible to decide about all households concerns like cultivated crops, methods of cultivation, allocation of labor and so on. They are also burdened with the risks of agricultural production. Hence, peasants' agriculture production in rural Sudan is subject to conditions, which cannot be influenced by peasants. However, they employ different means to ease these conditions (Grawert, 1998: 53).

2.6.1.2 Intra-Household Decision Making: Households as Units of Co-operation and Conflict

Kabeer's study "Revised realities" (1994) includes a very interesting article that focuses on gender and household economics, and discusses the bargaining process inside the household. Kabeer (1994: 109) points out that in the bargaining theory behavioral outcomes are expected to indicate rights and obligations as well as economic incentives. The structure of households suggests that the relationships within this household are long-term relations and not periodic or temporary relations. Thus, they give a sense of stability to household behavior. In Kabeer's words:

> "*The bargaining process thus generates interesting contractual relationships between different household members, specifies their rights and obligations to each other as the basis of household cooperation. Individual members are likely to observe the terms of the contract as long as they are better off than they would be should the contract break down. Attempts to renegotiate—and achieve success at negotiation—will reflect changes in individual circumstances which in turn impinge on relative bargaining power within the household Decision-making within the household is thus seen as the resolution of potentially conflicting preferences through a process of negotiation between unequals*" (Kabeer, 1994: 109).

What has been described by Kabeer is important in order to understand the bargaining behavior within households. What makes people co-operate within a household are not only individual interests but "*also powerful normative pressures backed up by the threat of social sanctions, which make the choice of household membership a social rather than a purely individual*" (Kabeer, 1994: 109). Kabeer cites Sen (1990) who extends the bargaining model in a way that more explicitly reflects issues of gender and power within the household. For Kabeer, "*Sen's household is a site of cooperative conflict*". This means the co-operation between household members will go on and have effect as long as it leads to outcomes that are preferable to those in the absence of co-operation (Kabeer, 1994: 109). Agarwal (1997: 4) also sees households as units of co-operation and conflict and argues that many co-operation outcomes become possible in relation to who does what, who gets what goods and services and how each member is treated. These generally constitute the main factors of the bargaining model.

The bargaining model within household economics emerged as a criticism of the unitary household model, which assumes that households' members seek to maximize utility based on a set of common preferences represented by an aggregate utility function and common budget constraints (Agarwal, 1997: 2). The criticism of this approach led to the emergence of a game-theoretic approach, which allows for individual differences in preferences in both budget constraints and in the control of resources within the household. Within this framework of the game theoretic model is the bargaining model. Schultz holds:

> "*Since the 1980s the utilitarian concept of the household where the household is conceptualized as a decision making unit under the umbrella of a benevolent director is contested by bargaining models within the game theory, anthropological evidence and feminist theories which construct the household as a space where patriarchal power is manifested*" (Schultz 2005: 410).

Schultz describes the household as an arena for bargaining and negotiating in which both parties achieve a desired result by co-operating, when one looks at the possible co-operation outcomes. Schultz sees differences in preferences concerning the co-operative solution as the main cause of conflicts in the household. Moreover, which solution ultimately succeeds is determined by the bargaining power of partners.

The intra-household relations and the social norms are also affected by the social norms that exist in the whole society. Many anthropologists argue that intra-household relations vary in form from one society to another. They point to its cross-cultural variations; they mostly agree to the idea that there are certain regional uniformities in the social relations that govern production, distribution, and consumption within the household. One of these regional uniformities is the "patriarchal system" that exists in northern Africa, the Middle East and some countries in Asia like Bangladesh and India (Kabeer, 1994: 115). Patriarchy as a concept is explained by Kandiyoti (1988: 275) in her paper "Bargaining With Patriarchy" as an overly monolithic conception of male dominance. The system is structured around cultural rules that focus on male responsibility to do the protection and provisioning of women and children. Kabeer names "*the practices of female seclusion, patrilineal inheritance and patrilocal residence interlock to produce corporately organized, patriarchal household forms. The social norms of male breadwinner/female dependent are reflected in men's privileged, albeit class-differentiated, clams to material and labour opportunities*" (1994: 115). Kandiyoti explains how patriarchy constrains women's bargaining power on the one side, yet opens up specific ways of bargaining on the other side:

> "*I will argue that women strategize within a set of concrete constraints that reveal and define the blueprint of what I will term the patriarchal bargain' of any given society, which may exhibit variations according to class, caste, and ethnicity. These patriarchal bargains exert a powerful influence on the shaping of women's gendered subjectivity and determine the nature of gender ideology in different contexts. They also influence both the potential for and specific forms of women's active or passive resistance in the face of their oppression. Moreover, patriarchal bargains are not timeless or immutable entities, but are susceptible to historical transformations that open up new areas of struggle and renegotiation of the relations between genders*" (Kandiyoti, 1988: 275).

Kandiyoti also points out that in this system women and men are assigned separate responsibilities in providing for the household. These responsibilities usually assign supplying all or most of the family food to the husband and other duties to the wife. It is common that women and men in this system co-operate in producing collective subsistence needs and use their residual time to pursue their own-account activities (Kandiyoti, 1988: 275).

Agarwal (1997: 14) adds to this discussion the fact that social norms among other factors influence the bargaining process, the outcomes and what is bargained over in the household even within one uniform society, e. g. within the patriarchy system. These factors are assumed by Agarwal to include ownership and control over assets, access to employment and other income earning means, access to communal resources, access to traditional social support systems like kinship, support from NGOs and the state, social perception about needs contributions and social norms (Agarwal, 1997: 8f.). The main assumption here is that these factors determine a person's fall-back position in the bargaining process and influence her or his ability to make contributions within relationships. Moreover, these factors affect women's and men's subsistence opportunities and access to resources from outside the family and thus the bargaining power and the access to subsistence within the family as well (ibid.). Her focus on social norms comes from the fact that they have a double effect, directly on the bargaining position and indirectly by affecting the other factors. She explains that social norms set the limits of bargaining (Agarwal, 1997: 15). Some social norms fall within an arena that cannot be discussed because it is agreed upon in the society whereas others are bargained over and can be discussed:

> "*Social norms can define which issues can be legitimately be bargained over and which fall in the arena of the uncontestable. At any given time for a given society some decisions would fall in the realm of what Bourdieu (...) (1977) (...) terms 'doxa'- that which is accepted as a natural and self-evident part of the social order, which goes without saying and is not open to questioning or contestation—the 'undiscussed, unnamed, admitted without argument or scrutiny'. A good deal of what is justified in the name of tradition would fall in this category ... In contrast to doxa is the field of 'opinion, of that which is explicitly questioned,' the locus of the confrontation of competing discourses*" (Agarwal, 1997: 15).

Bourdieu's "doxa" includes a set of varied but widely accepted norms and practices. Some of the norms address the gender relations and the bargaining power in the household such as norms, which define the gender division of labor within and outside the home, sometimes even whether women can work outside the home at all. Agarwal (1997: 15f.) argues further that these limits of bargaining may favor group over individual interest or favor some groups over others, say men over women, or favor some individuals over others, say older women over younger women. She claims that social norms mostly weaken the position of women in the bargaining process, when women are not allowed to work outside the home, when they ideologically construct women as dependents and men as sole breadwinners.

The contribution of Findlay and Wright (1994: 1) in the discussion of the household points to the debate that most empirical studies of poverty (focusing on income poverty) assume an equal sharing of resources between all household or family members. These studies reflect a situation where household members are assumed to pool their individual resources and these pooled resources are redistributed equally based on need. In such cases, a poor household is defined by its average level of resources when it falls below the poverty standards or line. In turn, an individual is poor when he or she is a member of a poor household. This has been revealed not to be realistic, since other studies strongly point to the inequalities within the household where income is not pooled or resources are not shared equally between men, women and children.

The discussion about this topic is enriched by the work of Seebens (2009: 61). His main theoretical argumentation is that individuals form households but retain their own personal interests and bargain with other members to accomplish their goals. The control over resources, individual contribution to household welfare or social status, all of which are associated with bargaining power, define the extent to which individuals can affect household decision making and distribution of resources. Thus, the higher the bargaining power the more the individuals gain from the bargaining process. Seebens provides evidence from other research that when women have more bargaining power they contribute more to the welfare of the household. For example, Seebens cites that "*food share tends to increase with increasing status of women*". He further discusses the effect of this on the welfare of children. The results show that women tend to care more for children, which is clear in the expenditure shares for this purpose.

2.6.1.3 Patterns of Income Allocation in the Sudanese Household

Grawert (1998: 106) describes income in the peasant household as a crucial factor for the survival of peasants in rural Sudan, and it is mostly generated from informal production activities and sale of crops and services in addition to the subsistence production.

In a study on income allocation patterns in the Sudanese households Schultz et al. (2008) and Schultz (2005) show four main income allocation systems. I would argue here that these systems are in place as the result of the bargaining process within the household. The position of women or men is determined within this framework. They also determine who is held responsible or who can make decisions.

The first income allocation system has one main breadwinner as the financial manger; a system, in which no allowance is paid to any of the household members. Schultz (2005) argues that the perception of the Sudanese society is well associated to the view of men as providers and managers of all family affairs. However, Schultz in her analysis and research findings draws attention to households where women turned into main breadwinners even with their husbands around.

The second system is the allowance system found by Schultz to include families, which distribute their income in form of a household allowance. Schultz explains:

> "*These families consist of one breadwinner or of two male breadwinners who share the responsibility of providing for the food. They give one woman a small household allowance to get the daily (small) shopping whereas they are responsible for getting the big shopping, are saving for emergencies, are paying foe school fees and so on. Some of the women get pocket money, some of them ask for money if they need a dress of money for Wajib or soap.*" (Schultz, 2005: 420).

The third income allocation system is the whole wage system; and in this case, the income earner or earners give all their money to a family banker who is responsible for all family expenses and who keeps the savings for the family. The findings of Schultz reveal that these family bankers are always female and they have a great influence on the financial decision making. They normally show a strong position in their family, through either age, income earned or personality (Schultz, 2005: 421).

The final system found by Schultz in the Sudanese society is the shared responsibilities system. In these households, income is not pooled in one place but responsibilities are divided between the income earners who are regularly found to be a man and a woman (2005: 422). The other family members can either use their incomes freely or give their incomes to one of the responsible household members (ibid.: 423). Schultz argues that this division of responsibilities is normally affected by gender norms, which assign certain work and responsibilities to female or male members. In all households fitting this system, a male member was responsible for the food supplies; however, they find this sometimes difficult; thus, women confessed that they sometimes help in taking care of the food needs of the family. Besides food, men are also obliged to pay for rent, health and the daily money for children. In most cases, women pay for what the husband cannot or does not want to pay. In addition to that, Schultz also found cases where women failed to keep the husband to his responsibilities and ended up taking the whole responsibility of the family (ibid.: 422).

2.6.2 Rural Livelihood Diversification and Coping Strategies: Emphasizing Mutual Economy

From the results of the research, diversification seems a general strategy the poor undertake in order to deal with poverty and vulnerability. However, while they deflect any specific shocks, risks, or stress, they also employ other sets of coping strategies in response to sudden situations. The whole debate about diversification and coping strategies is based on the principles of non-market claims and transfers in different ways such as gifts and livestock loans, meal sharing, migrant remittances and labor exchange. Adams explains: "*These principles are sustained in large part by the long-term self-interest of households in search of mutual insurance against livelihood insecurity*" (Adams, 1993: 41).

2.6.2.1 Diversification

Ellis and Freeman (2000: 15) define rural livelihood diversification as "*the process by which rural households construct and increasingly diverse portfolio of activities and capital in order to survive and to improve their standards of living*". Whereas this definition suggests that rural people diversify not only when they experience risks or shocks, from the perspective of other writers like Scoones (1998: 9) diversification aims to cope with temporary harsh conditions or more permanent alterations of livelihood activities, when other options fail to provide a livelihood. However, it is obvious that in the case of Al Dagag, diversification is a general strategy that the poor employ every day while what is described by Scoones are coping strategies. Diversification therefore may involve developing a wide income-earning portfolio to cover all types of shocks or stress. Moreover, for Ellis and Freeman (2005: 7) diversification happens when rural people try to diversify cropping patterns or by bringing together farm and non-farm activities as sources of income. Nevertheless, a number of the nonfarm economic activities (that depend on the off-farm production) may fail just as farming production or harvest may fail. Yet, the poor are forced to find other sources and diversify their sources of income outside agriculture and farming. For Ellis and Freeman (2005: 7), this process of diversification depends on peoples' capabilities and capital. Ellis and Freeman (2005) present evidence that the more diverse the capital and capabilities owned by the household, the greater is the capacity to manage risks and cope with shocks and diverse activities.

2.6.2.2 Coping Strategies for Shocks and Stress

The concept of coping strategy challenges the wide-spread assumption that the lives of the poor are simple and uniform and that they seek one single source of support. Chambers (1989: 3) argues that in fact the opposite is true! The coping strategies of those who are poor and deprived vary by region, community, social group, household, gender, age, season, and time in history. Most of the poor do not opt to put all their eggs in one basket. Rather, they reduce risks, increase adaptability and seek a degree of autonomy by developing and maintaining wider options, through the ability and willingness of different household members to do different things in different places at different times.

For Davies (1993: 60) coping strategies are "*an array of short-term strategies adopted in crisis*", while Wisner et al. (2004: 113) describe them as the manner in which people act within the limit of existing resources and range of expectations to achieve various ends. Coping strategies are often complex and involve a number of sequenced mechanisms for obtaining resources in times of adversity and disaster. They grow out of a recognition of the risk of an event occurring and of established patterns of response (Wisner et al., 2004: 119).

The aim of coping is to maintain the various objectives of the household, including livelihood security consumption, health and status; thus ensuring individual and/or collective wellbeing, at least based on Davis' study of coping strategies in situations of famine and decline in access to food (Davis,

1993: 60). Adams (1993: 44) points to four categories of transfers that may act to prevent the occurrence of food insecurity and other types of risks. These categories are ritual homage and alms, gifts, exchange transfers, and credit. Adams further explains that the ritual homage and alms giving are linked to certain religious norms and believes such as *Zakat*[12] in Islam. She defines gifts as "*a symbolic or tangible exchange of goods or services that carries with some obligation to reciprocate*" (Adams, 1993: 45). Gift exchange is regarded one of the most important means of reducing different kinds of risk in rural households. By gift-giving, social resources are transferred into a system of mutual insurance so that "*(s)he who is in need today receives help from (s)he who may be in need tomorrow*" (Adams, 1993: 45). Exchange transfers involve the immediate return of the initial goods and services provided. This could include labor or capital sharing arrangements such as threshing teams, which act to accomplish time intensive tasks more quickly together or for accomplishing any public work. Credit transfers demand a stricter schedule of repayment than the other categories of non market exchange. This credit could be for interest or it could be interest-free, deepening on the degree of intimacy between partners. The danger of social sanctions and public humiliation is usually enough to ensure the potential interest-free credit is repaid, as is the risk of suffer the loss of credit opportunities in the future (Adams, 1993: 47).

Fafchamps (1999: 7-20) identifies different sets of coping strategies. He differentiates between three categories: those that reduce the extent of the shocks themselves and consequently the exposure to risk; those that rely on the accumulation or liquidation of assets as protectors from stock; and those that share risks with others. The simplest way of dealing with risk is to reduce risk itself. This could include a variety of ways such as changing or modifying the surrounding environment. For example, most rural people avoid settling in areas highly affected by droughts; or when they settle in dense tropical forest, they remove much of the forest to reduce the risk of exposure to parasitic diseases and so on. It is well known that capital accumulation or liquidation can smooth consumption, but in the event of a series of shocks, individuals nevertheless run out of capital and are no longer able to absorb the shocks.

One possible way out of such a situation is to borrow. Nevertheless, borrowing from formal institutions in many cases has many constraints, which are unavoidable for the rural poor where banks and other formal financial services are not available or require a set of procedures and guarantees the poor lack and cannot handle. Many households in such cases borrow from informal sources like borrowing from a moneylender or relatives and so on. Rural poor also borrow cash or non-cash items like production tools or taking food from the grocery for credit and the like.

Risk sharing is the third coping strategy explained by Fafchamps (1999: 20) as risk pooling or as an aggregate approach for dividing risks among people in the household or community. For example when exchanging non-consumable capital among them, such as livestock in exchange with consumable capital like grain, villagers share risk among each other.

It is clear that the two classifications of Fafchamps (1999) and Adams (1993) complement each other. Together they provide a theoretical view about what rural people can do to cope with their vulnerable situation, especially when they are left without any external help.

2.7 Wellbeing and Security: "Living far from the Edge"

Wellbeing and security are what the poor are looking for. Wellbeing and security constitute the picture of life without poverty and vulnerability. Wellbeing and security are different but both are connected with poverty and vulnerability as they are also connected.

Literature on the topic agrees that the main objective of any development should be wellbeing for all, a concept connected to the work of Sen. In "The quality of life", he and Nussbaum (1993) link the concept to the concept of functionings. Sen (1993: 36) argues that the wellbeing achievements of a person might be realized as an assessment of the well-ness of the person's state of being rather than other behavior like the goodness of contributing to the country or others. The wellbeing of a person is connected to functionings, which are constituent elements of a person seen from the perspective of the person's own welfare. However, Sen and Nussbaum (1993) do not ignore that the wellbeing of a person is

---

[12] Islamic taxes that are distributed to the poor.

also 'other-regarding'. Generally, their argument states that these constituent elements that make a person's wellbeing are relevant to the functionings available to this person. These functionings vary between elementary ones, such as escaping morbidity and mortality, being adequately nourished, having mobility, etc. and complex ones such as being happy, achieving self respect, taking part of the life of the community, etc (Sen, 1993: 37) . Wellbeing then can be described as the experience of good quality of life.

Another important theoretical argumentation about wellbeing is that wellbeing and its opposite, ill-being differ from the concepts of wealth and poverty (Chambers, 1997: 10). Unlike wealth, wellbeing is open to the whole range of human experience—social, mental, spiritual as well as material. It has different meanings to different people, but most agree to include living standards, access to basic services, security, and freedom from fear, health, good relations with others, friendship, love, peace of mind, choice, creativity, fulfillment, and fun. Extreme poverty and ill-being go together as components of deprivation (Chambers, 1997: 10).

Chambers gives a very simple definition for security as "*the opposite of vulnerability*" (Chambers, 1989: 1). Thus, if livelihood is defined as "*adequate stock and flows of food and cash to meet basic needs*", security refers to "*secure ownership of or access to resources and income-earning activities, including reserves and capital to compensate risk, ease shocks and come across emergencies*" (WCED, 1987: 2ff., quoted in Chambers and Conway, 1992: 7). In the light of these two definitions, a household may be able to gain sustainable livelihood security in many ways—mainly those mentioned by Chambers and Conway (1992: 7), through ownership of land, livestock or trees, rights to grazing, fishing, hunting or gathering: through stable employment with adequate remuneration or through varied sets of activities. Livelihood security and wellbeing are long-term objectives involving the strengthening of a combination of the factors of capital, resources, activities, capabilities and social position to maximize future claims on resources.

3 Finance for the Poor: Theoretical Perspective

"*In fact, it is often argued that providing access to savings services is a much more valuable service to poor people than credit. The path out of poverty lies in building asserts, not accumulating debt*" (Ledgerwood and White, 2006: xxx).

3.1 Introduction

In agrarian and peasant economies, there is increasing need for credit (Adams, 1995). During the last decade, it has been recognized that the provision of financial services to the poor and small businesses in the informal sector has a potential of contributing to the development process, especially in developing countries. Moreover, the poor in developing countries like everyone else need access to a wide range of financial services that are convenient, flexible and reasonably priced (Helms, 2006: 17). The microfinance industry has seen remarkable growth for more than a decade; still it reaches only a small percentage of its potential market worldwide (Ledgerwood and White, 2006). After the enthusiasm in the 1990 about the impact of microfinance has on poverty alleviation, more recently the effects of microfinance as a poverty reduction tool have been questioned (Lont and Hospes, 2004; Bateman, 2010; Roy 2010).

The scope of this chapter is to discuss theoretical perspectives with regard to "finance for the poor", a concept that started to emerge with the attention given to the concept of finance in the discussion about economic development. The chapter starts by presenting theoretical efforts that discuss the question whether providing financial services is important for changing people's livelihood. The following section of the chapter presents the debate on the contribution of informal finance. The last part of the chapter is devoted to the issue of microfinance, its meaning, and its theoretical and policy implications and, most importantly, to recent debates that criticize the concept of microfinance point to many dilemmas that go along with its application around the world.

This chapter provides an overview how the financial landscapes have changed over time from the concentration on providing cheap credits directed to agriculture over the revolution of microfinance to the recent development where microfinance is even considered a poverty trap and poverty capital. This worldwide discussion is a basis for the later discussion of Sudan as one of the developing countries where microfinance is newly implemented.

3.2 Is Finance Important for Development?

Financial activities have faced doubt and critical judgment since man began to record history (Adams et al., 1984: 11); the motives and morals of lenders have been regularly questioned. However, part of these judgments can be regarded as prejudice that might obstruct the substantial advantages finance brings to the modern economy. Therefore, Adams et al. (1984) argue that the poor understanding of the advantages of finance has affected the regulation of financial markets, especially in rural areas in many developing countries.

The discussion about the importance of finance for growth and development reaches far; yet, arguments in the literature circle around two essential points of consideration. The first group of arguments relates to the question how the provision of finance can generate macro-economic development and the second group is about the connection between financial development and poverty alleviation at micro level. It is not within the scope of this research to investigate the effect of finance at macro level since this study focuses on how finance could affect the livelihood of people in rural areas on the household level in Sudan. Although I agree that these two levels are connected and influence each other. Thus, I would like to briefly present how finance could lead to development at macro level and in this will rely on the work of Drake and Robertson (1980).

According to Drake and Robertson, finance has a lot of potential for macro-economic development in different aspects; however, this has only lately been noticed and realized. For instance, economists usually argue that there is a positive correlation between economic development and financial development. Drake and Robertson clarify the logic behind that finance makes money available for many activities to take place. The use of money, *first*, gives a much greater scope for the division of labor in production, the use of money also enlarges markets over space and time and that in turn creates scopes of profitable divisions of labor by production type and production process. *Second*, financial instruments provide a bridge between ultimate savers and ultimate investors and create the opportunity for putting savings to the disposal of enterprises, thus promising to raise the total level of investment and hence income. *Third*, concerning indirect finance, it is accepted that the existence of financial intermediaries improves the allocation of resources by providing facilities to promote increases in aggregate savings and investment volumes (Drake and Robertson, 1980: 31ff.).

However, the picture is not that bright; all of the above are assumed to happen under perfect market conditions, which do not exist in many developing countries, where the economic as well as the financial environment typically is volatile, uncertain and at high risk. Thus, the question arises here how a positive financing impact can be sustained on markets in developing countries. How financial policies at macroeconomic level shape the financial landscape in empirical reality, I will elaborate in the case of Sudan in chapter 6. The main theoretical argumentation of providing finance for the poor will be presented next.

3.3 The Theoretical Context of Finance for the Poor

In this part of the research, I will present briefly the main lines of thought that over time have dominated the issue of finance and led to the existence of the current theories and practices. At the end I will focus on the financial sector perspective and the institution building approach as they are the most related to the case of the research. In this, I find it important to mention that the shift in theorizing and practicing finance for the poor is mirrored by the shifts in the meaning and measurement of poverty as discussed in the previous chapter.

The *first paradigm* of finance in development was developed after World War II and was prevalent into the 1970s. According to this view, development finance should not predominantly be concerned about poor target groups (Krahnen and Schmidt, 1994: 10; Adams, 1995; Schmidt and Zeitinger, 1994: 1). On the contrary, the focus of efforts in this time was on the *transfer of capital* to developing countries in order to fill what was considered a structural gap in capital formation. Development was seen to be the effect of accumulating capital used for macro-economic growth. Foreign funding was directed to finance large industrial and infrastructural projects. However, it was believed that economic growth would also benefit the poor by initiating a process of "trickle down" (Krahnen and Schmidt, 1994: 10). As is well known, this process did not happen in most countries. Rather, foreign financing only reinforced dualism, migration and poverty as far as the bulk of the population was concerned, even with the existence of high GDP growth rates in many countries.

The detection of these socially problematic outcomes let to a shift in donors' policy orientation. Krahnen and Schmidt (1994: 12) believe this to be the starting point for the *second paradigm* regarding the role of finance in development, which they name *financing specific target groups*. Based on the work of Schmidt and Zeitinger (1994), during the 1970s and into the 1990s the concept of "target group orientation" became predominant. Krahnen and Schmidt (1994: 12) and Schmidt and Zeitinger (1994) agree that this involves the idea that development aid efforts should be designed and implemented in such a way that they will directly benefit the poor segments of the population. At this stage, policy makers' attention became more directed towards social and human development than capital accumulation as it had been before. This capital was then supposed to be used to produce employment, income and better food supply (Krahnen and Schmidt, 1994: 14). It has been observed that planners of bringing capital in terms of credit to those who would use it to achieve such goals were looking for methods of credit distribution and quite naturally, asked the banking system to tackle this issue. However, banks proved unable to act as intermediaries for capital, which would come from abroad, from the government or the central bank. Consequently, new institutions were created; for instance, specialized banks for the development sector, for agriculture, industry and housing were established. Unfortunately, their work was also disappointing. Krahnen and Schmidt (1994: 14) explain this by the inefficiency of such institutions in achieving the desired outputs. In addition to high default risks, those development banks needed not only funds to lend to borrowers but also funds to operate as well as they needed technical assistance. All this led to the failure of the agriculture development banks in many developing countries.

As reported by Schmidt and Zeitinger, (1994: 2), in the 1980s new versions of guiding principle were strongly advocated and scholars called for the liberalization of the financial system. This led to *the third paradigm* regarding the financial sector in development, the *liberalization* paradigm. The ultimate hope was to create a financial system without interest rate ceilings and credit targets and the creation of liberal financial institutions that can provide credit and deposit facilities to poor segments of the population and at the same time survive economically. Liberalization gained particular recognition in the 1980s and then mainly consisted of establishing programs largely outside of the banking or the governmental sectors. The problems in dealing with banks were addressed and instead the liberalization approach led to the involvement of NGOs and all kinds of self-help groups using donor funds in offering financial services for the poor. The main potential of such institutions was seen in their capability to really reach the poor, small and unsecured borrowers, unlike government owned institutions (Schmidt and Zeitinger, 1994: 2; Krahnen and Schmidt, 1994: 15). However, it appeared that such financing schemes were extremely costly for donors, failed to reach many members of their target groups, and, most importantly, did not lead to the creation of institutions able to play a sustainable role in the lives of their clients (Schmidt and Zeitinger, 1994: 2; Zeller and Meyer, 2002: 4).

Consequently, in the 1990s two major lines of thought concerning the field of small and microbusiness financing came together in the *fourth paradigm* regarding the financial sector in development. These are the *financial sector perspective* and the *institution building approach* introduced by von Pischke (1991), Krahnen and Schmidt (1994) and Schmidt and Zeitinger (1994).

Krahnen and Schmidt (1994: 16) call the first approach "financial system development", for it attacks the policy of financial repression in most developing countries and it has led to a strategy of liberalizing and strengthening the financial system. This work is supposed to be done at both macro and micro level. At the micro level, it is argued that a financial system no longer controlled by unnecessary rules and regulations will be able to mobilize large volumes of savings and transform them into investable funds in the long term, once risks are fully understood (von Pischke et al., 1997). The concept of intermediation emerged from this work. This approach also calls against the fixing of interest rates at levels below what might be market rates (Krahnen and Schmidt 1994: 19).

The second approach of "institution building" argues that aid efforts should not be directed to the provision of financial services to the target group but rather to the creation of financial institutions, which would be both able and motivated to care for the relevant target group. The major hypothesis of this approach was that the main problem of finance provision in developing countries is primarily one of incentive-oriented financial institution building rather than one of the availability of "loanable funds".

The institution-building approach has dominated the finance sector development thinking until recently. The approach suggested upgrading informal institutions, downgrading the formal institutions and linking both. However, I would argue here that the focus in reality has been more on downgrading or restructuring of banks than on upgrading informal institutions. These approaches will be discussed again in chapter 4, where I tackle the issue of financial institutions.

Also, at this time started the work of Grameen Bank, which was established in the mid-1980s in Bangladesh and begun to attract attention from all around the world by providing microcredit for poor women, which will be explained alter in this chapter. Meanwhile, Bouman and Hospes (1994) called for mapping "financial landscapes". Lont and Hospes (2004: 4) describe the new approach of constructing financial landscapes as the first attempt to develop a theoretical methodological alternative to dominant, technology-driven approaches in the world of finance. They point to the time-spatial and social dimensions of finance. Their main argumentation is that financial transactions are elements of multiple contracts and cannot be understood in separation from multiple contexts, herewith reintroducing the anthropological notion of embeddedness (ibid.). Bouman and Hospes explain the metaphor of landscape:

> "*[It is] not only used to indicate the physical features of the financial landscape such as offices of banks, cooperatives, credit union, traders, pawnbrokers, self-help groups, NGOs and whatever other financial or quasi-financial institutions there may be. With the metaphor we wish to emphasize regional diversity and historical change in financial ecosystems. At the same time it stimulates us to explore what relations, norms, actions and processes influence, directly or indirectly the transactions of savers, borrowers and lenders*" (Bouman and Hospes, 1994: 1).

The concept of financial landscapes makes it possible to specifically focus on the connections and disconnections between different kinds of savers, borrowers and lenders within different contexts.

Bouman and Hospes (1994: 6) focus more on the behavior of the informal sector, which is not regulated by government rules and regulations. Their work is an extension to other efforts that by the 1980s had started to enlighten the importance of the informal financial sector in most developing countries. They point to the ignorance regarding the informal financial sector by consultants and government planners that argued in favor of regulated banks to provide finance. One can argue here that what has also been ignored is the fact that very few banks are providing finance for the poor in rural and remote areas. The existence of many money lenders, traders, pawnbrokers, and ROSCAs successfully working in such places underline the main argument for the need of the construction and mapping of the financial landscape.

3.4 Rural Informal Finance

Informal finance became a hot issue in the 1980s as a result of the efforts of the Asian Development Bank between 1986 and 1989 and the publication of the first collection of papers on informal finance in low income countries in 1992 by Adam and Fitchett (Lont and Hospes, 2004: 4). Moreover, informal finance also was emphasized in the work of Bouman and Hospes (1994) who argue for the restructuring of financial landscapes. In addition to that, the collection of studies on women's ROSCAs meant a new breakthrough in the field of informal finance for the anthropologists (Ardener, 1996; Bouman, 1994 [1]).

It is only recently that informal finance has been considered crucial in providing financial services for the informal sector, which covers such activities as small enterprises and home industries operating outside the context of official regulation (Bouman, 1994: 110). The informal labor market, mutual assistance in informal unregistered and indigenous associations, small businesses, informal trade, petty trade, street stalls for the sale of small products, operating locally and across borders without an official permit, illegal house building in slums and such activities exist in the informal sector and need finance. The majority of rural households engaged in such informal activities depend on informal intermediaries for their daily financial needs (Bouman, 1994: 110). Thus, the main role informal finance plays is to provide financial opportunities for those who are not able and unwilling to deal with formal financial institutions especially in rural areas where formal institutions are not available.

Krahnen and Schmidt (1994: 32) also include in their description of informal finance that loans and deposits are granted without collateral. In such cases, familiarity with the personal circumstances of the borrowers serves as substitute for collateral; also, social sanctions can serve as substitute for collateral. Typically, credit terms are adapted to the situation of the client. The total amount lent as well as the number and the frequency of payments goes in line with the expected cash flow of the borrower. For getting credit, there is only little, if any paperwork. In fact, this flexibility of loan terms and adaptation of loan management to the personal situations of the client are the most significant operational characteristics of informal financial institutions (Krahnen and Schmidt 1994: 32).

Adams (1992) and Schreiner (1997) both explain informal finance as contracts and agreements conducted without reference or recourse to the legal system to exchange cash in the present for promises of cash in the future. The notion of contracts and agreements defines finance as relations and networks as also applied in this research, however, this definition suggests that contracts always involve cash, which does not include all types of contracts and financial transactions in rural areas, for informal contracts also include non-cash assets like livestock and crop produce.

In the context of this research, informal finance includes contracts and agreements within financial relations outside the regulatory formal financial sector in rural areas. These contracts provide different financial services including small credits, savings and insurance for rural people for both consumption and production purposes in a high-risk environment. Thus, informal finance includes different arrangements ranging from being a member of a credit and savings group to buying daily needs from small shops on credit to loans to cover household needs like providing treatment in case of sickness of a household member. Informal rural finance also includes transfers and gift giving traditions that happen in most rural areas.

---

[1] Based on the work of Geertz (1962) and Ardener (1964).

It may be that currently there is a shift in the main aim of finance, which increasingly looks at indigenous financial arrangements. The debate about informal finance focuses on the local and indigenous strategies of people themselves which supports the definition of livelihood provided in chapter 2 that includes not only the use of local resources but also capabilities and strategies people themselves build to cope with their uncertain environment.

3.5 Products of Finance: What do the Poor Need?

Theories regarding finance of the poor aim to find the financial products that suit the poor. In most of literature about finance, credit seems the favorable product. The potential of savings is highlighted in the theoretical debate, yet rarely accomplished in practice. It is only recently that another product, insurance, has captured some attention, for it is needed by the poor as well. Giving more attention to savings and insurance besides credit might widen the aim of finance from only increasing income and employment to enhancing a sustainable livelihood since savings and insurance are important for building household assets and different forms of capital.

3.5.1 Credit: One Product Different Functions

The work of Abugre (1994) and Heidhues (1994) is central in describing the characteristics of credit as a financial product provided for the rural poor. For them credit should be small on average and provided with minimum procedures and therefore inexpensively; credit in these cases could be managed by community groups or informal groups whose use of social norms and peer pressure will ensure repayments.

Regarding the functions of credit, it is seen by most writers as a product which should be only directed to production and investment, thereby increasing income or providing employment. The desire to provide credit only for productive activities may be based on the belief that productive investments will create the income base for repaying the loans and paying the interest. Productive investments are assumed the precondition for sustained credit (Abugre, 1994: 169).

The main critique of this assumption is that a clear distinction between consumption and credit taken for production purposes may not be possible. Abugre (1994) and Heidhues (1994: 169) claim that there is no evidence that repayment is higher in cases of what is called productive loans. The distinction is misleading because it assumes that there is a strict division between consumption and investment application in poor households or that the distinction could be measured and monitored. This is difficult, given the fact that money is fungible which means that money meant for one type of expenditure can unnoticeably substitute for another. Borrowers are hardly able to distinguish consumption from production expenditures and lenders have no time and resources to monitor the use of loans. Consumption itself could be a legitimate objective of financial services (Heidhues, 1994: 169). For example, credit provided for meeting the cost of education could be considered both insurance and an investment instrument. One can argue here for the importance of both productive and consumption loans that the poor need. In the system of rural farm households, consumption activities are linked to production and vice versa, for instance the use of labor, land and capital are connected and not separate. The failure to recognize this fact prevents the financial markets from opening up to households' financial needs (Heidhues, 1994: 37). Consequently, many rural poor households are deprived from meeting an important financial need that might have higher priority at that time (Heidhues, 1994: 46)

However, the livelihood thinking has directed the use of credit to the demand of people and not only to credit for production purposes but also for smoothing consumption (Heidhues, 1994; Rutherford, 1999, 2009; Helms, 2006). Helms' "Access for all" (2006) also tries to answer the question how people use credit. Helms points to three main categories of events that call for spending more money than might be available around the house or in the pocket. These are *first* life-cycle events like birth, marriage, or death, *second* emergencies including sickness or injury, the death of the breadwinner, or the loss of employment, theft or any other emergency completely outside the household's control like war, drought, or floods; all of which create sudden need for cash. The *third* category includes opportunities to invest in businesses, land, household assets. Besides investing in businesses, Helms also recognizes the need of the poor to invest in costly items that make life more comfortable like better roofing. In his work "The poor and their money", Rutherford supports this argument and advocates the fact that the poor have multiple financial needs (1999, 2009).

Limiting credit to finance only productive means in absence of consumption loans or savings facilities is inappropriate and even counterproductive in building sustainable financial markets (Heidhues, 1994). For financial markets to be sustainable, two other complementary functions besides providing credit for investment and production need to be fulfilled. These two functions are the provision of savings facilities on the one hand and consumption credit and insurance on the other hand (Rutherford, 1999). Heidhues (1994), Helms (2006), Rutherford (2009) and Robinson (2009) all argue that, for households in high risk environments where food security is an issue, the provision of production credit only is not helpful and has in many cases led to the collapse of the financial market in many developing countries. According to this argument, what is mainly needed in rural areas is production credit accompanied by consumption credit that aims at preventing the occurrence of chronic food insecurity. Helms (2006: 22) states very clearly, "*poor clients need more than credit... Poor people need a range of options from credit (beyond enterprise finance), to savings to money transfer facilities and insurance in many forms*". Therefore, in times when households are at risk different strategies are undertaken; among them borrowing from informal and formal suppliers of credit and savings as mentioned above in chapter 2.

Another debatable issue about credit is that credit can be given to individuals or groups. Tying several borrowers to each other through the formation of borrower groups has become a common practice in credit extension to small and informal sector individuals and enterprises. Schmidt and Zeitinger (1994: 48) and Krahnen and Schmidt (1994: 63) emphasize that the group lending has emerged as a consequence of disappointments with the conventional individual lending. They explain group lending as "*credit technology which involves groups of borrowers in the process of grating and recovering loans*" (Schmidt and Zeitinger, 1994: 50). However, they distinguish between using the group method as loan guarantor, financial intermediary, or social network.

When groups act as loan guarantors, it is expected that groups of borrowers are supposed to assume collective and joint liability for each other's debts. If one group member fails to fulfill his or her payment obligations, the other group members will lose their right to obtain future loans from the relevant credit institution. The group acts as financial intermediary when a group is liable to the bank for the debt and it is the one lending out funds acquired from the bank to individual group members. Here the group is given the responsibility to carry out practically all of the key functions performed by a bank, namely borrower selection and risk bearing. In the third variant, the group rather plays a social role, where a potential borrower must belong to a group in order to be eligible for a loan. The groups are under moral obligation to exert peer pressure on group members who might fail to repay their loans including interest. Furthermore, by group lending transaction costs can be reduced (Krahnen and Schmidt 1994: 63).

Advances in credit reflect experiences all over the world that seek to be innovative in the provision of credit. The most innovative is the provision of loans for housing and the leasing credit as explained by Nagarajan and Meyer (2005: 29). They argue that especially in rural areas, people finance their housing needs by slowly accumulating building materials, then building the main part of their homes, and adding to it as they accumulate more materials. This process takes a long time and slows down the creation of assets. When basic housing and consumption requirements are not adequately met, external financing for economic activities tends to be diverted due to fungibility and it becomes necessary to unlock the passive capital in houses so it can be used as collateral for loans. There is clearly a need for more housing finance in most countries (ibid., 2005: 30). The other advance in the field of credit is leasing contracts provided also for the poor in rural areas. For Nagarajan and Meyer (2005: 30) leasing is now recognized as an alternative financial mechanism for reaching poor rural clients with limited access to long-term loans; it can be a means to acquire equipment and machinery needed to expand and diversify micro-businesses and farm businesses and to acquire capital assets through pay-as-you-go leasing contracts. Leasing may incur lower transaction costs compared to collateral-based long-term loans due to lower costs in developing and enforcing contracts in rural areas where asset registries and judicial systems for contract enforcement are poorly developed.

3.5.2 Savings and Insurance: The Other Side of the Finance Coin

3.5.2.1 Savings

Before Vogel's famous paper "Savings Mobilization: The Forgotten Half of Rural Finance" (1984) it was commonly accepted and assumed that the poor do not and cannot save. Vogel raises attention to the fact that the poor do save and even more so to the potential of savings in economic development. Since then the view has changed, and savings mobilization has been recognized as a major force in the theory of finance for the poor. Schreiner (2005: 3) explains savings as moving resources through time. This explanation includes both conscious and unconscious failure to consume. It is significant, that this description emphasizes the dynamic of savings. Thus, examples of savings include putting cash in a bank or buying other types of assets and resources for future use. People usually only think of the first example as savings, yet both examples move resources through time. Savings facilities allow wealth to be kept safe, in a form that preserves their value, in liquid and readily accessible form.

Supported by many other writers, Nagarajan and Meyer (2005: 26) provide the main practical and theoretical assumption in the discussion about savings, which also links it to the case of Al Dagag. They argue that the poor population living at risk may require access to savings facilities even more so than loans, since savings function as a good risk management strategy. Lidgerwood and White (2006: xxx) put it very clear that providing access to savings services is a much more valuable service to the poor: "*The way out of poverty lies in building assets, not accumulating debt*". It is now commonly acknowledged that households will deposit their surplus capital in financial institutions if the institutions are appropriately structured and offer savings products that meet their need (Fiebig et al., 1999: 3). However, not all households save by depositing their surplus in financial institutions; least of all in rural areas where such institutions rarely exist.

Different studies reveal that the poor are not only eager and regular savers they also have great need of safe deposit facilities and ways and means to shed liquidity (Helms, 2006: 24; Thankom et al., 2009: 8; Bouman, 1994: 117). They ordinarily start the saving process individually and at home. In short time, the saver starts to feel uneasy for many reasons like daily temptations of attractive consumption alternatives, and then there is the possibility of theft or fire. As well as fears from the potential claims of relatives once they know that he or she has accumulated a surplus of money. To shed liquidity, the poor have several options. They might deposit their savings with trusted person or institution, they might start to invest or diversify their investment opportunities, also they may join a traditional saving and credit association or buy gold or livestock, or they may start to save by building up debt claims.

Moreover, the main motive behind saving, as discussed by Fiebig et al. (1999), is insurance against different risks and shocks that might happen such as disability, disease, sudden income loss, seasonal variations and other contingencies. Moreover, savings could also be for wealth accumulation to finance household's long-term goals like social and religious purposes or for future investment. In addition, low-income earners with irregular income streams save in periods of high income to compensate during low income periods. The findings of Buckley (1997: 1085) show that savings constitute the basis for achieving financial independence and the way toward self-sufficiency to individuals, households and enterprises. It is of course not credit itself that lifts the poor out of poverty; it is their ability to save from income generated from the use made of credit. The importance of savings from the perspective of Zeller and Sharma (1998: 20) lies in its contribution for the accumulation of capital, which in turn can generate future income and enable future consumption. There is now sufficient evidence that the rural poor save to build a precautionary buffer to be used during lean seasons or to finance unexpected expenditure (ibid.).

In much of the discussion of savings, it is obvious that the distinction between the utilization of forced savings and the mobilization of voluntary savings is crucial. The utilization of forced savings perceives savings as an integral part of credit; savers learn financial discipline and qualify for credit by virtue of convincing savings records. The mobilization of voluntary savings assumes that savings and credit are integral components of financial intermediation and that savers already know why and how to save (Zeller and Sharma, 1998: 15). This in fact raises the issue of which must come first, or the sequential issue of credit and savings. Yet, the priority of one over the other—savings first or credit first—is debatable, however it is not an ideological issue in this research. Even though from IFAD's

(2007b) experience it appears that the practice of savings first has significant advantage in the way that savings first is more appropriate in subsistence agriculture and low-return activities while credit first is more appropriate in high-return activities. Savings-driven investments in low-yielding activities may generate the start-up capital for credit-financed activities with high returns. These, in turn, may generate profits and savings to be reinvested into low-return activities, including subsistence agriculture. (IFAD, 2007b)

There is proof that savings-based systems are more empowering for the poor than credit-based systems. Institutions that provide loans only and that appear weak or do not seem to be viable, provide the community with an incentive to deplete the household savings, which is most effectively done by failure to repay loans (Pischke et al., 997: 24f.; Thankom et al., 2009: 8).

In spite of the recognition of savings, still most of the financial institutions in rural areas do not provide savings facilities that match the demand for such service. Nagarajan and Meyer (2005: 28) support this argumentation as they argue that this is due to the high costs of formal savings. Rural savings mobilization involves very high costs and may produce small total volumes of savings. Nagarajan and Meyer (2005: 26) show that the rural poor generally peruse informal savings and other mechanisms to help mitigate some shocks. Moreover, the availability of cheap funds from donors and governments tends to discourage deposit mobilization. As a result, the volume of deposits mobilized by formal financial institutions has been low.

3.5.2.2 Insurance

Very few studies focus on describing insurance and its mechanisms in rural areas. Generally, insurance is considered to cover against such risks as the death of a family breadwinner, severe illness or a loss of an asset including livestock and housing, variability in output (especially as agriculture is largely weather-dependent), price and marketing uncertainty (Helms, 2006: 27). For Nagarajan and Meyer (2000: 31) large risks affect rural areas and cause considerable challenges that affect the outreach, sustainability, and impact of rural finance. While informal insurance can mitigate some risks, formal insurance is unavailable in most developing countries, especially in rural areas. Challenges in providing formal insurance in rural areas include: (i) difficulties in achieving scale and covering costs, (ii) low awareness of insurance, (iii) very few rural insurance products available, and (iv) the lack of an effective distribution system (ibid.).

Helms (2006: 28) views agricultural insurance as tricky as no evidence exists of viable programs. The problem associated with this type of insurance is that natural disasters can happen, and insured farmers might be less likely to pursue sound practices and therefore are more likely to lose their crops. Considering the fact that sources of risks in rural households are many and diverse, the timing and intensity of risks and their impacts in income are thus difficult to predict by households, which have no access to formal insurance schemes. This is considered the main reason for many households to diversify their income sources and pursue a range of strategies of self insurance. Heidhues explains: "*They save in the forms of cash, deposits, food, or other assets; they diversify production structure, cropping patterns and income sources, and they build networks of social relations*" (Heidhues, 1994: 36). However, in cases of intense and extended risks, risk-sharing or self-insurance mechanisms are not viable. It is then that the mere or even potential access to credit enables households to transfer part of their risks to the financial markets.

In discussing the informal risk management, Weerdt (2005) states that any form of endogenous networks can also be considered a form of protection against external risks and hazards of life; and that is insurance. These networks are based on such aspects as kinship and clan membership. Thus, they are considered a sort of informal risk management and include participating in reciprocal borrowing and lending systems. They play an important role in strengthening social networks, borrowing from relatives or informal sources, diversifying income sources and smoothing consumption. Dercon identifies informal insurance as intertemporal behavior in the face of risk and the existence of community and household-based mechanisms to cope with the consequences of risk (Dercon, 2005: 317). According to Yaron et al. (1997: 1), particularly insurance and access to income smoothing financial services can significantly contribute to the welfare of rural communities by mitigating the impact of seasonality and natural disasters on their incomes.

3.6 When Microfinance Came to Life

"In the 1990s we witnessed the birth of 'the new world of microfinance' a world consisting of policy makers and practitioners who believe that reaching the poor and building healthy financial institutions can go hand in hand..."[2] *(Lont and Hospes, 2004: 3)*

The term "microcredit" was first introduced by the Grameen Bank in Bangladesh, because of the failure to reach the poor by subsidized credit (Rahman, 2004: 29). Microcredit programs started with the main aim of lending to poor borrowers, primarily women, and promoted microcredit as an effective tool for poverty reduction and the empowerment of women (Rahman, 2004: 27). What the Grameen Bank has done is to provide small collateral free loans to jointly liable group members as a financial service delivery system to poor women.

The actual raise of microcredit as a global tool for poverty alleviation could be observed at the international microcredit summit 1997. Since then, a huge amount of funds have been directed to the sector as a result of the incorporation of the microfinance model into mainstream development agendas and microcredit programs in Asia, Latin America, and in Africa; later also introduced in North America and Europe. Subsequently, the concept of microcredit has been broadened to include other financial services like savings and insurance and has been named microfinance. Rahman (2004: 27) sees microfinance as one of the fastest growing sectors of the financial sector. For its success, in the new millennium the Grameen Bank has been viewed as a new policy framework and best practice (Rahman, 2004: 28). In 2006, the founder of the Grameen Bank Muhammad Yunus and the bank itself were granted the Noble Peace Prize.

Microfinance is provided in the form of small sized financial loans to people who usually fall outside the reach of formal finance (Zeller and Meyer, 2002: 1). Commercial banks usually ignore microfinance to avoid high transaction costs of servicing small loans and savings deposits. Moreover, most of the poor do not possess assets normally demanded as collateral, and are perceived as too risky to be granted loans. Thus, special microfinance projects outside of established banks target the poor, while particular interest is often given to women and micro-enterprises (GTZ, 2002: 1).

The main recent theoretical work to measure the performance of microfinance is the "Triangle of Microfinance" theory developed by Zeller and Meyer (2002). Their main theoretical argumentation directs policy makers and policy objectives to improve the financial sustainability, outreach to the poor and welfare impact of microfinance.

Zeller and Meyer state the main vision of microfinance:

"*Poor people in developing countries lack access to formal financial services and the problem is especially serious in rural areas. This constrains their ability to acquire assets, start businesses, finance emergency needs and insure themselves against illnesses and disasters. The pioneers believed that improved access to financial services would solve these problems, at least to some extent*" (Zeller and Meyer, 2002: 1).

Following this vision, governments and financial institutions started establishing village banking networks or microfinance institutions. Some institutions linked the provision of microfinance to other programs like education and health assistances; others only provided loans. Some worked hard to mobilize local savings; whereas other completely ignored the savings component. Several institutions used group lending in order to reduce transaction costs and achieve high repayment rates; others focused on the individual capabilities of clients. Various institutions also designed their loans to meet the need of specific groups like women; others gave different groups a chance.

Since the microfinance revolution started, millions of poor have gained access to financial services for the first time; but of course, poverty has not been resolved (Zeller and Meyer, 2002: 2). Although the microfinance vision stated above is well designed, practices have shown different trends. Only part of the microfinance vision of providing formal financial services to the poor is resolved, but it has also been revealed that much needs yet to be done, especially with the increasing poor populations in most developing countries.

---

[2] Lont and Hospes (2004:3) also refer to Rhyne and Otero 1994, Robinson, 2001, Morduch, 1999, 2000, Johnson and Rogaly, 1997, Schneider 1997.

Most of the microfinance programs have been small in scale compared to the demand of the poor, especially when counting the population of rural areas. Most of these programs were vulnerable to resources and management constraints. Most operate in a few locations and served specific groups of people; thus, they are subjected to risks of undiversified loans portfolios. Few were successful in mobilizing savings or becoming self sufficient and thus they increasingly become dependent on funds from donors or governments for their future existence (Zeller and Meyer, 2002).

Most of the microfinance institutions had collapsed after the pilot phase of the project, while the sustaining ones showed a dramatic decline in loan recovery. Zeller and Meyer (2002: 2) argue that this is not to say there were no successful experiences, but to say there were few successful experiences in specific countries that have been tried to replicate around the world with limited success. To recover, institutions within the microfinance sector started to compete by searching for the wealthier clientele groups in urban areas. Consequently, the loan products were designed to serve borrowers who can make small frequent loan repayments. Zeller and Meyer (2002) pose the question how such products are supposed to serve farmers and other clients who experience irregular cash flow. One can argue here that the microfinance vision was destructed by practices of these institutions; and, not surprisingly, the vision has never been achieved. This constitutes what is called the commercialization of microfinance and will be discussed later in this chapter.

According to the theory of the triangle of microfinance, what should be done is to put more emphasis on balancing sustainability, outreach and impact of microfinance. Zeller and Meyer (2002: 5) state that the current microfinance initiatives have not accomplished the desired degree of sustainability, outreach and impact. All microfinance institutions have tried to achieve one of the three objectives but many have failed to address all of them. Some institutions have produced large impacts but achieved limited outreach. Others may have smaller impacts but are highly sustainable. Furthermore, a trade-off between the three objectives has been pointed out by many microfinance institutions.

3.6.1 Microfinance and Livelihood

Since its emergence, the modern practice of development microfinance has been linked to poverty alleviation. Poverty alleviation is mostly seen as one of the objectives of any microfinancial services provision. Based on the work of Yaron et al. (1997: 1), providing microfinance for the rural population has two main objectives. These objectives are expanding income and reducing poverty by creating rapid growth in rural economies; objectives for which the authors consider finance the most promising tool (ibid.: 4). However, they define poverty quite narrowly as increasing income; also it remains unclear in their work if the increase in income will consequently reduce poverty. Moreover, what about the fact that in most developing countries the rural poor live in a very vulnerable environment that may further jeopardize any income increase? I argue here that the microfinance should not only target income poverty but should also address the livelihood of people.

I can detect but few attempts that argue for the importance of looking at the livelihood of people in microfinance programs. For example, Zeller and Sharma (1998: 7) discuss how credit and savings could positively affect people's standards of living and wellbeing. They give a clear picture of what finance can do for the poor at household level. They believe that credit and savings facilities can help the poor rural households to not only increase income but also manage their resources and acquire adequate basic necessities for their families. Credit facilities make it possible for them to exploit financial and other resources and take advantages of them. They further stress the importance of savings. For them, well managed savings facilities present incentives for households to build up funds for investment or future consumption. Moreover, credit and savings facilities enable farmers to invest in land improvement or agriculture technology such as high yielding seeds that increase income. Short-term borrowing or savings are often used to maintain consumption of basic necessities when household incomes decline temporarily after a bad harvest or between agricultural seasons.

Therefore, for Zeller and Sharma (1998: 17), the provision of financial services is an effective tool for improving the quality of life of the poor. They also give evidence on how well managed and innovative rural financial institutions have helped poor families to make permanent positive changes in the quality of their lives. This is done through human capital investment (typically school enrollment), holding assets to enhance women's empowerment, high off–farm income from micro-enterprises and household food consumption and improved nutritional status of children in countries like Bangladesh (the case of Gerameen Bank), Peru, Kenya and Ghana and many others. Further evidence of how microfinance can play a wider role than just increasing incomes is given by Zander (1997: 47). He points out that financial relations create assets in rural households. He argues that while increasing income is an important indicator of reduced poverty in the short term, assets-building of low income clients represents the most sustainable way out of poverty. Assets such as land, livestock and agricultural equipment may be directly productive, while housing and household furniture increase the social status of the poor. Moreover, Zeller and Meyer (2002: 1) argue in regard to both poverty and vulnerability that specifically microfinance projects help the poor to acquire assets, start businesses, finance emergency needs and insure themselves against illnesses and disasters. The importance of finance is considered to change the life and reality of the poor. The first book that provided clear linkages between microfinance and livelihood was the work by Lont and Hospes "Livelihood and Microfinance" in 2004, which constituted a major contribution. They believe that the two fields of livelihood and microfinance are connected, that savings and credit transactions are embedded in a bundle of financial and non-financial relations, most of which are socially regulated (Lont and Hospes, 2004: 3). They hold that every savings and credit transaction implies the use of combination of different resources or capital (ibid.: 11).

3.6.2 Commercialization of Microfinance

Commercialization of microfinance refers to the application of market-based principles to microfinance (Ledgerwood and White, 2006: xxvi). Commercialization is concerned not only with establishing specialized microfinance institutions but also with linking them to commercial funds. In their book "Transformation of Microfinance Institutions", Ledgerwood and White (2006) provide a detailed description of how the transformation of financial institutions takes place. For Ledgerwood and White (2006: xxvii) the transformation of a nonprofit organization into formalized regulated financial institutions is the most important way of commercialization. This process includes increasing cost recovery, achievement of operational self-sufficiency and the achievement of financial self-sufficiency and the full utilization of market based sources of funds which is realized when the microfinance institutions operate as profit institutions within the formal financial system. It is assumed to locate microfinance institutions in the legal and regulatory framework of the financial sector, which is important to mobilize clients' savings. Savings services are seen as critical for the commercialization process because donor funds have been experienced unsustainable (Ledgerwood and White, 2006). The third benefit that is expected by providing savings facilities and access to capital is increasing the outreach that is assumed to be the result of the two efforts. (ibid.: xxxi)

Ledgerwood and White (2006: xxxvii) also argue that besides the facilitation of savings, by expanding the funding base and increasing the number of clients, commercialized microfinance institutions are also able to diversify their ownership and governance structures, professionalize their staff, and improve management information systems and overall internal controls.

I would argue here that commercialization emphasizes the regulatory form of institutions, without proposing ways to serve the poor who are not able to deal with such institutions. Thus, when reading about the commercialization of microfinance the question arises what in the case of success is the difference between microfinance institutions and old-fashioned banks? When the starting point is that established banks have not been successful in helping the poor for the last two decades? According to Ledgerwood and White (2006: xxxvii) many skeptics believe that the commercialization of microfinance will eventually result in the profit motive replacing the social mission. They expect a shifting focus to provide loans to higher income clients instead of the poor. Critics have also questioned the high cost of transforming the financial institutions. This is the starting point for the following discussion about the death of microfinance.

3.7 When Microfinance Died: Microfinance as Poverty Trap and Poverty Capital

As I have now presented the theoretical perspectives and the experience with microfinance since its rise till the beginning of the new millennium, I will now go one step further in demonstrating recent incidents and findings. In this, I depend on the work of Wright (2000), Lont and Hospes (2004), Bateman (2010) and Roy (2010), who analyze the most recent efforts and results of microfinance around the world. This serves as a conclusion for this chapter. I would like to provide a general argumentation understood from these works before breaking into the idea that the vision of microfinance is exaggerated and hence its ideal never met.

Therefore, the main argument here is that microfinance is not as effective as it was planned to be and its impact on poverty is minimal. In his book "Microfinance Systems", Wright (2000) asks the question, is microfinance the solution or a problem? His main argumentation is that a microfinance program could have positive or negative effects on the life of people, especially women, depending on how these programs are designed to provide what he calls "quality financial services". Drawing from data in Bangladesh, he asserts that programs are most successful when they help the poor to help themselves. Moreover, in order for quality financial services to be successful they should not be designed to only tackle income poverty, since the poor need more than income, thus social issues like health and education are to be considered in the definition of poverty and the design of microfinance products (Wright, 2000: 8). Wright is generally in favor of diversifying microfinance products.

According to Rahman (2004: 31), one of the problems of microfinance is the fact that much of the legitimacy of the argument, which associates microcredit with poverty alleviation, rests on the perceived success of Grameen Bank. This bank has come to serve as a model of the virtuous outcomes of credit for the poor in rural Bangladesh. I agree and argue here that even if Grameen Bank can be counted as successful experience, this still does not ensure its success in other countries with different economic, social political and cultural backgrounds. I refuse the idea of an ideal model or best practices that do not address the local context. In addition to that, Rahman (2004) criticizes that most institutions measure the impact of microfinance on poverty by a very narrow term of impact. Rahman (2004: 32) reports measures of institutional performance, but no indicators of impact on clients. Moreover, the importance of sustainability is also measured for the institutions providing microfinance but not at client level impact assessment. These arguments are also supported by the work of Bateman (2010: 63). For Rahman (2004), the only survey that collected empirical data, which focuses on these challenges, is an unpublished study sponsored by the World Bank in Bangladesh in 1991-1992 (cited in Rahman, 2004: 32), which is considered the most rigorous on the impact of microcredit on the poor. Many writers evaluate the impacts of the microfinance using the data of this study. However, very confusing and contradicting conclusions have been reached. Some assessments find a positive impact, while others find it to be negative. For example, Khanker and Pitt (quoted in Rahman, 2004: 32) "*assess that increased incomes resulting from microcredit investments contributed to net increase in the household consumption of borrowers*". Contradicting to this, Morduch (1999, quoted in Rahman, 2004: 32f.) finds that those households with access to microcredit had no higher average consumption levels than the households in the control groups who had no access to credit, that the children of borrowers were not substantially more likely to be in school. Morduch's assessment confirms what Rahman (2004) found in the case of the Grameen Bank; that the borrowers used their savings and households assets for weekly installment payments of loans. Extracting resources from the households and redirecting funds from consumption needs to loan repayments resulted in further hardship of members of poor households. Rahman (2004) concludes that microcredit has the potential to improve households' conditions and living standards particularly for borrowers living over the poverty line. However, it has negative impacts for the poorest households particularly by increasing their debt burden.

According to Bateman (2010: 63), the criticism has recently become more serious when institutions like the World Bank started to doubt whether microfinance really is an effective poverty intervention:

> "*The high profile 2008 World Bank publication finance for all concluded that 'more research is needed to assert whether there is a robust and positive relationship between the use of credit and household welfare, including moving out of poverty'. For an institution that has been quite pivotal to the rise of the microfinance model, claiming that we do not know if the relationship between microfinance and poverty is even positive, never mind how robust it is, is pretty radical admission*" (Bateman, 2010: 63).

In relating microfinance to the key development triggers, Bateman (2010: 78) further discusses two recent important issues in the application of microfinance. One is the effect of microfinance on small enterprises and agriculture. Concerning the small enterprises, he argues that the importance of financing the enterprise sector comes from the fact that small enterprises are always considered the most important engines driving forward sustainable economic development. However, evidence from India shows that the growing focus on microfinance and small enterprises quite dramatically undermines the productive and overall efficiency of India's economy. Bateman further claims that most microfinance institutions in India have little concern for sustainable local development, being far more interested in maximizing profits and shareholder value through granting loans to whichever microenterprise can support their high interest rates and short repayment period.

The second issue of agriculture discussed by Bateman (2010: 80) concerns the controversial question, whether microfinance has an important role to play in agriculture. The common rationale sees a need to boost small farm production destined for home consumption and the local market, just as in the example of the first clients of Grameen Bank who received loans for rice husking, milk cow rearing and chicken farming. However, Bateman's presented evidence contradicts these in showing results how the aim was higher than what was achieved in reality.

Bateman (2010) also argues that in both developed and developing countries the most productive and socially efficient agricultural production structures are small family farms, which work for household subsistence or to serve the local market. Thus besides feeding the households members, a sizable portion of the agricultural production is destined for the local market. However, "*these small farmers showed a resistance to dealing with microfinance*" (Bateman, 2010: 82). They cannot deal with the formal financial institutions but have a need for credit. Therefore, they became a target of microfinance. Bateman again refers to the example of India to illustrate what he calls "a disaster":

> "*The eventual result was entrapment of several tens of millions of the very smallest subsistence farms in a vicious downward cycle of dependency and growing micro debt. In 2003, for example it was estimated that fully half of the small farmers in India were in serious debt... in fact, most farms in serious debt to a halt. Among other things, this was thanks to the 160,000 farmer suicides registered in India since 1997 one of the most grotesque statistics associated with the growing entry of microfinance into the agricultural sector*" (Bateman 2010: 83).

Bateman (2010) presents evidence from Mexico in Latin America and Malawi and Kenya in Africa. He concludes that the small farmers found it impossible to repay the high interest rates demanded by Mexico's microfinance institutions. In Africa, Bateman argues that most microfinance mobilized across the continent appears not to have been re-used into the crucial agriculture sector but into petty trading. On top of that, microfinance provided for family farms with growth potential, thereby contributing to the weakening of the agriculture sector. When targeted by microfinance institutions these borrowers tend to repay their microloans through one of their likely income streams or to sell their assets even this could be the agricultural land itself. The same argumentation is presented by Roy (2010).

Another interesting issue raised by Bateman (2010: 108) is the assumption that microfinance has the potential to help building and extending social capital in poor communities. Solidarity circles have been used as evidence of building and extending social capital and solidarity within communities like in the example of Grameen Bank. This is described by Bateman as "an illusion" for the fact that the central operating principle of the new wave microfinance model that was shaped by competition over maximizing profit, contradicts the essence of local solidarity, interpersonal communication, volunteerism, trust-based interactions and goodwill. He argues that in the world of Grameen Bank famous of high repayment rates there is high social pressure on borrowers, by socially banishing defaulting borrowers. Bateman argues that microfinance institutions often take advantage of those in poverty with very little social capital (Bateman, 2010: 110).

It is quite interesting to follow Bateman's elaboration and discussion how microfinance has died as a result of the commercialization of the sector which he calls the "new wave" of microfinance. He explains that development organizations are supposed to be nonprofit in the pursuit of development. However, in the majority of cases where public or nonprofit organizations were forced into the process of commercialization, negative results are the outcome (Bateman, 2010: 114). To make matters even more dubious, a group of "microfinance millionaires" has emerged in the process. Roy (2010: 27) calls this group the "micro sharks". They mainly constitute private individuals of the microfinance institutions who have opportunistically moved to convert their position as employees into stratospheric personal wealth (Roy, 2010: 123). In an interview with a senior CGAP advisor (quoted in Roy, 2010), it becomes obvious that there is little empirical evidence to indicate that microfinance is either sustainable or reduces poverty. Roy concludes from Rosenberg (2006: 1) who evaluates the microfinance portfolio of the World Bank and the UNDP that "*in both agencies, less than a quarter of the projects that funded micro lending were judged successful*". For all these problems, Roy (2010) conceptualizes microfinance as "poverty capital" to oppose Michael Goldman's idea (2005 quoted in Roy, 2010: 30) of "development capital", by which Goldman referred to the money that runs through the projects of the international development institutions such as the World Bank and the USAID and UN and mediated by NGOs and consulting firms.

Finally, from the work evaluating the success of microfinance discussed above, one can draw some conclusions, including the microfinance-critical work of Ackerly (1995), Hulme and Toye (2007), Kabeer (2001), Rahman (2004), Helms (2006), Bateman (2010) and Lakwo and Haan (2010). The general view is that micro-lending has reasonably positive impacts on households, but is challenged by severe ramifications:

— Credit has a positive impact on household income, but the impact on consumption, on health, on the nutrition level of family members, and on children's attendance at schools has been found unconclusive.
— Impact of microcredit on the poor has on average been small or negative related to the control group (in Malawi the impact was found marginal or negative on household income and household food consumption).
— Borrowing from microcredit institutions has had a negative impact on net crop incomes, mostly for the reason that it let farmers react to increase in input prices by borrowing rather than altering their farming strategies.
— The lending interventions normally impose severe sanctions on borrowers in order to achieve high repayment rates. Such sanctions and repayment pressure damage the cohesiveness of the group, undermine the empowerment of borrowers, lead to household debt building and create more poverty.
— Most of the loans women borrowed are controlled by male family members, despite of these women taking the burden of repayment. Other results have shown that micro-lending practices and repayment pressure of financial institutions cause intimidation of borrowers and an increase of violence against women.
— The average per capita calorie intake for households that never participated in microcredit programs was higher than for those who participated in such schemes.
— The lending outreach of financial institutions to poor borrowers has been marginal. Thus, the limited participation of the poor means that these project have little or no poverty reduction impact.

4 Financial Institutions: Variety of Arrangements

"*Microfinance is not fitting in the banks' culture, poor people smell, they are not dressed nicely and the staff of the bank cannot deal with them*" (Malcolm Harper on the conference "Lessons of Microfinance to be Learnt for Sudan", 6th of January 2010 Sudan Friendship Hall when describing the performance of banks in microfinance).

"*Banks collapse in all over the world especially in Africa and they are privatized in Latin America. One continent, which was an exception, is Asia, they reform their banks and it was a successful experience until the financial crisis of 1998. Few lessons of restructuring were successful; however under certain conditions—I was in Uganda and I know about that—they reform their banks; another example from Indonesia: the success emphasized with establishing village unites and these units graduated to be micro-banking units*" Prof. em Dr. Hans-Dieter Seibel on the conference "Lessons of Microfinance to be Learnt for Sudan", 6th of January 2010 Sudan Friendship Hall when describing lessons of restructuring banks).

4.1 Introduction

Financial institutions are the backbone of any financial system, since they are the central component of the financial landscape. Thus, the main objective of this chapter is to identify different types of financial institutions in developing countries. To this end, first a brief general overview of financial institutions is presented with focus on institutions working in rural areas and thus more relevant in the scope of the research. In Sudan, there have been continuous attempts to find out which financial institutions are most appropriate in helping the poor and leave significant marks in poverty alleviation through the provision of microfinance. Thus, it is important to discuss which institutions are better prepared to tackle the demand of the rural poor.

The main questions discussed in this chapter are: What types of financial institutions are available in rural areas? How and why are they classified? What is the difference in the performance of formal and informal institutions? Which institutions are serving better the poor and why? Further questions are raised regarding features and effectiveness of their operations to serve the poor in rural areas. The conclusion of this chapter deals with the question of how to build financial institutions to serve the poor.

Thus, this chapter serves as a theoretical platform that represents the international debate and experience of financial institutions around the world. This platform is considered crucial when investigating financial landscapes in Sudan.

4.2 The Structure of Rural Financial Markets

I believe that a discussion about financial institutions cannot take place without studying the financial market in which they exist. Thus, before starting the discussion I would like to briefly explain the concept of financial markets.

From the perspective of Drake and Robertson (1980: 10), Krahnen and Schmidt (1994: 5), Moll (1994: 72) and Heffernan (2000), financial transactions and the process of lending and borrowing generate financial assets, and depending on that, markets should exist to deal with these financial assets. Therefore, financial markets are like the markets for real goods in that the interaction of supply and demand determines the prices (rates of interest) and the coordination for the services provided by financial institutions to the non financial or the real sector of the economy. While the supply side of financial assets includes funds available for lending and other financial services provided by formal and informal institutions in rural financial markets, the demand side consists of the capacity of rural households to engage in financial transactions (Moll, 1994: 73; Heffernan, 2000). In his explanation of rural financial markets Moll (1994: 72) states that financial markets [1] consist of relationships between buyers and sellers of financial assets in the economy; these relationships take place between different parties through financial transactions such as lending, borrowing, saving, and insuring.

Unsurprisingly, these financial transactions incur costs of lending, which are supposed to be covered by financial institutions in their provision of finance. They include first the costs of funds, meaning interest paid to savers, depositors and other suppliers of funds and the administrative costs of managing savings accounts and deposits. Second the costs of granting loans meaning administrative costs for screening, monitoring and loan recovery and the costs of default. Lending costs consequently determine a financial institution's ability to attract more funds and to allocate these funds to borrowers (Moll, 1994: 76).

Generally, it has become apparent that underdeveloped institutions, inadequate availability or absence of reliable collateral security, covariant risks and seasonal fluctuations in demand for and supply of short-term financial resources and high costs associated with serving clients are characteristic for rural financial markets in developing countries (Yaron et al., 1997: 11). Moreover, as described by Conning and Udry (2005: 6), most of the literature describes financial markets as fragmented. Different segments of borrowers are observed across different loan types and lending intermediaries according to the characteristics of the borrowers, the lenders, the activities financed, and other variables in the trading environment. Also seen as typical for rural financial markets is the combination of limited access and choices. Institutions in the same market find themselves using financial instruments that substantially differ, for example interest rate charges, the type and quantity of collateral requisites on loans, resources spent on monitoring and implementing the terms of contract, and whether or not credit is tied to transactions on other markets (Conning and Udry, 2005: 6f.). These instruments are found to shape the access to finance and choices in the market and the financial innovations of many institution that aim to work in rural areas; they also determine what types of borrowers can be served under such conditions. Thus, borrowers, especially the poor, may find themselves excluded from access to certain credit instruments, or rationed to smaller loans than they demand and may then adjust by turning to substitutes available to them.

Another feature of the financial markets explained by Meyer et al (1992) and recently Fields (2007) is the financial market "dualism" that is explained by the existence of both formal and informal sectors. For Fields (2007: 1) the informal sector always arose as reaction to the domination of the single sector model. Thus, the co-existence of the formal and informal sector is considered the defining feature of the financial market. For Meyer (1992: 27), this to great extent happens in Sub-Saharan Africa where a large portion of households entirely relies on finance from the informal sector. Helms (2006: 35) agrees with the existence of the informal finance sector; but he believes that as a consequence of the microfinance over the past 25 years there has been a tremendous movement from informal toward formal providers.

Conning and Udry (2005: 11) list another attribute of rural markets, the heavy intervention from governments, which they have done since the earliest days of markets; but they classify times when this interventions are positive and leave positive and significant effects and times when they hinder the development of the market. For a positive type of intervention, they give the following example:

> "*For example, transaction costs between private parties may be reduced if the state is able to provide impartial and accessible legal mechanisms for the arbitration and enforcement of contracts.*" (Conning and Udry, 2005: 11).

On the other side, government interventions can constrain the development of the financial market (Conning and Udry, 2005: 12). This is mainly the case when governments have, for example, enforced strict 'anti-usury' laws that limited market interest rates or acted to prohibit or constrain the participation of certain types of intermediaries. In much of the discussion about this topic, it is regularly assumed that the state should take the responsibility to build a conducive environment for both financial markets and the rest of the economy through infrastructure, liberalization of markets, macroeconomic stability and so forth. According to Lapenu (2002: 299), the intervention of the state in the financial system may also be justified to cope with market failures and improve equity. In the case of market failures, the state's role is defined as the regulatory framework and fiscal and monetary policy, which is widely accepted as providing a public good. Under the liberalization policies launched in the devel-

---

[1] Financial markets are rural when they occur in rural areas. The participants of the rural financial markets are rural households and intermediaries operating between buyers and sellers of financial assets to bridge preferences for quantity, time, risk, and space.

oping countries, the main role of the state is to secure macroeconomic stability, limited to protect savers, provide insurance mechanisms, provide clear juridical and regulatory framework, and enhance political and macroeconomics stability. Most important is to provide an incentive structure so that all actors have a stake in a well functioning financial system (Lapenu, 2002: 317). However, in many developing countries the state has failed to take this role because governments seek more political gains (Lapenu, 2002: 299).

4.3 Financial Institutions: Continuum of Arrangements

Many writers have adopted Schmidt's and Kopp's (1987: 9) definition of financial institutions; "*financial institutions are establishments such as banks, which specialize in such functions as accepting savings deposits and granting credit, although not all financial institutions are in that sense, and not all financial institutions belong to the formal sector of the economy*". However, from the definition of finance applied in this research in chapter 3, financial institutions are institutions and community indigenous arrangements that bring together savers, borrowers and lenders in order to exchange financial benefits including loans, savings possibilities, and insurance and mutual aid opportunities.

I would like to briefly explain first the main and original model of Schmidt and Kopp (1987) and Krahnen and Schmidt (1994) that I consider the theoretical background for many studies. I combine this model with other more recent ones, most importantly in the work done by Nagarajan and Meyer (2005). This recent work seeks to explain the emergence of microfinance institutions (MFIs) and other new types like the apex institutions (Nagarajan and Meyer, 2005; Pischke, 1991; Bouman and Hospes, 1994; Coetzee, 2002).

According to the original model, financial institutions range between formal institutions in the formal sector of the economy and informal institutions in the informal sector; between these two types, a variety of other institutions exists depending on the degree of their formality or informality. The expression of continuum suggests that these institutions are grouped in different positions; moreover, even the degree of formality, semi-formality and informality differs between different institutions in every category. In addition to that, it not only suggests the description of the regulatory structure of these institutions but also implies and describes the distance between each category and the target group of the rural poor.

The model developed by Nagarajan and Meyer (2005: 20) is different and supported by other writers like Helms (2006) and Thankom et al. (2009). In this model, financial institutions are classified according to whether they are group based or individual based sources of funds. Thus, the source of funds is the criterion of classification. They first discuss rural retail institutions and differentiate between development banks, microfinance institutions (MFIs), member-based institutions (including co-operatives, credit unions, and self-help groups) on the one hand and informal finance on the other hand. Nagarajan and Meyer (2005) in their model include the wholesale institutions that are called apex institutions and have been established recently to work as intermediaries between the donors and the grass root institutions. The main role of these apex institutions is to support rural retail institutions.

Considering this classification, I would like to argue here that this recent work reflects on the changes that have taken place by the introduction of the microfinance sector and its institutions. Moreover, the emphasis on classifying member based institutions stresses the point that not only regulations should be used to classify institutions but also the sources of funds. This also comes from the findings of this research as people in Al Dagag showed different repayment performances when dealing with banks, NGOs and the informal institutions they are engaged in. In general, they were more committed to repay funds received from informal sources. Nagarajan and Meyer (2005: 20) state that in member-based financial institutions the members have the responsibility for owning, managing and operating. At the same time, they are the main or only customers of the same institution. Still the formality of the financial institution is not to be ignored. Thus, in my research, I tried to combine the two classifications of institutions.

The combination of the two models is presented in diagram 1:

Diagram 1: Classification of Financial Institutions

1) **Government and donor sponsored institutions**
   A) **Banks**
      — Commercial banks
      — Specialized banks
      — Development banks
      — Savings banks
   B) **Donor and government sponsored microfinance institutions**
      — NGOS and specialized Microfinance institutions (MFIs)
      — Donor sponsored programs
      — Apexes (wholesale finance formal finance)
2) **Member bases microfinance financial institutions**
      — Co-operatives
      — Credit unions
      — Self help groups mainly ROSCAs
3) **Individual and indigenous arrangements**
      — Moneylenders and traders
      — Family and friends

Formal Finance

Semi-informal Finance

Informal Finance

Source: Combining Krahnen and Schmidt (1994: 6) and Nagarajan and Meyer (2005: 20) models to the case of Sudan

4.3.1 Donor and Government Sponsored Institutions

4.3.1.1 The Performance of Banks in Rural Financial Markets

The main argumentation here is that banks have failed to provide financial services to the poor segment of the society. Many writers agree that banks have failed to serve the poor especially in rural areas in many developing countries (Adams, 1984; Pischke, 1994; Seibel, 1994; Olubiyo and Hill, 2000; Buchenrieder, 2000; Shete, 1999; Seibel, 1994; Nagarajan and Meyer, 2005).

In explaining why banks have failed to serve the poor, Seibel (1994) and Pischke (1994) point out that most formal financial institutions including banks are required to follow administrative procedures set by the government that might not help the poor. Banks administer their day-to-day financial requirements by lending to one person the money of another at reasonable costs to its customers and profit to itself (Bouman and Hospes, 1994). No efforts are made to actively promote savings, thus, their operations are restricted by their source of funds. Consequently, loans are usually restricted to sectors of the economy that already flourish. Banks offer loans, which are uniformly allocated in accordance with defined production goals. Loan terms such as size, maturity and grace period[2] are not individually determined. Furthermore, since they use their clients' deposits, they demand collateral requirements and installments tend to be short (typically on monthly basis) ignoring individual repayment capacities deriving from other sources of income. Generally, loans are strictly scheduled and strong penalties are enforced (Seibel, 1994, 2000). In addition to that, they provide minimal if any monitoring of production.

It is questionable, whether banks carefully balance costs, returns and the increased scale of operation (Seibel, 2000: 76). Olubiyo and Hill (2000: 248), Shete (1999: 477) and Vaessen (2001: 6) also reach the same conclusion about banks.

In addition, banks are usually not available in rural areas and few branches in the main cities are not enough to reach the rural population (Seible, 2000; Vaessen, 2001: 6). Furthermore, rural banks where they exist are faced with problems regarding the assessment of demand, number, location, and financial capacity of actual and potential clients (Seibel, 1994: 1; Seibel, 2000). All these characteristics make it clear that

[2] The additional period of time a lender or insurance policy issuer provides for a borrower to make payment on a debt without penalty.

banks as well as other regulated financial institutions are not suitable institutions to serve the poor in rural areas.

4.3.1.2 NGOs and Specialized Microfinance Institutions (MFIs)

Next I discuss NGOs and specialized microfinance institutions (MFIs) established by NGOs or banks to provide microfinance and apexes as wholesale finance institutions recently established in most developing countries to channel microfinance funds.

In providing financial services, NGOs are considered a special case, in that all over the Third World they have to resume what should have been done by governments' specialized institutions and banks. For Bouman and Hospes (1994: 12) and Cater (2001), during the past two decades, NGOs have shifted their policies from a welfare and relief course of action to a policy centered on income generation and increasing production; thus, they have become involved in providing financial services and credit has become a central feature of this approach. Sometimes such provision is organized in an "*integrated development approach*" (Bouman and Hospes, 1994) that encompasses marketing support, awareness building, skill training and education as well as other programs like health, nutrition and housing. Still, many issues remain open concerning NGOs' provision of financial services.

In spite of their advantages in serving the poor, NGO performance is not as expected due to many reasons. For instance, NGOs remain unfamiliar to the idea of liberalizing financial markets and remain reluctant to charge positive real interest rates. By this, they undermine traditional financial systems. NGOs largely lack the discipline required for the provision of sustainable financial services (Abugre, 1994: 158). Also questionable is the ability of their staff to manage the financial aspect, the sustainability of their projects. In addition to that, their overreaching to include the extra poor and economically not active poor in rural areas is doubtful. Bouman and Hospes (1994: 12) and Shete (1999: 482) raise similar concerns about the work of NGOs in providing financial services. More questions arise concerning their accountability to their sources of funding. This is mainly because NGOs remain highly dependent on donor funds and will often collapse if donor funding is discontinued.

In his discussion about the performance of NGOs in providing microfinance, Cater (2001: 5) explains that NGOs appear to enter in the microfinance field in a minimalist credit way; their growth is not linked to savings deposits.

NGOs operating in a community often assume that either financial systems do not exist and assume the operation of informal systems to be inadequate (Abugre, 1994: 167). NGOs usually have three typical ways of dealing with informal arrangements: They either ignore them, or seek to transform them into forms they can control or influence or try to formalize them and to pump more money into them. Abugre (1994) argues that although informal financial institutions might play a useful role, NGOs nevertheless consider them exploitive or too primitive or slow to create quick development. Thus, they might even destroy the informal financial arrangements that exist in the community. The most celebrated example of distrusting an informal financial mechanism is the picture of the local moneylender as an evil and exploitative character whose activities must be undermined not complemented (Abugre, 1994: 166).

Within the framework of discussing the recent advances in the financial institutions, Hishigsuren (2006: 7f.) takes the disadvantages of the NGOs further and point out what needs to be done since the realization of such problems associated with NGOs. A new approach of transforming NGOs into regulated MFIs supposedly takes place in some developing countries. This is also supported in the work of Lidgerwood and White (2006) and discussed as a basis of the commercialization process presented in chapter 3. Hishigsuren argues that when NGOs are regulated they can provide a wider range of financial services including savings, which would enable them to be self-sustainable and profitable, thus, not only to access this relatively stable source of local resources but also to expand their outreach by attracting a larger number of clients in different sectors (Hishigsuren, 2006: 7). Unfortunately, the initial findings of such efforts indicate that few transformed MFIs have taken full advantage of their ability to mobilize savings. Hishigsuren (2006) explains the model of institution transformation further and presents many cases and experience from Latin America, Asia and Africa, discussing achievements as well as disappointments that result from the transformation process.

4.3.1.3 Apex Institutions

Apex institutions are organizations that channel funds, with or without technical assistance, to retail financial institutions, often to target specific categories of borrowers (Nagarajan and Meyer, 2005: 24). Many function as conduits for governments and donors to finance MFIs. Levy (2002, cited in Nagarajan and Meyer, 2005: 24) examined 37 apex institutions in 28 developing countries. His conclusion points to issues equally relevant for agricultural and rural finance. Levy identified several expectations about what apex institutions will accomplish. This includes, (i) receiving large volumes of funds, repackaging them into smaller amounts, and passing them on to MFIs, (ii) building retail MFIs capacity, (iii) bridging the gap between MFIs and financial markets, (iv) improving donor coordination, and (v) supervising the borrowing MFIs. Most apex institutions have failed to build bridges to financial markets and there was little evidence of success in coordinating the efforts of donors in support of microfinance. Furthermore, many studies found that competing donors that offered funds at subsidized rates undercut the efforts of apexes. Therefore, the role of apex institutions in supporting rural MFIs at this stage of development is especially tricky (Nagarajan and Meyer, 2005: 24).

4.3.2 Member Based Financial Institutions

Member based financial institutions help the poor to get access to a useful lump sum through building up savings, which is in the centre of the formation of the group (Thankom et al., 2009: 10). Such arrangements are composed of a group of individuals who pool funds and lend primarily to members of the group. Examples of such institutions are the credit co-operatives and credit unions and the Rotating Savings and Credit Associations (ROSCAs). Considering the results of data analysis, ROSCAs will be focused on.

4.3.2.1 Rotating Savings and Credit Associations (ROSCAs)

The first recognition of ROSCAs within the social science came from the work of Geertz (1962) followed by anthropologists like Ardener (1964, 1996), Pischke (1992), and Bouman (1994) who contributed to a great extend in presenting ROSCAs to the world and form the basis of the discussion in this research. Helms (2006) and Thankom et al. (2009) and other writers also provide a general description of these institutions. Moreover, recent work of economists, for instance Fang and Ke (2006), investigate the insurance role of ROSCAs. In addition to that, the work of Kimuyu (1999), and Gugerty (2005) present cases of ROSCAs in east Africa with focus on Kenya; and Klonner (2003) studied ROSCAs in communities at risk. Most of the economical analyses of ROSCAs focus on two issues; first on the use of funds in purchasing durable goods; and second on the role of ROSCAs as insurance mechanism against risks. It is argued that while the formal credit market allows individuals to smooth their intertemporal income risks by borrowing and saving, ROSCAs provides an additional instrument for its participants to split contemporaneous income shocks amongst them (Klonner, 2001: 2).

Geertz (1962: 243) expresses the basic principle of the rotating credit association everywhere, as "*a lump sum fund composed of fixed intervals and as a whole to each member of the association in turn*". The main features are: the interest is not calculated, rotation is determined by lot or by agreement, membership tends to be small and a separate staff of officers does not exist. The members simply come together and agree among themselves to contribute fixed funds on a daily, weekly or monthly basis (Geertz, 1962: 243). Buckley (1997: 1085) and Ardener (1996) discuss the question who the members of ROSCAs are; and they agree that in such financial arrangements members usually know each other and have common bonds by location, ethnic group, approximate income level or type of enterprise activity. The members tend to meet on the day of payment, the meeting is often also a feast, small gathering of friends, neighbors and kin and particularly in the villages is commonly "*viewed by its members less as an economic institution than a broadly social one whose main purpose the streng-*

thening of community solidarity" (Geertz, 1962: 243, similarly Krahnen and Schmidt, 1994: 46; Buckley, 1997: 1085; Helms, 2006; Thankom et al., 2009).

Geertz (1962: 242f.) distinguishes between the most basic and simple form of ROSCAs and more complex structures and operations that exist in countries like China and Japan and in some countries in Africa. In Asia, the tendency is toward the development of complex methods of calculating interest payment and distributing those payments among the members of the association. In Africa, the tendency is toward the development of more complex leadership patterns and more internal organization and consequently toward increasing administrative costs (Geertz, 1962: 249).

Ardener (1964: 201) criticizes Geertz' (1962) way of thinking and points out that Geertz's basic principles upon which ROSCAs are founded is defined too restrictively and does not allow the inclusion of all the examples quoted by Geertz himself. She gives further examples from different countries and states that contributions are not always fixed and a member does not always receive the whole of the lump sum. Furthermore, the use of the term sum is not satisfactory, as it may seem to imply that contributions can be made only in cash and not in kind. In her paper, she also suggests that this variety in structure does not only appear between different communities but also within one community, the variety of arrangement makes it also difficult to have on comprehensive definition. Accordingly, she suggests a more simple definition for ROSCAs, which is "*an association formed upon a core of participants who agree to make regular contributions to a fund which is given in whole or in part, to each contributor in rotation*" (Ardener, 1964: 201).

Regarding the origin and the role of ROCAs in the economic development, Geertz argues that such institutions:

> "*form of symbiosis between the 'traditional' social structure of the immigrants and the more 'rational' one into which they have been suddenly projected has made possible the immigrants' adaptation to the new economic and political tasks with which they are faced, while at the same time minimizing the strain of transition and social transformation. The agricultural cooperative may thus be seen as an 'intermediate' institution which links traditional motivations to modern functions, serving at the same time to transform those motivations toward a more rationalistic basis*" (Geertz, 1962: 259f.).

Ardener (1964: 221) rejects Geertz' (1962) assessment of ROSCAs as "middle-rung" institutions, as products of a shift from a traditionalistic agrarian society to an increasingly fluid commercial one, as an educational mechanism in terms of which peasants learn to be traders not merely in the narrow occupational sense, but the broad cultural sense (Geertz, 1962: 260). Ardener (1964) admits that this might be true and applicable in some cases as in the case of Mba-Ise in Nigeria, however, in her view it remains unclear whether these associations are the product of such a shift; it may have been partly causative, but not completely since other factors might have intervened.

Ardener found that these institutions are not only linked to migrants but also to middle class women who contributed gold at that time. Moreover, in her book "Money Go Round" (1996) Ardener and other writers criticize Geertz' argumentation that rotating credit associations will turn more and more into specifically economic institution. They question if these institutions will necessarily be self-liquidating and ultimately replaced by banks, co-operatives and other economically more rational types of credit institutions (Geertz, 1962: 163). Ardener (1996: 1) disputes the assertion that ROSCAs, though useful in an intermediate stage of development would necessarily fade away as more developed financial institutions replace them. Her view is confirmed by empirical evidence; although ROSCAs may have become less important in proportion to other credit institutions in some places, they still have spread or burgeoned more vigorously than ever. They have done so in financial climates and cultural contexts where other credit systems have been unstable, due to the inability or unwillingness of creditors to meet their obligations. For instance, in Cameroon current economic activity, at all levels, depends heavily on participation in ROSCAs of a variety of forms and scales (Ardener, 1996: 2).

Another debatable issue about ROSCAs is the question if they can also exist in a prosperous formal financial system. Fang and Ke (2006: 1f.) who studied ROSCAs in China challenge the previous theoretical assumption that ROSCAs participants do not have access to formal financial markets. They argue that it is undoubtedly true that ROSCAs are more commonly observed in developing countries with underdeveloped formal financial markets; however, they show in their research that many linkages exist between ROSCAs and the formal financial sector in China. Moreover, they prove in their work that ROSCAs provide insurance to their participants even in the presence of the formal credit markets. Ardener (1996: 2), also in favour of this argument, believes that "*if ROSCAs are popular among the poor and in fluctuating economic conditions they also thrive among some relatively affluent economic strata. Indeed they are often popular with the intellectual and political élites who have easy access to formal banking system*". The question arises here, why are they that successful and sustainable? The answer to this question is presented next.

4.3.2.2 Outstanding Features and Advantages of ROSCAs

Rotating associations are important in the creation and accumulation of savings, which can serve as a basis for small-scale capital formation (Geertz 1962; Ardener 1964: 217; Krahnen and Schmidt, 1994: 47; Pischke, 1992: 326ff.). For Geertz ROSCAs are mechanisms enhancing basic savings habits of the people, thus unless aggregated national saving can be increased to cover or at least approximately cover the growth in investment, a developmental program implies persistent, runaway inflation will frustrate all efforts toward the realization of such programs (Geertz, 1962: 241). Geertz main explanation is that this increase in the national savings could not be achieved unless the basic saving habits of the people of a country can be altered, and an appropriate set of institutions should exist to serve the purpose of promoting individual savings, for organizing and making them useful for the savers and their communities (ibid.: 241).

ROSCAs create claims on resources that would otherwise have been used for immediate family needs, since it is hard to accumulate savings for investment or future consumption within a family, which gives ROSCAs another benefit (Krahnen and Schmidt, 1994: 47). One of the important advantages of ROSCAs over other institutional arrangements is that ROSCAs do not incur any managerial costs since at each meeting the contribution of each member will be given to one of them, so there is no money left needing to be managed (Krahnen and Schmidt, 1994: 48). The unique reciprocity way of thinking implies the function of peer monitoring, so every saver has an interest in seeing to it that the borrowers put the funds to sound use and are able to make his or her contribution (Krahnen and Schmidt, 1994: 49)

For Pischke (1992: 331) the main advantage of ROSCAs is that they work entirely on promise, trust and consent and members have intimate knowledge about each other. This creates relationships among members that permit the application of certain sanctions. The regular meetings can help members to observe each other's health and mood and provide indication of each other's current financial status (Pischke, 1992: 331). Abugre (1994: 167) argues that ROSCAs in Africa are superior to formal financial systems in several respects: they are adaptable to the conditions of members, do not require complicated loan processing and recovery procedures; and, therefore, tend to be less costly. They combine savings and credit and demonstrate types of relationships that build on behavioral norms and that are conducive to the participation of the poor; this also ensures that participants are disciplined and accountable.

In ROSCAs saving and credit is voluntary, which is why, as financial institutions, they exhibit a degree of self-sufficiency, self-regulation and self-control (Bouman, 1994: 377). From the features provided above, it appears that ROSCAs are well-established indigenous institutions found all around the word. ROSCAs can have significant benefits for their members and are apparently very valuable for those who do not have access to a well functioning formal financial system of banks and insurance companies, and indeed research in all parts of the world unambiguously shows that people use ROSCAs frequently (Krahnen and Schmidt, 1994: 49).

4.3.3 Individual Based Arrangements

The category of individual based arrangements includes two clusters: first individuals specialized in the business of providing finance to others, lending their own funds in a professional manner like moneylenders and traders; second loans and credit between family members, relatives and friends (Mcleod, 1992: 257).

4.3.3.1 Moneylenders and Traders

Moneylenders, landlords and traders are identified by Buckley (1997: 1084) as those individuals who spend a significant part of their time lending money usually for short periods of time and sometimes unsecured by any collateral. Moreover, moneylenders tend to work in local markets and have close relations to their clients, thus they provide their services to a small number of well-known borrowers. According to Bouman and Hospes (1994: 12) moneylenders can work on part-time basis; this category includes rich farmers, shopkeepers, teachers, input suppliers, millers and workers with a regular income or access to banks who replace the former professional moneylender of ill repute of high interest rate. They are in some cases famous of getting high interest rates but borrowers' transaction costs are low and disbursement is normally quick (ibid.), and they are often viewed as exploitative. Robinson (2009) argues that high interest rates, short time repayment, and small amount of loans make moneylenders not suitable for the borrowers' needs (ibid.: 29). From the perspective of Steinwand (1994: 300), commercially based moneylenders are institutions where the allocation of credit is mainly governed by economic principles. However, drawing from the theory of embeddedness and moral economy discussed in chapter 2, I would like to argue that economic behavior in specific societies might be tied by social norms and social capital matters causing to bond both lenders and borrowers and regulate their behavior.

The main theoretical debate about moneylenders is centered on the question whether they are exploitative or not and whether their operations are reduced by the existence of formal financial institutions. It is argued in some literature that the share of moneylenders in total loans portfolios has declined due to the expansion of other credit institutions, and more so because of their ill reputation of being exploitative. Steinwand (1994: 293) shows for the case of Thailand that when institutions like the Bank for Agriculture and Agricultural Co-operatives (BAAC) expanded their operations the role of moneylenders declined. Sharma and Chamala (1998: 107) find any decline in the role of moneylenders caused by moneylenders having long been considered exploitative, monopolistic and detrimental to socioeconomic development. However, in another discourse in the literature, these images are questioned and the traditional moneylenders are often found first to exist when formal institutions are already in operation and second to be better than the formal banking institutions especially because of their outreach to the poor and high repayment performance (Sharma and Chamala, 1998: 108f.). It has been revealed that villagers would prefer to deal with moneylenders among other institutions. Steinwand (1994: 302) answers the question why many villagers prefer dealing with moneylenders over banks and other institutions. Villagers prefer the convenience of the moneylenders as it takes only a few days to process the loan, moneylenders are much more flexible in loan extensions or rescheduling, and the transaction costs of moneylenders are comparatively low. The main advantage of this sort of informal providers is the fact that they are close to the poor which provides them with better information regarding the activities and characteristics of borrowers (Thankom et al., 2009: 10)

Helms (2006: 37) argues that in agriculturally dependent rural areas, traders, processors and input suppliers are important sources of credit for farmers. Pearce (2003) stresses the point that trader credit is widespread in rural areas where financial markets are shallow and poorly developed. Therefore, trader finance may appear as a good solution for rural areas that are not well served by formal financial institutions. Furthermore, while Pearce (2003) argues that trader finance may more likely be a compliment for formal financial markets and that both flourish in the existence of each other, Helms argues that the operations of moneylenders might be reduced under the influence of the formal institutions.

Still such transactions might also have problems. Pearce (2003) notes that traders offer very limited types of financial products—primarily seasonal credit and short-term advances that meet working capital requirements in rural areas but not start-up and capital investments. Trader finances are generally limited to clients with long-term relations and large producers, their contracts are often interlinked with production activities and in some cases are found non-transparent, and they do not provide other essential financial services such as deposits and insurance. Finally, poorer populations and those in remote areas may depend entirely on such traders for credit, thereby receiving less favorable terms and conditions.

In spite of the growing number of studies on finance and development, evaluations of the role of such individual based arrangements still lack detail such as empirical data on their methods of working, rules and regulations, the relationship between the lenders and borrowers, and the different socio-economic and cultural context in which they operate.

4.3.3.2 Family Members, Relatives and Friends

For Bouman (1994: 116) social networks that provide financial services include family, friends, neighbors, and tribal age groups. Bouman argues further that such networks change continually, in response to the challenges of new directions in the economy and the social fabric of society. With economic growth, they increase rather that diminish in size and scope.

For Steinwand (1994: 297), family loans constitute a significant portion of the whole credit arrangements in the Third World. Thankom et al. (2009: 8) stress the same idea and argue that reciprocal lending makes up the bulk of financial transactions for the poor. Transactions take place in a framework of mutual assistance and function according to the unspoken rules of the social organization, rather than according to fixed regulations. In principle, intra-family loans are interest-free. While it is possible to deny a loan request from a family member, it is impossible to charge interest (ibid.). For Steinwand (1994) the consequences of default range from the forfeit of land to conversion of the loan into gift, but cases of loan default are always dealt with within the family. However, McLeod's (1994) findings show that some of the transactions which occur between family members and friends sometimes carry an explicit interest charge because it is reciprocal. This is to mean they imply obligation to provide similar assistance to the same or another member of the group on future occasion (ibid.).

From the results shown by Steinwand (1994: 297), it becomes apparent that family loans are the most favored form of credit as they are cheap and convenient and are often spent on urgent expenses like in cases of accident or illness.

Part II:
Research Methodology

5 Constructing Grounded Theory

"My initial advice is: Just Do It! Get the experience, do not fight windmills, do not worry about justifying it ... well done grounded theory justifies itself" (Anselm L. Strauss, 1998: 19).

5.1 Introduction

This chapter describes the methodology, methods and procedures used to conduct the research. The chapter starts by highlighting the history of Grounded Theory (GT). In addition, the main philosophical roots of the methodology and the considerable changes that have taken place over time in applying the methodology are discussed. The next section of the chapter illustrates in detail the steps and procedures I have taken to apply GT. This includes different data collection phases, the methods of data collection and data analysis using the atlas.ti software for analyzing qualitative data. In this research, I have followed the GT methodology from the beginning to the end.

The chapter is rather lengthy as I seek to fill a gap in most studies using GT as methodology that do not provide detailed descriptions of how each step has been performed. I found this important and have thus tried to combine a detailed description of what I have done with an overview over the literature about GT and research methods. GT is not a method without complication. Some of these difficulties are caused by the need to go to the field and stay in the field for long periods, which is sometimes financially or logistically inconvenient. Reading about GT as a methodology, I realized that the process is not quite easy since I understood many of the stages only through doing them. This is another reason that has motivated me to write this chapter in detail.

5.2 Choosing a Qualitative Methodology

Over the past decades, qualitative research has left its mark conceptually and theoretically on social sciences. Since the past quarter century, a major methodological revolution has been taking place in the social sciences. A combination of social, political sciences and the humanities occur rapidly in a mutual focus on an interpretive qualitative approach to research and theory (Denzin and Lincoln, 2005; Berg, 2007: 2).

For Flick (2007: ix) qualitative research intends to study the world and how people construct the world around them. Qualitative approaches also seek to understand situations and experiences of people and do not focus on research settings in laboratories. It intends also to understand, describe and explain social phenomena by analyzing people's experiences, which helps understanding interactions and communications.

Unlike quantitative research, qualitative research refers to the meanings, concepts, definitions, characteristics, symbols and descriptions of things. If quantitative research tend to answer questions like what, how, when, how many, and where of an item, it is believed in quantitative research that the essence of this item is thus absent (Berg, 2007). It usually seeks answers to questions by examining various social settings and the individuals who inhabit these settings (Berg, 2007: 8). The research therefore is directed towards how humans arrange themselves and their settings and how inhabitants of these settings make sense of their surroundings through social structure and social roles and so forth. Qualitative procedures provide a means of accessing unquantifiable facts about people. This allows the researcher to share in the understandings and perceptions of others and explore how people structure and give meaning to their daily lives (Berg, 2007: 9).

Common between all approaches of qualitative research is *first* the data itself (Strauss and Corbin, 1990: 20). Data might come from different sources. *Secondly*, different analytic or interpretive procedures are used to arrive at significant findings or theories that might be tested or developed. *Thirdly*, in all approaches of qualitative research written and verbal reports are produced in different ways. The results reached depend on the type of qualitative research approaches that might vary between grounded theory, ethnography, phenomenological approach, life histories, and conversational analysis, all of which are used in different disciplines. The findings can be used firstly and most importantly to develop basic knowledge. Other uses vary between building up research instruments, developing policies, evaluating programs, and providing information for different purposes like commercial purposes, practitioners' guides, policies and practices, and several political ends (Strauss and Corbin, 1990: 21).

Some researchers argue that the data should not be analyzed, rather just be presented to give an honest account with little or no interpretation made by the researcher to avoid the researcher biases and presence. The main role played by the researcher then is to hear and report. The other group is concerned more about providing accurate description after systematically analyzing the data collected to make sense of it. Finally, a third group of researchers is more concerned about building theories. They argue that building theories will lead to building knowledge in a systematic way (Strauss and Corbin, 1990: 21).

For a long time the focus in Sudan was on quantitative research carried out by individuals and institutions. The aim of this quantitative research was to investigate in the major concerns of academics and policy makers, which included investigating percentages of poverty, impact of projects and studying different phenomena in urban as well as rural areas including microfinance. Yet, there has been a recent trend to conduct more qualitative research because descriptive information is needed not only to quantify poverty and vulnerability, but also to explain and provide dense explanation, deep understanding and details on how poverty is experienced especially in rural areas where poverty and vulnerability are entrenched. Therefore, this research aims to go deeper than providing percentages and statistics and to describe in detail how people handle their situations, social or financial resources, actors, institutions, relationships and networks and how they try to maximize their benefits from each. To be more specific, this research seeks to achieve better understanding of rural people's lives and realities. It tries to explore and explain different dimensions of livelihood in rural areas of Sudan with special focus on the village Al Dagag, in the North Kordofan State (NKS). The research mainly deals with rural people, their experiences, their attitudes, their livelihood activities and strategies. In addition to that, how they act and react to different formal financial institutions and how they establish their own indigenous institutions that serve their financial needs. Generally, the main aim of this research is to understand relationships between people as well as how people are connected to the institutions and arrangements in their community. Therefore, the type of the research problem required the use of qualitative methodology.

I started the research with a vision and a question, the vision was to conduct a village study that portrays the livelihood in the Sudanese villages and the question was if microfinance is useful to sustain the livelihood of rural people.

5.3 Grounded Theory (GT)

5.3.1 Brief History and Philosophical Roots of Grounded Theory

Considering the eight influential groups of thoughts in the development of the qualitative research over time, explained by Denzin and Lincoln (2005: 15-21) it is apparent that GT is discovered in the modernist phase or in the period of time which started with the post-World War II years to the 1970s. They consider this moment significant in shaping and formulizing qualitative methods:

> "*This was the golden age of rigorous qualitative analysis, bracketed in sociology by Boys in White (Becker et al., 1961) at one end and the Discovery of the Grounded Theory (Glaser and Strauss, 1967) at the other*" (Denzin and Lincoln, 2005: 17).

According to Denzin and Lincoln (2005), this golden age boosted the image of qualitative research by setting in a belief in the contingency of self and society, different from the period before when the "other" whom the positivism paradigm studied was alien, foreign and strange.

GT can be situated as a post-positivism, epistemological approach of qualitative analysis. GT emerged from the work of Glaser and Strauss in 1967 when their book "The Discovery of the Grounded Theory" was a distinctive historical turning point for doing qualitative research, for it argued that data should be systematically obtained and analyzed in social research. In their own words, Glaser and Strauss celebrate the moment of the GT discovery in the following way:

> "*We offer this book, which we conceive as a beginning venture in the development of improved methods for discovering grounded theory ... since previous books on methods of social research have focused mainly on how to verify theories*" (Glaser and Strauss, 1967: 1).

Charmaz (2006) explains the innovative defining components of GT originally done by Glaser and Strauss as simultaneous involvement in data collection and analysis, constructing analytic codes and categories from the data, using constant comparative analysis, advancing theory development during each step of data collection and analysis, memo writing, theoretical sampling and conducting the literature review after developing an independent analysis.

Philosophically, GT is considered a bond between two contrasting and competing traditions in sociology that are the Columbia University Positivism and the Chicago School of Pragmatism and field research (Charmaz, 2006: 7). Charmaz explains further that from the Columbia University GT imported the epistemological assumptions, the logic and systematic approach that reflect Glaser's rigorous codified quantitative research exercise. Additionally, Glaser also brought in the practice of codifying qualitative research methods, which entailed specifying explicit strategies for conducting research. He also introduced to the GT the construction of what is termed 'middle-range' [1] theories, which had been proposed by scholars in Columbia University.

On the other hand, Strauss's Chicago School inheritance also went into GT, as Strauss perceived human beings as active agents in their lives and their worlds rather than as passive recipients of larger social forces. He suggested that processes not structures were fundamental to human existence and human beings are the main actors in creating structures by their engagement in processes throughout their lives. Thus, Strauss introduced to the GT concepts of human agency, emergent processes, social and subjective meanings, problem-solving practices and the open-ended study of action (Charmaz, 2006: 7).

For Charmaz, the pragmatist philosophical believes brought by Straus to the GT reflect the thinking of symbolic interactionism, that is, a theoretical standpoint which believes that society, reality and self are constructed through interaction and thus count on language and communications. This viewpoint suggests that interaction is inherently dynamic, interpretive and addresses how people create, enact and change meanings and actions. It also indicates that people do think about their actions rather than mechanically respond to stimuli.

Mills et al. (2010: 429) explain that the methodology falls within the tradition of qualitative research, which includes in its tradition both the interest of positivisim in establishing how the world might be predicted and controlled, and the interest of interpretiationism on subjective realities experienced by social actors. The latter are concerned with lived experiences and seek varying accounts of those experiences in contrast to the positivist approach, which aims to seek out underlying variables and casual factors of phenomena. For Mills et al. (2010), GT has intellectual connections to symbolic interactionism. Symbolic interactionism is both a theory of human behavior and an approach to inquiry about human conduct and group behavior.

However, in the intervening time, many scholars have moved GT from the positivism in both Glaser and Strauss and Corbin's versions to the epistemology of constructivism (Charmaz, 2006). After referring to different old and recent books on GT, it can be concluded that there is no one simple way of doing GT. I found myself in a position that I needed to specify which boulevard to walk through to reach the end of my research. Thus, it is worth mentioning that I take the side of constructivist GT thinking and specifically follow the work of Kathy Charmaz (2006). Charmaz goes in line with Strauss' standpoints in the sense to consider GT though an open and flexible method, but still includes a systematic process that should be followed. In her book on GT (2006), she provides a simple and practical guide to construct grounded theory. Charmaz believes that GT serves as a way to learn about the worlds we study and a method for developing theories to understand them (Charmaz, 2006: 10). I agree with her that the "discovery" of theories that is introduced by Glaser and Strauss is something related only to a very few theoretical underdeveloped areas of social science. Still GT can be used to study certain phenomena in our world that we are part of and that we seek to understand. This reflects the constructivist way of thinking.

Constructivist GT is explained by Charmaz (2006: 3f.) as a method that uses systematic procedures of data collection and analysis that allow constructing a theory that is grounded in data. Thus, analysis of data yields concepts that the researcher constructs. Constructivist GT is explained in Charmaz' words:

---

[1] Middle-range theories consisted of abstract rendering of specific social phenomena that were grounded in data (Charmaz, 2006: 7)

> *"We construct our grounded theories through our past and present involvements and interactions with people, perspectives and research practices... Research participants' implicit meanings, experiential views and researchers' finished grounded theories are constructions of reality... in keeping with Chicago school antecedents, I argue for building on the pragmatist underpinnings in grounded theory and advancing interpretive analyses that acknowledge these constructions*" (Charmaz, 2006: 10).
>
> *"Unlike their position (classic GT works of Glaser and Strauss), I assume that neither data nor theories are discovered. Rather, we are part of the world we study and the data we collect*" (Charmaz, 2006: 10).

Thus for her GT is:

> "*GT methods consist of systematic, yet flexible guidelines for collecting and analyzing qualitative data to construct theories 'grounded' in the data themselves*" (Charmaz, 2006: 2).

Although I share Charmaz' approach regarding the GT process, I will also reflect on my own research procedures that I have undertaken according to the possibilities that were available to me. Punch (2005: 157) stresses that in the case of GT the research does not start with a theory that is used to generate hypotheses to be tested. It starts with an open mind, aiming to end up with a constructed theory. The notion of generating theory comes from the fact that the main theoretical categories or concepts developed throughout GT research are and should be grounded in the data. This discussion represents an important concept brought by the GT thinking that is the theoretical sensitivity.

5.3.2 Theoretical Sensitivity

Theoretical sensitivity is discussed in GT because of the shift from the theoretical thinking about discovering underdeveloped categories and theories, and constructing theories based on previous knowledge or experience in the topic studied. In conducting this research, besides my previous educational and practical experiences in the field of rural development; viewing literature before, during and after I go to the field was helpful. I quote here a supporting sentence from Charmaz that GT and specifically the coding process is about to keep your mind open and not about going to the field with no prior ideas and skills. It was crucial to realize that "*there is a difference between an open mind and an empty head*" (Dey, 1999: 251, quoted in Charmaz, 2006: 30). Strauss and Corbin emphasize the theoretical sensitivity in their books (1990 and 1998). They argue that the basics of qualitative research provide a simple and direct way how to apply theoretical sensitivity. They link this term to the researcher's awareness of the meaning of data (Strauss and Corbin, 1990: 41). In their words: "*One can come to the research situation with varying degree of sensitivity depending on one's previous reading and experiences with or relevant to an area*". They explain further that theoretical sensitivity refers to the attribute of having insights, the ability to give meaning to the data, the capacity to understand, and the capability to separate the pertinent from that, which is not. All this is done in conceptual rather than concrete terms (Strauss and Corbin, 1990: 42). They also discuss different sources of sensitivity, such as professional, personal and analytical sensitivity. Moreover, they provide varied ways to help in holding to the reality of the phenomena rather than thinking imaginatively about them; these include periodically stepping back and asking questions, maintaining an attitude of skepticism and following the research procedures (Strauss and Corbin, 1990: 42).

Theoretical sensitivity, thus, is the heart of constructivist GT. GT then is not about discovering theories but about providing fresh insight into existing knowledge (Mills et al., 2010: 429). This applies to my research since the area of rural livelihood and financial relations are not underdeveloped, yet, for the specific case of Sudan qualitative research is required that generates concepts embedded in the data collected from the rural people themselves, something rarely done in Sudan. Also, most of the research conducted in this field relies purely on quantitative methodologies. In addition to that, the microfinance revolution in Sudan that has been taking place since 2002 and is sponsored by the Central Bank of Sudan (CBS), led to pour a huge amount of money into the microfinance sector. Nevertheless, most of the studies conducted rely on quantitative methodologies that serve providing statistics and that I believe is not enough to explore both demand and supply sides of microfinance.

What is more, for my research, theoretical sensitivity helped me to gain insights; it developed my ability to do initial coding, and feeling familiar and comfortable with the topic. It helped me also to know about literature in advance and different opinions and theoretical perspectives of writers, thus to know where to go when I felt the need to read about a specific category; many issues emerged from the data itself that forced me to go back and dig for books and literature about these new topics. At the beginning of the research, I only read about the main concepts of finance, microfinance and livelihood generally. However, later from the interviews, many other details and specific issues and new categories emerged, for examples the debate about the traders' dilemma, the importance of social capital as an insurance mechanism and the linkages between the financial and social capital of rural people.

5.3.3 Evolution of Grounded Theory

The main influential point of the evolution of the GT is the divorce between the two scholars Glaser and Strauss that materialized when each took different theoretical and practical standpoints. For Charmaz (2006: 8), Glaser kept on his earlier exegesis of the method and thus keeps distinguishing GT as a method of discovery. As it is clear that Glaser stresses the idea of emerging categories and theories from data with a minimal role of the researcher, the role of the researcher then should allows data to be self-explained, thus, the emergent categories and theories to be self-developed, assuming that "all is data". Mey and Mruck (2007: 45) argue that as Glaser stresses and supports the classical GT as the original approach, different ways of—in his words—, "*remodeling GT*" are considered as misuse of GT.

Meanwhile, Strauss' co-operation with Corbin (Strauss and Corbin, 1990, 1997, 1998) moved the method towards a different position. Strauss leans on symbolic interactionism and regards GT as a methodology to be adopted and modified while doing research. Strauss advocates for the concept of theoretical sensitivity, where the researcher is allowed to find alternatives while analyzing (Straus and Corbin, 1990). Strauss and Corbin rely on the idea that systematic theoretical coding, theoretical sampling, and the constant comparison of data are the basics of GT research. In their view, the systemic coding procedures provide reliability and validity. Strauss and Corbin aim to build a skeleton or axis for developing grounded theories. They used different terminologies of axial coding where categories and concepts developed during the open coding are investigated and related to either a phenomenon, casual condition, an action or interactional strategies, attributes of the context, or the consequences of these actions and interactions. For them, the axial coding is the main coding that attempts to explore which types of phenomena, context, causal and intervening conditions and consequences are relevant to the domain under study (Kelle, 2007: 140).

Even with Glaser's opposition to Strauss' and Corbin's model of GT, Strauss and Corbin succeeded in establishing a solid and powerful standpoint for the method that led many scholars to follow their steps. Recently scholars like Charmaz (2006) and Bryant and Charmaz (2007) have viewed GT as a container into which different content can be poured, but the principles of GT such as coding, memo-writing, theoretical sampling and comparative analysis are still followed.

GT is an inductive method when discovering theories; however, an element of deduction might have been introduced by the work of Berg (2007). Berg's model (2007: 287) allows both inductive and deductive methods. In this case, GT emphasizes induction, deduction and verification as integral parts of inquiry and it accepts the duality between deductive (i. e., generalization from a prior conceptualizations) and inductive (i. e. inference of particular facts or observational evidence to general principles). Mills et al. (2010: 430) discuss the same reasoning logic of induction and deduction. The GT model established by Berg also shows another divergence of views that allows reviewing literature while choosing the case to study, developing the research design, identifying data analysis strategies, collecting the data, and during the analysis. Thus, literature review is not only conducted after the data collection and initial steps of analysis, which supports the theoretical sensitivity discussed by Strauss and Corbin (1990).

In the same debate about the combination of induction or deduction of GT, Punch (2005: 158) cites that the contrast between theory generation and theory verification is not so sharp in practicing GT. Researchers may start without a theory and have the aim of creating one, it is not long into theorizing process before they also find themselves in need to test theoretical ideas which are emerging. Thus, Punch argues that theory generation may rely also on gradual verification. In other words, GT is essentially an inductive technique, but it uses deduction as well. That is to mean, GT stresses induction as the main tool for theory development; however, in developing a theory deduction might be unavoidable (Punch, 2005: 158).

To show how the use of GT has changed recently and become more open and flexible in accepting different thoughts, and to reflect the constructivist way of thinking I would like to present the work of Bong (2007). This research contradicts the main idea of the original version of GT that one should not start with theoretical assumptions. Bong (2007: 258) even starts with a hypothesis that directs the research from the beginning into connecting the main research categories. Her research categories are cultures and religions from one side and women's rights discourse and activism from the other side in Malaysia (Bong, 2007: 262). Bong who is a women's rights activist assumed from the beginning that they are related. These research categories were already theorized in the literature. Thus, Bong has presupposed an integral relationship between these categories prior to data collection. Even if this in a strict sense contradicts the original version of GT, it, however, gives an example of how flexible and how different GT can be compared to the original version.

In addition to that, one more point to the evolution of the GT is that, when GT started, it was used more for research about health, nursing and evolving medical technologies and treatments. Since then some people always link GT with such fields of inquiry. But GT has been spread from its original use to other social sciences and to practitioner fields including at least accounting, business management, education, and social work (Strauss and Corbin, 1997: vii). The GT Reader (Mey and Mruck, 2007) and the latest Sage Handbook of GT (Bryant and Charmaz, 2007) are evidence to show how GT can be used in different disciplines and by different researchers to investigate different phenomena. These recent developments are complemented by the introduction of computerized programs to analyze qualitative data within the framework of GT.

5.4 The Process of Conducting Grounded Theory

The steps of constructing GT in this research advanced gradually, as I have developed my knowledge about GT when conducting the method.

5.4.1 Data Collection

Generally, this research is a qualitative study of an illustrative case of a village that is based on systematically gathering information about Al Dagag to permit the researcher to effectively understand the phenomenon of financial relations and at later stages the social relations. Thus, in this instance, the case consists of a community that is defined by Berg (2007: 297) as some geographically delineated unit within a larger society. It is small enough to permit considerable cultural homogeneity to diffuse interactions and relations between members and to produce a social identification by its members (Berg, 2007: 297). Case studies of a particular communities can be conducted to provide the researcher with understanding and awareness of what things are going on in the community, why and how these things occur, who among the community members takes part in these activities and behavior, and what social forces may bind together members of this community (Berg, 2007: 297). This is assumed by Berg to provide deep understanding and thick description of a phenomenon or behavior of people and organizations that exist in the specific community (Berg, 2007: 285).

With regard to data collection, I have conducted three phases of data collection, which will be explained next. I visited the village Al Dagag during the three phases as well as Khartoum, El Obied, Al Rahad, and three other villages in the Al Rahad locality in NKS, namely Kabaka, Mandoor and Rehood Al Nabag[2] (cf. appendix 1).

---

[2] These visits to the other three villages were not performed to extend the data collection areas or sample but to understand some issues regarding the final evaluation of IFAD project in the North Kordofan State as will be mentioned later. The result of analyzing interviews done in these villages is presented in Apendix 1.

5.4.1.1 First Phase of Data Collection

A purposive sampling technique was used in choosing Al Dagag as a case study for this research. The rationale behind selecting NKS is that the severity of poverty in Sudan differs considerably depending on regional differences and NKS is one of the poorest states in Sudan.

To elect one village, I conducted a short survey in 2007[3] to choose the village for the case study. Since the main initial idea was to study microfinance provided by banks and NGOs, I visited International Fund for Agriculture Development (IFAD), Agriculture Bank of Sudan (ABS) Khartoum, CARE international, Plan Sudan, Agency for Cooperation and Research Development (ACORD) and Food and Agriculture Organization (FAO) headquarters in Khartoum. These institutions are the main developmental institutions that provide financial services in rural Sudan. The main questions I addressed were about their area of work and the reason behind selecting these areas. The main findings were that Kassala, Port Sudan and NKS[4] were mentioned as the main areas for the high degree of poverty and vulnerability.

The selection of Al Dagag was conducted with the help of the IFAD officers in El Obied in an interview with the general coordinator. The main criteria I provided is that the selected village must show great differences of financial services and relations. Visiting Al Dagag for the first time in May 2007, I was accompanied by Ulrike Schultz. The main aim of this visit was first to check the criteria I set for selecting the village and second to introduce myself. However, since I was accompanied and recommended by IFAD officers, the introduction was not so helpful. This is because most people thought that I came to evaluate the project, thus I was directed to interview the people who were showing better repayment rates and performances. During this visit, besides many informal conversations I conducted five in-depth interviews with respondents who are members of the village fund committee or who have been selected by them. I also conducted a long interview with the village *Shaikh*[5] and one group interview, as the *Shaikh* suggested that he should invite some people from Al Dagag to give me more information about the origins of the village, the tribal system and the native administration system. I conducted the Participatory Rural Appraisal (PRA) method of transect walk to visit most of the residual, agricultural, and livestock herding places, and the social services facilities, and held a very interesting group interview with women, as I invited most of the village women to a coffee gathering. I decided to do so as I had learnt during my first days that it is common to meet for coffee.

The entire first visit was about familiarizing myself with the village and the villagers, so not so many in-depth interviews were conducted. When I analyzed these interviews, I found out that since I prepared a very long and rigid set of questions for conducting interviews, I got very limited, specific and short answers. Besides, from the individual interviews I conducted I got the impression that the IFAD project has been very successful; however, from the coffee gathering I observed that when I was asking about the IFAD project some women seemed not happy and started whispering. That opened my mind to a problem of getting information about a project from the project coordinators or those whom they selected for interviews; something I had to change in my next visit. Furthermore, my positionality was not appropriate from the beginning since I was introduced by IFAD officials to the village project coordinators who introduced me in turn to the people. On top of that, I even lived in the house of the coordinator of the village fund, which further made villagers link me to IFAD. What I realized later is that some people really wanted to meet me to tell me their experience with IFAD; others ignored me because they did not repay all their debt, and feared that I would put pressure on them. During my next visit to Al Dagag, I had to think about a different positioning and introduction to the villagers and of course different interview settings.

---

[3] However, the official research period started 2008.

[4] In most of the statistics provided about different regions of Sudan by these institutions the regions of Darfur and all the Southern regions are excluded.

[5] The head of the native system at the village level.

5.4.1.2 Second Phase of Data Collection

This time I used my position as a lecturer at Ahfad University for Women, in Sudan. I decided to supervise an Ahfad student field trip of 20 female students working in the field of rural development and rural extension to Al Dagag. This helped me in two ways: on the one hand I was linked to Ahfad and the students, this helped many people to believe me that I am not part of IFAD project.[6] On the other hand, the Al Dagag village satisfied the criteria for villages set by the rural development program of Ahfad University.

Changing my introduction and position in the village helped me to a great extent and made the Al Dagag people accept me in a way different from the first visit. Doors were opened to me and more open conversations were taken place. For instance, during my first visit people were talking about how IFAD fought *Shail,* which is the local money lending system. Some of the respondents of my first visit told me that it does not take place at all in Al Dagag, especially Rugaia who is the coordinator of the credit committee of IFAD village fund. During my second visit, interviewing Shaikh Ahmed who is a shopkeeper I realized that *Shail* still takes place in Al Dagag. Surprisingly during my third visit in 2009 after the end of the IFAD project, all respondents told me about their experiences with *Shail* and *Shail* traders. I even interviewed the same Rugaia in her function as a *Shail* trader.

Being born to a grandfather from one of the ethnic groups of the area helped me to become accepted in the village. At the same time, as an outsider or an "urbanized lady" as they called me, I was able to extract much information about rural livelihood because people assumed that I do not know about their situation so they started to talk in detail and explained many things to me.

During this phase, I focused on conducting semi-structured in-depth interviews with respondents who were not selected by IFAD project coordinators. As a result, more topics and themes were emerged and I realized that there was much more informal finance taking place in the village than I expected in the beginning.

I also adjusted the interviews to be more open; still I had a prepared set of questions. Moreover, the analysis of the first interviews and observation during the first introductory visit helped me introduce new issues or themes that I did not consider from the beginning. For example, I started focusing on people who repaid their loans to the IFAD project late and those who did not repay at all, and how this impacted on their household situation. In addition, I asked about how they act and react to different personal emergencies like the one I attended in my first visit—the death of an Al Dagag child migrant in Al Gezira State.[7] Later on, I realized that microfinance and other financial relations could not be studied in disconnection from other factors like emergencies and disasters. The results of analyzing interviews at the end of that stage directed the main focus of the research do discuss not only livelihood patterns but also vulnerability of people to different emergencies and natural disasters.

During the second phase of data collection, I conducted 15 interviews, however, I let the students also conduct interviews that I transcribed but never analyzed later because I could not feel attached and could not make sense out of them as with the ones I conducted myself. They lacked the flexible way of interviewing I developed, which for instance included developing questions from answers that boosted the conversation, since students were only asking the questions I had prepared.

Moreover, I realized that the time I spent in Al Dagag was not enough to do more in-depth interviews besides all the other activities I participated in with the students. I felt I lacked many pieces of information to make the puzzle complete, and till then I had never reached saturation of questions leave alone cases or categories.

---

[6] The field trip was designed to achieve many things: firstly to change my positionality, to help me to conduct more interviews, and get more involved with the villagers, since students conducted meeting and conversation on issues like primary health care, eradicating harmful practices, community mobilization and so on. This also as I planned for, helped the students since I provided them with training about how to conduct interviews, something new at Ahfad university since questionnaires were always used before.

[7] This child was 18 years old and had migrated to the Al Gezira state to work there during summer. He drowned in the Nile River while bathing.

At this stage, I started to use atlas.ti, a computer program to analyze my interviews as I had got experienced and trained in how to use it. Thus, I analyzed 10 interviews using atlas.ti. During this phase, many initial codes were produced showed in Table 1:

Table 1: Example of Initial Codes Produced during the Second Phase of Data Collection Using the atlas.ti Computer Program

Agric: Comparing production by seasons
Agric: Cost
Agric: Hibiscus as women crop
Agric: Hiring farmers, time, reasons and payment
Agric: Moving to live in the agricultural filed
Agric: having different Seasons
Agric: Technology used
Agric: The whole family work together
Agric: Working for money
Al Dagag people political belongingness
Al Dagag water services
Al Dagag: Food habits
Al Zakat in Al dagag
Are Al Dagag people poor?
Borrowing: Shops
Borrowing: Relatives and friends
Children work
Children sending money
Comparing sources of income
Comparison of different sources of credit
Credit: Types
Credit: Amount of money
Credit: Benefits
Credit: Continuing taking credit
Credit: Family member credit
Credit: Group formation
Credit: How it worked out
Credit: Islamic modes of finance and if they are satisfactory
Credit: Not taking at all
Credit: Number of loans
Credit: Paying back
Credit: Procedures

I kept on writing my ideas about codes in memos and observational notes and diaries at this stage of data collection.

Another interesting point that emerged at this stage of data collection was the way people talked about poverty. I did not ask whether people perceive themselves as poor or not; however, when I asked about livelihood patters and activities people started to talk about diversification of income sources and the fact that the income from agriculture is not enough and the reasons behind that. Then I found them talking about how people with stable source of income like salaries or large assets like livestock are considered better off while others considered as poor or destitute. So I decided later to investigate this further.

5.4.1.3 Third Phase of Data Collection

My third visit was the major, most focused and longest data collection period. During this phase[8], I intended to fill gaps from the analysis of interviews conducted in the two previous visits. At this time, I gained more detailed knowledge about the village, the concepts, and the method of GT. Since I stayed longer, I tried to be involved in the peoples' lives more than before. That is why I conducted 38 individual in-depth interviews. Indeed, I conducted two interviews per day, one starting with drinking the early morning tea with the family, and staying over to eat the breakfast meal at 11:00, if they stayed in the house. In cases where they were going to the field, I carried my papers and pencils and went with them. I was welcomed to all houses and could conduct in-depth interviews and observe many issues. The second interview was held in the afternoon. I usually stayed over to eat the lunch meal at 3:00 and in some cases, I started later and stayed up to almost mid-night.

Something I had learnt from the previous visits was that in participating in their meals I showed that I was involved and I respected their situations. By refusing to eat or to come to their invitations for meals, people were likely to consider me to be looking down at them. Thus, I participated with them in all their daily activities; I went with them to the agricultural fields, and to the Monday market in the Al Semaih village. In many cases, I helped in doing domestic work, and when I found them cleaning their crops I was also engaged. Like when many respondents were talking about the importance of *Nafeer*[9], I asked to be involved in one for cleaning hibiscus to understand how they do it, who comes and all the other issues surrounding this event. In some cases, I had to conduct the interviews in the agricultural field since I could not find the people at home. Some people like Alshaikh have even moved to live in the field with the whole family. In fact, sometimes conducting interviews in the fields was even better since in the houses many people could be involved in the discussion, even neighbors who have come to visit, something I could not avoid in many cases. However, conducting long interviews helped me to tackle the situation. In some cases, I was waiting for the visitor to leave, was asking the daughter to prepare me some tea or was sending the son to make my next appointment. Khadiga, Abualgaseem's wife, I had to interview under a tree outside her house, since she wanted to tell me things that she did not want to say in front of her husband like the fact that she is involved in a *Sandouq*[10]in Um Rowaba.

It was important for me to be involved and to be trusted by people in Al Dagag. That is why I attended all events I was invited to, such as weddings and other ceremonies, and to events, I was not invited like the funeral of the one year old daughter of Alnaeem, one of my respondents, in which I participated just like the other people and stayed in the house of the funeral for several hours. Hereby, I realized that *Wajib* done in the village is different from how it has been taking place recently in the cities; for instance, I have learnt what is *Khulud*[11]. I was also involved in things that were not related to my research and I was also consulted in cases when people needed help. For instance, I was invited to a meeting that was held by the youth association in Al Dagag and attended a meeting of the *Shaikh*, solving some problems of people. Being part of their lives helped me to understand many issues related to how people in Al Dagag act on and react to different events. This also facilitated my stay in the village and helped me build up long-term relationships[12].

In this stage of data collection and with the help of two teachers from Al Dagag, I could design and conduct a survey to get general information about every household in Al Dagag to develop a village pro-

---

[8] I was accompanied by Ulrike Schultz who attended some of the data collection procedures and one field work assistant.

[9] Group work done for free for one of the villagers to help him or her to overcome an emergency like cleaning or harvesting crops that he cannot do alone or hire workers to do the job in short time.

[10]The name of the Rotating Savings and Credit Association (ROSCA) of women in Sudan, sometimes named *Khatat*. Both are Arabic words and indicate the meaning of collecting certain amounts of money by a group and distributing it in rotation.

[11] A small vessel filled with crops or sugar or coffee brought to the women who have an occasion like birth, given by the people with whom she is socially connected.

[12] This relationship did not end with the end of this research. Thus, a trust relationship was built between me and the people of Al Dagag. I went out of Al Dagag feeling that I was always part of the village. I was even given a piece of residual and agriculture lands, because people believe that this will make me return to the village.

file. Thus, every household has been asked about issues like the number of household members, the educational level of each member, if they are migrating or permanently stay in Al Dagag, the number of males and females, number of children, number and types of livestock, size and ownership of agricultural land. However, I did not use all this information, but it helped me to understand many issues.

What I have said above is to give a brief overview about the different stages of data collection, what I have done and the main results of each stage. Next, I will describe steps and procedures of the GT in the course of my research process.

5.4.2 Memos and Observational Notes

Since the earlier stages of the research, I wrote observational notes or ethnographical diaries in form of pieces of information or questions to reflect my ideas. Gradually some of these observational notes seemed important and I started to develop them into memos in the last phase of data collection. Later on, some of the initial notes and diaries were developed into memos, as I will give examples. Most observational notes I wrote were about how people behave towards me and towards each other or in specific situation. This later directed me to the main research categories and later to the relationships between categories. The following examples show how I wrote the initial notes and diaries. Later I will present an example of the initial memos. However, any part of the empirical chapters could be an example of the final memos that I combined together in the stage of the writing-up.

This part of the first ethnographic diary I wrote on the first day I slept in Al Dagag:

"*Al Dagag is a 'real' Sudanese village, where houses are built of hatch and no public electricity or safe water available.... However, it is located on the main road which links the capital of the country to the capital of the state. How will this help the people and facilitate their daily life? ...*"

Another part of an observational note that later developed into a memo is about the event I described above that later led me to focus on and develop one of the main research categories "helping each other":

"*While I was meeting with the women in the coffee gathering, we heard bad news about a 16-year old kid who had died. Women started screaming, crying, and running to the house of the funeral ... I had to follow them, in fact I was shocked for the way they behaved, however, I was wondering at night that, immediately when they arrived to the house of the funeral, some of them started to cook, bring drinking water and prepare tea for others... For the next two days, I could not meet any of them, unless I went to the funeral house. Most of them were working there, talking and bringing food to the house. Since the child was young and died in Wad Alhadad, in Al Gezira, I was asking myself, what was he doing there? ...*"

This observational note later developed to a memo. It helped me in my second visit to put a clear description of how they build their social relations and how and why they are engaged in these social networks. The memo I developed from the analysis of interview later led to the emergence and explanation of a category that is "helping each other". In this category, I describe how the help people give to each other is considered as one of the main insurance mechanisms that they resort to in cases of risks and stress. The same category of helping each other with other categories turned later to be one of the main theoretical categories that is social capital. Social capital as a concept already exists in the livelihood and other literature. However, the category emerging from the analysis of the interviews reflects different patterns, attributes and behaviors than what have been mentioned in the literature.

The following memo indicates how memo writing was developed through the research process and helped in developing categories:

"*Answering the question about how the money is used they get from Sandouqs, most respondents mentioned that they are paying for Wajib inside or outside Al Dagag, or for any emergencies like birth giving expenses or sick child... Dawa who is a second wife and lives in her own house uses the money for maintenance of her house. Bakheta bought one golden ring to save her Sandouq's money. Amna gave the money to her husband as loan that he will repay later; Khamesa mentioned the same but added that if he did not repay she will take money for Sandouq from him. Three women used the money to buy livestock, mainly sheep and goats. Most of them when they receive the money they pay for two or three next turns. Even if Batoolay thinks Sandouqs are problematic sometimes, she also thinks it is so useful for saving or dealing with an emergency. Umalhasan said she used the money to buy Sorghum to feed her children...*"

From this piece of detailed information, where I presented all what has been mentioned by every respondents using the code list (will be explained later in this chapter) I developed Diagram 3 and the category of "the utilization of *Sandouq* funds" presented in chapter 10. In the final version of this memo in chapter 10, I located this discussion in the literature about the topic using the most well known theoretical literature from Geertz (1962), Ardener (1964, 1995), Pischke (1992), Krahnen and Schmidt (1994), and recently Klonner (2001) and Schultz et al. (2008), the latter is mainly about *Sandouqs* in Sudan, in order to reflect the use of literature in this research.

I set every memo to discuss one category this later helped finding connections and relationships between categories. For example, the category of "the utilization of *Sandouqs* funds" is linked with "women and livelihood", "the intra household decision making", "intra household allocation of resources", "savings", and the "*Wajib*" categories.

5.4.3 Data Collection Methods

I did not intend to perform a triangulation; however, I found it important to check on the individual interviews by combining other methods like group discussion or observation. Combining methods in this research was not conducted to check the findings of one method against the findings of the other method as the triangulation process described by Punch (2005: 241). Rather, it is used to get more data about certain issues when it shows a degree of controversy and disagreement between respondents in individual interviews or to get general information about the village. Like in the case of discussing the impact of microfinance at a household level, results of interviews revealed controversial findings. Therefore, it was important to conduct a group discussion about the issues in order to understand the reason behind such differences. Other methods were used when considered appropriate to get information that is more general. For example I used the PRA method of transect walk to understand how land is divided between farming, residual and other purposes. Group interviews were conducted to a get general overview about arrangements like *Sandouqs*, whereas elite interviews were conducted to get general information about categories emerged from data like the description of some characteristics of the financial market in Sudan that has not been thoroughly described in the literature. Thus, the need to include further methods to make the data more comprehensive is the main rationale behind using different data collection methods. Consequently, I used in-depth interviews, focused elite interviews, focus group interviews and PRA methods of ranking and transect walk. A detailed list of all individuals, experts, and group interviews I conducted in Al Dagag, El Obied, Khartoum and other places I visited in Sudan is provided in appendix 2.

5.4.3.1 In-Depth Semi-Structured Individual Interviews

I have followed the idea of Mills et al. (2010: 496) that semi-structured interviews are designed to address a number of questions or themes. I conducted individual in-depth semi-structured interviews to get in-depth information about the research respondents. Semi-structured interview are designed to be between the structured and unstructured forms of interviewing. Even if some questions and themes are prepared in advance, still many others will evolve as the interview progresses. The interviews were open for many new themes to emerge during the interview process. All questions were open-ended; questions that I asked not in sequence or order but as the issues were raised. This helped because as suggested by Mills et al. (2010), semi structured interviews are used when the researcher aims at comparing participants' responses while simultaneously seeking to fully understand their unique experience. Examples of in-depth interviews questions will be provided later in Table 3 when presenting an example of open coding; this example reflects how questions are developed within the context of the interview and the discussion with the respondents[13].

---

[13] A list of all respondents and the dates of interviews is provided in appendix 2. Names of respondents were anonymized.

5.4.3.2 Focus Group Interviews and Participatory Rural Appraisal (PRA) Methods

Focus group interviews facilitated not only new data but helped to countercheck the individual in-depth interviews. In the group discussions rich data was collected specially regarding livelihood patterns. Group members were correcting each other; they were discussing and also exchanging information between themselves. Thus, it made a balance between different opinions and views gathered through in-depth individual interviews.

I tried to get members of homogeneous groups to avoid extreme behavior and reactions. However, I selected also respondents with different livelihood patterns and standard of living. Like the group, I interviewed regarding livelihood capital in Al Dagag. I tried to choose some of the village leaders and better-off people and at the same time some very poor respondents.

Considering the time limits, conducting group interviews helped me save time and get information, which I used to fill any gaps in individual interviews. I did not intend to calculate or quantify the amount of earnings and expenses in the households; however, I found it important to give a general overview. Thus, I conducted a group interview with a group representing both the better-off and the very poor; this assisted me in getting general and average views about income and expenses. Form this group interview I developed table 5 to present estimated income expenses and savings in the Al Dagag household.

The process of sampling was not difficult for the group interviews with members of *Sandouqs* since I interviewed all members of one group together. These group interviews helped me to control data collected from individual interviews and to get the main principles upon which *Sandouqs* are formulated.

I conducted the PRA method of ranking and comparing different financial institutions in Al Dagag in form of group interviews. This helped me to a great extend to get a comparative view about financial institutions, also from the individual interviews, it was difficult to arrange or rank these institutions according to specific criteria.

However, with all my efforts to systematically organize focus groups, this did not prevent the domination of members over others. Some respondents were talkative and dominant in the way they express their views, while others were not.

5.4.3.3 Observation

Besides conducting interviews, observing was another everyday task. All interviews were supplemented by observations. Observing when studying people's life is not avoidable. I generated most of the field notices out of observing what happened in the village, observation was also used to develop the set of questions or to integrate new cases. For example, I often passed Asha Alnoor's shop, which is located in the center of the village on my way to different houses. I was sitting there talking to the shopkeeper, people came to buy from the shop and I was listening to their conversations. I did that after I discovered the importance of the transactions people have with the shopkeepers. So after sitting there for hours I identified different patterns of dealing with different people, also I selected some people to be interviewed or re-interviewed.

Through observation I was able to extract the meaning of things; for instance after I had learnt about the classification of people in Al Dagag I started observing how their houses are different. I was observing and writing notes about how the houses were built or how they were arranged and organized or what people ate, where they kept crops and livestock as well as other detailed information. Some of the observations I used later to understand the classifications destitute, poor or better-off people, as respondents had suggested.

To provide an image of how the village Al Dagag looks, of people, resources, and other village life aspects and details I have observed and mentioned throughout the research, I have documented this in a picture album provided in the appendixes.

5.4.3.4 Expert Interviews

I also conducted some expert interviews with microfinance practitioners and representatives of organizations like IFAD and ABS[14]. The main aim of interviews with microfinance practitioners was to fill the gaps in the literature regarding specific topics since not much literature is available about Sudan generally or specifically about the financial landscape in Sudan. The interviews with IFAD and ABS and other organizations aimed at background information about the IFAD project in Al Dagag. Each interview was designed differently and was focused on specific issues. Thus, these interviews were conducted to gather specific information about the financial landscape in Sudan with emphasis on NKS and to get insights on experiences and description of microfinance that is not available in the literature. Different interview guides were prepared for interviews with different people.

These are the only interviews I could record since for the setting of interviews in houses or in open spaces, this was not possible. For instance, when I interviewed Abdelhameed we were sitting beside the *Hafeer*[15] and he did his work besides talking to me, so it was not possible to record the interview. Most of the interviews I recorded earlier in the early stage of the research I could not understand because of the noise of the people or the wind or animals. Therefore, I decided to write by hand, and conducting long interviews, the fact that I was staying long time with each respondent and the possibility to meet them since I was living in the village enabled me to write down comprehensively. When I missed some information as I was sometimes transcribing interviews regularly, I had the chance to visit the person again on my way to another interview or meeting them during other events and ask about the missing information. Even after I came back to Berlin, I was able to call and ask for any missing information. I also found the interviews I recorded during the first visit not clear or people were shy to use a recorder, or some were not comfortable. I found that the best interviews I conduced were the ones I did not record, people talked freely and openly.

Besides interviews and observation, I attended a conference about the future of microfinance in Sudan, held on 6th of January, 2010, in Khartoum. Besides the governor of the Central Bank of Sudan, two international experts were invited, Malcolm Harper and Hans-Dieter Seibel, who presented cases about microfinance from all over the world.

5.4.4 Sampling Techniques: Purposive and Snowball Sampling

According to Berg (2007: 44), purposive sampling is conducted when the researchers use their special knowledge or expertise about some group to select subjects who represent this population. Purposive sampling is carried out to make sure that certain types of individual displaying certain attributes are included in the study. Decisions about choosing and putting together empirical material (cases, groups, and institutions) are made in the process of collecting and interpreting data. Following Flick's (2006: 125) explanation that selecting categories and cases is performed according to their expected level of insights for the developing theory, the criteria of selection were defined in relation to the theory. Since the main question regarded financial relations, I selected respondents as they were using or involved in different financial institutions and arrangements, formal or informal. However, I tried to include a variety of respondents for example destitute, poor or better-off or men and women. In selecting the sample purposely, I was not concerned about representativeness, but about what each case will add to the discussion. In conducting the purposive sampling my aim was to get a deeper understanding of each case and thus the main topics of the research. Meanwhile I used the snowball-sampling technique as well, in order to locate respondents with certain attributes necessary in the study. Thus, in every stage of data collection, I selected new cases or conducted more interviews with previous cases following what is called the theoretical sampling emerged in the work of Glaser and Strauss (1997) and illustrated next.

---

[14] See appendix 2 for names and positions of the microfinance experts interviewed

[15] The main source of water in Al Dagag; it is a big man-made water reservoir where rain water collected.

5.4.4.1 Theoretical Sampling: Continuous Integration of Cases

The meaning of the theoretical sampling is illustrated in the fact that I always felt in need to integrate more cases. By integrating new cases, I was seeking to elaborate on the research categories to illustrate this further I will present some examples.

In the first phase of data collection, I started with clients who were selected by IFAD village fund coordinators. Analyzing these interviews show very positive views about the project. After learning that such a positive view may not be accurate, I asked for the list of all clients and within this target group, I conducted simple random sampling of beneficiaries. Moreover, I have heard in some interviews that there are some clients who went to jail for not repaying their debt to the IFAD project. Therefore, I asked for their names and conducted interviews with them, which sometimes revealed different information, and opposite to what I found when interviewing only clients with acceptable repayment performance.

I realized that "People talk in Al Dagag" which helped me to a great extent in selecting cases. I was engaged in many conversations when people start to talk about the experience of others. I added the case of the Mohamed family (three respondents) because I had heard about their situation from other people. When people were talking about the poorest people in Al Dagag, they were referring to them.

From the analysis of the first interviews the question came up regarding those who did not take loans from IFAD, why they did not and how they felt about this, who they are and how not taking loans had affected them. However, I also tried to choose people who are involved in other financial relations like *Sandouqus, Shail*[16] and others.

With the emergence of some categories, I also felt a need to add more respondents who I thought might provide better understanding of these categories. For instance, from the beginning, I wondered whether it is relevant to investigate about emergencies and disasters in Al Dagag, their effects and how people react to these situations. However, I found myself forced to do so because of the tremendous effects of these shocks and disasters on people's lives. After this, I selected some cases of people who suffered from personal emergencies like Abdalla's wife, Hadia and others. These people who were more affected by the general disasters or who lost all their crops in the last year flooding as *Khour*[17] Abuhabil I developed this sample as I was categorizing these emergencies and disasters.

In addition, I realized that since I went to Al Dagag the first and second time in summer, I thought studying the phenomena at different times and seasons will provide me with more insights. Thus, the third visit was in November. In addition to that, when I realized that men migrate to different regions in summer, I added males who migrated to different regions, for instance Khartoum and Al Gezira. I interviewed them in Al Dagag to see if there are any differences in the work they do there or the amount of money they earn or they remit. For instance, I interviewed Abualgaseem, Alshaikh, Alnoor, Mustafa and others.

It was also revealed from the analysis of the second phase interviews that respondents classified themselves into destitute, poor and better-off as mentioned above. Consequently, a need emerged to include more cases to show differences, so I decided in the third phase to focus on this issue and consider it as one of my categories. Therefore, I integrated cases reflecting destitute, poor and better-off households. Another issue emerged as the fact that most destitute people are women, so I included more cases of destitute women who are head of their households. At this point, I started to also interview the heads of households who have been beneficiaries of the IFAD project; however, since most of them are men, I later integrated female respondents to get more views about, for instance, intra household relations and decision-making.

5.4.4.2 Introducing the Sample of the Research

50 households were selected purposely within the theoretical sampling procedures described in the previous section. Diverse households with diverse composition, resources, livelihood strategies, living

---

[16] Money lending system in Al Dagag-

[17] A small seasonal river-

standards and backgrounds were selected to provide a wider picture of Al Dagag as a case study of a community. Selecting people through the theoretical sampling process was not an easy task. The central unit of analysis of this research is the household[18]; thereby interviews were conducted mainly with the head of the household or the person in charge in the absence of the head of household. Even when I selected beneficiaries from the IFAD project, I intended to include those who are the head of their households and even others in big families.

The educational status, marital status, sex and age are not main criteria of selecting respondents; however, they give a general view about the respondents. Briefly, the majority of the respondents was illiterate or did not finish their primary education, only two finished their secondary schooling and got special education and training to be teachers and only one of respondents is a university graduate. The majority of respondents is married, three are divorced, three are widows and one is single but remains head of the household, since he is the oldest son and his father is dead. To give a general view about the age range of the respondents, out of the 50 respondents, 8 are around 20 years old, 20 are around 30 years old, 14 are around 40 years old, 8 are above 50. Therefore, the majority of the respondents is between 30 and 50 years old.

Moreover, the main criteria for selecting the respondents did not include sex because even the efforts of ABS and IFAD were not directed to target a specific sex, plus all other financial opportunities are equally presented to women and men. Even with the existence of *Sandouqs*, which are perceived as women's arrangements, still men are allowed to join through their women relatives. Out of the 50 respondents, 31 are females while 19 are males. The need to include more female respondents emerged gradually as the theoretical sampling progressed as mentioned above. I also included some inhabitants who do not belong to the *Gawama*[19] tribe to get a more comprehensive view about social and financial relations and I found most of them are women who are married and brought to Al Dagag by their husbands. Thus, these two factors enlarged the number of female respondents.

The main criterion used to select respondents was their involvement in any financial institutions and arrangements. Selecting respondents who join informal financial institutions was not difficult since the majority of people in Al Dagag do. All respondents dealt with one or more informal institutions, which are many and diverse in Al Dagag including ROSCAs (*Sanoduqs*), indigenous money lending systems (*Shail*), and different loans and transactions that take place among relatives and friends or with shopkeepers. I focused on including respondents with experience of taking loans from formal institutions mainly ABS, which is the only formal institution they deal with, or semi-formal institutions, mainly the IFAD project.

Hence, in introducing the 50 respondents it is of major importance to mention that 42 are from households who are beneficiaries of the IFAD project while 8 of them are not. It is also worth mentioning that 6 of these 8 applied for but did not receive loans, while the other 2 never applied. However, most of them were involved in the training provided by the IFAD project. In addition to that, 17 of the 42 respondents received loans from both the ABS and IFAD village fund, 7 only received loans from IFAD village fund and 12 received loans only from the ABS.

Only two respondents were never involved in the *Shail* contract, three interviewed as *Shail* traders, and two had taken *Shail* in the past but recently stopped. All respondents borrowed money or other types of assets like crops from their relatives or friends, and they borrow or buy goods on credit from shops in Al Dagag. 24 women out of the 31 interviewed are members in *Sandouqs*.

It is significant that all respondents with no exception are involved in *Wajib*. All respondents mentioned that they pay and receive *Wajib* within or outside the social networks, they are involved in. In addition, all respondents called for or helped in *Nafeer*, even though one stated that she had not recently been involved in any *Nafeer*, but had in the more distant past.

Therefore, in selecting the sample of this research, I was guided by the principle of theoretical sampling procedures and the need to gradually add more cases that I believed to help in constructing a

[18] When I started this research, I was thinking about the household as the unit of data collection and data analysis but later it was revealed from the analysis of the interviews that it was necessary to convert this concept into one of the main research categories. Thus, from the data the relevance of such concepts like composition of household and the intra household decision making emerged. What is also important to mention is the fact that households are also revealed to be the main units of social relations in Al Dagag.

[19] The majority of Al Dagag inhabitants belongs to this tribe.

grounded theory that illustrates the financial and social relations in Al Dagag and locates them within the structure of rural livelihood in the village.

5.5 Data Analysis: Using the atlas.ti Computer Program

Generally, the collected raw data in form of transcripts was not immediately available for analysis. Rather it required some sort of organizing, processing, and translating before it could actually be analyzed. Transcription of interviews and field notes was done, but not for the whole detailed interviews at the first phase of data collection but only part of them; however, in the third stage, the entire lengthy interviews were transcribed. Also for the fact that all interviews were conducted in Arabic language, I had to translate all of them in order to insert them into the atlas.ti computer program. I personally transcribed and translated all the interviews. However, the translation process was not easy since I had to use some English words even if they are not said in the same way in Arabic, which is the respondents' language, such as the word vulnerability. Even if this process was long and exhausting, it helped to do it in person because I was reading and rereading them for many times, as I translated, transcribed, organized and then typed them in word document files before conducting the open coding.

5.5.1 Coding Procedures

5.5.1.1 Initial Coding: Breaking Data Down

The way different GT scholars explain the coding process is almost similar. For Charmaz (2006: 47) the main steps in analyzing data are initial, focused and axial coding; she holds that at least two phases of coding should take place, initial coding and focused coding. She defines initial coding as naming segments of data with labels that simultaneously categorize, summarize and account for each piece of data (Charmaz, 2006: 48).

During the initial coding process I always went back to the example of the "lady in red in the popular restaurant" mentioned by Strauss and Corbin (1990: 63). This example explains in a very systematic, however, simple way how coding can take place;, it is the process of breaking the data down, conceptualizing, and putting them back together in a new way; thus helps to make the data understandable and comparable (ibid.: 57). This mainly means taking parts of the transcripts, a sentence, paragraph or an observation, and giving each incidence or idea a name that represents the phenomenon. This is performed by asking questions like, what is this, or, what does it represent. I conducted an initial analytical comparison through the initial coding process between incidents in different interviews, I was asking myself, is this similar or different to what is mentioned in the previous interviews?, and then I give it the same or a different label.

Using the atlas.ti computer program made the initial coding easy and systematic. Naming codes can be carried out in different ways; sometimes using in vivo codes which use the terms used by participants themselves like the term *Guran,* which was used repeatedly by respondents when they were describing the money they share in case of death. However, most of the initial code names were borrowed from the reviewed literature (constructed codes), especially in the part of interviews that talk about sources, types, and uses of credit. Initial coding aims at expressing data and phenomena in the form of concepts using sometimes line-by-line and paragraph-by-paragraph, at other times depending on the sequence and connectivity of stories told by respondents (Charmaz, 2006: 48ff.). For coding, I used sentence-by-sentence coding, and sometimes I used incident--by incident especially when respondents were talking about personal emergencies that they experienced before. However, I found out later that I had lost much detail when using incident-by-incident coding, thus, I went back and used sentence-by-sentence coding.

In Table 3, I present an example of open coding. All codes are linked substantially to parts of the interview texts called quotations. At the end of the initial coding process, I had hundreds of codes. By using the atlas.ti software, I developed a code list that I could even print out. In the code list all codes exist, moreover, all quotations cited by different respondents are presented under each code. The benefit gained from this code list is that I could see all codes together, and for every code, I could also see the quotations coming from different interviews. This helped to build a final code list where codes are elaborated by what respondents have said about them. This was also so helpful in comparing later between cases and categories.

Table 2: Example of the Open Coding

Part of the Interview with Aisha Al Daw (December 2009)	
……., they formed the groups and told us about getting credit either from the bank or from our village fund which they established. I decided to take from the bank first because they give me more money than the village fund. I told them I want a fridge, they laughed at me and said no it is better for you to take sheep for rising. I did as they told me and I took a loan for 1000 Pound to buy 10 sheep, but it was not good.	Group formation done by IFAD Sources of credit, Who decided to take credit?, Comparison of credit sources Negotiating types of credit Agreed but not feeling comfortable to the type of credit, Amount of loan, Uses of credit, How credit worked out?
What happened? I failed to keep them, because I could not find a good person to keep them, some I lost others died and only two left for me. I could not pay back the money in time, but I used the money from selling my crops to pay back not only the 1000 Pounds but also the profit.	Failure to keep livestock (credit), Reasons of failure (credit), not paying back (defaulting)
It was a problem and I was depressed because I failed, you know that failure is not something good, it is bad. **What happened?** What could happen? I returned back to farming my land, then me and Rogaia one of the member of my group, thought to get credit from the village fund to do juice and cakes.	Consequences of failure Coping with failure Group members, working together Sources of credit, intentional use of credit
We got 50 Pound in Ramadan. **For both of you?** No, for each one but we were working together, we sold a very good quantity.	Amount of loan, Time of loan, group remembers, working together, how credit worked out?
We were selling here in Al Dagag and the near villages too "al heela wa al halal" (hila is the village and halal is the plural and means the surrounding villages) when Ramadan finished we collected all the money we got and divided it between us	Place of business, Al hila (Al Dagag) Making profits, profits divided between group members
after we paid back the loan to Batool with 3% profit.	Paying credit back, paying profit margin
Was the profit good considering the capital you started with? Yes it was good,	Profits were good
how did you use the profit? I used it to buy kitchen utensils big plates or dishes and 3 pots.	Uses of profit
So you paid back from the work you took the loan for? Yes, this time I paid from the business itself not like the livestock raising when I had to pay form my crops income.	Paying from the same business Paying from other sources: crops income
Then Batool came to my house and she gave me 120 Pound she said "take this money and do any investments with it, then pay it back with 3% profit again" she put the money in my hand and closed it.	Credit application procedures, amount of credit, type of credit, profit margin Credit application procedures,
Part of the Interview with Rafeea Khamis (December 2009)	Perception of oneself as poor, reasons of being poor, suffering: lack of livestock
Are you poor? Yes I'm poor, **why?** I'm suffering, I miss so many things, **like what?** Livestock, I want to have more than 10 and they are my own livestock, this make my hand higher in the house,	Household relations: higher hand
if I need something I will take one livestock and sell it in the market by myself and get the money and he cannot talk to me one word	Savings, types of savings, uses of savings, who use savings in the household, household financial relations
I want to have much gold like 8 or 10 gowaish, then I'm rich and all people see this and say this women is rich.	Perception of better off (richness) Others perception of better off (richness)
In the village not like in cities, here people they say for the women who does not have gold, her hand is cold.	Village compared to cities Perception of better off (richness) in villages, cold hand
Are the people in Al Dagag people? They are divided some are better than others, but the majority are poor, and they need to travel searching for work. **What do you mean by travel?** All men travel in summer	Classification of Al Dagag people Perception of poor people in Al Dagag Migration as sign of poverty Migration: only men migrate, time of migration,
it is not good it is something bad, then when one of my kids is sick in the night I have to call someone to help me I'm stranger	Perception about migration, Consequences of migration, Perception of oneself as stranger,
and I have to be careful with people sometimes it is so difficult to do that,	Coping with being stranger

5.5.1.2 Focused Coding: Categorization

Using the code list explained above, I started the next step of the coding process, the focused coding. Following Charmaz (2006: 35), focused coding means using the most significant and/or frequent earlier codes to shift through large amounts of data. Focused coding requires decisions about which initial codes make the most analytic sense to categorize your data incisively and completely. This is described by Flick (2006) as grouping codes around abstract phenomena discovered from the data itself. Codes now represent the content of a category. (Flick, 2006: 296).

I started this step by first reviewing and sorting the initial codes by first merging similar codes and sometimes renaming them. Then I started grouping them depending on their significance to the research topic and themes.

For instance, I grouped the initial codes "taking loans from friends and relatives", "taking *Shail* in September", "buying on credit from the shop", and "taking cash loans from the shop", together in the focused code or category of "indigenous financial arrangements" and also introduced it into the discussion of the main coping strategies of people in Al Dagag. To give another example, the codes "money contribution in case of birth giving", "giving gifts in case of weddings", and "providing labor in case of child death" and some other codes to describe a focused code or category of "*Wajib*" (in vivo code). Another example is grouping the codes "providing labor in case of building a house", "providing help in case of harvest", "providing help for cleaning hibiscus" with some other codes as focused code or category "*Nafeer*" (in vivo code). Both categories of *Wajib* and *Nafeer* later constitute the main essence of "helping each other" as insurance mechanism. Each of these categories are described in terms of their properties of why, how, when, to whom they are done, what the results are, what the returns, if the returns are reciprocal, if the reciprocal returns have to be of the same type of help and what will happen when the expected returns are not realized.

When I conducted the focused coding, I also conducted constant comparisons of cases and their experience as suggested by Glaser and Strauss (1967: 23). Thereby evidence collected from different respondents was confronted against each other. I looked for replications and I tried to develop patterns of behaviors of respondents with regard to categories. The code list I produced from the initial coding helped largely in doing the comparative analysis. Comparison of cases is essential for developing patterns and I find the work of Babbie (2004: 370) helpful in doing so. Babbie (2004) suggest six questions in the process of developing patters of behavior. These are *first*, frequencies, for example, how many respondents are engaged in this behavior: *second* magnitudes, meaning the levels of behavior: *third* structures or types of certain behavior, whether they are related to a particular manner. The *fourth* question is about processes or the order among elements; that is how a certain behavior begins or ends; *fifth*, cases of behavior and *sixth*, the consequences.

During this step, I developed the most important memos in form of questions I was asking while reading the transcripts. This helped in the next step of axial coding to build the relationships between categories.

5.5.1.3 Axial Coding

During the next step, I needed to reflect on the relationship between categories. This is described by Strauss and Corbin (1990) as axial coding. By axial coding, the researcher builds up a dense texture of relationships around the "axis" of a category. Thus at this stage of theoretical coding, I described the context, causes, strategies and consequences for the main categories. I found the set of questions prepared by Flick (2006: 300) very helpful in conducing the axial coding. The axial coding also relates categories to subcategories and specifies properties, dimensions of a category, and reassembles the data you have fractured during initial coding to give coherence to the emerging analysis (Charmaz, 2006: 37). For instance, the codes directly derived from the data like *Nafeer* and *Wajib* mentioned in the previous section, move towards the main category of "helping each other", and then to very abstract category or axial code of "social capital as insurance mechanism" that embraces the theory of livelihood. Finally, in the final stage of axial coding the theoretical category of "social capital" is linked to many other categories. For example, social capital is recognized as important for fighting both poverty and vulnerability in Al Dagag. Moreover, the importance of the social capital comes from the function it plays as insurance mechanism and coping strategy in times of stress and, thus, is seen as significant for sustaining rural livelihood. From another side, the analysis of interviews revealed the connection of the social capital to the financial capital. This comes from the fact that the resources exchanged within the social networks are mainly financial and supported by reciprocity. When conducting the axial coding I located the discussion on the theory of social capital, the findings of the research is supported for example by the work of Bourdieu (1986) about the conversion of types of capital. Next, the entire discussion about social capital led me to put more focus on this capital than other forms of livelihood capital, since it is not existent in livelihood theory, which treats all forms of capital in an equal way. It is worth mentioning that at this stage of the research I tried to find the connections between the main two categories of the research, which are the sustainability of livelihood, and the practice of microfinance and other financial relations. The use of literature at this stage of axial coding followed the explanation of Strauss and Corbin (1998) and Charmaz (2006).

In summary, for me this advanced coding step implied three levels; *first* to find the relationship between the main categories, *second* to produce a conceptual framework, and *third* to write down the story that constitutes the theory I have constructed by interpretation of the data. Charmaz (2006: 38) describes this step as a sophisticated level of coding that follows the codes you have selected during the focused coding. Theoretical codes specify possible relationships between categories you have developed in your focused coding. They help you to tell an analytic story that has coherence. Thus, the most relevant categories to the research questions were selected and explained further. In this step, I followed the work of Charmaz (2006), Strauss and Corbin (1998: 127) and Flick (2006: 301).

Conducting the coding process in this way assuming that systematic coding procedures is important to achieve a degree of validity and reliability in the data analysis as described by Babbie (2004: 292). This is especially assumed because the connections between codes and between categories are built depending on the data itself.

At the end of this step, I wrote all the empirical chapters using the findings of analyzing interviews in orientation to literature and theories already existing about the topic. I produced chapters that connect what I have found in the data and what I have read in the literature about the topic, in my view this constitutes "the story" of the theory constructed. A final chapter of conclusion and summarizing the theory constructed from data follows these chapters. In this chapter, I focus more on how the theory of livelihood is remodeled or constructed to be relevant to the case of rural areas of Sudanand on to what this research has added to both the livelihood approach and financial relations including microfinance thinking and practice. In this concluding chapter, the relationships between the main theoretical categories become obvious.

To conclude the discussion about coding, although it is often mentioned in the GT books that the different phases of coding are neither distinguishable nor separate phases, I realized that it is not appropriate to conduct the focused and theoretical coding before you finish the initial coding for all interviews.

Another point is related to the saturation point which Strauss and Corbin (1998: 136) explain to be the point when no new information emerges during the coding process considering the limits of time and money available for conducting the research (ibid.: 292). This is the point when there no new dimensions, conditions, action or interactions, or consequences are seen in the dataStrauss and Corbin (1998: 143) explain the theoretical saturation as the point when no further relations are found in the process of category development. Thus, it is supposed to determine the limits of the data collection and lead to analysis being explained theoretically. However, in reality there is always a possibility of new information or relations that could still emerge (ibid.: 136), that is to mean there might never be such a point for *all* categories. In this research for many categories there was no new information emerging in data especially when elaborating microfinance or the livelihood activities in Al Dagag. For other categories, the data was enough to elaborate and explain them within the scope of the research and find relationships that were important for the theory building. However, some categories could be taken one step further to be investigated in greater detail in further research, for instance the concept of household in Al Dagag.

Generally, using the atlas.ti computer program has helped to a great extent. For instance, the use of atlas.ti allowed me to attach codes to quotations or parts of the subscribed interviews. It also allowed writing memos and observational notes, displaying collected data in a condensed, organized format. It was used for printing out all codes, or single codes with their linked quotations; it saved time and effort compared to working with pen and paper and you can view all your codes and quotations from different interviews in one place; and that allows for analytical comparison that is always considered the essence of conducting GT.

Part III: Discussion and Results: Theory Construction

6 Contextual Analysis of Livelihood and Financial Landscapes in Sudan

"*Sharia traditions of no interest, profit sharing Musharaka and Murabaha, have no potential to microfinance if the lenders do not share the loss*" (Malcolm Harper on the conference "Lessons of Microfinance to be Learnt for Sudan", 6th of January 2010 Sudan Friendship Hall when describing Islamic microfinance).

"*I do not understand fully what is Murabaha but if it is Islamic them it is good*" (Alnaeem answering a question about *Murabaha*).

6.1 Introduction

This chapter attempts to critically reflect on rural livelihood as well as financial landscapes in Sudan. Description of poverty and vulnerability are presented in the first part of the chapter. In the following part, the Sudanese financial landscape is scrutinized. As the term 'landscape' implies, not only one aspect will be discussed but the description will rather consider all features of financial markets, different financial relations between borrowers, lenders and savers, financial systems and policies, financial institutions and so on. To understand the reality, earlier reform efforts will be explained, such as liberalization, structural adjustment programs and the Islamization of the financial sector, that I suppose are still going on and have effects on the financial sector. The microfinance revolution taking place in Sudan since 2002 is also presented in this chapter as well as the discussion about providing finance within the Islamic principles and modes.

6.2 Sudan's Livelihood Context: Poverty and Vulnerability

Generally, all the literature about Sudan in this research refers to the time before separation; there are no recent statistics and other information available for after separation.[1] However, even before the separation, information about the South was not always available, since it was considered a war zone. Sudan is located in the south-eastern end of the African Sahara (Library of Congress, 2004). It is subdivided into 26 states; of which 16 states comprise Northern Sudan and 10 States (26 % of the total area) comprise the recently seceded South Sudan. According to the African Development Bank (ADB, 2010), North and South Sudan's population was estimated to be 41 million in 2007. Sudan borders nine countries and reflects the religious, ethnic and cultural diversity of the region. Arabic, the official language, is spoken by 60 % of the population, although English was the official language in the South even prior to secession.[2]

The Sudan had been involved in one of Africa's longest-running wars since it became independent in 1956. The signing of the Comprehensive Peace Agreement (CPA) in January 2005 brought to an end more than two decades of hostilities between the North and the South. The CPA between the Government of Sudan and the Sudan People's Liberation Movement in 2005 resulted in the creation of a new Government of National Unity in Khartoum and the Government of South Sudan in Juba, to form a confederation system for governance under the slogan of 'one country, two systems'. The CPA is founded on a vision of wealth and power sharing that seeks equity, guarantees political rights and civil liberties, aims to prevent political and economical monopolies, and provides for a reformed and fully developed system of governance in which all Sudanese are equal. Yet, the CPA entitled the people of the South the right to vote for unity or separation in 2011. The results of the self-determination referendum showed that 98.83 % of all voters from South Sudan chose independence in February 2011. The separation of the two countries took place in July 2011. Conflicts are still going on in the process of defining the borders between the North and South, which is highly contested due to its rich natural resources of oil fields, mineral deposits, fertile land, and access to water (UNA-GB, 2011; ADB 2010).

---

[1] The separation took place during the third year of this research.
[2] In most cases no separate data is available for Sudan and South Sudan yet, numbers for Sudan before separation are provided unless otherwise indicated.

Although Sudan is near the bottom of all the lists prepared by the United Nations (UN) or other organizations, it still has the potentiality of growing economically and socially, considering the unexploited natural resources. This enormous diversity of resources in a huge country shows, on the one hand, the assortment of human and natural resources like types of soil, climate differences, and other rewards (MOF, 2002). On the other hand, it shows how difficult such a country is to be managed in a way to ensure equity and prosperity, as they are not realized given the current circumstances. ADB reports (2006) that since the signing of the CPA, the country has slowly been shifting from managing conflict to pursuing pro-poor development. Yet, significant political, economic and social challenges continue, including many trials for the resolution of the conflict in Darfur and in other regions, which are considered central to improve the security, the humanitarian situation, and the success of the recovery and development efforts in all parts of the country. After the separation of the two countries economic difficulties are expected in the northern Sudan due to the loss of the oil revenue (PaanLuel Wël: South Sudanese Blogger, 2011).

At the center of all, there has been prevailing deprivation reflected in poverty, vulnerability, regional inequalities and disparities and competition for natural resources in Sudan. Despite the persistent real GDP[3] growth, poverty remains widespread and deep and the inequality levels appear to be escalating. Many efforts have been made towards institution building and capacity development to accelerate the delivery of the peace dividends; however, translating this peace into tangible poverty reduction outcomes has proven to be a challenge. In the Human Development Index Sudan before separation was ranked low as 154 out of 177 countries (UNDP 2010). This reflects such aspects like the average national enrolment rate in primary education, which is 58 % but drops below 20 % in several parts of country. The average infant mortality rate was 105 per 1000 live births in 2000. Moreover, due to deep regional disparities, not least in war affected areas, the country has over 4 million internally displaced people. The maternal mortality ratio averages 1,107 deaths per 100,000 live births. IFAD (2004, 2007b) also reports severe deficiency in safe drinking water as well as prevalence of infectious diseases and low production of the labor force, which all are considered as causes and effects of widespread and deepening poverty.

Sudan has been undergoing serious economic problems, as mentioned in the Sudan Economic Report of the Central Bank of Sudan (CBS, 2007) and the ADB report (2006). The performance of the economy at a macro level has been unbalanced and significant regional disparities persist. Like other African countries, Sudan has experienced disappointment with the results of the structural adjustment policies in the late 1980s and beginning of 1990s; most experts believe that poverty has actually increased since then (expert interviews 1, 2 and 3). In addition, in the years before separation the focus of the government budget has been on the oil sector, withholding attention, budget spending and investments from other sectors like agriculture and the industrial sector. The latter is characterized by limited inter-industrial linkages but also high dependency on agricultural inputs (ADB, 2006; MOF, 2002). It could be reasonable if all or most returns from the oil sector are used to achieve the overall goal of poverty reduction before the separation. In addition to that, there is growing rural and urban unemployment. Rural-urban migration and migration to other countries especially the Gulf area have been described in the literature as a brain drain and with under-utilization of different types of resources is considered one of the main problems.

The economy is at considerable risk also due to rising prices and inflation. Not surprisingly, because of the rising world food prices, the inflation rate jumped from 7 % in 2007 to 16 % in 2008. A number of short-term policy adjustments have been implemented to reduce inflation, including removal of import duties and administrative fees for cereals (ADB, 2010).

Public financial management has also become a challenge at all levels of government, especially at the state and local level (Library of Congress, 2004). The government has started to implement measures to improve public financial management as well as transparency. It is worth mentioning that Sudan is one of many African countries where corruption plays a devastating role in the country's economic development.

It is cited in the ADB report (2006) also that the financial sector struggled to manage falling reserves and a depreciating exchange rate. Moreover, Sudan has a debt overhang problem with most of

---

[3] The GDP growth is stated in MOF (2002).

its debt ratios remaining above the indicative limits for sustainability. Although Sudan has been attracting FDIs and private capital flows, its access to granting loans has been very limited largely because of the debt situation with the main creditors including the ADB. Other macroeconomic features show negative performance like the worsening balance of payments; slow growing exports as well as unequal and deteriorating terms of trade. In addition to that, Sudan's growing isolation, particularly from the donor community, has made the economic crisis even worse (ADB, 2006). The country's failure to pay outstanding debts has led to tense relations with donors who reduced the inflow of development assistance. One principal result has been widespread poverty, while groups that are close to the regime own lots of wealth; others live in miserable conditions.

Vulnerability is another dimension of deprivation that persists in Sudan as well in other developing countries and negatively affects people's livelihood. The IFAD report (2007b) states that throughout the last three decades, the country has suffered from environmental degradation, unpredictable seasonal rainfall, floods and droughts in marginal dry lands, which constitute 85 % of productive lands in the country. In addition to that, chronic food insecurity might prevail in many times in specific regions and might lead to famine. IFAD (2007b) also claims that inadequate development strategies to deal with vulnerability and slow forecasting capability and climatic unpredictability are among the root causes of poverty and vulnerability in Sudan. The critical situation has been worsened by political instability and the growing conflicts over natural resources in regions like Darfur, Kordofan and Blue Nile.

Describing the agriculture sector connects the discussion between poverty and vulnerability. In terms of growth, while agriculture is the largest sector contributor to GDP (MOF, 2002), its share in GDP has recently declined from 41.9 % in 1996 to 32.4 % in 2002. This is mainly due to the difficulties encountered in reforming the sector and to the growth in other sectors (IFAD, 2004: 3) as mentioned above. Even with the potential agriculture has in the country's economic development, it is technically limited including unsuitable practices in the traditional rain-fed sub-sector, low land utilization ratio, soil erosion, low human capacity to use modern and improved agricultural technology, as well as inadequate control of pests and plant diseases. As a result, of these constraints at the level of production, horizontal expansion and maximization of output are influenced and food security is at risk as harvesting is still done manually in many rain-fed areas and labor shortages lead to wastage of crops.

The problem of lack of data and research is particularly relevant for the case of Sudan, in order to address the difficulties facing development management. To start with, the basic instruments necessary for compilation of resource information on macro-economic statistics are either non-existent or, at best, of poor quality. Moreover, scarcity of trained personnel and logistical support for research, data collection, management and analysis is considered to be another problem. That is the main reason why the available data about Sudan is neither recent nor complete.

All what has been mentioned above generally applies to the whole country; however, with regional inequalities, especially rural areas are viewed to be much worse off than urban ones. IFAD (2007b: 1) indicates that some 20 million people were living below the poverty line of less than US-$ 1 a day. About 19 million people—85 % of the rural population—are estimated to be living in extreme poverty. Recent statistics released by the UNDP (UNDP- Sudan 2011) on Sudan give more information about poverty in the country, even though many important statistics are not available like the percentage of poverty in rural areas. However, in the reports that discuss the status of the Millennium Development Goals (MGDs) in Sudan by 2010 released by the UNDP-Sudan, it is stated that by 2010, 46 % of the population in northern Sudan lived below the poverty line. Moreover, the report shows the significant variation of percentages regarding the MDG components across states. Just to give an example, the northern Sudan gross enrolment rate has reached 71 % with a wide disparity among states ranging from 93.7 % in Khartoum to only 36.1 % in the Red Sea State (UNDP-Sudan 2011).

The only source of information available for describing rural poverty and vulnerability in Sudan in general, are the IFAD reports of 2002, 2004 and 2007. The IFAD (2007b) report 2007 specifically describes rural poverty in Sudan as deep-rooted. In the IFAD reports (2004, 2007b), rural poverty is understood by criteria such as when most of rural populations struggle to feed themselves and their families and have little or no access to safe drinking water and health services. Rural poverty is closely related to agricultural production that mainly depends on rain for subsistence. 30 % of the rural population does not have access to health services and almost half do not have access to sanitation and safe water. 63 % of deaths among children under five are caused by pneumonia (26 %), malaria (21 %), diarrhea (9 %) and malnutrition (7 %). About 47 % of people are illiterate, with only 50 % enrolment rates in primary schools followed by high dropout rates. State spending on health and education is estimated at 0.7 % and 1.8 % of the GDP respectively.

Not only because economic growth has been unfairly distributed but also because of the economic and social devastation caused by the conflict in certain parts of the country, severe inequalities in terms of access to basic services, infrastructure, income opportunities, justice and political protection exist between regions (IFAD, 2007b). People living in rural areas have been or continue to be affected by drought and conflict (west and south) are the most vulnerable to poverty (IFAD, 2007b). A rapidly growing population puts significant pressure on already fragile ecosystems, a situation which has been intensified by the displacement of people, by either natural disasters or conflicts. In addition, soil erosion, loss of soil fertility and damage to watersheds affect rural resources (ibid.). According to IFAD (2007b), agricultural productivity on which livelihood in rural areas depends is decreasing as a result of lack of technological and financial support in rain-fed areas, thus food security and livelihoods are threatened in turn. Malnutrition, tuberculosis, malaria and other epidemic diseases have gone out of control. Consequently, small-scale farmers and herders in the traditional rain-fed farming and livestock sectors are more vulnerable than those in irrigated areas. In addition, those without land depend on cash earnings from casual labor, such as collecting firewood and making charcoal (IFAD, 2007b).

Even the features and measurements of rural poverty and vulnerability vary between irrigated and rain-fed regions. In the irrigated areas, poverty is defined by IFAD (2004: 8f.) in terms of size of landholding, type of land tenure, type of crop and market channels available while vulnerability is related to fluctuating prices and availability of markets. Reforming exercises of rehabilitation of irrigated schemes have pointed out that the main causes of poverty in these areas are the spontaneous planning of scheme operations; escalating degradation of the physical infrastructure due to lack of maintenance and development funds; non-payment of services charges, e. g. water; and poor water management. In traditional rain-fed areas, poverty is defined in terms of food self-sufficiency, livestock holding, and cost of access to water and availability of off-farm income. Households in these areas are highly vulnerable to climatic changes, pest outbreaks, and to competition over open access natural resources that in many areas have developed into and armed conflicts and in specific places even wars (IFAD, 2004: 8f.).

Within rural communities, households consisting of elderly or disabled people, or households headed by women with young dependants possessing no assets and labor power are the poorest; plus, women and girls are the most disadvantaged members less than one third of them have access to education (IFAD, 2004). Not surprisingly, herders and smallholder farmers in rural areas are trapped by the limited size of their land property, low rates of productivity and inability to improve their incomes. There is also strong evidence that because they have limited access to credit, distribution and marketing channels and because of their inadequate technical knowledge and poor skills in production and marketing, it is difficult for farmers and herders to escape low productivity and income. Seasonal migration hunting for wage labor opportunities on mechanized and irrigated farms and in urban areas has become widespread (IFAD, 2007b).

The country's poorest areas include the southern Sudan, with the exception of Western Equatoria, the transition area between northern and southern Sudan, including the states of Blue Nile, Southern Darfur and Southern Kordofan, and the states of Gedaref, Kassala, Northern Darfur, Northern Kordofan, Red Sea, Western Darfur and White Nile (IFAD, 2007b). Most of these states suffer not from lack of resources but rather mismanagement and misallocation of resources as well as inappropriate macro-economic policies that directly affect people's lives.

Next, considering all this as a background I will focus on the financial sector, which is at the center of study in this research.

6.3 Financial Landscapes in Sudan: Puzzled Between Liberalization and Islamization

Even if the statement made by Ibrahim and Arbab (2006) is frustrating to introduce the financial sector in Sudan, unfortunately it is completely true. Ibrahim and Arbab (2006) argue that not only the available data but also the documentation of practices and previous experience of the financial sector in Sudan are very incomplete and disappointing. Lack of statistics, lack of openness to the international experience and information, supremacy of the Central Bank of Sudan (CBS), are among the features of the financial sector in Sudan. For Ibrahim and Arbab (2006) finance to the poor is not getting enough attention. They also state problems such as absence of specialized staff and organizations and excessive concentration on financing well-established micro and small scale enterprises instead of financing individuals. These points are also cited in the interviews with experts (expert interviews 1, 2 and 4).

Finance for development in Sudan has passed through distinguishable periods of time, during each of which different reform efforts were made to shape the provision of finance for development. Since 1900 the financial sector in Sudan had been controlled by three or four foreign banks branches, until independence when Sudanese banks were started; for instance the Agricultural Bank of Sudan (ABS) 1959, then followed by the CBS in 1960 as well as other commercial banks that financed only commercial activities. In the era of the 1960s toward the 1970s, the green revolution dominated financial policies in the agricultural sectors. However, many problems associated with this experience led to directing the development policies toward looking for other alternatives. Between the 1980s and the early 1990s, the World Bank (WB) and the International Monetary Fund (IMF) launched their structural adjustments and market liberalization programs. After and during the 1990s a shift toward the poverty alleviation issues took place that brought up the millennium development goals and the microfinance revolution was initiated as a promising exercise to alleviate poverty and sustain livelihoods.

Banks are the main institutions that shape the financial landscape in Sudan. In addition to a few newly established foreign banks, the Sudanese banking system comprises both commercial and specialized banks. Commercial banks incorporate both government-owned and private sector banks, the latter as a result from the liberalization process. Specialized banks target particular sectors, such as social development, agriculture, animal resources, and industrial development, or specific groups such as farmers. According to CBS statistics, there are 23 banks operating countrywide; with 535 branches scattered unevenly among states: 34 % in the Khartoum State; 20 % in central states; 14 % in eastern states; 11 % in northern states; 10 % in the Kordofan states; 8 % in the Darfur States; and the remaining 3 % in southern states (Elhiraika, 2003).

Liberalization and Islamization of the financial sector are the main macro-polices taking place in Sudan. The liberalization of the financial sector is assumed to have a negative effect in the context of Sudan. Elhiraika and Ahmed (1998: 8) argue that one of the major limitations of liberalization is the assumption that there is complete certainty that production and consumption decisions are separable. The household includes production and accordingly decides how much labor to hire in or out, how much to lend or borrow, and how much to consume of home produced and purchased goods in order to reach a desired utility level. The assumption of a perfect capital market implies that credit supply and demand are simply controllable, things not realized in Sudan. In There is also uncertainty in the agrarian credit market in Sudan. Thus, efforts to liberalize the banking sector have led to squeezed lending by commercial banks to agriculture, mainly because of the relatively high risk attached to relatively low or even negative real rates of returns on agricultural finance. Meanwhile, the supply of agricultural finance by these banks has dropped remarkably.

A microfinance expert (expert interview 1) argues that liberalization brought on the one hand strength to the well-established institutions and traders. On the other hand, liberalization affected the small producers and traders negatively. Moreover, the strength for the well-established sector is not even fully realized. These strength could have been fully realized when business is performed in the right and untraditional terms. Unfortunately, the private sector in Sudan has always been composed of a group of traders who accumulate money and make only trade in a very traditional way, not using any business approaches. Consequently, liberalization and structural adjustment processes were not so successful in restructuring the financial markets. Liberalization and structural adjustments mean two things: deregulation and privatization. The aim of this policy was that private and large-scale producers get good a chance to have more funds from banks and link up by trickling down financing small producers especially in the agriculture sector. However, this never materialized in Sudan; instead, a negative phenomenon took place with huge amounts of money coming through privatization. These funds reach only the well-established traders who refrained from involving with small producers and preferred to buy directly from the market during harvesting time with the least prices. By doing so, they dismantle the panic of involving with small producers who are not sure to pay back. Consequently, liberalization affected small producers by depriving them of access to more funds from banks and from large-scale producers or traders. This was negative considering the considerable number of small businesses working in the informal sector and their contribution to the economy in Sudan.

Besides the liberalization efforts, the financial sector of Sudan is completely Islamized. Under the Islamized financial system, all financial institutions in the formal sector have to be conducted under Islamic principles, including microfinance services, which, given the experience, have different scope and features. This brought to the surface the concept of "Islamic microfinance". The Sudanese banking system has been fully Islamized since 1990 (UNICONS, 2006: 17).

6.4 Principles of Islamic Finance

The current concept of Islamic microfinance rests in the general framework of providing finance following the principles of Islam. The Islamic understanding became more important with political Islam. Accordingly, financial institutions in Muslim societies are generally governed by Islamic principles. Islamic finance evolved from Islamic *Sharia* laws, which are laid down in the *Qur'an*: charging interest is prohibited and described to be usury or *Riba*; same as gambling *Maisir* and ambiguity *Gharar*. Income must be an outcome of productive economic activities based on the principles of profit-and-loss-sharing contracts. That is why, for millions of Muslims, banks are institutions to be avoided. *Riba* in the *Qur'an* is defined as excessive interest, i. e. any fixed or guaranteed interest payment on cash advances or on deposits.

The main reason behind the prohibition of interest in Islam lies in the fact that Islamic financial practices originate in the main belief that money is not an earning asset in itself; it is considered to be a medium of exchange not a product itself. Islamic laws are supposed to emphasize ethical, moral, social and religious factors to promote equality and fairness for the good of society as a whole. Principles encouraging risk sharing, equal individual rights and duties, property rights, and the purity of contracts are all part of the Islamic code underlying the financial system.

An advantage of the profit-and-loss-sharing features of Islamic finance lies in the fact that it requires a high level of disclosure and transparency, which allows the market to assign the appropriate risk premiums to companies, thereby enhancing the potential for market discipline to take effect (Ozturk, 2008).

Around the world, Islamic finance has developed considerably over the past 20 years and can be considered as one of the fastest growing segments of the financial market in the Islamic world. Because of its features, (mainly profit and loss sharing and other features, see Ozturk 2008), Islamic finance has experienced major transformations and growth especially since 2000. Its volume has reached almost $ 1.5 trillion, with an estimated annual growth of 20 % and is expected to continue expanding at an even faster rate especially after the previous collapse of the conventional financial system (Ozturk, 2008). From the view of Ozturk (2008) and Chapra (2008), after the last financial crisis, more people consider Islamic finance as a more efficient, equitable and even sustainable form of finance since it has not been affected during that crisis as much as the conventional finance. Ozturk argues that Islamic finance also encourages business and trade activities and generates fair and legitimate profit as well as establishing close links between financial flow and productivity.

Islamic finance is provided through a number of financial modes and contracts, which have been developed to satisfy the Islamic doctrine and provide acceptable financial returns. These modes of finance have been established to replace the conventional approach of interest-based transactions. The existence of more than one modes of finance is viewed to be an advantage over the conventional system, especially for the fact that many and specialized modes of finance are available for every economic sector. For instance, *Muzara* for serving the agriculture sector and *Musana* for providing funds for the industrial sector (Ahmed, 1993) (cf. glossary for more details). In addition to that, there are also *Musharaka, Mudaraba* and *Ijara*, which constitute the partnership modes of finance and so many others. However, the most common and used mode of finance is *Murabaha* which is a sales-based mode of finance (Ahmed, 1993).

I will explain here two modes of finance; *Murabaha*, the most used mode in Sudan, and *Musharaka*, which represents the real meaning of Islamic finance; however, used in a limited way. Other modes of finance are explained in the glossary. *Murabaha* is the sale of a commodity at a price, which includes a stated profit known to both the vendor and the purchaser. This can be called a cost plus profit contract. The buyer in deferred payments usually pays the price back. Under *Murabaha*, the Islamic bank purchases, in its own name, goods that an importer or a buyer wants, and then sells them to him at an agreed mark-up. This technique is usually used for financing trade, but because the bank takes title to the goods, and is therefore engaged in buying and selling, its profit derives from a real service that entails a certain risk, and is thus seen as legitimate (Ahmed, 1993). Meanwhile, *Musharaka* is a partnership, normally of limited duration, formed to carry out a specific project. It is therefore similar to a Western-style joint venture, and is also regarded by some as the purest form of Islamic financial instruments, since it conforms with the underlying partnership principles of sharing, and benefiting from, risk. Participation in a *Musharaka* can be either in a new project, or by providing additional funds for an existing one. Profits are divided on a pre-determined basis, and any loss shared in proportion to the capital contribution (Ahmed, 1993).

Ibrahim and Arbab (2006) estimate that in Sudan *Murabaha* accounts for more than 50 % of total volume of finance while all other modes including the profit and loss-sharing or partnership contracts constitute around 34.6 %. This share of partnership modes is considered unsatisfactory, putting in mind that these modes of finance are expected to reflect the main principles of Islam more than others. The unsatisfactory use of partnership modes is also discussed in expert interview 3 with an expert in Islamic microfinance in Sudan.

Some problems of Islamic finance are described in the literature, if scattered, yet an overall evaluation of the whole experience is not available. Especially in countries like Sudan where Islamic principles are applied to all aspects of life, this lack of comprehensive analysis is regrettable. Islamic finance takes for granted that it is the most suitable system to be used and any debate to assess its impact is seen as doubtful. The main two problems seen are the ignorance of the *Musharaka* mode of finance and the fact that finance under the Islamic principles in Sudan is provided only in short-term not in long-term loans (expert interview 3). In Sudan, Islamic banks usually do not provide medium or long-term finance because of inflation; most of the finance is short-term for a period of one year at most. When discussing the impact of this on the Islamic financial markets, the microfinance expert (expert interview 3) holds that if Islamic banks are not able to generate long-term sizable deposits, they will not be able to extend long-term loans that are believed to be necessary to achieve developmental goals.

6.5 Microfinance in Sudan

In this subchapter, I would like to describe the microfinance sector in Sudan and highlight the main debatable issues. I will start with the main aim, the dispute over microfinance clients and its impact. After this, I discuss features of the microfinance sector.

6.5.1 Aim and Clients

The UNICONS report (2006) explains, that the

> "*microfinance aim is to cover critical gaps in formal financial systems in order to specifically address the problem of poverty in a manner sensitive to the needs of the worst off and consistent with gender equity. Microfinance is expected to reduce poverty by increasing incomes of the poor and providing sustainable livelihoods, through accumulating assets and reducing risks. It is also expected to create employment and increase investment opportunities for production. Moreover, microfinance is assumed to participate in the financial sector development by linking formal and informal financial sectors in Sudan*" (UNICONS, 2006: 11).

One can argue here that this aim is wide and all encompassing. Microfinance is seen as the solution of not only poverty but also vulnerability. Whether this aim is realistic is a question not yet answered in

Sudan (expert interviews 2 and 3). It is not clear whether microfinance can impact on income, employment and assets of the poor who are not even specified.

A debatable issue in discussing microfinance in Sudan is who the clients of microfinance are. It is also acknowledged in the UNICONS study (2006) that although Sudan has diversified experience with microfinance projects scattered throughout the country, only in very few cases there have been serious attempts to include the worst-off sections, promote sustainability, and mobilize accompanying resources to serve the poor. It appears from the expert interviews (mainly expert interviews 2, 3 and 4) and the conference I attended in Khartoum in 2010 that the topic remains debatable. It is obvious that the idea finds support that for microfinance to be successful it should be provided to economically active poor. For instance, according to an expert (expert interview 3) microfinance should be understood as a very rewarding business with a profit margin even after deducting costs. He believes that not all of the poor are capable of doing business, managing money and repaying funds; for him if this fact is not considered then microfinance is not going to give credit, but will rather put poor and vulnerable people in debt. Consequently, poverty and vulnerability will be deepened. He explains further that the poorest of the poor should be served by *Zakat*, charity, from family and friends in order to get out of poverty once they have an economic activity they could be involved in with microfinance services. I argue here that the expert's view comes along with the commercialization thinking that I discussed in chapter 3. In this case, the objective stated above for the provision of microfinance as well as the link between microfinance and the alleviation of poverty and vulnerability in Sudan is irrelevant. The obvious results of such financial behavior are the exclusion of the poor and the ignorance of the social aspect of microfinance. Thus, poverty alleviation could not be the desired aim.

The expert interviews have emphasizing significant results of the way microfinance is practiced in Sudan. It is stated that microfinance in Sudan has a limited impact when poverty alleviation is concerned. In responding to the question about the main impact of the microfinance on poverty alleviation in Sudan, both microfinance experts (expert interview 1 and 3) have given disappointing answers. Both state that microfinance is misunderstood and exaggerated if it is supposed to alleviate poverty in Sudan; microfinance can only alleviate poverty of 10 % to 20 % of the economic active poor and cannot reach the very poor. From another point of view, the Deputy Director of the Microfinance Development Facility (MDF) (expert interview 2) realizes a recent shift in government and the policies of other institutions toward dealing with this problem. Farah cites an emerging and undeniable fact that many sectors of the society are excluded from the formal microfinance services and raises the question of what should be done for correction; and further recommends that either ways to include the poorest of the poor need to be found or the aim of alleviating poverty should be revised.

6.5.2 Features of Microfinance

As repeated in most of the literature on features of microfinance in Sudan (including the study conducted by UNICONS, 2006)[4], microfinance is still at an "infancy" stage in Sudan, despite of its potentials in development. It is estimated that the supply of microfinance covers only about 1-3 % of the potential demand (UNICONS, 2006: 11). In much of the discussion about microfinance products, it is stated that microfinance in Sudan is still credit-oriented, due to very few efforts of mobilizing savings and the only recent development in the micro-insurance sector (Ibrahim and Arbab, 2006). For the MDF expert (expert interview 2), savings and insurance are the weaknesses of microfinance efforts in Sudan. This can be explained by the fact that only banks are allowed to take deposits because government laws and regulations control their operations. He argues that credit is now given to diversified businesses, not only to small and micro-scale enterprises but also for construction, education, and consumption purposes.

[4] The report financed by the CBS to be a base study to formulate a vision for the development and expansion of the microfinance sector in Sudan

6.6 Microfinance Institutions in Sudan

The debate about financial institutions continues in Sudan. Questions are asked with regard to which financial institutions are ideal to provide microfinance and what should be the role of government. Until now, the government and banks' efforts in developing the microfinance sector have remained significant in Sudan, and it is clear that the government is fully involved in the sector. In 2002, the CBS engaged in the microfinance sector and directed all banks to allot a fixed percentage (10 %) of all bank resources to the productive families programs, which is microfinance program work with the objective of reducing poverty in Sudan (CBS et al., 2008: 38). This percentage was increased to 12 % by 2006 (ibid.). The initial efforts by the CBS needed four years to be realized; it was only in 2006 when a vision and financial strategy were developed to support the microfinance system in Sudan.

However, divergent views about what should be the role of the government in the microfinance sector in Sudan were presented in the expert interviews. They consider intervention of political power in the financial market problematic, since politicians have their own political agenda, and are interested in microfinance when elections are approaching. They also believe any intervention by the government to limit the existence of a liberal competitive financial market (expert interview 4). At the same time, the government intervention is seen as significant when it comes to providing funds in the initial stages to support the microfinance sector during "takeoff stage" (expert interviews 1 and 2). After that, the demand and supply should control the financial market; and then to be successful, microfinance should be left to the private sector. Another opinion is that, the intervention of the government of Sudan is successful when establishing specialized microfinance banks such as Gudaim[5] bank in NKS (expert interview 1).

Likewise, while banks remain working mostly in urban areas, NGOs and rural development projects have continued to be the essential providers of microfinance to the poor in rural Sudan. The government in one way or other also regulates the work of NGOs, INGOs and most of the national institutions like the social funds providing microfinance. This prompts the question whether this is the second era of subsidized credit in Sudan. Meanwhile, the informal finance arrangements are considered the main providers of finance for the rural poor.

6.6.1 Government and Sponsored Institutions

Government and sponsored institutions in Sudan comprise of apex institutions, banks, NGOs and social funds.

6.6.1.1 Apex Institutions

The creation of apex institutions is considered an important effort of the CBS to support the microfinance sector in Sudan. Consequently, a Microfinance Unit (MFU) was established as one of the apex institutions in Sudan. The MFU is supposed to be a regulatory institution to ensure the realization of the CBS's vision and objectives within a time framework of five years starting 2007 (CBS, 2007; expert interview 4). After that, the authority of the MFU is supposed to be delegated to the Microfinance Development Facility (MDF), another apex institution, as a private institution to take over what has been started by the MFU. The MDF was already established in 2008, still, in January 2010 (when I conducted expert interview 2) it was under construction using initial capital from CBS and international donors like the World Bank with the main objective to support microfinance formal institutions through technical support and wholesale financial loans (expert interview 2).

The MFU and MDF are expected to perform certain duties to draft policy guidelines for microfinance providers, which are being applied in setting up working partnerships with the banking sector. In addition to that, it is supposed to promote awareness and dialogue among microfinance practitioners and stakeholders, support linkages between commercial banks and NGOs and Community Based Or-

[5] When I visited Gudaim Bank in El Obied in 2010, it was under construction and had not yet started providing any financial services.

ganizations (CBOs) at branch level and amendment of the policies of the CBS concerning microfinance. The MFU is liable for promotion, awareness raising and thematic debates on microfinance, among others via a monthly forum of microfinance practitioners and stakeholders in Khartoum. The MFU supplies newspaper reports and debates and hosts a weekly radio program in which bankers and other stakeholders are invited to share their experience. (MFU website; expert interview 4). In reality, the MFU started to provide wholesale finance to microfinance institutions. The MFU is involved in Islamic partnership contracts with 9 banks, the Social Development Foundation (SDF) and three other developmental associations working in the Kordofan and the River Nile State. These projects provide 20 % of the total capital of the Family Bank to be the first bank in Sudan specialized in providing microfinance to poor families only (expert interview 2).

6.6.1.2 Commercial and Specialized Banks

The Sudanese Savings and Social Development Bank (SSDB) was the first bank and considered the pioneering financial institution for providing micro loans and mobilizing micro savings in Sudan (CBS website). The main aim of this institution is to reduce poverty; however, this bank only works in Khartoum and the surroundings. In order to do so, the SSDB targets those who do not have any sources of capital to start a productive business. The bank focuses its efforts to help women as the poorest of the poor, following the Grameen Bank experience where 96 % of clients are women (CBS et al., 2008: 37).

Some specialized commercial banks have been providing small scale and microfinance services for the previous 15 years. Following the successful experience of the SSDB, the Faisal Islamic Bank started to provide microfinance for already operating small-scale enterprises in the 1980s. Since then, the sector has expanded especially after the intervention of the CBS in 2002 as explained above. The Agriculture Bank of Sudan (ABS) is most important in that it also serves as an intermediary for INGOs and UN agencies. Most of these banks do not work in rural areas but are based in urban areas. While some commercial banks have also been engaged in the microfinance sector, their outreach has remained minimal. They include the Sudanese Islamic Bank, the Faisal Islamic Bank, Albaraka Bank, and the Islamic Cooperative Development Bank (CBS et al., 2008: 37).

6.6.1.3 Performance of Banks in Providing Agricultural Finance in Sudan

From the description of the livelihood in Sudan presented earlier in this chapter, it is undeniable that the economy of Sudan heavily depends on agriculture for employment, production and consumption. The main argument here is that most of the small farmers in the rain-fed areas have access only to non-banks financial institutions. It is mentioned in expert interview 1 that for the small farmers especially in remote rural areas the formal institutions are not reachable. The most obvious efforts of providing microfinance for the rain-fed sector are made by the ABS (Elhiraika, 2003: 25), however it only works in the main cities or in some villages when used as intermediary for some NGOs or INGOs.

Even with the available natural resources—in terms of land, water and livestock—agriculture in Sudan presents the best opportunities for future economic growth and development. However, up to now, the country's agriculture is largely traditional and is characterized by low and fluctuating productivity, which means that modernization and development are of the essence. Moreover, availability of funds to make new production inputs and technology accessible to farmers is considered by many writers as crucial for the development of the agricultural sector. Moreover, it is also realized that the efforts of banks in providing finance to agriculture have yielded very disappointing results (Elhiraika, 2003: 25).

Three papers are central for this discussion, the first written by Elhiraika and Ahmed (1998) reflects on the experience of agricultural credit under economic liberalization in Sudan; the second focuses on the experience of Islamic agricultural finance in Sudan (Elhiraika, 2003). The third is written by Ibrahim and Arbab (2006) and explains the reality of agriculture finance in Sudan, however not presenting any analytical or impact assessment.

In the view of Elhiraika (2003: 24ff.) financing agriculture is a serious challenge to governments in developing countries for decades. From independence up to 1990, formal agricultural finance in Sudan entirely relied on government and donor sources (ibid.). Thereby, the focus was on big and mechanized schemes mainly Al Gezira (central Sudan), Al Rahad (Kordofan) and Halfa (north-east Sudan). Scheme administrations were responsible for the disbursement of cash and kind advances to tenants. After marketing the cash crops, the administration deducted the amount of credit owed by each farmer before he/she received his/her proceedings. However, because of failure of the scheme administration to repay credit, the CBS accumulated huge amounts of debts. Outstanding loans to agriculture stood at SD (currency at that time) 17 bn. (3.4 % of GDP) in 1981 and SD 85 bn. (2 % of GDP) in 1989 (ibid.: 28.).

To correct growing internal and external imbalances in the agrarian credit markets and to achieve desirable growth and stability, a National Economic Salvation Program (NESP) was launched in 1990. With economic liberalization as an overall objective, the program assumed to achieve varied objectives among them to reallocate resources to enhance production particularly in agriculture and to achieve financial stability. Successfully, by 1992 several price and exchange rate controls were removed within a credit policy to encourage and increase bank lending to agriculture. Nevertheless, banks mainly faced a problem of small budget available and later more problems concerning bank performance (Elhiraika and Ahmed, 1998; Elhiraika, 2003).

Elhiraika (2003) relates this policy shift to the full adoption of Islamic modes of finance, which took place at the same time. He argues that the liberalization and the Islamization of the financial sector led to a notable increase in formal agricultural loans from just about 1 % of total bank credit in the 1980, to about 30 % in the period 1992-1997. However, this is mainly considered a result of the NESP initiatives to activate agriculture to enhance food security; consequently, the number of bank branches in rural areas was more than doubled. Nevertheless, the same credit policy was steadily relaxed later and as a result, formal bank lending to agriculture started to decline; because of that, government and donor support had to be raised again.

The NESP also directed commercial banks to take over the task of agricultural finance both by lending to farmers directly and indirectly through a Commercial Banks Consortium (CBC). In addition, the ABS was expanded horizontally and vertically but most importantly, its branches increased from 15 in 1990 to 118 in 1994 (Elhiraika and Ahmed, 1998). This is mainly because ABS was the only formal agency specialized in farm credit prior to 1990. The government owns the bank and it is now the most geographically widespread bank in the country. At that time, loans by ABS increased from S£ 0.33 billion in 1989 to S£ 7 billion in 1991 and S£ 13 billion in 1992 with focus on food crops. The bank's outstanding debts amounted to S£ 3.8 billion in 1992, with a loan collection rate of 73 % for mechanized farming, 61 % for irrigated agriculture and only 18 % for traditional rain-fed agriculture. Two other specialized banks were established, the Farmers Bank and the Animal Resources Bank (expert interview 1). At that time agricultural insurance was introduced for the first time in 1994 (Elhiraika and Ahmed, 1998).

Critical issues emerged with implementing the NESP especially in the traditional (crop and livestock) rain-fed subsector that contributes almost two thirds of agricultural output but receives a tiny proportion of formal finance (ibid.). Another significant result was the reduction of the CBS funding to agriculture and its replacement with finance by the CBC and the privatization and commercialization of irrigation services corporations; hence, commercial banks were released to determine their lending policies regarding agriculture still under the control of the CBS.

Comparing before and after commercial bank involvement in agriculture, evidence indicates that the percentage of commercial banks lending to agriculture averaged about 1 % of total bank credit in 1980-1989, and then jumped to 27 % of total loans in 1991 and further to 33 % in 1998 before falling to 17 % in 2001 (Elhiraika, 2003: 29). Elhiraika (2003: 29) argues that this behavior of bank lending to agriculture is due essentially to the formal credit policy of credit ceilings and subsidies for agriculture until 1997. The same happened in most developing countries and was criticized by Adams (1984) and his followers in the 1980s, as mentioned above in chapter 3. Because of realizing that the percentage of poverty in the country was on the rise, banks were directed to lend at least 5 % of funds raised by branches to rural borrowers in order to boost the availability of finance. The progress of commercial bank loans to agriculture was considerably reversed, pursuing the relaxation of the financial policy toward agriculture in 1998-2001. The amount of agriculture finance decreased. Another major question was also raised, concerning the impact of the NESP and the macroeconomic and financial policy shifts on farm households' participation in the credit market, but no data has been provided to answer this question.

To explain further, the core problem of bank performance in financing agriculture has been disappointing; Ibrahim and Arbab (2006) argue that commercial banks generally view agricultural loans as risky, costly to administer and less rewarding, as they do not allow quick circulation of funds. Against the background of perceived high demand for operation, credit and intense regulations by the central bank have been problematic. The nature of the agricultural production system, which is subject to various environmental hazards and price uncertainties, might represent a major factor influencing bankers' attitudes towards agriculture and hence constrain the supply of formal farm credit. This proposition is particularly forceful when interest rates are not free to sufficiently make farm loans profitable. Comparing returns on agricultural loans with those on non-agricultural credit, it is observed that returns on farm loans are lower than returns on non-farm credit.

Ibrahim and Arbab (2006) argue that with the disappointment with providing financial services for the agricultural sector, a partial and gradual recognition of the importance of providing finance for small and micro-enterprises (SMEs) sub-sector started in the middle of 1990s. The full recognition of microfinance for the SMEs sub-sector started with the 1994/95 financing policy. Craftsmen, professionals, petty traders and small producers including productive families were considered one of the priority sectors for banking finance, together with the agricultural, industrial and export sectors. Consequently, the financing policy of the year 2000 specified that each bank should allocate a percentage not less than 7 % of the total banking finance to this sub-sector which has been raised to 10 % by 2002 (Ibrahim and Arbab, 2006). Due to scarcity of information, no readily available answers exist, whether there is any feasible impact of such programs or how successful it is or not.

Beside the efforts made by the CBS, the Ministry of Finance and National Economy (MOF) has always been involved in the agricultural financial market through supplying funds for capitalization of specialized state-owned banks and lending through both banks and agricultural corporations such as the Sudan Cotton Corporation (Elhiraika, 2003: 27). At the side of these above mentioned institutions, the MOF also worked with international donor NGOs and INGOs, such as the UNDP, that are also involved in the provision of farm finance in some areas of the country. External funds are presented to agriculture through the MOF that has worked as a management body to administer these funds; however, some these institutions, such as IFAD, are engaged in direct micro-credit to small farmers in various parts of Sudan.

6.6.1.4 NGOs

NGOs providing microfinance in Sudan are viewed as better than banks in reaching the poor; however, their operation has been limited in its outreach and sustainability, moreover as it heavily depends on donor funds. With few other studies and reports of IFAD, the Sudan Microfinance Policy document (2002) will be used as the main sources of data for this part of the research. According to the Sudan Microfinance Policy document (2002: 17) and as far as microfinance is concerned, NGOs have been much closer to grass root operations than banks. They have been directly working with communities and CBOs, adopting more flexible financial methods. They tend to have simpler procedures, they normally ask for flexible collaterals, some have created successful links with formal banking systems, and most of them finance variety of activities, not only economically productive ones. Furthermore, NGOs offer their services in livelihood packages of training, community development and community awareness rising; the same practice Ibrahim and Arbab (2006) view as inappropriate. Moreover, conditions for providing financial support include group lending and a Grameen Bank-type of group guarantee, together with the Islamic *Murabaha* finance system.

PLAN Sudan, IFAD, the Dutch University Gadaref Assistance Program (DUGAP), the Agency for Cooperation and Research in Development (ACCORD), the Sudanese Development Association (SDA), the Port-Sudan Association for Small Enterprises Development (PASED), and the Women's Union are a few examples of NGOs working in Sudan. The example of IFAD providing microfinance in Al Dagag will be illustrated in chapter 9.

So far, out of all NGOs, experience shows very few profitable and sustainable microfinance models for rural areas in Sudan (Ibrahim and Arbab, 2006). To explain more, success varies considerably between NGOs. Some NGOs have found it difficult to change from a 'beneficiaries' oriented approach to a 'clients' based approach, in other words, shifting from grants to credit. Most NGO operations are restricted in their limited geographic coverage. Due to their dependence on external funding, some NGOs have faced problems of sudden phase-outs, which adversely affected the sustainability of their programs. They spread all over the country, making quantification of their finance volume and their impact a challenging task. Most of them provide small loans for tiny projects such as food processing, livestock rising, selling of drinking water, petty trading, and so on.

6.6.2 Informal Finance in Sudan

In Sudan, the informal sector is considerable; taking into account masses of small farmers, producers and small and micro-enterprises to whom only non-bank institutions may be accessible. Small farmers and producers have to provide some amounts of self-finance. If self-finance is insufficient they resort to informal institutions (expert interview 1). In such cases, informal finance represents the only opportunity to cover any money shortages.

Informal finance exists in the agricultural market due to the ability of small farmers to satisfy the requirements of banks including collateral, records, and so on. It is estimated that together with self-finance informal finance provided about 80 % of financial requirements of agricultural operations in Sudan (Elhiraika and Ahmed, 1998; expert interview 1).

All experts who were interviewed came to the agreement that till today semi-formal and informal arrangements are more available and accessible by a wide range of borrowers in both urban and rural areas in Sudan. From the perspective of Farah (expert interview 2), informal finance is not only present in rural areas for long time but it can also be considered to be part of rural people's culture, and exhibit the generosity and closeness of rural communities in Sudan. They provide significant sources of funds, mainly for consumption. However, some arrangements like *Shail* are more profit-oriented. The important thing to be recognized about informal financial arrangements mentioned in expert interview 1 is that they deal with rural target groups and have an outreach of 100 %, considering arrangements like *Shail*, *Sandouqs* and borrowing from relatives and friends.

6.6.2.1 The Sudanese's Model of ROSCAs: *Sandouqs*

Sandouqs[6] are considered member based financial arrangements, which are self-administered. They constitute the rotating savings and credit associations ROSCAs in Sudan and constitute the most popular and widespread social and financial community arrangements. Ardner (1964) and Rehfisch (1980), both agree that *Sandouqs* were introduced in Sudan during the 1940s. Ardener (1964) argues that middle-aged women introduced them to buy gold while Rehfisch explains the founding of *Sandouqs* with the aim of obtaining scarce goods mainly sugar, tea, and others, which were severely rationed at that time.

Rehfisch (1980) explains the original type of *Sandouqs* in Sudan as a group of women who agree to keep a little portion of their domestic consumption of sugar and tea and pool these amounts. They meet weekly or fortnightly and the collected goods are given to one of them in rotation. The meeting is usually held in the house of the woman whose turn it is. She has to provide refreshments to the group also in form of tea and sugar. The rotation is set by lot, the order of rotation is flexible (ibid.: 694).

Three examples of such institutions are given by Rehfisch (1980: 693); one is a group among intermediary school girls, each member pay a certain amount of sweets; it is seen as a social institution among school girls coming from one area and latter joined by members from other areas aimed at maintaining solidarity and social interaction. The second *Sandouq* described is among women who live in the same street or area, most of them relatives; they vary in their economic status from being better-off to others who are poor. The third group is organized among male civil servants who graduated from the same university and contribute money. They join the group mainly for its financial gain.

At that time, *Sandouqs* were mainly seen as female institutions but always there also has been male participation, Rehfisch (1980: 695) calls them "associate members" for they did not attend meetings but sent their contributions through their wives or sisters and received their share in the same way.

These basic associations described by Rehfisch (1980) hardly have any formalized structures since one woman is the informal leader with the main responsibility of chairing meetings and serving as a link between members (ibid.: 696). In the case of contributing sweets, sugar and tea, no sanctions

---

[6] A *Sanadouq* is an Arabic word meaning a box used to save things.

were put against default members, but rather the default member asked to compensate later after the group considered the main reason behind the failure.

El-Nagar[7] (1980) states that ever since the 1970s, the scale of operation of *Sandouqs* has increased. They remained popular in finding money to meet unexpected expenses or to save. She gives evidence that the number of *Sandouqs* as well as the number of their members increased since that time (Rehfisch, 1980: 703). Also through time the purpose of *Sandouqs* has been altered, Ibrahim and Arbab (2006) argue that *Sandouqs* nowadays fall within a self-managed system in which individuals contribute an agreed sum of money at regular intervals. The pooled amount is distributed in predetermined order, and used mainly (sometimes not wholly) for small businesses (rent, purchase of equipment/utensils, working capital, etc).

The recent empirical work done about *Sandouqs* in Sudan is a paper written by Schultz et al. (2008). This paper investigates urban and semi-urban areas in the Khartoum State and provides a general description of *Sandouqs* in Sudan. It reveals that *Sandouqs* are common in both urban and rural areas; they are not connected with one place or one group of people. Schultz et al. (2008: 23) explain that *Sandouqs* are one important saving alternative; women rely on among other options like keeping cash in a box or buying gold. Moreover, *Sandouqs* are popular means of saving for all groups of women, wherever they reside; either in villages, in settlements of displaced people, as well as in urban areas. Not only this; *Sandouqs* also are found to be common among different social classes of women.

One interesting issue raised by Schultz et al. (2008) is the one about sources and uses of *Sandouq's* money. They state that although the money saved comes from different sources, either from the women's own income or from part of the household allowance given by their husbands (ibid.: 25), only women decide how to spend money saved in *Sandouqs*. Commonly the money saved is invested in female goods or things that display female status and security. However, the discussion showed that the uses of *Sandouqs* funds are gradually changing, since more women are starting to spend the money on household needs like school fees or heath emergencies and some other women use the money to start businesses. The study reveals that the patterns and behavior of women within households are changing in line with the change of the common image of men as the only household breadwinners.

A microfinance expert (expert interview 3) holds that *Sandouqs* fund are used for both production and consumption. He believes that even if consumption *Sandouqs* help women, *Sandouqs* used for production purposes still can be appropriate for providing funds to start small business. He gives an example of a *Sandouq* of 10 women who are employees in Khartoum. They monthly contribute S£ 500 each, in a fund of S£ 5000 to start a small business. He states that having a steady income has helped them, because the salary of one month is not sufficient to start a business and get profit out of it. He also argues that *Sandouqs* are very traditional arrangements, which were good in the past, but not suitable for today. However, this is questionable since from the findings of this research *Sandouqs* are considered very significant in mobilizing local savings; a task most formal institutions have failed to do.

From the descriptions of *Sandouqs* provided by Schultz et al. (2008: 30f.) it is clear that *Sandouqs* in urban and semi-urban areas are considered purely financial institutions emphasized by the women themselves and do not fulfill other needs such as mutual aid or social exchange. What is considered important is that women persist that there are no conflicts over the order of rotation and there is no default. Schultz et al. (2008) argue that this emphasizes the social closeness and trust between members.

6.6.2.2 The *Shail* System in Sudan

Unlike other money lending, *Shail*[8] is always linked to farming. *Shail* contracts are performed when a farmer asks a rich man for credit against the promise of his next crop at a price decided upon by the two parties, usually below the expected price at the next harvest (Brausch, 1964: 344f.). The farmer expects the merchant to be responsible for all matters concerned with handling crop such as providing empty bags for packing, harvest, transport and storage, and also risks of loss during to storage. At the same time, other services are rendered by merchants to their farmer-partners such as needed technical support

---

[7] Who provided a postscript in Rehfisch's paper (1980).
[8] *Shail* is an Arabic word meaning taking or carrying.

(ibid.). The moneylender supervises and advises the cultivator during the season and at harvest time so that the work is done with care and efficiency. Furthermore, the moneylender may be expected to lend extra money for medical emergencies, weddings, birth ceremonies, etc. In cases of outstanding loans, the lender might under fear of communal exclusion, make further loans to a default cultivator. Sometimes he might be ready to write off the debt if the cultivator's livelihood depends on it. This is considered one aspect of the moral obligation, which moneylenders by tradition and sometimes by preference accept, once a steady credit relationship has been established (ibid.).

In their explanation of *Shail* Elhiraika and Ahmed (1998) add to Brausch's ideas that *Shail* could be understood be system of crop mortgage under which the borrower in advance sells a certain part of the future crop in exchange for a loan from a village trader, a landlord, a relative or a friend. They emphasize the thinking that *Shail* is always linked to farming. Kevane (1993: 516)[9] argues that *Shail* takes place only during the growing season, when the farmer is in greatest need of cash and food.

What differs in Brausch's (1964) and Kevane's (1993) description and the one of Elhairaika and Ahmed (1998) is the emphasis on the close supervision of lenders and their engagement in other types of contracts for satisfying any consumer needs for the borrowers during the contract time. Elhiraika and Ahmed (1998) argue differently that the relationship between the lender and the borrower is not that close, or in some cases, that there is no direct monitoring of borrowers, and no loans for consumption are provided.

In the literature about *Shail* mentioned above, it is realized to represent a very old individual-based indigenous financial arrangement that regularly takes place in rural Sudan. Elhiraika and Ahmed (1998) conducted an empirical research on *Shail* in Sudan and conclude that in absence of institutional loans, farmers resort either to share-cropping or *Shail* credits to meet their financial needs. They argue that besides the normal borrowing from moneylenders, traders and shopkeepers, *Shail* is a well established money lending system in rural Sudan (Wilmington, 1955; Brausch, 1964; Adam and Apaya, 1973: 104).

According to rules of lending and borrowing within the *Shail* system as discussed by Saleem (1987), lenders may not operate across villages and borrowers normally determine the purpose for which loans are used. Although subject to negotiation, the lender has the upper hand in determining the amount of cash to be received by the borrower and the amount of future crop to be delivered; thus, they enjoy monopolistic power with no risk-sharing efforts, as the borrower is obliged under all circumstances to honour his commitments. However, it is common for contract terms to be renegotiated to allow cash or delayed repayment; in such cases additional interest may be charged. Elhiraika and Ahmed (1998) assume that sufficient knowledge about the borrower is a prerequisite and hence there is no collateral.

The debatable issue about *Shail* is about whether it is exploitative of the farmers or not. Different views have been presented about this argument; writers like Wilmington (1955)[10], Brausch (1964) and Adam and Apaya (1973: 104) argue that *Shail* is exploitative of the farmer and *Shail* has often been recognized as a exploitive transaction benefiting only the *Shail* trader leaving the farmers in worse situations than if selling their produce in the market after harvest time. Adam and Apaya conclude

> "*Little institutional credit is available to the farmer for production and marketing purposes and he is not able to obtain consumer credit from institutional sources at all. Consequently, the tenant turns to village merchants and other operators of traditional credit... The terms on which he obtains credit from the traditional system are not fair to him, but he continues to borrow from this because alternative sources are not available*" (quoted in Kevane, 1993: 517).

This argumentation is contested by Kevane (1993: 515) who states that *Shail* has been misrepresented in consistency with a broader perspective that discourages informal finance in Sudan. Kevane argues that the ill reputation of the informal credit for peasant farmers in a predominantly Islamic country like Sudan is due to the assumption that this type of lending is usurious and this is against the Islamic religion. For Kevane (1993) the high interest rate in the *Shail* system serves as insurance for the lender against the high risks related to agriculture like a bad season with very low rain that normally happens. Kevane (1993) states that such types of financing use personal resources of the merchants, aiming to

---

[9] Kevane's paper (1993) "Is *Shail* a Shil?" is considered central for the discussion about *Shail* in Sudan.

[10] This was the first scientific work discussing Shail in Sudan as quoted in (Kevane, 1993)

generate profits that might reach up to a total of 100 % of the crop's value. Even if this is considered a big burden on the farmer, however, it might be true that such high interest rates might play a major role as incentive for lenders to be engaged in such risky transactions (ibid.).

Kevane provides evidence from different parts of Sudan and research conducted by other writers (Kevane 1993: 516) to challenge the widely propagated myth, and to show that, first, *Shail* presents a significant source of finance to many farmers with no access to other sources. Second, as has been revealed from different rural areas of Sudan presented by Kevane, *Shail* has been embedded and sustained in many of these areas for long time.

6.6.2.3 Loans from Relatives and Friends

Loans from relatives and friends are free of interest loans taking place between family members, relatives, friends, neighbours and so on. What it is mentioned by expert interviews 1 and 2 is that such transactions are the same as described by Bouman (1994), Steinwand (1994) and Thankom et al. (2009) in chapter 4. They constitute a large proportion of the credit transactions. Normally, the provision of loans of this type in certain parts of Sudan is made via kinship.

The case of the village Al Dagag will be presented in the next four chapters. In chapter 7 and 8 the livelihood concept in the context of poverty and vulnerability is elaborated. Meanwhile in chapter 9 and 10 the experience of the IFAD project in providing microfinance and linking their operations with ABS is illustrated in detail. In addition to that, detailed descriptions of *Sandouq*, *Shail*, loans from relatives and friends are presented.

7 Portray of Rural Livelihood in Al Dagag

"*In summer we migrate me and my older son to Khartoum... we do any type of work that is available for us there*" (in-depth interview with Alnaeem, 2008, Al Dagag, NKS).

"*We just eat for surviving and we do not buy things other than food and water*" (in-depth interview with Omima, 2009, Al Dagag, NKS).

7.1 Introduction

In this chapter, I intend to describe the Al Dagag village within a general analysis of the North Kordofan State (NKS) to show how Al Dagag as part of the state reflects the main features of livelihood in NKS. The chapter starts with describing the geographical location of both the state and the village. One of the questions, which arises in this discussion, is why NKS is considered one of the poorest regions of the country despite the existence of such an extraordinary endowment with natural resources. Even if it shares a considerable percentage of the country export, it attracts little attention in the developmental efforts. Government interventions to help the poor are rare, and consequently people live in a miserable situation and suffer chronic deprivation. Thus, this chapter tries to describe how rural livelihood is constructed and sustained in such a situation.

Primary information about NKS and Al Dagag is provided in the next sub-chapter to show what type of rural settlements are there, who the inhabitants of the state and the village are, what types of administrative systems and services such as education, health and basic infrastructure exist. This information is considered crucial when the livelihood patterns of people are at the center of the discussion. They also mainly reflect the human and physical capital that constitutes people's livelihood.

In the main descriptions of rural livelihood in the literature, rain-fed agriculture obviously is considered the major economic activity of most people of the state and Al Dagag; however, it is conducted under quite vulnerable natural conditions. The main argumentation realized here is that agriculture in Al Dagag reflects the inheritance of not only land but also farming technologies and strategies. Modernization of the sector is not realized and this consequently results in decreasing agricultural production and change in the types of crops produced, that NKS is famous for. As a result, agriculture is never realized as a sufficient means of survival. People then need to bridge the gap in income by diversifying their sources of income by using the available opportunities of off-farm employment, non-farm employment and migration during summer. Generally, households in Al Dagag strategize their patterns of livelihood only to survive; very few reach the stage of investing or building businesses. Therefore, people in their hunt for wellbeing and security are forced to diversify their sources of income, thus, most members of households are engaged in different livelihood activities. Within this framework of livelihood patterns women play a significant role in securing rural livelihood in Al Dagag. Women combine the triple roles of reproduction, production and constructing the social capital that is always viewed as important for sustaining people's livelihood. Women generally have access to resources and they are farmers besides performing other production activities in summer. They have access to agriculture land, production and income earned.

What is also realized to determine the livelihood of rural people in Al Dagag is the structure of households and how it shapes and reshapes people social relations and networks. Households in Al Dagag are found to be too complex to set boundaries between them or to be identified in a social system that is guided by social norms like tribalism and familisim. Households in Al Dagag combine both the spatial and kinship features. Within these households and between them many different social and economic behaviors take place.

In the following sub-chapter, the economic arrangement in the household is in the focus and found to include such aspects like household sources and uses of income, household needs and expenses. The patterns of bargaining and income allocation within the household have been found influential. This deals with how members of the household divide not only labor but also financial responsibilities and distribute resources. It becomes clear how the social system giving men the attribute of being breadwinners is changing in the society since women are revealed to have an increasing and import role in taking household responsibilities.

The household savings are discussed in the last sub-chapter to reflect on savings as household financial behavior. Generally, it is found that all respondents do save with no regard whether they are destitute, poor or better-off. The analysis of how people save and in which items they prefer to save is presented. However, it is also revealed that many changes take place due to repeated natural disasters that have been taking place until now. This shifts the use of livestock from being the main livelihood pattern in the area to be the best saving opportunity; still, the changes of the types and number of livestock significantly affect the volume and type of savings each household holds to be used for future emergencies.

It is worth mentioning here that the classification of the people into destitute, poor and better-off is done by the people themselves and discussed in detail in chapter 8 about poverty and vulnerability in Al Dagag.

Generally this chapter exhibits "the portray" that describes the rural livelihood of the Al Dagag village, shows how complex and diverse rural livelihood needs to be.

7.2 North Kordofan State and Al Dagag Village at a Glance

Map: North Kordofan State

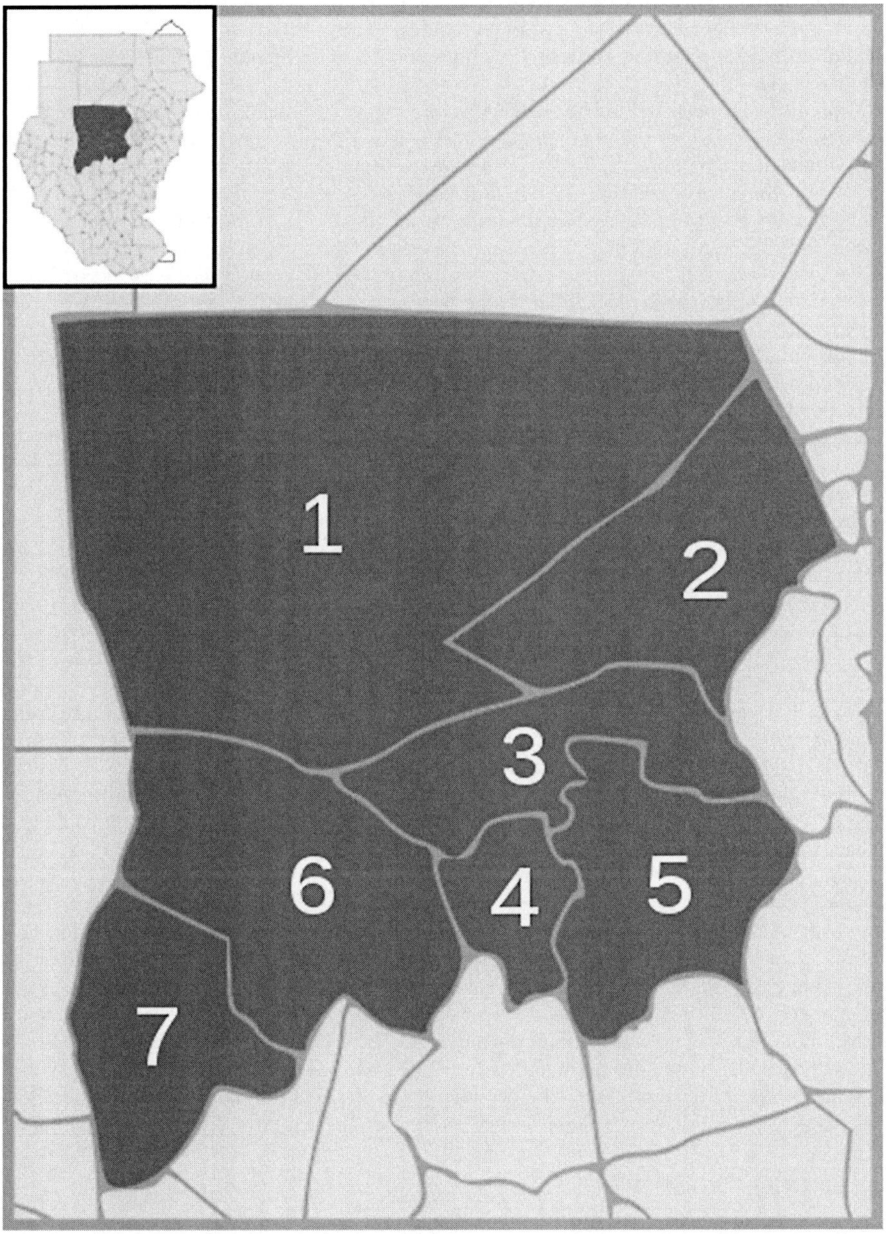

1—Sowdari; 2—Jabrat Al Sheikh; 3—Bara; 4—Sheikan; 5—Um Rawaba; 6—En Nuhud (now divided into three districts En Nuhud, Wadbanda and Abuzabad); 7—Ghebeish. Source: commons.wikimedia.org

7.2.1 Geographical Location and Types of Settlements

NKS is one of the three states that constitute the Kordofan region in Sudan. The other two states are the South Kordofan and West Kordofan States. They differ to a great extent concerning population groups or tribes[1] as well as the environmental and climatic deviations distinguishing each of the three states.

Quite little has been written about NKS as one region of Sudan. Moreover, despite the fact that it contributes significantly to the national economy, it draws a minimum share of the developmental efforts by the central government. This may be due to the fact that most of the population of the state supports the Umma party and the Al Mahadi family, which is one of the main opposition parties to the current government. For instance, North Kordofan supplies 30 % of the total non-oil exports of Sudan (Elbashir, 2008: 30). Additionally, there are 97 forests in NKS, which produce a large amount of various forestry and non forestry products that constitute a sizeable portion of the export of Sudan (IFAD, 2008). In addition to that, the Kordofan region is considered to be the first in Sudan with regard to livestock wealth and considered the main livestock producer for the national and export markets (Ministry of Agriculture NKS, 2009). The livestock wealth is listed as 15.8 million in 2006 statistics. The state is endowed with an important livestock terminal market in El Obeid, which is the main trading point for herds.

The state borders the North Darfur State in the Northwest, the Northern State in the North, the Khartoum State in the East, the White Nile State in the Southeast, the West Kordofan State in the Southwest and the South Kordofan State in the South. This locates NKS in the center of Sudan; it connects the capital with not only Darfur but also neighboring countries like Chad and Libya. The capital city of NKS is El Obeid located in the southern part of the state. Other major cities are Um Rowaba and Bara.

The most recent governmental report (The Central Department of Statistics, 2008), shows that NKS is divided into nine localities which are sub-divided in turn into 36 administrative units (NKS, 2008). Al Dagag is located in the Al Rahad Administrative unit, which is part of the Um Rowaba locality in the southern part of the state. Al Dagag is situated five kilometers from the Al Semaih village, 15 kilometers from the town Al Rahad, 60 kilometer from the city Um Rowaba and 87 kilometer from the state capital El Obeid. The main road that links Khartoum with El Obeid and goes further to reach Darfur passes Al Dagag. The village is located in a heavy sand area; even though it is planted with *Neem* trees mainly brought in the IFAD rural development project in 2001, it is surrounded by agricultural fields of sandy soil and it is 3.5 kilometer from *Khour* Abuhabil, a seasonal stream (Village Profile Sheets, 2008).

Different types of rural settlements exist in NKS, which vary in size of population, number of households and social services available. They are: (i) the major cities and towns like El Obied, Um Rowaba and Al Rahahd; (ii) around 45 large villages of over 1,000 households, which have shops, weekly or twice weekly markets, schools and health facilities and often administrations like the Al Semaih village; (iii) around 450 large rural settlements with 500-1,000 households, which are villages with a number of facilities, including schools, mainly primary schools, shops and some kind of health services, but do not have permanent administrations,; (iv) 800 and 970 medium and small settlements of 5-500 households spread around the area and surrounded by the cultivated areas of the households; these villages usually have primary schools, one or two shops and minor health facilities. Al Dagag is regarded one of these villages (Village Survey 2010); (v) 280 settled and nomadic settlements of fewer

---

[1]The main reason behind using the term tribe and not ethnic groups is the fact that the term tribe is mentioned by the people in Al Dagag. I have been looking for a definition of the term tribe, and in Stiansen and Kevane (eds.), "Kordofan Invaded" (1998), different authors use the term tribe when talking about the Kordofan Region. And in the same book, Abu Shouk (1998: 120) states that scholars have not come up with a universal definition of the term tribe. This can be explained by the fact that all attempts must necessarily fail to accommodate all variations in space and time. Definitions have also reflected their authors' individual objectives and preferences. Abu Shouk regards tribe to be a group of individuals bound together by kinship ties either through common ancestry or intermarriage The same definition will be applied in this research as it really represents the perception of the people in Al Dagag.

than 50 households; these include both permanently settled people and nomadic settlements which have an average of 15-20 households (Ministry of Agriculture, 2009: 8ff.).

7.2.2 Inhabitants of NKS and Al Dagag

According to the fifth population census 2008 in Sudan, the total population of NKS is 3,300,375 (The Central Department of Statistics, 2008) including an increasing number of migrants from the Darfur and South Kordofan States escaping the conflicts there. In addition to that, there is a high annual population growth rate of 1.55 % (ibid.). Most of the population of NKS is sedentary living in rural areas; the nomads constitute a very small percentage (Elbashir, 2008: 30). The rural population comprises 75 % of the total population and consists of nomadic herders, agro-pastoralists, and sedentary farmers and horticulturalists (IFAD, 2004: 18f). Average household size is estimated at 5.5 persons but this varies with far larger households among the nomadic and semi-nomadic communities. (IFAD, 2004: 18f.)

As far as the tribal affiliation is concerned, *Dar Hamid* and *Gawamaa* dominate the Um Rowaba locality where Al Dagag is located. However, Um Rowaba shows a sizable portion of ethnic diversity. That is because besides these two major tribes others like *Nuba*, *Bedaria, Maagla* and *Kawahla, Bazaa, Shanabla* and *Beny Jarra* also settle there. Furthermore, *Bedereyia,* and other minor groups such as *Gaaleen, Shygeya* and *Danagla* who are originally from northern Sudan also live there.

From the village survey I conducted in 2010 in Al Dagag, the population is estimated to be 691 persons clustered into 143 families or households. In Al Dagag, women constitute 51.81 % of the total population (Village Survey, 2010). The average number of children under 18 per household is five even though there are many households with seven children.

Consistent with the village survey (2010), individual in-depth interviews and the interviews I conducted with Al Dagag's *Shaikh*, (2008, 2009), it is noticeable that in Al Dagag more than 80 % of the population are *Gawamaa* and belong to the sub clan of *Gamreea;* the other 15 % are either *Gawama Fedialya* or *Gawama Seraiheea*. Those who are not *Gawama* constitute only 5 % of the population and are mainly from other tribes like *Bagara, Jafra, Shanabla, Bedaireea, Nuba and Bargo;* constituting only individual cases.

The dominance of one tribe in Al Dagag can explain the strong social relationships and networks that exist between people in Al Dagag and as most of respondents repeated the phrase of "*In Al Dagag we are one big family*" this is taken into account when discussing social capital in chapter 8.

7.2.3 Administrative Systems

Generally, there are two administrative systems in NKS, which are the local government system and the native system. The local government system covers both rural and urban areas, whereas the native system is based only on rural areas (Ministry of Agriculture, 2009: 8ff.). Both systems have come through different developments regarding their structure and function. Currently, and according to the law of local administration system each system has a specified role to play, but both systems are supposed to work in harmony for the welfare of the people and promotion of peaceful coexistence or social integration among their affiliates (Ministry of Agriculture, 2009: 8ff.).

Native Administration was established during the British colonial rule (1920) to assist the colonial government to restore order, peace, and assist in collecting taxes. Afterwards, native administration as a traditional government system played an important role in the allocation of agricultural lands, settlement of disputes, organization of land and natural resource use, and conservation of the natural environment (Ministry of Agriculture, 2009: 8ff.).

The native administrative system used to be heritable from one generation to another. It consisted of three levels, first the tribal structure of the *Shaikh* who constitutes the unit at the bottom of the native system performing in a village, part of a village or a nomadic camp. Second, the *Umda* who is supposed to administer a group of *Shaikhs* who live in the same geographical area; and third, on the top of the structure, the *Ameer* who is considered the head of the native system for one or sometimes more than one tribe. The Um Rowaba locality has one *Ameer* for the *Gawama* who controls 36 *Umda*. Every *Um-*

da is responsible for 12-15 *Shaikhs* (Interview with *Gawama Ameer* and Al Dagag *Shaikh*, 2009). Native Administration leaders are entitled to perform duties such as to restore peace and order; environmental conservation and protection of forests; collection of herds' tax and supervision of nomadic and routes to avoid potential conflicts over resources. Moreover, they are entitled to perform tasks like the resolution of conflicts through means that assure sustainable and peaceful coexistence; other tasks commanded by the local authorities; and functions that were added recently by the current government, which is to stand for and work for the empowerment of Islamic principles in all aspects of life. Even if the native administration is still more appreciated by the majority of population in Kordofan, it has only limited juridical authority over the people who live in their jurisdiction area. (Ministry of Agriculture, 2009: 8ff.)

Although different procedures are taken by the current government to change the native system or to replace it, still decisions made by the native system bodies are highly respected by all communities in Kordofan. What I have understood from the interviews I conducted and observations done while living in Al Dagag is that the native system is more embedded in the lives of Al Dagag people than the local government system that is located in the Al Rahad town and does not play any role in the daily life of the Al Dagag people. Despite the existence of the public committee which is ignored by many inhabitants in Al Dagag, most respondents wondered if the government is existent aside from collecting taxes and *Zakat*[2] fees or solving problems that go beyond the ability of the native system and which have to be reported to the state police. Generally, the current government established a public committee to gradually replace the native system (Interview with Al Dagag *Shaikh,* 2009). However, in the case of Al Dagag this never happened. Members selected from the village however are recognized by Al Dagag inhabitants to be supporters of the current government. Their main tasks are to connect the village with the Al Rahad administrative unit and to handle local official transactions like issuing primary documents for land registration or residency certificates and most importantly reporting to the security authority in the administrative unit in Al Rahad (interview with the Chairman of the Al Dagag Public Committee, 2010). The committee was not always active in Al Dagag and with no functions in the day-to-day livelihood of people. However, since 2009 a new committee was elected that is getting more involved in the life of the Al Dagag people. Still all members of the committee are believed to support the current government and they are considered by the Al Dagag people to be part of the government security forces. In the interview with the general Chairman of the Al Dagag Public Committee, he stressed the fact that the main role of the committee is to empower the principles of Islam in all day-to-day aspects of life. This may be the main reason why most residents of Al Dagag ignore the public committee. As stated by one respondent:

> "*We are already Muslims, and we are poor what we need is development but not someone who forces us to do whatever he wants in the name of Islam without considering our poor situation and our lack of simply the daily basic needs. The soul of Islam is that Alraee (the government) should not leave Alreea (the people) poor and humiliated. If this committee is good then they have to think about building the school or raising funds for building health center*" (in-depth interview with Abualgaseem, Al Dagag, 2010).

7.2.4 Services in Al Dagag

This section deals with services provided in Al Dagag that include health, education, market facilities, transportation, housing, and electricity. It aims to show that the lack and inappropriateness of these services are considered one of the main attributes of poverty and vulnerability.

In regard to health services in Al Dagag, in absence of any proper statistics, the interview with the health assistant Isa shows that there is a high rate of mortality of children under five years and a high rate of children and adult malnourishment. Diseases like malaria, typhoid, bilharzhia and diarrhea are wide-spread and frequent in their occurrence. Children specifically die of diseases like diarrhea

---

[2] Islamic taxes which are imposed on Muslims who have capital savings, assets or livestock (Grawert, 1998: 197).

and malaria. Isa claims the lack of save and clean drinking water and the absence of any sanitary system are the main reasons of all health threats in Al Dagag.

Contrary to this, the Ministry of Agriculture (2009) declares that all types of health facilities such as health units followed by smallest health centers that provide only primary health care called dressing stations, well equipped health centers and hospitals are available in NKS (Ministry of Agriculture, 2009: 16). However, all hospitals are located only in the large cities and towns, and big health centers are located in larger villages. That means the people living in remote rural areas who are the bulk of the population lack health services (Osman, 2002). They have to travel long distances to reach the nearest health center or hospital in absence of a proper public transportation system. The Al Dagag people are an example for this since the nearest health center or hospital is located in the Al Rahad town 15 km away and the nearest health center in the Al Semiah village 5 km from Al Dagag. Available in Al Dagag is one health assistant and a midwife who have been trained by the IFAD rural development project in 2003 (IFAD, 2007a; in-depth interviews). They work at their homes providing primary health services and, more dramatically, both have not been trained and equipped to treat most of the serious diseases or cases that have to be transported to Al Rahad or Al Semaih. Moreover, the medical assistant provides his services to two other villages besides Al Dagag; thus, he is not available at all times. As he states, he offers primary health services, such as in cases of minor emergencies, nursing, providing environmental awareness, children vaccination, and the circumcision of boys. He gives medicines only in case of specific diseases like malaria.

Education services are in no better condition than the health services provided in NKS, although the government reports show substantial numbers and percentages like the existence of 1750 pre-school and primary schools, 135 secondary schools (NKS Government, 2008: 73), plus the availability of adult and high education in NKS (Suleyman, 2002: 10). These numbers are far less than what the population needs and most of the schools are far to reach from rural areas. Additionally, not all villages have primary schools, and sometimes a number of villages share the same primary school in absence of any public transportation connecting villages, towns and cities. Secondary schools are only available in the large villages, towns and cities. The number of teachers, classrooms and other teaching facilities is not sufficient to serve the number of children living in NKS. Consequently, the quality of education services is very low. In Al Dagag, only one primary school exists with seven classrooms (even though the primary schooling in Sudan composes of eight classes). This school is not only for the Al Dagag population but also for three neighboring villages; thus, the classrooms are overcrowded. Moreover, the teachers are not motivated; this is not only the case because of the low payments but due to the instability of payments and mistreatments from the local administration. Additionally, most of the teachers live outside Al Dagag and are privately transported every day. Results of the poor education services in Al Dagag are obvious in such factors as; of the total population, 58 % are illiterate and 14 % only got either *Quranic* education in *Khalowa* or primary education. The majority of persons who started primary education did not finish the primary schooling (Village Survey, 2010). The percentage of drop-out schoolchildren is not only very high but also increases rapidly since young boys are starting to migrate to search for work in towns and cities (interview with the principle of the primary school, 2010).

As a result, poor health and education facilities reflect the main features of human capital in Al Dagag and reveal that people in Al Dagag are subjected to many factors that help in the deterioration of their livelihood. Bad health conditions affect their ability to work and their illiteracy determines their knowledge, skills and adoption of new technologies that can positively increase their production. Moreover, the high rates of school drop-out and children mortality impedes the future of the area.

In Al Dagag, there are only three small grocery shops, three bakeries and one butcher scattered in the village; these are supposed to satisfy the inhabitants as buyers and consumers. The shops sell the main and basic needs of any household of Al Dagag like sugar and coffee, different types of crops, onion, cooking oil, etc. However, as has been mentioned by many respondents, if they have cash money they tend not to buy from these shops since their prices are much higher than in the markets in Al Rahad or Al Semaih. Nevertheless, most of the time they need to buy on credit because of the seasonality of income. The nearest market to Al Dagag is the Al Semaih market that only opens one day per week, and is called "Monday market". Many respondents prefer to go to the Al Rahad market for selling their crops because it is big and permanent, and it is the main market in the locality where many large-scale crop traders operate. Some respondents prefer to go to the Al Rahad market for consumption goods also, as it provides the cheapest price alternatives to buy household needs and higher prices to sell crops; however, the availability of the public transportation is regarded as a barrier.

Public transportation on the main road is available but not all the time, so private cars that charge higher prices are used to connect Al Dagag to the nearest cities, towns and even villages.

Considering media and transformation of information, radio represents the main way of receiving information while television sets and satellite units are only available in very few households, mainly of the better-off. There is but one common place for watching TV with satellite that respondents name the "watching club"[3]. Isa, the health assistant, owns the only watching club in Al Dagag, as he has procured it as a loan from the IFAD credit project. The mobile networks cover most of Um Rowaba locality (Ministry of Agriculture, 2009: 16). In Al Dagag, it is observable that many, including the destitute, own mobile phones[4].

Housing is another critical issue of rural life in Al Dagag. Most houses are built of thatch or the leaves of millet straw or *Doom* trees. However, after the big fire that burned almost the whole village in 2001, IFAD introduced a new technology of building rooms out of mud in shape of huts; still the roof is made of thatch. Mud is used to construct the lower part and thatch for the top part of the hut (named locally as *Durdur*). This in reality has helped to lessen the damages caused by fire, which is regarded by many as the main shock threatening their life and assets. Very few houses have rooms built completely out of mud or at least the roof built of iron sheets. Regarding ownership of residence land, the same applies like for agricultural land; it is registered with the *Shaikh* to show ownership of land; however, the registration is not authorized officially and no official documents are provided.

The village was planned after the big fire of 2001 and consists of four parts, north, south, west and east, as they are called by respondents. A very big piece of land is kept empty in the middle of the village for future community service buildings like a health centre. There is one mosque in the middle of the village that has been under construction since I visited Al Dagag in 2007. The primary school and the big storage room built by IFAD are located in the southern part of the village.

Inside the private houses, there is only very simple furniture; many beds are made of metal or wood and chairs. Few people have cupboards for clothes and even fewer have cupboards for kitchen utensils, the latter a sign of wealth. One refrigerator is available in the whole village owned by Asha Alnoor, which she also obtained by a loan she got from the IFAD credit project in Al Dagag. All people can use it for keeping small things, or buying ice or cold water or soft drinks. Most people use charcoal or wood for cooking and only two women have gas stoves, even though the IFAD rural development project introduced the experience of mud stoves; however I observed that people talk about mud stoves but they do not use them. Asked why, most respondents expressed the opinion that they are too slow and not practical. In-house sanitation does not exist in many houses, only few people have toilets.

In Al Dagag, there is no connection to the main public electricity network. Only few people have their own generators. One big generator is owned by the health assistant Isa, who received it as a loan from the IFAD credit project in Al Dagag in order to convince him to stay in the village, for he is the only health assistant there. Many houses are connected to that generator by a lease contract of payment of five Sudanese pounds per lamp, most of them from the better-off group. The average people have a maximum of two lamps per household. However, the general generator works only in the evenings between 7:00 and 11:00 o'clock.

These descriptions of services in Al Dagag not only show the lack of main facilities needed by rural people. They also reveal the simplicity of life in Al Dagag, since people live using minimum services, which is very different from the life in the nearest cities. IFAD is the only organization that has intervened to enhance these services. IFAD trained the health assistant and the midwife, provided the only electricity facility in Al Dagag, introduced the new technology of using different and less risky building materials, helped to a great extent in building the primary school and provided carts as loans to help making transportation more available. This reveals that the work performed by the IFAD development project in improving people's living situations has been considerable. IFAD provided the basic services

[3] A watching club is a place that is connected with satellite where people go to watch television for money, mainly because this is not available in every house in the village.

[4] Maybe this is due to the fact that income from seasonal migration and other remittances are received as credit for mobiles.

that should be provided by the government. Moreover, most loans were directed by IFAD to finance public services such as transportation, health and education to great extent have had a positive impact on people's life. However, these facilities provided by IFAD are still very basic and insufficient, besides the absence of any monitoring, maintenance and sustaining efforts after the withdrawal of IFAD.

It is obvious that any improvements in these services can have a positive impact on people's life. For instance, availability of appropriate health facilities will decrease impacts of shocks related to health and thus might increase household labor; and proper education facilities might enhance the human capital of the village. The provision of proper and cheap transportation will reduce the cost of production and thus increase income.

7.3 General Livelihood Patterns and the Natural Environment

Agriculture represents the major economic activity of most people in North NKS. The total available land is estimated to be 24,000,000 feddan, but only 4,800,000 feddan are under cultivation (Ministry of Agriculture, 2009). NKS is best known for its production of millet, groundnuts, sorghum, Arabic gum and livestock, yet it also contributes significant amounts of hibiscus, pumpkin, tomato, hot pepper, okra, watermelon, and fruits of citrus, mango and guava to Sudan's major marketing centers (Ministry of Agriculture, 2009). The most important crops produced are sorghum and millet, which represent the main cereal crops in NKS. Sesame and groundnuts are the main cash crops. Some other crops including watermelon are cultivated in the area and used in summer to cope with shortages in drinking water. Focusing on agriculture makes NKS famous of its crop markets all around the state with one central market in El Obeid where varieties of crops are available to cover the demand of not only NKS but also other states of Sudan (NKSGovernment, 2008).

NKS is divided into four ecological zones, desert, semi-desert, arid and, semi-arid (Hassan and Hamed, 2004), with average rainfall ranging from 75 mm in the extreme north over 100-200 mm in the middle to 350-450 mm in the southern parts (ibid.). This information is important when discussing livelihood, since it makes it clear that drought is a common feature and in fact takes place every 3-5 years. The climate change in the area reflected in the drought between 1983 and 1992 and again in 2001 has extensively affected the natural resources of the state (NKS Government, 2008: 1).

The accessibility of water is a considerable difficulty in NKS, since there are no accessible permanent, natural sources of water and only a few seasonal passing streams. There are two sources of water in NKS for human, animal, agricultural and industrial needs, which are rainfalls and ground water (Elbashir, 2008). Rainfall is the sole source of surface water whether in form of surface reservoirs, valleys *Wadi* or shallow wells. Rain water annually supplies water for small seasonal rivers *Khours*, this includes *Khour* Abuhabil that passes near Al Dagag, and valleys which gather into small surface reservoirs *Berak*; *Hafeer*, medium reservoirs *Turdah* and large water reservoirs *Rahad* like the one in Al Rahad, the town is named after. The ground water resources are great but not used (Elbashir 2008: 29f.; NKS Government, 2008: 1). This is why I address the problem of accessibility and not availability. Natural and man-made *Hafeer*s are scattered all over the area where soil condition permit (Ministry of Agriculture, 2009: 15).

In Al Dagag, rainfall is the main source of water used for livestock, people and agriculture. Rainfall water is collected in Al Dagag's *Hafeer* that was established in 2001 with financial and technical help provided by Save the Children organization. IFAD also participated by walling up the *Hafeer* and provided money for maintenance and cleaning for three years (2002-2004). The department of water supply is part of the local government and was involved to pay the monthly salary for one *Hafeer* guard and unsurprisingly collected fees paid by people when they take rain and not treated water from the *Hafeer*. Despite the fact that the *Hafeer* was initiated, planned, and dug by the poor themselves with the help of thee two mentioned NGOs, it is important to note that all respondents consider the price of water a significant household expense and calculate it as just as important as the money paid for food. Water for agriculture also comes from rains and the flooding of *Khour* Abuhabil; since few people own pumps, they wait for the flooding to cover their agriculture land near the *Khour* and start growing after, the land then is very fertile. This depends on the rainfall since the *Khour* is seasonal. Moreover, in many times when the *Khour* floods at different times this might damage the whole crop cultivated.

7.4 Livelihood Patterns in Al Dagag: Making a Living

Respondents were asked individually and in groups interviews to rank the main livelihood patters in Al Dagag. Not surprisingly, agriculture appeared in the top of the list, followed by off-farm labor, other patterns listed after these two. Surprisingly seasonal migration is considered an important household livelihood pattern.

7.4.1 Agriculture: Natural Inheritance

By using the term "natural inheritance", I intend to reflect the fact that respondents in Al Dagag did not only inherit the agricultural land but also the farming system and practices. In addition to that, as I observed in the village they did not adapt to any innovations provided by IFAD or other organizations. Although they started using these innovations at the beginning of the project, as time passed by, they went back and used their own indigenous and inherited practices.[5] Just to give an example I have observed that even if the water harvesting[6] innovation introduced by IFAD was very successful in increasing agriculture production it still has not been recently used by respondents.

When ranking the main livelihood patterns, all respondents revealed that they are farmers with no exception of being men or women. Even those who were not originally farmers are now involved in farming activities. Abdalla is an example since he was a herdsman before but recently started farming. He argues, "*When rains are good I get very good production and then I earn very good income that is much better than the one I get from herding*". Thus, agriculture com-es at the top of the rank as the main source of labor and income; however, due to the climatic changes agriculture is viewed to be depending on whether season and rains are good nor not. Thus, rain-fed agriculture alone is not enough.

What I have found in Al Dagag is consistent with the theoretical concept of "peasants" who are described as small agricultural producers who, with the help of simple equipments and the labor of their families, directly or indirectly produce mostly for their own consumption (Bernstein et al., 1992: 30; Grawert, 1998: 24). Factors distinguishing this type of small farmers' households are basically the use of simple technology, use of household labor and subsistence production. Thus, households in Al Dagag represent the peasants' households described in most literature about poverty and agrarian structure and rural livelihoods. In addition to these factors, the concept of diversification is also important to describe peasants' households in Al Dagag. As all respondents pursue diversified livelihood activities, a pure farming household is not existent in Al Dagag (Village Survey, 2010). This typically confirms the theoretical argumentation of Ellis (2000: 3) and Grawert (1993: 24) that in many rural areas of the developing countries farming on its own does not provide a sufficient means of survival; this is also the case in Al Dagag. For this reason, most rural households are found to depend on a diversified portfolio of activities and income sources. Among other reasons, natural hazards like rain shortages are counted to be one of the main reasons behind low agriculture production in Al Dagag.

Consequently, agriculture is usually combined by other activities like petty trading or off-farm labor. Nevertheless, what is different in the case of Al Dagag from what is mentioned in the literature is that raising livestock is not considered as part of agriculture or even as part of the livelihood patterns as Ashley and Nanyeenya (2005) and Ellis and Freeman (2005: 243) and other literature hold. Livestock is perceived as a separate activity from farming, and is neither integrated directly in, nor considered as an essential input into the farming system as explained in the literature by Ashely and Nanyeenya (2005). Livestock is mainly considered as the best saving opportunity as it will be discussed later in this chapter.

Children sometimes help in the farming activities but as many respondents pointed out, they are allowed to help only in school vacations. Those not enrolled in schools and the unmarried girls who stay at home work during the season. However, I have observed that children work more than what respondents

---

[5] The IFAD rural development project also provided agriculture extension services and training focused on improving the farming technologies.

[6] As explained by farmers it is a farming technique to collect the water when the soil permits and cultivate the land after.

report.[7] At some times of the year, it is possible to find the whole family working together cultivating the household's land. In some cases like Batoolay, Alshaikh and others, the whole family moves to live in the agricultural land in harvesting time.[8] Children still go to school normally using the household donkey as transportation, so they can be able to bring the water from *Al Hafeer* after the school. Many respondents declared that, unlike in the past, the number of children per household has recently been linked with poverty. The household is considered very poor or destitute if the number of children is high and especially if they are still young.[9] While in the past, households with high number of children were perceived as better-off since children contributed to household agricultural activities. Most respondents stated that nowadays they tend to send their children to school, which they regard to as a huge spending obligation. Asking respondents why they insist on the importance of sending their children to schools, the majority of respondents declared that they do not want their children to be farmers, instead they want them to be educated which is assumed to allow them to get official employment opportunities referring to few official employees as examples. However, to a great extent, this contradicts what has been mentioned in theories about peasants' households, that the enormous value peasant society characteristically attach to children is based on the material importance of children as a future labor force for the household and for its agricultural production over time (Bernstein et al., 1992).

7.4.1.1 Agricultural Land

Generally, I can claim here that the availability of land is not an issue in Al Dagag. People inherited their farms, not all the land is cultivated and even those who are landless can still rent for little amounts of money. This is understandable from the fact that only six of the 50 respondents I interviewed do not own agricultural land; however, every one of the six rents a piece of land from others. Besides, it is interesting to note that five of the six respondents are women who use to rent a piece of land for their own farming not for the household. Generally, in Al Dagag women have their own agricultural land. These five women rent land even if their husbands own a piece of agricultural land.

To explain this further, the ownership of the agricultural land is a well-known issue although it is not discussed in the household. Normally the land of the male head of the household is separated and known as the "household land". Even if women usually help in cultivating this land, still the male head of the household controls the production and income from this land. The agriculture production and income from the household land are used for household basic needs, mainly food and water. This is consistent with Kabeer's (1997) explanation that women in East Africa contribute to the cultivation of the household fields, while the control of earnings from these fields is in the hand of the husband.

Moreover, I found that this pattern of behavior is accepted and well known in Al Dagag. Generally, it fits Bourdieu's concept of doxa that constitutes norms that remain undiscussed, unnamed and admitted without argument and scrutiny (as explained in chapter 2). As quoted from most respondents "*we do not say this is my land and this is your land; however everyone knows his or her land's boundaries, size, production and income which are used separately*". Most women in Al Dagag have their own smaller piece of land that they cultivate by themselves in the afternoons without help from men, unless it is urgently needed.[10] Moreover, women own full control over the production and the income from selling the produce of their land.

Generally, ownership of land in Al Dagag is inherited from the father or the mother. Consequently, land scarcity is not a significant factor underlying the choice of livelihood pattern, as it has been

---

[7] The work of children is not only observed in farming but also in the households. Some responsibilities like bringing water from Al Hafeer are assigned to them.

[8] That is mainly because they believe it reduces the cost of transporting crops twice from the land to the house and then again to the market. They need to transport crops due to the fact that some crops need to be cleaned like groundnuts, dried like hibiscus or prepared like dried okra. Additionally, they state that they can use their time in working instead of doing other things like long social visits and so on. Alshaikh, who is one of those who never applied to get funds from the IFAD credit project and his wife who was never involved in a *Sandouq*, mentioned that the cost of living in the farming land is less than when they stay at home

[9] An example for this type of household is the one of Mustafa Mohamed who has 12 children and considers himself and other people with similar number of children to be destitute.

[10] All men in the afternoon stay at home while women go back to their land.

clear from the literature (Ellis and Freeman, 2005; Bernstein et al., 1992). Even if the ownership of land is well known, however, is not officially registered. Respondents only have initial and local documents kept by them and the village *Shaikh*, but they do not have any official documents from the government of the State. This in fact endangers any future developmental efforts aiming to make Al Dagag part of the Al Semaih agricultural scheme that the residents of Al Dagag are looking for and put effort to attain, since to be part of that scheme people need official documents and the documents they have are insufficient.

Few respondents do not rent land from others, but mostly they use the uncultivated part of the land. The normal price for renting land is S£ 20 per *Mukhamas* for the whole season which respondents consider not much. However, most respondents rent part of their land to other people and they consider it a source of not only cash income but also of crops that are exchanged in share-cropping arrangements, i. e. crops in exchange for renting land. This enhances availability of land. Female respondents can use the uncultivated part of the household land or they are able to rent a piece of land as mentioned above. However, in some cases of polygamy, wives normally have separate pieces of land for avoiding problems that can emerge from working together or distributing the income between the households of two wives. For instance, Haloum, with her husband Jaber, has a big piece of land but because her husband married another wife, she cannot use the land to avoid any trouble with the other wife; instead she rents her own land. Generally, the rent is paid in advance, the contract is flexible and can be ended at harvesting time, or be renewed, or just cancelled.

Most respondents possess small holding sizes of land in the range of 2-12 *Mukhamas*[11] divided between the sandy soil surrounding Al Dagag and the clay soil near *Khour* Abuhabil, which is the nearest and accessible seasonal water stream. People like Rugaia, Abdalla, Hassan, Asha Alnoor, and Ali have larger land holdings averaging 10-22 *Mukhamas*. It is obvious that the size of the agricultural land holding is never used as criterion to distinguish poor and better-off people in Al Dagag.[12]

Very few respondents bought their land for money; Khamesa is one of the few. She explains this by being a stranger (not from the *Gawama* tribe) who was brought by her husband to Al Dagag. She wanted to have her own land to make her feel more settled and secured. Her answer to the question about the amount and sources of money for buying her agricultural land shows how financial and social relations as well as household's savings can foster the accumulation of natural capital. She states that she bought the land in 2008 for S£ 50 for one *Mukhamas*. She explains that she saved S£ 20 given to her by her husband, she asked her relative who works in Khartoum and he sent her S£ 20 and then she borrowed the remaining S£ 10.

What is obvious and respected by all respondents is the fact that most women are able to possess or rent a piece of land but preferably in sandy soil more than the clay soil. Since men possess the "household land", they prefer to have clay soil land that is more fertile. This may be due to the reason that women use to grow hibiscus, which is regarded as a female crop and grows only in the sand soil land. Another reason could be that sandy soil land is nearer to the village while the clay soil land is located far away. The preference for clay land on the side of men can also be explained that the clay soil land is located near *Khour* Abuhabil, thus both rains and floods can be used for irrigation, thus, it can produce more. This pattern is generally accepted because the production and income from this land is used for food and water in the household.

Most respondents do not use the whole land every year; they cultivate only part of the land. Some of them cultivate part of the land until the land is not fertile enough, then they shift to cultivate the uncultivated part of the land for the next 4-5 years, which constitutes the traditional rotation system. Another reason revealed by many respondents for not using the whole land is that the land is so big that they cannot cultivate it all, unless they hire farmers, which they cannot afford. Quoting Um-

---

[11] *Mukhamas* is equivalent to 2 feddan.

[12] For example, Ali who has 21 *Mukhamas* is considered poor but not destitute. The main reason for considering him not so poor is that he has five grown-up children. most of whom work outside Al Dagag and not as farmers; for instance one of them works in the Ministry of Agriculture in South Kordofan. Mohamed's children help him by sending regular amounts of money. Abdalla and Rugaia possess the largest land holding in Al Dagag since they have 27 *Mukhamas* in clay soil land and 30 *Mukhamas* in sandy soil land inherited from both their father and mother. Still Rugaia is considered as better-off because she is a teacher in the Al Dagag primary school and she does not have children; thus she does not have so many expenses.

belal who is a widow and owns 10 *Mukhamas,* which she inherited from her husband, "*I normally start cultivating using my maximum efforts and I stop in the limits of my efforts, always not all my land is cultivated because I work alone, only my children are helping me*". Umbelal has five children; two of whom are married and thus financially responsible for their own families, while the remaining ones living with her are still young.

To sum up, although agriculture land holdings are rather small in Al Dagag, still not all the land is cultivated due to shortages in water, labor force, finance and modern technology. The question arises here what agriculture production can be expected under such circumstances.

7.4.1.2 Agricultural Production

Generally, the agricultural production in Al Dagag depends on whether the season is good or bad. Other factors are also present like the type of the soil and the irrigation system, availability and accessibility of water, lack of labor and lack of finance for agriculture operation at the beginning, during or at the end of the season. Generally, all these problems lead to low agriculture production.

The main types of crops produced in Al Dagag depend on the type of soil they require. In clay soil land, respondents said that they grow crops like tomato, watermelon, okra, sorghum, eggplants, cowpeas, hot pepper, onion and cotton, which has recently been introduced in Al Dagag. While in sandy soil land, respondents grow sesame, hibiscus, millet, and groundnuts.

Most respondents regard hibiscus as a "women crop" that is grown, cleaned, dried and sold by them. In addition, it is the ideal crop for saving since after being dried it can be stored for long times. Most women respondents claimed that they clean the hibiscus, dry it and keep it so they can sell it in small quantities to the shopkeepers in Al Dagag or at the Al Semaih Monday market. The income from this crop is used for both household needs and female needs like kitchen or house utensils like bed sheets. However, many women have to use the income to pay for school fees, food when the household head/husband is not around, for emergencies: and the majority of women said they use it to pay *Wajib*. Hameeda who is one of those who are poor but not destitute (because her brother works in Saudi Arabia and her sons are grown up and working) gives an example that she sold part of her hibiscus production for the Muslim festival *Eid* in 2009 and the other part when she was sick in the same year. In many cases, the hibiscus and other crops are used for exchanging grocery from the shop, so respondents may pay not in cash but in crops. These in generally are the main uses of income from agriculture production owned by women in Al Dagag.

Normally, most respondents do not sell all their agricultural production at harvest time in case they get a good production. They divide the whole production into four parts: one to be sold immediately for instant household expenses, the second part to be used in the near future for subsistence, the third part is kept as savings for any emergencies, this represents normally only a small amount. The fourth part is kept to be used as input seeds for the next season. Different crops are used differently; i. e. crops like okra and sorghum are normally kept for the household subsistence, as they constitute the main food in Al Dagag, while millet, sorghum, sesame and hibiscus are considered cash crops that are sold immediately or in the future seeking higher prices. I find this household behavior to diversify strategies to ensure the maximum utility of agriculture production explained by Ellis (2000). The saved part of the production is also regarded as savings for any future shocks or disasters.

The transportation of crops is another issue to be discussed. Some respondents would prefer the trader to come and collect their crops since when they take their crops to the Al Rahad market they have to pay one pound per sack for transportation, then five per sack as taxes and another five as *Zakat*. This amount is a lot of money in relation to the prices at harvesting time and the amount of production, especially in bad seasons. Respondents were looking for prices that cover the cost not only of production but also of transportation and taxes. Thus, where to sell crops depends on calculating the cost of selling as well as the cost of production and taxes.

The technologies used in agriculture are very traditional hand tools. People in Al Dagag do not use animals like cows for ploughing since they do not have any cows[13]. Nevertheless, some who got good production in the previous year can rent a tractor in the next year to plough and lodge the land. Still many cannot afford to rent a tractor.

---

[13] Even the richest man in Al Dagag who owns cows still does not use them for plowing

I find it important to give a general view about the amount of agriculture production or income to show how agriculture production is affected by the season. I find it even more interesting to show how different the seasons can be, using respondents' classification of good and bad seasons. In addition to that, it is revealed that the occurrence of bad seasons respectively could lead to a natural disaster.

In comparing the production of the year 2009 and the previous year 2008 to get a general picture of the affects of seasonality of rains on agricultural production in Al Dagag, all respondents agreed that the last two seasons were "bad seasons". The main reason behind a bad season is a rain shortage. Still people say that the 2008 season was better than 2009 in terms of agricultural production. Other types of shocks that occurred, besides the rain shortage, include crops failures, which happened in 2009 as a result of insects and crops diseases like *Sharoopa* and *Santa* that regularly occur. In 2009, there was crop failure for two crops, which are sorghum and millet, and the production of sesame and hibiscus was smaller than expected. If one bad season affects the agriculture production that is used mainly for subsistence a repetitive bad season extremely endangers the sustainability of livelihood in Al Dagag and might lead to serious food shortage.

To give some examples of respondents reflecting how bad seasons affect the agriculture production, Hameed and Hashim said that they got only two sacks of sorghum out of two *Mukhamas* whereas normally they used to get 15 to 20 sacks[14]. Basheer who is one of the better-off people, compares his income from agriculture: In 2008 he earned S£ 1,200 while in 2009 only S£ 200. In this context, he was addressing the question, "*how can I and my family survive by such small amount of money till the next season*?" Abualgaseem who is considered destitute, mentioned that he cultivated six *Mukhamas* of sorghum in clay land but got exactly nothing since he lost the whole production. He continues to say, "*After a long season, in which I worked so hard, now I sit with you and I have not even two pounds in my pocket*".

When the season is bad all people suffer in Al Dagag since agriculture is the main source of income. However, those who have other and steady sources of income are better-off and thus are not equally affected. Rugaia explain: "*This year I lost my whole production of sesame, millet and sorghum, but at least I have Hail (support) to live from*"—by *Hail* Rugaia means her salary as teacher—"but *others they will be suffering so much*". This reflects the degree by which people are vulnerable to natural disasters, which will be explained more in the next chapter. The poor and destitute are more affected than the better-off who have other steady sources of income or more accumulated savings.

Going through what has been presented so far, agriculture production is little and mainly used for subsistence, for households consume a large segment of the agricultural production. This makes people vulnerable to food shortage in bad seasons because they depend on rainfall for irrigation. In cases of rain shortage or other types of natural risks, most people in Al Dagag are left with very little production. Bad seasons can generally lead to a devastating food shortage. Rugaia expected this to happen if 2010 is also a bad season, and it was[15].

7.4.2 Occasional Off-farm Labor

The second rank in the list of livelihood patterns is off-farm labor. It is occasional since farmers tend to exchange their labor on other farms or work as day laborers when they are in urgent need for daily income besides cultivating their own land. However, it is performed by almost all respondents at one point of time in their life. Besides, no respondent mentioned that he or she is working as a laborer permanently. Occasional off-farm labor is not the sole source of income for any of the respondents I interviewed.

Normally, who performs such a type of work are those who are destitute because they cannot cultivate their own land due to their need for a daily income and do not have savings to be used in such situations. In addition, this also includes the poor when they do not have enough production that

---

[14] Moreover, using the water harvesting experience introduced by IFAD the same land of Hameed produced even up to 25 sacks per *Mukhamas*.

[15] As announced in the USAID and FEWS Net report 2011, NKS was one of the states affected by drought and the area is considered to have only minimal food insecurity for 2011-2012 (USAID and FEWS Net, 2011).

can be used for household subsistence till the next season. Having land or not is not distinguishing those who need to do day labor and those who do not, as has repeatedly been mentioned in the literature about landless peasants. The main criterion is the need for urgent or daily income.

Moreover, most of those who are better-off hire laborers during the rainy season. For instance, Abdalla, and Rugaia who used to hire laborers at one point of the farming process since they both take care of large size family land and are sick and unable to work by themselves. However, even the poor sometimes resort to hire laborers when they get some extra income like in the case of Aldur. When Aldur's husband works as a driver in public transportation, he is normally away from the house. Her children are still so young that she cannot do the whole farming activities by herself or with their help. Thus, she uses the income from her husband's job as driver to hire laborers. Another reason is by Khamesa who considers herself a stranger in Al Dagag since she is not *Gawama*. She finds it difficult to perform the farming activities; therefore, she hires farmers. Still, not learning farming makes her feel separated and excluded from most women's activities and gatherings, as she expresses.

Occasional labor is hired by the head of the household at any time of the season to help in different stages of farming. Laborers usually work in two shifts, the first one is called *Dahwa*, starts early in the morning and ends in the afternoon; the second shift *Sarba* starts in the afternoon and ends with sunset. The agreement is conducted through unwritten contracts after negotiating wages, work to be performed and time limits. For example, people might agree to pay for the whole season or by *Mukhamas* or only for specific tasks like harvesting or weeding. They are paid by *Dahwa* and *Sarba* sometimes on a daily basis. In a few cases, laborers are paid in advance, but this is unusual. Maximum earnings for *Dahwa* are S£ 10 whereas for *Sarba* laborers receive S£ 7. *Dahwa* is more expensive than *Sarba* since it is supposed that workers are more active and full of energy in the morning. Furthermore, *Sarba* is always believed to be done by women and normally women are paid less than men are in Al Dagag. Answering the question why women are paid less than men are, respondents said that women cannot do all the heavy tasks performed by men. Additionally, it is stated that women get tired more easily and have many excuses to avoid work like a sick child and so on. However, only women perform some types of work like cleaning crops, mainly groundnuts after harvesting. Hassan used to hire women from other tribes like *Nuba* who are famous for strong bodybuilding, as he expresses.

Some respondents work as laborers more often than others who work only in cases of emergencies in the household. This distinguishes the poor from the destitute. Analysis of interviews also shows differences in that the destitute always need to work as laborers while the poor do so in cases of emergencies to cover any gap in expenditures, but otherwise cultivate their own land. For instance, Alradeea has her own land but is not able to cultivate it, because she needs daily income since she is divorced and takes care of her children alone. While Umsalama has four children and her husband cannot migrate because of his age, and therefore, she chooses to work as a laborer in cases of emergencies before buying from the shop on credit, which is respected by her as a choice that she will make when she cannot find any work to do in the village.

Most old women mentioned that they used to work as laborers when they were younger and had young children, but now they no longer need to because their children have grown up. However, I also came across old women working as day laborers.

Those unable to hire laborers but in urgent need call for *Nafeer*; in this case *Nafeer* represents the indigenous mechanism to provide insurance as will be explained later in chapter 8. Many times people ask for *Nafeer* when they feel they will otherwise lose the crop. Normally, this is done for those who are in need for help and do not have money to hire laborers, but even the better-off people in many times call for *Nafeer* in Al Dagag. The main reason is the fact that reciprocity guides this behavior, and consequently if the poor need the help of the better-off they come to help them also when the better-off are.

To sum up, most respondents have to work as laborer at some time or other, the regularity of this distinguishes the poor and the destitute. The better-off normally are in need and able to hire laborers, while *Nafeer* which is a social capital arrangement, is done to help with any urgent needs. However, it can also be given to the better-off since reciprocity is the guide.

7.4.3 Seasonal Migration in Al Dagag

Seasonal migration of men during summer is graded next in the rank of livelihood patters in Al Dagag. Unlike occasional off-farm labor, which both men and women can perform, only men can migrate.

Before discussing the seasonal migration in Al Dagag it is worth mentioning other types of migration that take place in the village, first migration to other countries, mainly the gulf area of Saudi Arabia and the Emirates. However, residents from Al Dagag who migrate to other countries are only few cases. A second type of migration includes permanent migration to other cities in Sudan. They constitute a slightly higher percentage than the first category, but still less than the seasonal migration. Both first and second type migrants permanently live outside Al Dagag. Most of the second type are educated, have formal jobs mainly in universities, the Ministry of Agriculture, insurance companies and the tax department and live in cities like Khartoum, El Obeid, Umm Ruwaba and towns like Al Rahad. The third type of migration only occurs in case of a severe drought. In this case, migration is considered one of the coping strategies that will be discussed later.

The fourth and most regular type of migration is the seasonal migration of male residents looking for work outside Al Dagag. Since this category is present in most households in Al Dagag, it deserves special focus. In this case, migration is considered more a livelihood pattern than a coping strategy (however it combines both functions); remittances are considered a source of income as presented in table 3. This is consistent with the theoretical argumentation of Ellis and Freeman (2005) and Dolan (2005) who consider migration one of the livelihood activities as explained in chapter 2. Generally, one can argue here that this type of migration in Al Dagag matches the explanations of the new economics of labor migration (NELM) approach discussed in detail in chapter 2. In the NELM model the decision to migrate is not made by isolated individual actors, but by the household. In this case, migration has been informed by the need to maximize individual expected income and by the need to minimize risks and to loosen constraints threatening families, households and communities.

The main dimensions of the seasonal migration are who migrates where and why, what type of work migrants do , how they live at the destination, what facilitates migration and how households organize themselves in the absence of the head of the household.

Farming takes place in the time between June and October, and again between November and February. In summer that is between February/March and July most men migrate to other cities and towns like the Khartoum State, Wad Medani, Wad Alhadad in the Al Gezira State where income opportunities are available. Only men or older sons migrate, women stay in the household looking after the children and doing some types of work at this time. Migration of men in this way reflects one feature of the social system where men are considered the household breadwinners. This is also discussed by Agarwal (1997, cf. chapter 2). Moreover, women's mobility within this social system is curtained both by familial and/or childcare responsibilities in addition to social norms that do not easily accept women's mobility in rural areas. It may also have to do with the behavior of the labor market that also is affected by the social norms in favor of men. For instance, Alradeea who used to go to Khartoum in summer for work mentioned that she would say in the village that she has gone to visit her sisters in Khartoum. In Khartoum, she performs such work as washing clothes for other people or providing domestic help; but she will not admit this in Al Dagag.

In most cases, the head of the household and his sons migrate at the same time, sometimes even to the same place: in other cases to different places, as they tend to reduce the risk of not finding work there. Another factor related to who migrates in Al Dagag is that most of those who migrate are normally farmers who do not have any or just basic skills of doing specific non-farm work. Thus, when they migrate they perform minor jobs available for them that do not need any pervious training. As respondents revealed that the type of work they do during migration is mainly making building bricks; working in cafeterias or supermarkets, selling water, mobiles and clothes in markets and driving public transportation cars, two are a plumber and an electricity technician, even though they never got any formal training. Most men mentioned that they normally perform any type of work available for them when they migrate.

The main reason behind such behavior is the need to bridge a gap in income when there are no farming activities available. Thus, the main pushing factor is the need for income to cover household expenses when there is no other option available. Migration here is a household strategy enabling households to overpass a gap in spending (cf. Haas 2008). Remittances are sent to the families in Al Dagag. Most of respondents send the remittances in form of mobile credit to the shopkeeper who either gives it to the family in cash or lets them buy things from the shop. Sometimes, if many migrants from Al Dagag work in one place, they send the money with one of them to Al Dagag and share his travel expenses.

Seasonal migration in Al Dagag is also affected by the occurrence of bad or good seasons. Even if all male respondents said that they would migrate at any time, I found out that if the season is good, fewer tend to migrate looking for work. Those who tend not to migrate in good seasons are from households that accumulate greater amounts of savings to pass this time. Additionally, when the season is bad, most men migrate and some respondents mentioned that very few men only the shopkeepers or the very old men are left in the village. Migration in this case takes place with no regard to whether the households are poor or better-off, own land or not.

At the destination respondents face many types of risks such as not finding any work, being paid less and the risk of doing heavy duties in combination with low food intake that in many cases leads to sickness. Most respondents mentioned that they normally work from early morning to late in the night because their work is evaluated and paid in cash based on the daily production and not by numbers of hours. Moreover, normally they eat whatever is available at the work place.

The role of social capital in the migration process in the case of Al Dagag might strengthen the argument of the NELM model that migration takes place within a social context wherein family and social relations influence migration behavior (Cross et al., 2006: 107). I find it relevant to describe how social networks play an important role in finding work in other places and later in helping households in the absence of the head of the household.

In Al Dagag, social connection shape what type of work can be found and in selecting the destination place of migration. For instance, one would ask his relatives about where to find work; others follow each other to the destination place. This is mainly why most of them migrate to the same places every year and for many years. Migrants tend only to migrate to places where they can find relatives. So, few will go and are followed later by others, mainly relatives. Some migrants call their relatives when more workers are needed at the destination. There the group of Al Dagag migrants live together to reduce the cost of living. Since no organizations or intermediaries are involved to facilitate the migration process, people tend to resort to their previous social networks or build new ones at the destination. Another issue that shows the importance of social networks in migration is that migrants tend to build social connections with the employers.

In regard to the question of how households organize themselves when the household head is migrating, it became clear that first of all they live on remittances. Migrants tend to send money back home as they divide the income they get in two parts, a smaller part for their own consumption and a bigger part to be sent to the family. Most households at this time of the year survive on this money sent by the head of the household or other migrants of the family. The money send is used for household basic needs mainly for food and water. This is consistent with the NELM model, which states that remittances are the most essential motive behind migration (as elaborated in chapter 2). The money is sent to women and most of them confirm that they try to save a small part sometimes in cash but usually put into *Sandouqs*. In a few cases, respondents mentioned that they could even buy livestock from the remittances. Generally, what has been mentioned here contradicts the assumption of the NELM model described by Stark (1991) and Sander and Maimbo (2003) that remittances are invested in new technologies or to make a transition from subsistence to commercial production. In the case of Al Dagag, seasonal migration remittances are still used for subsistence.

When men migrate women are responsible for spending the remittances but in an agreement with the head of the household. This goes in line with a contractual way described by the NELM model that characterizes the behavior of partners in a larger context of the household where migration is not an individual action or strategy.

Social relations play another crucial role concerning the issue of how households organize themselves when seasonal migration takes place in Al Dagag. Analysis of interviews revealed the fact that women resort to their social connections in the absence of the head of household. Extended family members in or outside Al Dagag help in cases of emergencies and in case the migrant delays sending money. In fact, most men mentioned that they migrate without much fear about their families mainly because they know that they will be supported and served by other male or female members of the extended family. For instance, Fatima Ibrahim mentioned that she borrows from relatives when she faces any emergency in the absence of her husband. Good relationships to the shopkeeper are also an important source of financial help at this time. Most women borrow from the shop or buy on credit in the absence of the head of the household and pay back when they receive the money, which normally is every other week.

7.4.4 Non-Farm Work, *Shail* and Wage Employment

Non-farm work is performed regularly in Al Dagag. This mainly refers to the construction of houses and petty trading which is defined by respondents as selling goods in small amounts. In many cases, these goods are presented on a table called *Tablia* located outside the house doors or in other common places. Other types of nonfarm work are cutting and selling firewood or dry grass used for building houses, making and selling charcoal, money transfers using mobile credit, driving transportation cars or lorries, working as butcher, driving donkey carts, working as baker, and shop-keeping.

Some people in Al Dagag (six respondents[16]) are classified as crop traders, mainly *Shail* traders or shopkeepers in Al Dagag. Only one respondent I interviewed (Asha Alnoor) is a crop and *Shail* trader and shopkeeper at the same time. In fact, her *Shail* trading facilitated the business of crop trading since *Shail* traders used to collect big amounts of crops for cheap prices from *Shail* contracts. Therefore, some of the *Shail* traders in Al Dagag are crop traders. Indeed, the number of *Shail* traders has been rapidly increasing in the village; some people tend to save mainly to give *Shail* in September. Thus, the increasing number of *Shail* traders makes it possible to include it as a livelihood pattern in Al Dagag. This issue will be illustrated further in chapter 10.

Particular types of work are regarded as exclusive women's work. In addition to being farmers and housewives, women perform such work as handicraft. For instance, most female respondents are involved in making *Nasee*, (a rope made of *Doom* tree leaves, used for building houses and roofs out of grass), making and selling charcoal, selling breakfast at the school and selling food stuff like powdered okra in small quantities as door–to–door vendors which is called *Tyjarat Sabat*, which means basket trading. This category is also included in the trading work. Generally, trade and *Shail* specifically are considered significant in Al Dagag and the number of people performing such activities is increasing. For instance, the number of *Shail* traders makes it possible to include it as a considerable part of the non-farming livelihood pattern in Al Dagag.

Wage employment opportunities in Al Dagag are mentioned at the end of the ranking of livelihood patterns, mainly because they constitute only individual cases in the village. Not so many people are formally employed; opportunities available in Al Dagag are primary school teacher, midwife, guard of the *Hafeer* and health assistant. They are the only ones who get monthly salary from the government and are viewed by the respondents as better-off. Although they have their salary, all of them are farmers besides doing other types of work. Among other examples, Rugaia is a teacher, farmer and in summer, she does handicraft work, while her husband works in Khartoum. Isa, who is the Al Dagag health assistant, also owns the only TV watching club in the village and is a farmer as well as his wife.

To sum up the discussion about livelihood pattern in Al Dagag, it becomes clear that the general livelihood pattern is agriculture since all of respondents mentioned that they are basically farmers with no regard to sex, age, or education. However, during summer, men tend to migrate looking for labor employment while women do other types of work in Al Dagag. Besides these two activities, respondents pursue different types of other activities like occasional off-farm employment, and non-farm business and wage employments. This classification is to some extend similar to Dolan's (2005) classification of livelihood activities mentioned in chapter 2. However, the classification of respondents in Al Dagag varies from the model of Dolan in the way that livestock is not considered part of agriculture. In addition to that, the case of Al Dagag stresses the existence of the occasional off-farm labor. Both Dolan's explanation and the case of Al Dagag agree on giving weight to trade and considering migration a livelihood pattern.

To conclude, what Chambers (1997) theoretically expresses about local livelihood strategies in the developing countries cannot be ignored when explaining the case of Al Dagag, for he argues that livelihoods of the

---

[16] I interviewed three of them mainly as *Shail* traders, thus two interviews were conducted with each of the three respondents.

poor are diverse, complex, dynamic as well as unpredictable. The poor have not only one source of support but several. They combine different sources of income and assets to ensure their survival and sustain their livelihood. People use all resources, capabilities and opportunities available to them and maintain a portfolio of activities, as different household members carry out different livelihood activities (Chambers, 1997: 163).

7.5 The Role of Women in Securing Livelihood in Al Dagag

Going along with the results of Seebens (2009) discussed in chapter 2 in a group interview with women at a coffee gathering revealed that they, to a great extent, invest in the wellbeing of the members of the household. This result was later confirmed after analyzing individual in-depth and group interviews with respondents and village leaders. Not only at household level but also at community level women play a significant role. It is clear that women are not only involved in reproduction but also in the agriculture production considered a source of household survival. According to their statement, they work more than men do, since they combine both productive and reproductive roles. In addition they made it very clear that they are the ones who keep the norms and tradition of "helping each other", mainly by upholding the culture of *Wajib* with significant contributions as will be explained in chapter 8.

Women's triple roles, i. e., productive, reproductive, and community involvement, are similar to what has been explained in Moser's Gender Planning Framework (Moser, 1993; UNDP, 2001: 43) discussed in chapter 2. In Al Dagag, almost all female respondents are farmers and besides that engaged in other economic activities as mentioned above. They participate in all community activities like digging and constructing the Al Dagag *Hafeer*. If the social relations are considered crucial in all aspects of life; in Al Dagag they are mostly done by women. Thus, women in Al Dagag might be considered the main actors in building and keeping social relations functioning. Women enhance *Wajib*, are involved in *Nafeer*,—some types of *Nafeer* are even performed mostly by women.

Women in Al Dagag have the right to own agriculture or residual land which they cultivate by themselves, something which is not accepted in most other rural areas in Sudan, for instance in eastern Sudan (reflection on my own personal and work experience). Since women earn their own income, they pay for important expenses in the household; this is also seen by most of them as the main reason for having a "word" in the household. It is mentioned that women master most of the household issues especially in the period during which men migrate to search earning possibilities. During this period of time, women also do other types of work as mentioned above.

Respondents like Rugaia, Dawa, Zainab and Asha Alnoor claim that women are now in a better situation after the IFAD rural development project was introduced to the village 2001. This is mainly attributed by them to the chance to get credit but also to the involvement in literacy classes and training programs in different issues like reproductive health, handicraft and food processing. Female respondents think that this has allowed them to have the skills of doing different types of work. The new Al Dagag *Hafeer* has made life easier for all women since they no longer need to collect drinking water from Al Semaih or other *Hafeer*s very far, thus, saving time and effort—even children can collect water now. Rugaia additionally claims that now women have started to do men's work like being a crop or *Shail* trader, which was men-only before in Al Dagag.

Another interesting question is whether nowadays women are more empowered[17] to do things. For instance, women claim that they are now allowed to go to the market especially if the head of the household is not there, unlike in the past when such behavior was not acceptable. Women argue repeatedly that they have played a major role at all times in agriculture. They actively participate in crop production, planting, weeding and harvesting sorghum and millet in their own land in the household land. Additionally, most women in Al Dagag have full responsibility for the *Jubraka*[18] gardens near or inside their houses, where vegetables and some other crops are cultivated. They also play an important role in livestock rising, looking after animals near the homesteads, milking and watering them when

[17] I used the word strong to explain women's empowerment to respondents.
[18] *Jubraka* in Al Dagag is defined as a small piece of land cultivated by women to grow different crops for house consumption, to be sold for neighbors, or to be used for *Wajib*.

this is done in the compound; they take care of all the young livestock until they are old enough to go and graze on their own.

With regard to the division of labor within the household, I can argue here that while men help as responsible heads of households, women in Al Dagag play major roles as well.

7.6 The Concept of the Household in Al Dagag

7.6.1 Structure of Households

In Al Dagag, a household can be defined as people constituting one family who live in one house. People use terms like household *(Bait)* or family *(Usra)* interchangeably. A household normally consists of a married couple and their children if they have any. However, the concept of households in Al Dagag is more complex than that, because there are many relations between nuclear family households and the extended family households, which are connected together to great extent in the meaning of households in Al Dagag. This confirms what Kabeer (1997: 115) described as a bundle of relationships through which its primary reproductive activities are organized, as presented in chapter 2.

Normally in Al Dagag, the nuclear family household[19] is located within the extended family household. The extended family household is always a big house built on a large stretch of land; inside the extended household different smaller households of nuclear families exist. Within the compound, doors are open between separate nuclear families households. The extended family household has one door to the main road. This constitutes the spatial structure of households in Al Dagag.

The household of the extended family is normally composed of an elder married couple and all unmarried children and they have a separate house within the household. Married sons occupy small nuclear family households within the compound of the extended family. Married daughters usually move to live in their husbands' family household. Every extended family household is named after the name of the elder man, for instance one household is called *Bait* or *Usra* Mohamed. Within this big household, Mustafa Mohamed, Alnoor Mohamed and other sons of Mohamed constitute separate nuclear households which are also named after the head of the household like *Bait* or *Usra* Mustafa Mohamed. Thus, the name of the head of the household is considered important in distinguishing between households. It is observed from the above discretion that the household in Al Dagag has a double meaning of extended and nuclear household and the relations between them need to be considered.

In case of death of the elder man, normally the oldest son will take the responsibility; only in few cases it is the elder women.[20] These attributes show communal rules governing the composition of households. In Al Dagag and with regard to the marital relationship normally the eldest man is considered the head of household; however, in some cases women that will be explained later in this chapter are considered heads of households

On the other side, the parental relationship is apparent at the two levels of extended family household and the nuclear family household, normally parents are responsible for their children until they are married and live separately. However, in many cases, the married sons are responsible for the very old or sick parents and unmarried sisters. This structure of nuclear family households located within the extended family household makes it difficult to distinguish relationships within the household or to determine responsibilities in Al Dagag.

Households in Al Dagag are complex to be identified as many and diversified relationships take place. Normally not only the married couple and their children live in the nuclear family households but it is also common to find other relatives there. Most of the inhabitants of the village belong to one tribe (*Gawama*) and one sub-tribe or sub-clan (*Gamreea*), so they feel they already belong to each other. It is formidably true what they have repeatedly mentioned, "*in Al Dagag we are one big family*". Therefore, it has often been difficult to set boundaries between households in Al Dagag.

---

[19] In this research the term household is used to describe the household of nuclear families, unless otherwise specified.

[20] In both cases the name of the household is the name of the elder man who died.

I would like here to use the household of the above mentioned Mohamed family to show this complexity.

First, the elder couple of the family is dead; the sons are Mustafa and Alnoor plus other sons who are part of the extended family household. Every nuclear family household has a separate place or house with a fence and door inside the big household, which has one door to the street. Every married male is the head of his own nuclear family household. Despite the fact that each nuclear family household has a separate space, I never experienced this physical boundary since people spend the whole day together. Only at night, people go to their own compounds. During the days, I spent with them, I have observed that people cook separately but eat together, separated between women, men and children. I could also observe a sense of reciprocity in this because women rotate for example in preparing the porridge and who will bring the sauce. This does not only show how people support and help each other but also how difficult it is to define a household and its members in Al Dagag. People go to the field together. They also work together; for instance, when I visited them for the first time, the whole family was cleaning the hibiscus of one of them. In addition, I have observed that women take care of the children of other women during their absence. Every time I visited them I used to meet Um Balaina who later became one of my respondents. Um Balaina is the sister of the wife to Alnoor Mohamed; she is divorced with five children and she is supposed to live in her own house. However, Um Balaina spends most of the day with her children in the house of her sister, they eat together and they stay until when at night they go to their own house, which is in the extended household compound of her former husband Hejazee Hamed. However, Um Balaina is used to share the food with her sister to whom she brings sorghum or dried meat for meals. Even if Alnoor Mohamed seems unhappy about this, as I observed, he told me that his sister-in-law is welcome to his house at any time and stressed the fact that she shares her food with them but would be welcome even if she did not. Um Balaina does not have agriculture land but rents a piece of land from Alnoor Mohamed. Even if by this he is helping her, she still has to pay rent.

Thus, I can say that many relationships take place within and between households that make it difficult to set boundaries.

Next, I would also like to present what is common and what is relevant in the case of Al Dagag to the theoretical discussion of households. Generally, what is common between this type of household in Al Dagag and the description provided in the literature, for example by Chambers and Conway (1992: 8) and Bernstein et al. (1992: 91), is that household membership is extended to mean all persons living under one roof; even if occupying a separate housing unit, having either direct access to the outside (or to a public area) or a separate cooking facility. In fact, they have a separate hearth but shared dishes since they cook separately but eat together.

Another element, which is apparent in the other definitions and consistent with the case of Al Dagag, is the help household members give each other. People living within an extended family household help each other in many aspects of life, for instance in their farming activities or domestic work. On the one hand, within a nuclear family household in Al Dagag members are generally entities of respect and understanding following a mutual interest of providing wellbeing to all members of the household (described by Schultz, 2005; Schultz et al., 2008), which, nevertheless, I find that people are forced to do by their worry to survive.

On the other hand I cannot ignore the conflicting interests and preferences that cause tensions in the households that I have observed in many aspects, especially concerning bargaining over distribution of resources and income allocation. Thus, following mutual interest of survival is not to say there are no conflicts of interests, but to say that even with the existence of these conflicts, what people are looking for is the welfare of the whole family, especially the children to pass any stressful times. This will be elaborated further when discussing patterns of income allocation later in this chapter.

One can argue further that generally the behavior of helping each other and the notion of households as entities of respect pursuing mutual interests can be described as part of the "doxa" (Bourdieu, 1977; Agarwal, 1997) as explained in chapter 2. Thus, helping each other within the household falls in the arena of the uncontested and naturalized part of the social order. Nevertheless, this is not to suggest an absence of the contractual nature of households or exclude the conflicts of interests that emerge in most households I studied in Al Dagag. Consequently, I found the type of household applicable in the case of Al Dagag to match Sen's model of household as a household of co-operation and conflict described in chapter 2.

7.6.2 Women-Headed Households

Generally, in Al Dagag households headed by women represent cases of divorced and widowed women. In a few other cases, the wife took over the main responsibilities even in the presence of her husband; however, she was not named head of the household. In the case of a divorced couple, the divorced husband is still financially responsible; but in practice, often women like Alradeea find themselves taking over the household responsibilities completely. In cases of divorced and widowed women, the age of children determines who is counted as the head of the household. If the children are grown up, then the older son is considered the head of the household. However, this is sometimes contested as in the case of Agba Alnoor who despite grown up sons considers herself the head of the household because she makes all decisions and she is sure that they will always follow her guidance.

The cases of Asha Alnoor and Fatima represent the few cases when women took over the household responsibility. Both are not officially called head of their household but they are the main breadwinners. Asha does business and earns more than the husband earns, thus she is taking the responsibility while the husband contributes a little share. Fatima's husband is mentally sick; thus, she has to take the responsibility.

Not surprisingly and in line with the literature (Seebens, 2009: 6), female-headed households of widows and divorced women are often considered destitute. The main reason discussed by Seebens is that women secure less land rights and then produce less than male-headed households. However, the land issue is not relevant in the case of Al Dagag. To show how female headed households differ from others in Al Dagag I would like to compare some of the female-headed households with destitute male-headed households in Al Dagag. I will use the female-headed households of Alradeea and Hassina, and the male-headed-households of Balla Ali[21] and Abualgaseem. From this comparison, it becomes apparent that female-headed households are poorer than male-headed households. They are in fact some of the poorest households in Al Dagag, mainly because in the case of female-headed households, only the female is responsible for all matters. One of the reasons for this is that women cannot do all types of work performed by men. For instance, they cannot migrate looking for work outside Al Dagag because of social norms that determine the mobility of women. Consequently, this leaves not a lot of room for diversifications of livelihood patters as for destitute male-headed households. In addition, in case of the two destitute male-headed households, the presence of the household land and the agriculture production out of this land was still supportive especially in good seasons.

It is important to note that female-headed households mainly resort to social networks like kinship and neighborhood as these connections present a very important source of security. A call for help by *Nafeer* from a widowed or divorced woman is more respected. The case of Hassina who is not *Gawama* shows that even within the group of female-headed households there are some differences. Her case reveals that when a female-headed household is at the same time considered a stranger this household often lacks the necessary support and is worse off than other female-headed households are.

In the many occurrences of polygamy in Al Dagag, the wives normally have separate households. I did not come across a case of sharing one household or sharing the cooking facility between wives of the same man. Even if in a polygamous family or household every wife constitutes her own household, the husband is still considered the head of all the households. Examples are the households of Shama and Zainab where the two households are located within the extended family household.

7.6.3 Household Income

It is not within the limit of this research to quantify and calculate the income[22] or to investigate cash inflow and outflow of households under study. Whereas it most important to show generally income resources, uses of income and whether the aggregate of these earning is enough to cover the household needs or not. Howev-

---

[21] The husband of Redeena whom I interviewed; I could not interview the Balla Ali himself, as he was working in the Al Gezira state at that time.

[22] I use the term income as defined by Ellis (2000: 10) and differentiate cash and in-kind components of income. Moreover, it not only represents the earnings that people get from work as it also includes *Shail* and remittances.

er, a brief estimation of income, expenses and savings is conducted in a group interview with the village leaders in order to give a general overview of household incomes, expenses and savings in different seasons of the year. Consequently, the following table was designed in a group interview to get an average view. These calculations are based on an average household, as the number of average people in Al Dagag is six persons per household. These calculations are based on what is considered an average season that is not extremely bad or extremely good. However, an average season means when farmers get agricultural production that is enough for some months but not to cover the expenses of the household till the next season since this is normally the case.

Table 3: Estimated Income, Expenses and Savings of an Average Household of 6 Members in Al Dagag, NKS

Income	**Relevant Months**	**S£**	**Percentage of the Total Income**
Agriculture	July-Oct/Nov	990	57.23
Non-farm activities	During the year	240	13.87
Seasonal migration	February-June	240 per month	13.87
Shail	September	100	5.78
Remittances from other relatives	January-June	50	2.89
Renting two or three *Mukhamas* agricultural land		60	3.47
Women's income from handicraft, collecting and selling dried grass and wood, making and selling charcoal and others	February-June	50	2.89
Total income		**1730**	**100.00**
Expenses			
Food and water	All year	650	37.57
Education		150	8.67
Health		250	14.45
Wajib		80	4.62
Paying back *Shail*	October/November	200	11.56
Land preparation and inputs		150	8.67
Other expenses (e. g., traveling tickets)		200	11.56
Total expenses		**1680**	**97.11**
Savings including livestock	February-July/August	**50**	**2.89**

Source: Group discussion with Al Dagag 21.12.2009
Note: Savings indicate the cash saved or cash used to buy livestock, crop savings is not included in the savings but in the agriculture production.

To my surprise in the survey presented in table 3, *Shail* is listed as a source of the household income and not as credit and later in the expenses also considered as expense that has to be paid. This reflects that *Shail* regularly takes place in most households and is considered a stable source of income in September. Moreover, people calculate the repayment of *Shail* as expense using the current prices which is double than what they have been receiving.

Considering that the main source of income is rain-fed agriculture, it is unsurprising that household income is characterized as subject to significant seasonal fluctuation, which forces people to engage in many activities to diversify their sources of income. The income coming from other sources than agriculture is sizable in summer. The income from seasonal migration is regarded between S£ 40 and S£ 100 to cover the expenses of one or two weeks and it depends on how much the migrants earn and the type of work they find.

Unsurprisingly, a huge amount of the household income is spent on food and water, which reflects the degree of vulnerability. Other expenses considered significant are expenses for health and education. The money paid for *Wajib* was difficult to be calculated since it depends on many factors that will be presented in chapter 8; among them the type of occasion and the relationship with the person. However, the major discussion was about why *Wajib* is not considered a source of income since it is done more regularly than *Shail* and is regarded a considerable expense. The main answer was that while they regularly give *Wajib* they never expect it or consider it an expected income. Although Wajib takes place in a framework of reciprocity, however, when people normally give, they still do not expect a return at a specific time. Calculating *Wajib* as income would mean to break one of the main rules guiding the social behavior of helping each other, is is against what has been discussed by Baker (2000) as the ethics of social relations. It would mean that the relationship is considered built on focusing on what you will get out of the relationship more than what you will give. It is also obvious from table 3 that in a season that is not bad or good but average, people in Al Dagag can still make savings although in a good season they can save more.

To recapitulate, people in Al Dagag not only live from a very small income but they are also challenged by unstable income and vulnerability to many shocks and disasters. Concluding the discussion about household income, I found out that some results are similar and others are different from the classification provided by Ellis (2000: 11f.) when he classifies three types of income, farm, off-farm and non-farm income, where earnings from farming activities include only the cultivation of land. However, in the case of Al Dagag it does not include livestock as mentioned by Ellis because this is regarded as savings; also this category in Al Dagag includes income respondents get from *Shail* contracts something I could not find in any of the literature about livelihood. In Ellis' (2000) model, the off-farm income includes off-farm labor or working on other people's farms and also earnings from local environmental resources such as firewood, charcoal, selling house building materials. However, the income from using local environmental resources mainly comes in summer in Al Dagag when no farming activities take place due to scarcity of water or when there is an emergency and the need to spend more than expected. Finally, Ellis (2000) considers the non-farm income to include salary employment, self-employment and remittances within national or international boundaries. This also applies to the case of Al Dagag where the remittances especially from seasonal migration in summer are considered crucial for household survival.

7.6.4 Household Needs and Expenses

Generally, from the interviews, three levels of financial behavior in households in Al Dagag have become apparent; firstly, people need to provide the basic needs of food and water in the household. The second level regards coping with an emergency like child sicknesses. Thirdly, people try to save some money for any future emergencies and sometimes for investments. These three levels of financial behavior are found in most households depending on the amount of income and on the frequency of shocks and disasters. It also depends on the number of people living in the household.

With no difference between poor and better-off households, all households calculate their food expenses per week, since they buy most households' needs from the Monday market in Al Semaih. The average of household food expenses per week is between S£ 50-150 for the better-off and S£ 15-50 for the poor and destitute.

Normally, household needs are very simple in Al Dagag. It all goes around food and drinking water. What people usually buy every Monday are things they need for preparing meals such as onions, oil, flour, sugar, and sometimes meat. Those who own donkeys pay much less than those who do not when transporting water from the *Hafeer*. Those who do not have donkeys spend about S£ 2-2.5 per day for water for a big household. Other expenses are school fees for students in the Al Dagag primary school, which is calculated S£ 2/month for one student for teachers' beverages, and S£ 11/year for registration. Secondary school students who study in Al Semaih or Al Rahad live in the school and parents have to pay S£ 27 per student per month for food, S£ 75 for school fees per year and some money for personal expenses. Those who are sitting for the Sudanese secondary school certificate have to pay S£ 92 exam registration fees. In both cases, parents have to buy all the books, uniforms, and other school needs. Further expenses are paid for *Wajib*. Furthermore, *Wajib* is also done outside Al Dagag and tickets for traveling are counted as substantial expenses. There are expenses for *Eid* and other Muslim festivals when people spend money on clothes and preparations items. Likewise, they need to rebuild their houses every year since they use non-durable materials. The bulk of the expenses occur in the beginning of the season as people spend a significant amount of money for land preparation and buying inputs. At the end of the season, more expenses occur selling their crops that include transportation and taxes.

Summing up, people in Al Dagag spend what they have and what they can earn; although their needs are so basic, they still cannot afford to cover all of them.

7.6.5 Patterns of Bargaining and Income Allocation

Maybe due to differences between rural and urban areas, I could not classify households in Al Dagag following the four types of income allocation systems that have been distinguished by Schultz et al. (2008: 19) and Schultz (2005: 418). Alternatively, it might also be because the households in Al Dagag share some homogeneous features of ethnicity and class more than the households studied by Schultz. However, many households showed combinations of several income allocation systems. Generally, all the households I studied reflect similar attributes of shared responsibilities and some attributes of income pooling or whole wage system on a few occasions; however, this happens in a general social system where men are considered breadwinners as explained in chapter 2. Indeed, I did not find any households that follow only the system of whole wage allowance, which may be due to the cultural background considering men as the ones with full responsibility, even though women work and contribute to the household basic needs.

Nevertheless, women respondents said they would contribute only when they know that the man does not have any or sufficient money. The shared responsibility is obvious because there are some financial needs that should be covered by men, such as the basic needs, mainly food and water, and others by women, which are often less prioritized needs like education. I have observed from analyzing interviews that spouses sometimes share these responsibilities when one cannot fulfill his/her own. The question arises here who sets priorities and decides about what needs are necessary while others are not. It is revealed from the interviews that men decide which expenses to cover and which they leave to women to take care of, but within the norms of the society that view men as the provider of food and water, which is in line with the findings of Schultz (2005) discussed in chapter 2. Thus, it is always the men who are responsible for food and water and women for other things. Quoting Abdalla as an example for something repeatedly mentioned by other male respondents, "*I'm the man of the house, I'm responsible for covering all household expenses, I keep the money and I buy the household needs. If she needs anything she tells me, even if she has money of her own, I do not ask her to spend in the house unless she wants to.*"

However, it would be sub-complex to describe all respondents' households as pure shared responsibility systems, especially in some cases when the children work inside or outside the village. They give or send the money to one of their parents and sometimes they divide the money between the two. This shows some sort of income pooling where members give their income to the one who is responsible. However, the fact that some children divide the money between their mother and their father also supports my argument that women and men have separate purses within one household. On certain occasions the whole wage system applies for then the whole money will be given to one of them to cover the expenses like in case of child sickness.

I found the cases of Asha Alnoor and Fatima presented above (as female headed households) consistent with the attributes that Schultz (2005) and Schultz et al. (2008) use to describe households where women have taken over the whole responsibility; however their husbands are working and participating but in a minor way. In case of Fatima her husband is mentally sick, while in the case of Asha, her husband works and shares in the households needs, but not to the same degree. In addition, when Asha's husband lost his work, she helped him get a loan from IFAD to start a new business. Asha describes herself as responsible in the household for all the income and expenses; she did not fail to keep her husband to his responsibility, but she found herself quite successful in doing business and now she has more income than her husband does. Still officially, she is not the head of the household. Mainly widows and some of the divorced take full financial household responsibility. For example, Agba Alnoor says: "*After the death of my husband I am now responsible financially for all my unmarried children, even if they are working still, they have to give me the money and I decide how to spend it*".

The social norm of men as the main breadwinner is still considered by respondents but I have some doubts that it takes place the way they describe it. These doubts developed when more thoroughly investigating the role of women in the household. Most respondents stated that the eldest man is considered the head of the household and is normally the responsible person for covering all main household expenses, especially for food and water. When both male and female respondents were directly prompted about who is responsible all mentioned that men are financially responsible. However, in reality, women take a significant part of the household responsibility. In many cases, they contribute when they know that their husband has no money, when their husband migrated in search of work, or when there is an urgent need, especially for buying food. Therefore, I can strongly argue here that the whole household's responsibilities are shared between income earners, especially considering the fact that women have their own income.

What I have described above also reflects aspects of co-operation and conflict in households. For instance, most of the male respondents consider education of their children less important than food and water while the majority of women perceive it as crucial and an urgent household expense. That is why often conflicts occur when a child is discharged from the school for not paying the school fees. Most men consider children's education expenses women should pay whereas women contest this. However, when children are discharged from school, the mother is often the only one who reacts by borrowing or selling her crops, otherwise the father will force the child to stay at home.

Another aspect that describes how the bargaining takes place is the process of decision-making. Generally, I found out that in most cases, husband and wife make financial decisions jointly and discuss together. Even if an agreement is not reached, still the discussion will take place. It also depends on the issue under discussion with no regard to whether it is perceived as the responsibility of the man or the woman. However, in some cases, such as the case of Aldur, husbands do not discuss financial matters with their wives. Aldur did not even know when he applied and received loans from the IFAD credit project. However, she protests that both of them had to handle the situation when he could not pay back. Few women like Batoolay said that they involve their children in their financial decisions. Agba Alnoor, a widow, said that she discusses with her children; however, she will make the final decision even if she has grown up (unmarried children). She decides how to spend the household income; for example, she states, "*When I say this money is better used for buying a sheep, they listen to me and they do what I say*".

I also observed from interviews that conflicting interests within the household lead to such behavior like not telling how much income or cash everyone has in the household. Some knew how much the other partner has; others did not and would not tell. However, generally they know how much agriculture production each one has produced. Most women do not tell men how much they have. They keep the money out of reach of their husbands, because they fear that if their husbands know they will stop spending in the house, knowing that women will not save the money if there is an urgent need for it. Abualgaseem's wife Khadiga mentioned that she will not tell him, because then he will say, "*I do not have money*", and she would have to pay for many things. She did not even want to say that she is involved in a *Sandouq* in front of him; she waited till we were outside to reveal. On the contrary, all male respondents know that women always keep some money aside, some men ask their wives for money when they do not have, others feel ashamed of doing so. For instance, Abdalla said his wife would tell him how much cash she has because she knows that he will not ask her to pay for anything. He continues: "*I do not need to tell her that, when I do not have money she will realize that by herself*". In case they take the money from their wives as loan, sometimes they might pay it back; many times, they even do not if they have promised, but in this case, when a woman asks for money for her own needs, the man will give her.

Married sons are responsible for their new families but still contribute to the household income but not on regular basis. They give priority to their new families even if they live in the same household. In case the parents are very old or sick then their sons are responsible for them. If the parents are still working, they take care of themselves. They can still resort to their married sons whenever they are in urgent need and in some cases; sons give their parents money when they have excess of money. In a few cases, like in the case of Rugaia, children give their parents a fixed amount of money monthly.

Some respondents like Hashim are responsible not only for their small family but also for some members of the extended family like their grandfathers, grandmothers, or unmarried aunts. Hashim is married and lives in the extended family household where his old father and mother live. Since they are quite old, he and his wife take care of them and he is financially responsible for every member of the household. In case of Alnaeem, the only unmarried respondent I interviewed, he is financially responsible for his old mother, father and his unmarried sisters.

Shopping is also a distinguishing factor when financial responsibilities are discussed in the literature (Schultz, 2005: 417). In most cases, men go to the market and buy the household needs; however, some women are given the money to do the shopping. However, this used to not be the case in the past when women were not allowed to go to the market. Most women mentioned that it is better for them to be given the money to decide. Zainab said this is better for her because then she can save some money to pay other things that men normally do not pay. Some women like Um Mohamed and Khamesa do not like to go to the market although they are allowed to do so. They feel uncomfortable because there are many men there and they prefer to send one of their sons when their husband is not around. In reverse, men do not like to give their wives cash, since they do not know on what items women spend the money. They only give their wives cash when they work outside Al Dagag and even then, this still needs to be negotiated. However, some male respondents like Hafiz believe that women manage money better than men do. Hafiz states, "*When I go to the market I use all the money I have, but when my wife goes she usually comes back with all what we need plus some cash money back*".

I would like to conclude this discussion by arguing that despite the general social attribute of men as breadwinners, the income allocation system opens up areas of negotiation and bargaining because there are no crosscuts for who is responsible for what. In addition, women have their own income and they exercise control over the use of this income. Moreover, as I said above, all this takes place in households that suffer chronic poverty and vulnerability, where people have not many options and only look for survival. These current trends construct a new way of thinking and new behavior in the Al Dagag community, which reflect, as I believe, a change that takes place with regard to the view of men as breadwinners. The conflicts arising within the households reflect resistance to the new trends. It is obvious that there is a shift from looking at men as breadwinners to patterns of more shared responsibilities where women have more room to contribute to the welfare of the household. This is obvious in the way that women are taking many and increasing responsibilities in the household. Behaviors that were not acceptable in the past are becoming common now, like women going to the market.

7.6.6 Household Savings

In this part of the chapter, savings will be discussed as a financial behavior, which takes place in most households in Al Dagag. All respondents, regardless whether they are destitute, poor or better-off, mentioned that they saved at one point of time. As it will be explained later, the type and volume of savings is used to distinguish the destitute, poor and better-off people in Al Dagag.

With regard to the discussion of who saves in the household, many respondents mentioned that even if the savings are done individually they still constitute the "household savings" which can be used for any household emergency regardless who saved. This is mainly because savings are used to cover the cost of emergencies and all members of the household should contribute in such a stressful time. The other issue is that agriculture production from the household land is the main source of "household savings". However, some women also save separately from the household savings, one option being a *Sandouq*.

Generally, women save more than men because they do not have to use all their income to cover household expenses and therefore it is easier for them to have surplus money. Some women believe that their husbands save money for emergencies while the majority of men believe that all women save regularly. Even the destitute like Umbelal and Alradeea save some of the produced crop for emergencies although they do not save cash money and if they do it is the form of *Sandouq* that puts them in a commitment to pay. They also save more in a good season. Most respondents state that savings depend on whether the season is good or not. In bad seasons not many, sometimes no savings at all are kept. Thus, it is observable in Al Dagag that savings as well as the other aspects of peasants' life depend on the quality of the season.

Some of the better-off are the *Shail* traders who mentioned that they save mainly to invest the money. Asha Alnoor, Zainab, Farhana and Rugaia believe that it is better for them and more rewarding to invest their savings in business and trade. Thus, they save to invest the saved money not like the poor and destitute who save to cover expenses in the case of an emergency. As in the case of Asha Alnoor saving part of her profits has always helped her to upgrade and sustain her businesses. Moreover, she did not only use savings to develop an existing business but in other times, she used them to start a new business. She also keeps other people's savings when she is asked.[23]

7.6.6.1 Savings in Livestock: Changes of Patterns

The majority of respondents prefer to buy livestock or save in crops. The main reason for saving in livestock is that they grow up and breed, and in both cases, they generate more money that can be used for any emergencies. Furthermore, livestock is saved in order to get higher prices in the future. However, it is not common to sell milk in Al Dagag, because this is believed to be shameful, unless the person is a destitute like Umsalama who used to sell the milk for money. Rather the milk is used in the household as it is used as one of the important components of most meals.[24]

This matches the findings of Ashley and Nanyeenya (2005: 243) that one of the main roles of keeping livestock in rural areas is mainly to enable household savings. Raising livestock then is therefore not considered an occupation or livelihood pattern. Whereas livestock are commonly purchased with money, it does not need to be spent immediately and can therefore serve as savings. Thus, livestock plays the role of banks, but it is even better than the bank since livestock grow and breed in a fast mode. Moreover, livestock can simply be liquidated and turned into cash and bring other benefits to the household, which the bank does not. In addition to that, banks are not available in rural villages and people refrain from dealing with banks with regard to savings (ibid.).

In contrast to what has been mentioned in the literature about rural livelihood and the history of NKS, the role of livestock has changed to a great extent. From the individual interview and the interviews with the *Ameer* of the *Gawama* tribe and the former and current *Shaikhs* of Al Dagag and other elderly people, it is clear that rising livestock or herding was the most important livelihood activity of the first inhabitants of Al Dagag in 1918. At that time, agriculture was considered as secondary livelihood pattern. However, since the severe famine in 1983/84 things have changed gradually. Followed by the drought of the 1990s, people tend to do more farming than rising livestock as a source of income, and agriculture has become the main livelihood pattern in the area by now.

Consequently, livestock raising is not considered an occupation or a livelihood pattern used to provide a steady source of income like mentioned by Ellis (2000), but it is rather considered a way of saving. Thus, represents one way the poor use to reduce vulnerability to shocks and disasters.

Another change that took place in Al Dagag as a consequence of the natural disasters is the type and number of livestock raised. The main livestock available in Al Dagag includes goats, sheep, and

---

[23] With regard to how they keep their savings, most respondents mentioned that they keep their cash savings by themselves while few said that they keep their savings with somebody else like Asha Alnoor.who is allowed to use the money for her business under the condition that whenever they need it they can get it. This is free of interest. Others said they save with Mansora, the *Shaikh*'s wife. Both Asha and Mansora are also *Sandouq* organizers. Most women respondents mentioned that the reasons for choosing these two for keeping cash savings are the same as for choosing them to be the *Sandouqs* organizers as explained in chapter 10.

[24] Also milk is used to extract yogurt or fat called *Samin* which is used as a food component. The traditional dish in Al Dagag consists of a porridge *Asida* made from sorghum, which is served with one of many different sauces, *Mulah* made of fried onion, water, dried and powdered meat, and *Samin* made of dried okra powder or of sour milk, or porridge with milk, sugar and *Samin* for evening meals.

chicken and donkeys,[25] as the former and the current *Shaikhs* of Al Dagag explain. In the past their grandfathers had more cows and camels which are more expensive than sheep and goats; at that time the wealth of the man was counted by the number of cows and camels, the more he had the richer he was. The number of sheep and goats possessed by households in Al Dagag has also drastically decreased. Livestock possession range between 2 and 23 but the majority of households has 4-10.[26] The Al Dagag *Shaikh* mentioned that in the past people used to count their sheep possession in hundreds of livestock, and at that time livestock was considered a source of income. Most households raise their own small number of livestock at home; in this case, any member of the household will take care of them but normally it is women and children.[27]

The ownership of livestock is perceived as joint ownership; however, it is also considered who bought the livestock. This is well known and discussed in the household, as some respondents answered, "*The livestock are mine*", others said, "*They are ours*". Omima continued, "*I had a small sack of hibiscus, I sold it and bought the chicken*", thereby insisting on her ownership. However, livestock will be liquidated as soon as an emergency comes regardless the owner.

To conclude, evaluating the consequences of recent natural disasters, major changes concerning types of livestock raised and livestock possession compared to the history of the area were observed. The number of livestock is much smaller than before and the possession of expensive kinds of livestock like cows and camels by which NKS was famous has changed to goats and sheep, which are considered much cheaper. Due to these changes, raising livestock is now regarded as the best saving opportunity rather than a main source of regular income. The main expected consequence of this change is an increasing vulnerability of people in Al Dagag.

In the conclusion of this chapter, I would like to link what I have described about rural livelihood in Al Dagag to the main thinking of the livelihood approach. People in fact manage their livelihood strategies and options in the absence of any help from specialized institutions and use local resources and capital available to them. Decisions about diversification of patterns of livelihood are taken within the household and by all household members in the context of limited opportunities looking for survival at a very basic level. Moreover, considering the many changes taking place it is obvious that these changes to a great extent affect the livelihood patterns of the people, their activities, and capital; and make them dynamic as they respond to changes. One can argue here that these changes and the dynamics of livelihood constitute an addition to the definition of livelihood provided in chapter 2. Changes in all forms of capital and resources, in people's capabilities to attain only minimum living standards, in people's and households' attitudes toward shifts in their life, and changes in institutions' behavior are to be considered in the definition of livelihood. Thus, livelihood does not only encompass forms of capital, activities and access that determine the living gained by people, but also how the shifts and changes in these aspects affect what people are able and capable to gain.

---

[25] Hassan uses the donkey with a cart which he got as a loan from the IFAD credit project as a means of public transportation within Al Dagag and to reach the nearest villages. He judges this as one of his main sources of income. Very few respondents' households do not have donkeys, mainly because they are used for bringing water from the *Hafeer*, transporting crops, dried grass, wood and people. However there is a considerable number of households who do not have livestock with the exception of having donkeys. Only one person who is considered better-off/rich has a little number of cows and two camels.

[26] The current prices of livestock are different depending on their type, sex, age and size. An average size goat could be sold for S£ 70-75, while an average size sheep could be S£ 120-150. The main source of money for buying livestock mentioned by respondents is agricultural production. Few got the livestock they possess now as a credit from the IFAD credit project.

[27] Sometimes livestock are kept in a separate place within the household called *Zareeba* (a separate place inside the household for keeping livestock). Otherwise they will be given to a herdsman to take care of in the open spaces around Al Dagag called *Al Khala* (valley or open space). The herdsman is normally a family member or close relative, he is paid sometimes in livestock. for instance when taking care of 20 sheep and goats for two months he will get one sheep or goat. Normally the animals are taken to the *Hafeer* to drink; this costs S£ 1 for 20 livestock.

8 Poverty and Vulnerability in Al Dagag

"*The poor person is the person who does not have a 'decent life'—Hayat kareema*" (Part of Hassan's perspective of the poor in Al Dagag, in-depth interview, 2009).

"*In Sudan Wajib is one of the important institutions which structure the social life of the people, give them security and reinforce social networks*" (Schultz et al., 2008: 26).

8.1 Introduction

From what has been discussed in the previous two chapters, it is revealed that poverty prevails in Sudan and the situation is even worse in rural areas. NKS is one of the poorest regions in Sudan, where poverty is linked to rain-fed agriculture. As noted in the IFAD project document of Western Sudan Resource Management (2004), at household level poverty is maintained through a low input/low output agriculture that renders smallholder farmers vulnerable to de-capitalization because of drought and conflicts over resources.[1] Older people and female-headed households are poorer and more vulnerable because of limited opportunities of labor, education and mobility. At community level, poverty is sustained by poor access and underdevelopment of services, especially health, education, water and roads that undermine the long-term investment in productive capacities of inhabitants. Destruction of farming and grazing land by local communities undermines long-term investments in any productive capacity. According to the household survey conducted by IFAD (2004), destitute households lacking both assets and labor power constitute around 25 % of the total NKS population. Poor households (those owning few assets and characterized by high vulnerability) are about 30 %, while less poor households (households that can satisfy their basic needs but may be vulnerable to a serious crisis) make up about 26 % (Sidgig et al., 2007: 11). This reveals the severity of poverty and vulnerability in NKS, on community and household level.

In this chapter, the three main categories, which emerged from data analysis concerning poverty and vulnerability, are discussed. These three categories are poverty, vulnerability and wellbeing and security. Respondents themselves do not mention the world vulnerability as there is no exact matching word in the Arabic language.[2] Generally, vulnerability in Al Dagag is described as exposure to shocks and natural disasters.

The first sub-chapter is devoted to drawing attention to how people perceive themselves and others within the context of poverty and vulnerability. Interesting in this discussion is the classification people have developed to distinguish between destitute, poor and better-off people and households in Al Dagag and what attributes are linked to each category; how they are seen by themselves and by others. The answer to the question, who are the most vulnerable people in Al Dagag, is revealed to show that most people in Al Dagag are considered vulnerable but to different degrees, depending on the classification of people as destitute, poor and better-off.

In the following sub-chapter, the main reasons of poverty and vulnerability are discussed, before shocks and natural disasters taking place in Al Dagag are presented. While they are called shocks in the literature, in Al Dagag they are called emergencies or in Arabic *Tawaree*. The word emergency is used by all respondents to describe the personal shocks that might happen in any household to include such stress that urges more expenses than usual like sicknesses, disabilities and death. Happy occasions are also included like weddings and birth giving. In the last sub-chapter I will show the distinctiveness of the rural societies where social networks are significant for sustaining people's livelihood. Two main theoretical categories of coping strategies and social capital as insurance mechanism are described under the discussion about the meaning of wellbeing and security in Al Dagag.

---

[1] The IFAD perception of poverty and livelihood is described in the IFAD report (2009: 5). For IFAD rural finance is "one of several important areas for investment in poverty reduction through agricultural and rural livelihoods development. In addition, access to financial services can be instrumental in coping with income shocks such as severe weather events, increases in commodity prices and unexpected life events. While rural finance is not a panacea for poverty reduction, access to financial services plays an important role in empowering poor people to create their own pathways out of poverty."

[2] This is called in Arabic *Al tarood lel* (exposure to) *twoaree* (emergencies) and *kawareeth* (disasters).

8.2 Perception of Poverty in Al Dagag: Destitute, Poor and Better-off

Generally, what is going on at the state level is mirrored at the village level, in Al Dagag. The description provided by respondents for their situations in Al Dagag is consistent with what has been described in the introduction of this chapter. Thus, the situation in Al Dagag is not an exception of what is going on in NKS.

In the main course of data collection and analysis, it became apparent that poverty is a topic that people in Al Dagag talking about even if not asked, since it is linked to their livelihood and their daily life. People describe their situation and find linkages between changes in the surrounding environment and the severity of poverty and vulnerability. In addition to that, what respondents have generally described confirms what is explained in the livelihood approach including the discussion about capabilities and different types of capital. People do not ignore the importance of income but also include other needs and other forms of capital, not only the economic, in discussing poverty and vulnerability. Besides, it is revealed that the language used by the poor themselves matches the language of the capabilities approach since respondents talk about what they have and what they do not have, what they are able to do and what they are not able to do. Moreover in discussing poverty, the question arises if what people have (resources or capital) affects what they can do (capabilities and livelihood strategies) and vice versa; thus, how different types of capital affect people's capabilities and strategies and consequently influence their livelihood.

Almost all respondents stated that in Al Dagag most households and people are considered poor. Their poverty is generally described by the term "*they have nothing*"; most respondents explain the term "having nothing" as lack of "steady income, savings and assets". People explicitly and regularly used the words "income" and "savings"; while they did not mention the exact words of assets or capital in describing poverty, the analysis revealed many aspects mentioned by people could fit in the meaning of assets or capital that is used in the livelihood approach. To explain further, I grouped some aspects mentioned by people around the meaning of assets or capital and Sen's meaning of capabilities. For instance, education, ability and accessibility of labor, adoption of technologies, water supply, and many other services could to some extent represent different types of capital. Consequently, they determine people's capabilities. Moreover, in their explanation they always stressed the term "steady" which also reflects the desire for sustainable livelihood and expresses the vulnerability of people. What is also interesting in this discussion is that the term of "having something or nothing" is used further to classify people into those who have more and people who have less. Thereby, savings and assets are considered as the crucial conditions to be better-off.

Many of the respondents claim that nobody in Al Dagag is rich but some are better-off than others are. Hameed explains: "*Even the few rich people in Al Dagag should be regarded as better-off but not as rich compared to the rich people living in urban cities, who have nice houses and cars*". In contrast, those who have less are considered poor although most respondents argued that not all the poor live at the same standard. As a result, the category of the poor itself is classified further into poor (*Miskeen*) and destitute (*Modam*). To sum up, people and households in Al Dagag are poor because of the lack of (steady) income, savings and assets. In addition to that, they are classified into better-off, poor and destitute according to these factors.

How do people perceive themselves and others? There are a considerable number of respondents who consider themselves poor. In contrast, very few of the respondents classified themselves as better-off like Asha Alnoor, who is proud of her successful businesses. However, mostly respondents who are better-off, when asked to classify themselves, say they either live in average living conditions or they use the phrase of "*we are better than some people and worse than others*". This might be because they compare themselves to the rich people who live in the urban cities, for example Hassan.

To show how people do not use only income as measure for their poverty I will use the Hassan as example. Hassan is considered by others as better-off because he is a university graduate who worked in the Gulf area for long time and came back with "*knowledge and money*". However, in his words, "*I have an average standard of living; I'm better off than some people and worse than others*". According to Hassan, the poor constitute the majority of the Al Dagag population. He specifies that in Al Dagag 99 % of the people are poor and destitute; the one remaining percent only consists of 4 persons who are better-off. These are mainly Hafiz, Asha Alnoor, Basheer and Shaikh Ahmed.

In the same line of reasoning of how people classify themselves, I found that they compare themselves with other people either in Al Dagag or in urban areas. To illustrate, some poor respondents, in describing their situation, compare on one side between themselves and the better-off in Al Dagag, on the other side they refer to people in cities. Alradeea who identifies herself as one of those who "*have nothing*", not even any kind of livestock explains: "*I have nothing but what is worse is when I see other people having more and better than what I have, at the same time I cannot have the same, then I'm poor... I feel this more when I go to Khartoum where people are much better than us*". Umbelal who works for money since her children are young also mentions, "*when I compare my children with other ones, my children are hungry and have no shoes and nice clothes, I always felt ashamed, because it is not their fault it is mine*". Omima who believes that she is one of the poor compares herself to both the better-off and the destitute saying, *"I'm in the middle, not rich and not poor... I'm not destitute because I have one goat and donkey and the father of my kids is alive staying with us and works to bring me things... I'm not rich because I do not have many livestock or a shop"*.

Therefore, the result of analysis indicates that the poor identify themselves as poor by distinguishing themselves from others in Al Dagag. At another level, this shows that the poor are aware of the differences between their situation and the situation of the rich people in urban areas.

People describe the better-off as the ones who have a steady source of income like a salary, a successful trade, or grown up and educated children who work outside Al Dagag. The households of the better-off differ from other households because these income sources help people to accumulate assets, which can be used in the case of an emergency or for investing in economic opportunities. It is clear that the education of children is realized as important since a household with a number of educated children employed in formal positions, especially in the capital city, are considered better-off or sometimes poor, but never considered destitute. Traders and shopkeepers, especially the *Shail* traders, are identified as better-off people since trading is considered a profitable investment that provides a higher and a steadier source of income than agriculture. Some respondents who are considered better-off combine more than one attribute like in the case of Basheer who in addition to his educated children working in Khartoum, is a successful crop and livestock trader. Besides there are few cases of people who are formally employed like Rugaia, Farhana and Hamed who are considered better-off. To give another example, Dawa, the midwife, perceives herself not as poor because she has the skills, knowledge and training to do other work than agriculture. She explains that before working as midwife, she was poor but now she is not. It is clear here that people in Al Dagag consider education and knowledge important when classifying people; this reflects how important the human capital could be for sustaining livelihood.

Generally, what is shared between all better-off households is that they tend to be secure in terms of income, have saved assets and are therefore less affected by emergencies and disasters. In addition, concerning agriculture they get more production because they can hire laborers regularly, rent tractors for weeding, and buy enough inputs. This is mainly because most people in Al Dagag depend on agricultural production to cover household consumption of food and water. Hassan is for instance considered better-off also because he owns a water pump and normally produces more than the others. In 2010 when I visited Al Dagag, there was a severe crop failure due to rain shortage and crop diseases. People were very worried how to get the sorghum needed for food for the next season but Hassan had a good production of sorghum because of his water pump.

Considering the fact that livestock is the best savings opportunity, people are classified according to the number of livestock they possess. For instance, the richest man in Al Dagag is identified by having the biggest number of livestock. He is also the only one in the entire village who possesses species of cattle and camel.

In contrast, the poor are identified by having less livestock than the better-off people. Thus, the poor and destitute are identified according to their low income, their inability to farm their own land, since most of them are not able to buy inputs or do the weeding at the beginning of the season due to the lack of money. Beside this, they need to take any work available to get a daily income, which would help to cover their households' needs. They are also classified as those who have less ownership of assets. Furthermore, the destitute are identified and well known in the village. When I asked about who is considered poorest, the answer was given by name. Most respondents described the destitute as those who cannot find the daily food for their children. Accordingly, they are those who not only have no regular source of income but also have fewer assets or none at all. For instance, Hassan believes that "*the Modam (destitute) is the person who has to work as laborer because he cannot cultivate his land and in case he cannot find work, he fails to get his daily expenses; then he and his family will be starving*". Hassan further defines the destitute person as "*the one who cannot sleep at night thinking about what his family will eat tomorrow*", a destitute is therefore a person who does not have a decent life or in Hassan's words: "*Haya kareema*". The number, age, education and employment of children are also used to distinguish the poor, since most poor and destitute households have bigger number of young children.

To illustrate the difference between the poor and the destitute further, I refer to what is stressed by many respondents. For instance, Kaltoom, Agba Alnoor and Batoolay are considered poor but not destitute because they do not have any steady source of income on the one hand but they have their children working in the capital on the other hand. Dawa explains: "*Poor people differ, there are some people who do not have even food for today, they normally have many children, this includes people like widows and divorced women who are the worst or old women without kids they are Modameen, others have few assets like small amount of crops or one to two livestock they can sell them and buy food they are Mosakeen*". I have also found that most of the poor own livestock of 2-5, mainly goats and sheep, whereas most of the destitute either do not have any livestock or just have one donkey and some chicken.

Respondents think that a poor person is somebody who does not have enough agricultural production to cover the expenses of the household of food and water until the next season. However, some of these people are considered not destitute because they have some sort of savings to resort to or are able to do other types of work in or outside Al Dagag. A destitute person is perceived as one who does not even have enough food for all members of the household, in other words, he/she is the one who has to get his/her income on a daily basis from working for other people besides farming in their own land.

On the other hand, it is observable from what respondents said that *Shail* is used to distinguish the poor from the better-off and the regularity of taking *Shail* is also used to differentiate poor from destitute households. Whereas some of the better-off are the *Shail* traders, the poor are those who are in need to take *Shail* since they have less or no savings to depend on in case the agricultural production is not enough for household survival. Consequently, they need to take *Shail* in September to cover the basic needs of the households such as food and water in addition to other expenses. Moreover, those who are in need to take *Shail* every year are seen as destitute while the poor depend first on the few assets they possess before resorting to take *Shail*. This means that the poor do not take *Shail* as regularly as the destitute do.

Most male respondents associated their poverty with their need to migrate looking for work outside Al Dagag. Alshaikh who has five young children states that this is psychologically disturbing in the way that they have no other options available in Al Dagag and they are worried about not finding the work or being less paid outside Al Dagag. Moreover, migrants suffer from being away from their families and complain that in other places they do very hard work for very little income.

Respondents also mentioned the number and the type of meals as a distinguishing factor. Some respondents reveal that the poor eat two meals or sometimes one meal per day while the better-off eat three meals per day. In regard to the type of food eaten, few respondents believe that the difference is obvious. The difference emphasizes mainly on whether people can regularly buy fresh meat and fruits, which is possible for the better-off, or cannot afford, which is the case for the poor.[3] However, I can observe that it is not a significant issue in differentiating between people. Meanwhile, the number of meals is more significant; since I find it relevant to many respondents who repeatedly mention it.

To conclude, even with all what I have discussed above, it seems not easy to identify the better-off from their living conditions. Despite all this discussion, entering into most of Al Dagag houses I could observe only a slight difference concerning the content of the household like furniture, the places for keeping livestock inside the houses, the building material, types of meals or the organization of the household. Most of the households are similar regarding these aspects, only slight differences like having big and nice cupboards for clothes and kitchen utensils or the number of beds and chairs could be observed. Moreover, people in Al Dagag share the same social services, they drink the same water, they do the same livelihood activities, and they are challenged by the same environmental problems. This also explains Rugaia's statement that even if she is better than the others, she still lives just like the poor.

---

[3] I found out that the poor also eat meat but dried meat that can be kept for long times and used in small quantities to prepare one meal.

8.3 Identifying the Vulnerable in Al Dagag

Whereas the focus on defining a poor person is mainly steady income, followed by savings and assets, the vulnerable person is defined specifically as the person who has no or few saved assets to sell in cases of shocks and disasters. The majority of respondents states that the vulnerable person in Al Dagag is the one who does not have savings in money, crops or livestock to be used in the future in cases of emergencies and disasters. This falls in line with ideas of Chambers (1989: 1) and Swift (1998) presented in chapter 2 that vulnerability is measured in terms of assets people control.

However, this also reveals that the meanings of poverty and vulnerability are interlinked to some extent in Al Dagag. When defining a poor person as mentioned above, it is clear that the use of the word "steady" also indicates the vulnerability dimension. This obviously includes what have been discussed in the literature for instance by Naudé et al. (2008) who explains vulnerability as when people are exposed to fall into or remain in severe poverty. From the respondents' point of view about who is the vulnerable person in Al Dagag, vulnerability is defined as their exposure to unexpected contingencies, risks, emergencies and disasters that might distress their life. Indeed, the term emergency or *Tawaree* in Arabic is used by most respondents to describe sudden events that can happen in the household or to any of its members that needs more expenses than expected. This is the same like the words "shocks or risks" that are used in the literature.[4]

Respondents differentiate between emergencies that are personal and natural disasters. Emergencies are regarded as any stress that happens to them individually or to any member of the household; or starts individually and spreads to other households. Thus, emergencies are either individual or general. Respondents presented many examples of individual emergencies such as deaths, accidents, sicknesses, discharging children from school for not paying the school fees and so on. Paying *Wajib* is also considered an emergency since it is an unexpected expense that needs to be paid. An example of general emergencies provided is the outbreak of fire that normally starts by carelessness of some people and in many times ends up burning the neighboring houses.

Natural disasters are caused by uncontrollable natural hazards and affect all people in the village like droughts.[5] Both emergencies and natural disasters are normally believed to be serious matters and to threaten the peacefulness of people's daily life.

This goes in line with the definition of vulnerability by Chambers (1989) as mentioned in chapter 2, that vulnerability means defenselessness and exposure to different types of stress and risks and implies the difficulty to cope with them. In addition to that, the definition of vulnerability provided by the respondents in Al Dagag fits Wisner's et al. (2004: 11) explanation that vulnerability is identified as the factors that determine the degree to which people's life, livelihood, property and other assets are put at risk by discrete and identifiable events in the nature or in the society. However, regarding the meaning of vulnerability in Al Dagag the focus is not only on food shortages or famines as illustrated by Sen (1987) or Ellis and Freeman (2005). Although people are concerned about food shortages because they mainly produce for subsistence, respondents also provide a wider definition of vulnerability than that of acute food insecurity. Respondents include many emergencies like paying school fees or sickness. The inclusion of paying *Wajib* reflects the fact that people are also concerned when emergencies happen in other households. This broadens the definition of vulnerability to cover more than only food shortage. Thus, people not only die in famine as explained by Sen (1980, 1982), they could also physically die from sickness, accidents or tribal conflicts or socially from not contributing to the social life in the village. This argument is supported by Swift (1989). By living on such vulnerable conditions, people live on the edge as described by Ellis and Freeman (2005).

To conclude, reviewing the respondents' perception of poverty and vulnerability, poverty is mainly characterized by the lack of a steady and sufficient income and the lack of savings and assets, while vulnerability is perceived mainly as lack of savings that can support a household when it passes through any future hard-

---

[4]Many writers used the terms risks and shocks and some like Dercon (2005: 10) define both as shock used to mean a realization of a risky process. In the literature the term shock is used to reflect rather large deviations form expected outcomes, usually in a negative way, although positive shocks may exist as well. Sometimes terms are used interchangeably like risks, stress, contingencies, for example in Chambers (1989).

[5] The term disasters is used in most literature about the topic and defined by Wisner et al- (2004: 3) as caused by natural hazards

ship. It is clear that the theoretical argumentation discussed in chapter 2 is very clear in the case of Al Dagag that vulnerability is not the same as poverty but they are both connected and linked to lack of steady income and savings. Poverty makes people more vulnerable mainly because the poor have less income than required to save assets. Other factors like being forced to take *Shail*, illiteracy, lack of skills and a great number of children are also raised; for they aggravate both poverty and vulnerability.

With regard to who is poor and who is vulnerable, the answer to this question is raised from the definition of poverty and vulnerability provided by the respondents above. It is obvious that the majority of the Al Dagag population is poor and all of the population is vulnerable to different types of risks. However, they are vulnerable to varying degrees, depending on different factors that determine their ability to cope and resist, mainly the assets they have. In Al Dagag, these are the household's possession of livestock, physical and human assets in addition to the social relations and connections. The more access people have to these resources, the less vulnerable they are.

Moreover, given the definition of the economists of poverty as the failure to reach a minimum acceptable consumption level of food, one can argue that this definition does not include all of what the respondents in Al Dagag have mentioned about their situation. The theoretical perception focuses more on the income to buy food and disregards other types of capital like human (e. g., importance of education and other social services), and natural (e. g., land, types of soil, climate, rains, etc.). In other words, the type and measurement of poverty explained by the economists does not capture the whole meaning of poverty in Al Dagag considering how people define poverty and how they differentiate between destitute, poor and better-off. However, even in the case of Al Dagag, income is considered central to the discussion of poverty. Having low or high, stable or fluctuating, seasonal or steady income distinguishes the poor from the better-off, but within a framework that includes many other factors.

The perception of people in Al Dagag with regard to poverty and vulnerability is more consistent with the discussion provided within the livelihood theoretical thinking of writers like Chambers and Conway (1992), Chambers (1995, 1996), Ellis (2000), Ellis and Freeman (2005), Scoones (1998), and others presented in chapter 2. What people in Al Dagag are looking for is what has been described theoretically as wellbeing by Chambers when he refers to the human experience, not only the material but also the social, spiritual and mental. The opposite of people's situation in Al Dagag is conceptualized as a secured life that is described by having a better standard of living. This better standard is described by the Al Dagag people in terms of a stable source of income, access to basic services, security, and freedom from fear about how they will survive the next day, health, good relations with others, friendship, peace of mind, choice, creativity, fulfillment and fun. Moreover, people in Al Dagag added the dimension of not being forced to take loans from anyone or to be indebted to anyone or any organization.

The most relevant definition of livelihood mentioned in the theoretical debate that can be used for the situation of the people in Al Dagag is the one provided by Ellis (2000: 10). According to Ellis, livelihood includes assets of different kinds, activities and access that are mediated by institutions and social networks. These factors determine the standard of living for each rural household. How people use these assets, which activities they undertake, what type, and how important the existence of institutions and social networks is—these are the main questions addressed in the case of Al Dagag. Another crucial theoretical argumentation relevant to the case of Al Dagag is the link between assets and the options people possess to pursue alternative activities and opportunities that can generate the income level necessary for survival. One can think of the human assets, financial assets and other types of assets, to show how they are important in shaping the livelihood opportunities in Al Dagag.

8.4 Reasons of Poverty and Vulnerability

In the light of how the people in Al Dagag describe their poverty and vulnerability, it is important to draw attention to the reasons and causes of such phenomena. Almost all respondents think that the main reason for poverty in Al Dagag is their dependency on rain-fed agriculture as their main source of income considering that rains are seasonal. Thus, they lack any regular source of income that enhances savings and capital or assets. Many other factors are stated to worsen this situation.

One respondent, Rugaia who is one of the better-off believes that the lack of capital, investment mentality, and opportunities in Al Dagag are the main causes of poverty. She argues that because of the hardship people in Al Dagag cannot think about any investments even when they have a good season. They rather tend to save instead of investing.

Some respondents think that the main cause of poverty is the competition of poor and rich people over resources and opportunities. They gave the example of the IFAD credit project. They believe that IFAD provided credits to the better-off instead of targeting the poor, pointing to the problem of élites capturing the outreach of the project.

The *Ameer* or the head of the native system of the *Gawama* tribe in North Kordofan mentions some other causes of poverty in Al Dagag and names the main cause of poverty in the cultural heritage of being consumers but not investors, for people in NKS have subsistence economy since they produce only for their household consumption and all activities are directed to survival not to investment. He thinks that the people in Al Dagag do not inherit the gene of making money, investing and taking risks. Furthermore, he argues that NKS and specifically the Al Rahad locality used to be one of the richest localities in the past. They had a huge number of livestock that included expensive species. However, he argues, no money was used for investment but rather for consumption that left the new or the current generation deprived, vulnerable and poor. Additionally, he explains that the climatic change caused disasters like droughts and desertification and has thereby affected to a great extent the livestock possession in the area. The *Ameer* also mentions that the famine in 1983/84 and again in the 1990s resulted in the highest loss of natural resources in the area in history. Furthermore, he thinks that this has led to changes in the types of crops grown in the area, the vegetation cover and the water availability in the area. Furthermore, respondents also mention natural disasters like drought as reasons of poverty and vulnerability. He gives another cause of poverty, which is the rapid and uncontrollable increase in prices of the main consumption goods not only in NKS but in the entire country that is not matched by any increase in incomes.

Many other factors are viewed to play a major role in the deteriorating situation that people live in. Respondents like Dawa and Rugaia argue that both poverty and vulnerability become severe in the absence of any financial support. They emphasize on the provision of financial support that is directed to enhance agriculture in terms of loans designed to provide agriculture inputs and loans to start the season or loans to enhance the water supply improvements that they assume to lead to significant increases in agricultural production. Others realize their need for finance to be directed towards improving agricultural technologies and systems. The use of pumps is specifically pointed out as a means to reduce both poverty and vulnerability to seasonality of rains and thus having steady agriculture production and income. For instance, Haloum argues that people of Al Dagag are poor mainly because they do their farming activities manually and they do not have machines like pumps and tractors. She believes that if she had a tractor and water pump she would not be poor. In addition, she compares Al Dagag with other villages in the Al Semaih mechanized agriculture scheme and thinks that those villages are much better off than Al Dagag.

Kaltoom, one of the poor and others respondents mention further factors, as they think that the main cause of deteriorating living conditions is that people are lazy and not hard workers, especially men working only until midday. Conflicts like competition between the better-off and the poor over resources are also mentioned repeatedly.

Respondents view the lack or inappropriate social services to be an additional factor that worsens their living conditions. Poor social services like health, education and poor infrastructure and services like transportation and electricity are considered among other factors. It is unforgettable what Hassan mentions, that even if he has some money and wants to send his children to better schools he cannot because there is only one primary public school in Al Dagag. According to Hassan, the poor quality of education provided in the primary school in the village is one of the factors that worsen the degree of poverty of Al Dagag people. Many respondents think that they are getting worse because they are not educated, sick and further have no money or savings to cope with such situations.

In addition to that, respondents explain another factor that makes them poor and further contributes to their deteriorating conditions to be their need to take *Shail*. They believe this makes them even poorer. Being indebted to the *Shail* traders is perceived by most of the respondents as not only the cause of poverty and vulnerability but also as a cause of the deterioration of their situation. To give an example, Amna, who is one of the destitute and used to take *Shail* every year, explains that the poor person might become destitute when taking *Shail* because she had to repay using the production of the whole season for the very little money from the *Shail* trader. Amna explains further that if she is not forced by her situation to take *Shail*, then she can sell her crops for higher prices and keep some as savings and as seeds for the next season. Amna expresses her feelings when crops are collected for repaying *Shail*, "*Even if I need and take Shail it is so bad that I almost get a heart attack when they come to collect the crop I spend the whole season cultivating*".

While the IFAD project in Al Dagag helped a few people to graduate out of poverty, at the same time the project was repeatedly mentioned as a cause of poverty. Some of the respondents report that taking loans from the IFAD project through both the ABS and Al Dagag village fund left them worse off than before. Besides the rigid and confusing procedures of the project, loans were not significantly directed toward agriculture but were used for consumption and not for production. Thus, respondents had to sell their assets or borrow to repay their loans to the project. Respondents like Hashim said in his own words that the loan he received from the IFAD project was the starting point of his deterioration.

Some respondents refer to religious and supernatural phenomena in explaining why some people are poor and others are not. They mention that poverty is caused by God to test their belief and patience. They believe that they cannot do anything to fight poverty as long as God is the source. They depend on the religious belief; insist that anything bad or good, which happens to people, comes from God. They believe that their bad situation will be over when God permits and wants it. People refer to their belief as a coping strategy that helps them cope with any time of hardship, knowing that God will help them. In some cases, they add the phrase that "*even if we are poor of money we are rich of belief and patience because we depend on God.*"

Some respondents like Hassan, Fadelalla and Haloum also stress the problem of migration of young boys without completing their education as a cause of poverty.[6]

To sum up this sub-chapter, people in Al Dagag perceive the main cause of poverty and vulnerability in their dependency on rain-fed agriculture, the severe climate changes and decreasing percentage of rains over the recent years. Other reasons identified include lack of technology, lack of financial support, lack of social services, poor infrastructure, *Shail*, natural disasters and competition between people over resources and finally some cultural and religious factors.

8.5 Emergencies and Disasters in Al Dagag

I would like to start by presenting the table 4 that summarizes and differentiates between emergencies and disasters mentioned by respondents in Al Dagag. Generally, every type of emergency or disaster produces different consequences and impacts. The most common impact of individual and general emergencies includes loss of people, reduction of labor, and loss of assets among others. While the most immediate effects of general and natural disasters are crop failures, food shortages, and loss of assets, the most reported is the reduction of income. Thus, the reduction of income is perceived as the most serious and the most significant impact of emergencies and disasters. This falls in line with the theoretical argumentation of several writers like Morduch (1995) and Dercon and Hoddinott (2005) who stress that emergencies and disasters affect income and thus consumption. Their effects on volume of accumulated assets possessed by households are also stressed.

---

[6] To give an example; when Haloum's son knew that the family would sell the only goat they had and use for milk for his youngest brother in order to pay the fees of his secondary examination, he preferred to migrate to Khartoum and work there with his relatives and friends without even telling his parents.

Table 4 Main Emergencies and Disasters in Al Dagag

Emergencies and Disasters
Individual Emergencies:
Sickness including unexpected abortion of pregnant women
Loss or disease of livestock
Children discharged from school for not paying fees
Accident
Death
Injury
Going to jail for not paying back financial debts
Loss of other assets (by fire theft or others)
Urgent need to pay for *Wajib* in or outside Al Dagag
Having no children
General Emergencies:
Fire
Low crop prices
Natural Disasters:
Rainfall shortages and drought
Insects and crops disease
Flood of *Khour* Abuhabil at an unexpected time
Reduction of land fertility
Desertification

8.5.1 Emergencies in Al Dagag

Generally, individual emergencies related to health are the mentioned most by respondents. Different types of sickness are the most stated personal emergencies. However, sickness of children is considered more threatening than that of an adult. Deaths of children or adults that occur frequently in Al Dagag are regarded as the most painful and affecting emergencies. For instance, Agba Alnoor considers losing the husband the most severe emergency she ever passed through, since he was sick for a long time and they had to sell most of the household's assets for his treatment. Accidents/injuries on the main road are also pointed out as major emergencies. Accidents that happened to people might lead to death, physical disabilities or minor injuries that affect the household by losing part of the labor force permanently or for some time. The need to pay financial debts accumulated by one of the household members is also considered an emergency. This is mainly because in these cases most of the family members have to collect the money for paying the person's debt or the penalty payment. This is also linked to the experience of many people who went to jail for not repaying the debt to the IFAD project in addition to few other cases that are not linked to IFAD.

Furthermore, most respondents regard the need to pay for *Wajib* as an emergency that needs immediate attention. This is illustrated in the meaning of emergency that respondents provided above. This is mainly for the fact that paying for *Wajib* is backed up by reciprocity and mutual aid; thus, respondents feel obliged to contribute in any happy or sad occasion happening to relatives, neighbors, friends, or any other members of the social networks they are involved in. Within the idea of *Wajib* also falls the need to receive or comfort any sudden guests. This can fall within what Fafchamps (1999) calls "ritual risks" (cf. chapter 2) where social pressures oblige people to participate in expected or unexpected customary expenditures.

Other individual emergencies are the discharging of children for not paying school fees or other events that need urgent reaction such any urgent need to travel for any occasion. In addition to that, damaging crops by livestock of other people is also regarded as an emergency that regularly happens in Al Dagag.

The general emergency mentioned repeatedly by almost all respondents is fire, which is declared by all respondents the main and most regular general disaster taking place. Respondents count consequences of losing the house and most of household assets and furniture due to fire. Carelessness when using firewood for cooking plus using candles for light in absence of electricity are the main reasons. The other major general emergency is the instability of prices, mainly sharp decreases in prices during harvesting time believed to be distressing for all respondents. The immediate consequence of such emergency is low income that affects the household's financial situations until the following season. At that time, much supply of agricultural production is available in the markets leading to low demand and thus low prices.

What is emphasized by most respondents is that in cases of emergencies *Wajib,* considered as help they pay to each other, is regarded as important in order to overcome such stressing times.

8.5.2 Natural Disasters in Al Dagag

While people resort to helping each other in individual emergencies, this is considered difficult in the case of natural disasters, which are also common in Al Dagag and leave more significant consequences. This is mainly because in cases of natural disasters most or all people are affected. Therefore, they are not able to help each other and depend on help coming from outside Al Dagag.

The most mentioned natural disaster is drought, which is caused by rain shortages. Droughts lead to serious food and water shortages and in severe cases when occurring repeatedly, like in Kordofan in 1984/5 or 1990, might lead to a famine. The immediate consequences of droughts include low agricultural production, damaging the vegetation cover that is used to feed livestock and shortages of water supply for both agriculture and domestic activities such as cooking and drinking water.

Natural disasters also include over flooding of *Khour* Abuhabil or floods at an inappropriate time that damage crops. In addition to that, floods also lead to other problems such as separating part of the land, which is located between *Khour* Abuhabil and one of its branches. In cases of floods, reaching this land is impossible and has, in the past, led to deaths of many persons who were trying to get to their land swimming.

Respondents consider polluted drinking water a general disaster that they have to live with. It is believed to have severe effects on health of the entire population, but mostly children. This goes in line with Fafchamps (1999) who includes poor infrastructure as a risk found to deepen rural people's vulnerability.

The main emergencies and disasters in Al Dagag are significant in their effects on the livelihood of people since they affect people's capabilities and influence the main livelihood activities in the village.

Concluding the discussion, I would like to point out to that the set of emergencies and disasters in Al Dagag is not so much different from what has been mentioned from the literature in chapter 2. They deepen people's vulnerability as argued by Chambers and Conway (1992) and Fafchamps (1999) because they accumulate over time and thus leave a quite devastating impact on individuals and households. They leave most households in a miserable situation that forces them to react, cope and manage their lives to find a way out of the "edge" as explained by Ellis (cf. chapter 2). The only difference is that respondents stress and focus on *Shail* and paying back debt for themselves or for family members as individual emergencies, such as receiving unexpected guests. This shows on the one hand how strong the social relations of people are, but on the other hand, also that excessive social relations could cause an emergency that urges them to pay extra or unexpected amounts of money that they might not be able to afford.

8.6 "*Having a decent life*": Reflecting Wellbeing and Security in Al Dagag

Respondents never mention security or wellbeing as a concept in the talk about their poor condition; I had to ask them to get an idea about what such concepts mean to them. In addition, I find it complicated to describe the meaning of security in situations of chronic poverty and vulnerability. I realized how complex the discussion about security could be from what respondents answered to my question what security and wellbeing mean to them. The main term used by respondents is to have a decent life or "*Haya Kareema*". This decent life as described by them consists of firstly a sufficient and steady source of income, secondly the possession of savings like money, livestock and crops that can help in cases of emergencies and disasters. These attributes of *Haya Kareema* fall in line with Sen's (1993) explanation of the constituent elements of functionings presented in chapter 2. However, the set of functionings is to some degree different in the way that it is more specific to the life of the Al Dagag people and their situation unlike Sen's more general set. It is obvious that the meaning of security and wellbeing for Al Dagag people comes from the above definition of poverty and vulnerability. This is also clear from the inclusion of many of the terms used by respondents to describe poverty and vulnerability like education, health, *Shail*, and others.

In addition to the need for steady income and assets, respondents mentioned the existence of a strong family systems and social connections to be causes of security. This I could also extract from the analysis of interviews and it emerged when talking about many other issues. Many respondents repeatedly stress the importance of social relations as their way to fight poverty and vulnerability. This confirms how Chambers (1989) and Chambers and Conway (1992) explain security as something that strengthens not only assets and income but also the social position to maximize future claims on resources as discussed in chapter 2.

What respondents in Al Dagag have added is that the decent life is also defined as a situation when people are not forced to borrow from other people on any aspects that put them in debt, most specifically taking *Shail*. For example, the decent life for Abdalla, Fadil and others is defined as a situation when people own assets and better farming facilities like tractors and water pumps, shops, cars, and a lot of crops and are not in need to borrow in order to survive. Thus, if credits from *Shail* contracts or the IFAD project are used only for consumption and not to enhance agriculture as stated by respondents, it is considered threatening the security of people by putting them in debt. This stresses the need for credit for production (mainly agriculture) as well as credit for life cycle events and other consumption options. In the frame of reference, some respondents added the fact that when they are not in need to take credit for immediate consumption they are able to make the decisions regarding household expenses because they are not indebted to anyone. They can invest and increase their income, but this is only when they have better agriculture facilities and thus production.

Decent life also includes other things for the respondents. For instance, for Bakheta who has been cultivating the household land since her husband married another woman and works in Khartoum, it means, "*having enough food for one year*". The case of Um Bakheta and her definition of security represent how different factors and categories are connected. The decent life for Um Bakheta, who is destitute, is "*when you do not need help from other people, when you do not need to work for other people and when you do not need to take Shail*". Um Bakheta has seven very young children, most of them go to school, and received credit from the IFAD credit project to raise livestock but the livestock became sick and died. She then had to repay from the household agricultural production income. She and her husband used to take *Shail* every year. Um Bakheta's statement briefly reflects that security and wellbeing are when one owns resources that are enough for self-sufficiency and survival. Other terms employed when discussing the decent life are: having steady salary, full household storage rooms, livestock like cows and camels, educated children, comfortable houses, nice clothes, clean and healthy food, clean water, and not being tired and not needing to migrate.

To conclude this subchapter I would like to take the discussion one step further and refer to Chambers and Conway, (1992, cf. chapter 2) who argue that in the absence of external help to enhance people's wellbeing and security, an internal mechanisms is employed by the poor themselves to adapt to their situation. The term internal in this case does not only include the household but is extended to include relationships between households and the village society as whole. Accordingly, what is discussed next is how people survive in such poor and vulnerable situations in the absence of any external help. What are their coping strategies? What is the role of social relations, which is stressed by respondents as significant in enhancing security and wellbeing (decent life) of the poor and thus assumed to affect the sustainability of their livelihood?

8.6.1 Coping Strategies

I would like to argue here that survival or as respondents call it *Al Maeesha* (to continue being alive) is positioned between death on the one end and wellbeing and security on the other end. People then live in chronic poverty and vulnerability and basically look for remaining alive in such situations. However, this also connects to the argumentation of Wisner et al. (2004: 119) that by coping households also seek the maintenance of other human needs such as respect, dignity and the maintenance of family, household and community cohesion.

Moreover, applicable to the case of Al Dagag and in consent with Wisner et al. (2004: 113) and Dercon (2005: 11), coping is defined as managing resources of different kinds in unusual or adverse situations and to deal with contingencies. I would also suggest depending on the case of Al Dagag to group these resources into physical, financial, human or natural resources, which are available in the surrounding environment as argued by Wisner et al. (2004: 113) and presented in chapter 2. What is also observable from the case of Al Dagag is that the coping strategies of people are sequenced as different emergencies and disasters prevailed. Moreover, households establish patterns of responses that they can use to deal with different types of emergencies and disasters.

To illustrate further, the responses to emergencies and disasters by household are diverse depending on the type of emergency and disaster. In addition, it depends on the type and amount of assets and the presented opportunities for income diversification that each household possesses. Households do not just suffer the consequences of emergencies and disasters but they develop different and suitable strategies to reduce their impact. This is not to say that these strategies are always successful but normally people combine more than one coping strategy at one time to reduce the effect of different emergencies and disasters.

The main coping strategies stated by respondents are diversification, saving in livestock, migration in cases of droughts, reduction of consumption, borrowing, selling assets, and finally tolerance, patience and depending on God as the last resort. I have already discussed diversification and savings in livestock in chapter 7. Here I will focus on the coping strategies that were not included in the discussion of patterns of livelihood. In addition, diversification and savings in livestock might be better understood as *insurance* mechanisms because they constitute general behavior expecting any emergency to happen, unlike *coping* strategies that are conducted after the occurrence of the shock or disaster.

Migration in case of drought is seen as a main coping strategy for people in Al Dagag. Normally, the whole family migrates to other states seeking agricultural work or other types of work. In many cases, families migrate in groups which means many families can migrate together to the same destination place. Respondents state that they normally tend to migrate to states like Al Gezira or other states along the Nile River where there are mechanized agricultural schemes and water availability is assured.

People tend to distinguish between two types of drought that lead to such type of migration. They distinguish between severe droughts "*Al gafaf al kabeer*" (big drought) and less severe ones "*Al gafaf al sageer*" (small drought). They give examples of severe droughts that hit the area in the mid 1980s and in the beginning of the 1990s. During the two severe droughts most of the Al Dagag families migrated due to severe food and water shortages. In the cases of less severe droughts, the consequences are not so devastating; thus, a lesser number of families normally migrate.

In the cases of these two severe droughts, the whole region of Kordofan was affected. Respondents mentioned that families from Al Dagag were generally welcomed at the destination places. They were welcomed as guests in the houses of the original inhabitants. Their children were welcomed in the schools and they could smoothly engage in the labor market. Hafeez remembers those days as good days they spend in Al Gezira, although she mentioned that when they heard the situation got better in Kordofan, they immediately came back. She said that on return she possessed two sacks of sorghum and the cash equivalent to S£ 160 today; she feels happy to remember that.

Another coping strategy is the reduction of consumption. The majority of women said that the reduction of consumption is the immediate coping strategy in many emergencies. People tend to buy smaller amounts of households needs than usual, for instance they buy food in smaller quantities than normally. For example, they buy half *Ratul* sugar for the day instead of one *Ratul* per day, which is normally consumed. Hameed, who has seven children, revealed that people in cases like a drought reduce their food consumption by eating two and sometimes one meal instead of three. Hukum Al Gadeer who has six young children mentioned that sometimes they eat only one meal per day and drink a lot of coffee instead. Generally, people in Al Dagag drink a lot of tea and coffee with much sugar. This is also considered a coping strategy, mainly because people claim that drinking a lot of coffee reduces appetite and a lot of sugar gives energy. In addition to that, they buy less new clothes, furniture or utensils during a drought. Omima gives a statement about reducing food consumption: "*We just eat for surviving and we do not buy things other than food and water*". Omima is destitute and takes *Shail* every year. Most male respondents confirmed that generally women spend household money carefully, which is believed to be a coping strategy.

In some urgent emergences like sickness, respondents tend to borrow money. Some respondents stated that they borrow from the shop or from relatives and friends before they sell their livestock. Many respondents borrow from people who have surplus of money like Rugaia or start buying on credit in cases of income or food shortages. Generally, there are no formal financial institutions in Al Dagag to provide financial help in cases of such emergencies or loans for consumption; thus, people have to deal with institutions in the village like shops, relatives and friends and *Sandouqs* for women or *Shail* in September. Consequently, most of those who received credit from the IFAD project eventually used the money to cover costs of emergencies like most of those who got livestock as credit sold it later when they faced a difficult situation. Moreover, a significant percentage of the money received from *Sandouqs* is used to cover household needs or an emergency as will be discussed in chapter 10. Furthermore, the collected fund of *Sandouqs* is often borrowed by one of the participants who is passing through a difficult time or who experiences a sudden emergency, which is also considered as one of the main conditions of joining *Sandouqs*. Taking *Shail* in September is also included by some respondents in this category, *Shail* will be discussed in detail also in chapter 10.

When the above mentioned coping strategies fail, respondents tend to sell some of the household assets. However, this sequence is not always the case. The majority of respondents revealed that they sell part or all of the household assets in cases of emergencies. Most people start by selling crops stored for the time of emergencies. Abdalla for instance sold one sack of sorghum for S£ 130 and part of his tomato production when his wife was injured in an accident. He also sold some of the family livestock when his brother went to jail. Some female respondents stated that they sold their gold in the past but only in case they are sure their husbands do not have any money to cover the costs of the emergency. Alradeea, who is divorced and has two children, mentions that she already sold most of her house furniture the same year. The reason is that she does not have anyone outside Al Dagag to send her money. However, in some cases, selling the household furniture is considered shameful. Mustafa Mohamed who belongs to the destitute category refuses to sell household furniture. He argues that most of the household furniture is normally considered female goods, thus it is shameful for the man to sell it to cover household expenses.

Other strategies are also mentioned, however, to prevent shocks. For instance, because of the frequency of livestock robbery, people thought of building up a place to keep livestock that is called *Mehjar*. In this place, everyone can keep their livestock for free; the place is guarded by the villagers in shifts. Recently, for dealing with fire they built houses out of mud and started a *Gameea* (a type of saving association that will be described in chapter 10) only for the case of fire. This *Gameea* consists of a group of people who collect small amounts of money in case fire occurs to one of them.

The last coping strategy mentioned by respondents is having faith in God. Most respondents reveal that when nothing works, they just pray to God and have faith that things are going to become better. However, for many respondents they keep doing so every day and not only in emergencies as they feel insecure and vulnerable most of the time. They consider this a coping strategy because it gives them tolerance and patience. The expression of "God is generous" exactly in their Arabic words "*Allah Kareem*" is used by all respondents repeatedly.

When respondents are asked to rank these coping strategies in relation to the emergencies using the PRA method of ranking, respondents rarely agree on the order of coping strategies. However, in summary, the main results of ranking coping strategies are: Which type of coping strategy is used mainly depends on the type of emergency people experience. Different coping strategies are used during different emergencies; some emergencies require immediate action while others can wait longer. For example, the first resort in cases that need urgent response like sickness, accidents, injuries, and when children are dismissed from schools for not paying school fees, is to borrow from the shopkeepers, relatives and neighbors, thereby counting in mind the help they will get by *Wajib*. In case of fire or imminent loss of crops, respondents use the help of others in sort of *Nafeer*s or ask for money contributions. In cases of food shortages, most respondents resort to ask their relatives outside Al Dagag for money, followed by reducing consumption, and at the end selling household assets. The main coping strategy to pay *Wajib* and any future expected or unexpected emergency is using savings in livestock, money or crops. In cases of severe disasters, people tend to migrate to other places as the final coping strategy available to them.

Concluding this part one can argue here that many coping strategies are employed in Al Dagag; however, I find it unmistakable that they are supported and strengthened by their social relations and connections that play a significant role in dealing with poverty and vulnerability.

8.6.2 Social Capital in Al Dagag: "Helping each other" as an Insurance Mechanism

Being part of social networks and being committed to help each other is the most important coping strategy and an insurance mechanism in Al Dagag. This is in line with most of the theoretical argumentation in this field which suggests that communities faced with risks engage in social networks that are used as mutual insurance (Goldstein et al., 2005). Contributions of people are perceived as significant during an emergency and are considered very helpful by the majority of respondents. In Al Dagag, for instance, families eat together in cases of food shortages, as Abdelrahmen states "*If I know someone does not have food for his kids, I take my food and go and eat with them*".

The meaning of social capital for the Al Dagag people is not far from what has been discussed in chapter 2, that social capital comprises social relationships and networking of people. What I have found in Al Dagag fits the theoretical meaning of social capital in that it stresses the idea that social capital is available in and through social networks that involve the exchange of different types of resources in reciprocal manner (Bourdieu, 1986: 248; Baker, 2000: 1; Bartkus and Davis, 2009: 4).

Moreover, I found out that these resources exchanged could be financial like money, which is important, yet could still be of other types. The financial resources coming out of social resources could be varied in types; it does not only include money, and gifts but also includes things like labor, visiting each other, exchanging information or ideas and business or work opportunities as it has been mentioned when seasonal migration was discussed in chapter 7. However, all these types of resources are called "help" by respondents, as they repeatedly state, "*we help each other*". It is also clear that beside financial resources, the mutual help or labor is the most important gain from social networks. The financial capital is built through and connected to social relations; this idea is also supported by Baker (2001). Bourdieu's (1986) meaning of social capital is also applicable, considering that social networks could be understood cumulative of actual or possible resources that are exchanged and linked by the members of a social network and governed by social contact.

The main finding with respect to types of social networks in Al Dagag is that different types of networks exist varying in their size, structure, norms and other aspects. Moreover, most of these relations are established within the tribal system that is strongly embedded in the village.

The majority of respondents classifies the social relations and networks starting from the far to the closer social networks; these include tribe, sub-clan, neighbors from the same tribe and sub-clan, extended family, and then nuclear family members. Other relations also exist but are considered inside these cycles such as friendship, or sometimes outside these networks with the few people who do not belong to *Gawama* in Al Dagag or outside.

Diagram 2: Social Networks in Al Dagag

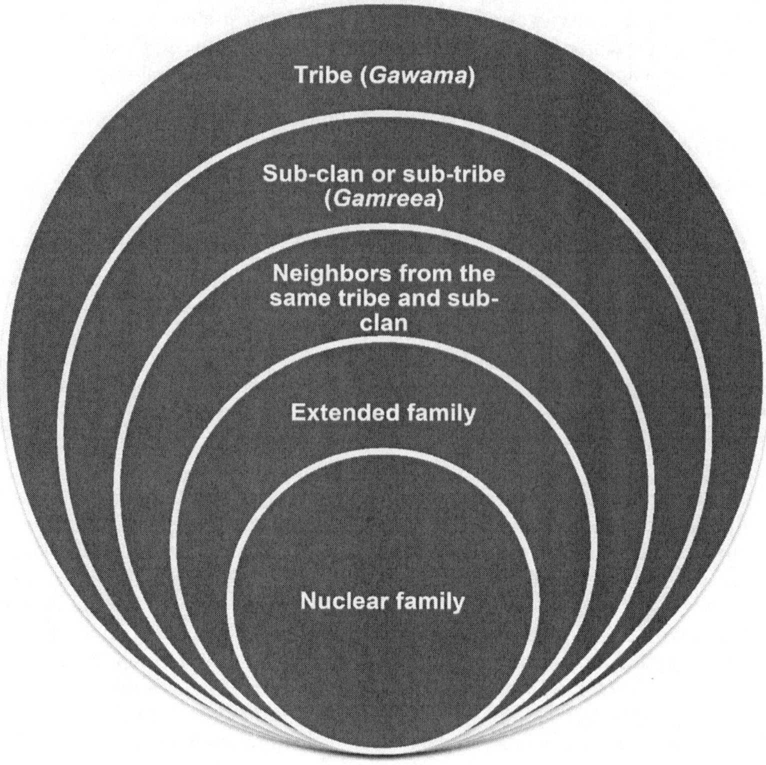

Source: My own classification depending on data from individual and group interviews in Al Dagag.

From diagram 2, it is obvious that with regard to the size and structure of networks the biggest social network constitutes respondents belonging to the same tribe. Consequently, most of the norms and values within these networks belong to the norms of the tribe. Accordingly, "strangers" or people who are not *Gawama* are not treated the same in many aspects of relationships and benefits. The sub-clan is also respected, and constitutes the second level of network thus who are *Gawama Gamreea* are closer to each other than those who are *Gawama* but not *Gamreea*. Additionally, this reflects stronger social relationships than the tribal connections. On the next level, come neighbors who live next to each other and belong to the *Gawama* and/or *Gamreea*. The next network level involves family members of the extended family that are born to one grandfather and live in the extended family households. Next, come members of a nuclear family who live in the nuclear family household and share responsibilities toward each other. This constitutes the strongest relationship in Al Dagag.

The degree of household involvement in any of these networks reflects the degree of help that a household gets out of the networks. In other words, the closer the network is, the stronger the connections and the greater the help that can be gained. Fafchamps and Lund (2000) and Weerdt (2005: 199) argue that the risk is shared within the confines of small networks more than at the level of the community, which also supports my findings.

These are the well known and respected social relations; however, some relations could be built outside these networks. Taking into consideration that most of Al Dagag's population belongs to the same tribe, other networks outside this connection are not many. For example, people could have relationships to neighbors who do not belong to the sub-clan, but still they are bounded by the tribal connections. Hassan's wife stated that when going to the agricultural fields she would leave her young children with her neighbor who is not *Gamreea,* instead of leaving them with her mother who is old, sick, impatient, and lives far. Few respondents revealed that in a case of emergency they could resort to their neighbors better than to family members who live at a distance. The neighborhood connection is also clear in the social relations and connections that exist between people living in one part of the village. For instance, connections between people who live in the northern or the eastern part of the village are involved in relationships that people from other parts might be excluded from, for example the *Gameea* and *Karama*[7]. Other social networks are friends who might also be close. In general, the existence of few people from other tribes makes studying social relations between different tribes in Al Dagag impossible, thus comparing between social relations within and without the tribal connection could not produce significant results.

Generally, people are closely connected to each other in Al Dagag and this is reflected in the degree of involvement in each other's life. Other factors also reflect the strong social relationship such as the easiness of transformation of information within the community. I observed that everyone knows everyone, if anyone asks any child in the street about any person he or she will definitely know her or him and where her or his house is located in the village. It is further obvious in the way people visit each other either in the case of social occasions or in the habit of visiting each other on a daily basis. For instance, many respondents mention (I have also observed) that they see or visit each other on a daily basis just to make sure that everyone is fine. It is normal to start the morning with a visitor who is coming to say good morning; people might also stay and drink some tea and talk about many issues like time of going to the agricultural fields or any news of other neighbors.

What is also considered important when discussing social networks is the benefits members gain from joining the networks. The majority of the respondents repeat the phrase of "*in Al Dagag all people are relatives, we are one big family*". The main essence of this phrase reflects the social relations is that people help each other to pass any emergencies mentioned above. Adams (1993) argues similarly about exchange transfer as described in chapter 2. For the majority of the respondents, the main benefit of any social relation is the "help" they get from them. People in Al Dagag, define social relations as the help they get from each other on different occasions and when people are in need of help. These social relations are reciprocal in the way, "*if you help someone today, he is obliged to help you tomorrow*". These social networks include financial help as well as help in other manners like providing labor or taking care of children and other needy family members.

However, the resource exchanged most frequently in different emergencies is money and that makes it difficult to differentiate between social and financial relations in Al Dagag since both are linked to a great extent. This represents Bourdieu's (1986) idea of conversion of forms of capital. This becomes for instance evident in social institutions like *Wajib* and *Nafeer*. Although they are mainly considered as arrangements that reflect the notion of "*helping each other*", they still imply significant financial benefits. It is also supported by the work of Schultz et al. (2008) who show that such institutions like *Wajib* could be considered both social and financial institutions. They constitute an obvious example of how social relations can provide financial help that is needed by households. This adds a detailed explanation to what has theoretically been mentioned in the literature about the role of social capital as insurance mechanism, here using the case of Sudan. This will be more clarified in the next sub-chapters that describe in detail the mechanisms of social relations in Al Dagag, which are *Wajib* and *Nafeer*.

8.6.2.1 Wajib

The word *Wajib* is an Arabic term used to describe obligation towards other people in case of social occasions considered as "duty" that must be done. In Sudan, *Wajib* is an important community arrangement as explained by Schultz et al. (2008: 26), "*in Sudan Wajib is one of the important institutions which structures the social life of the people, gives them security and reinforces social networks*". In the village, as well, *Wajib* is a practice that is generally accepted by both men and women in order

[7] Money sharing to buy some goods to be distributed among the contributors.

to share the burden of financing big feasts when very many people are invited to come to join and particiapte (Schultz et al., 2008: 26). For Schultz et al. (2008) the whole Sudanese society is largely involved in *Wajib* relations, which concern small amounts of money or different kinds of gifts from guests at certain social occasions like marriage, birth, death, circumcision and various religious festivals. However, the concept of *Wajib* in Al Dagag is more complex than its simple immediate meaning of small contributions of money or gifts to be given in different social occasions.

The concept embraces the essence of social networking in Al Dagag and reflects the way social networks are arranged. Reciprocity guides *Wajib* behavior since resource exchange within the social networks is reciprocal. This is supported by what has been found by Schultz et al. (2008: 10f.). Interviews reveal that *Wajib* has been embedded in the culture of the people for a long time as it reflects their beliefs in helping each other in emergencies. However, I believe that it is more regular and constitutes a social norm in rural than in urban areas.

Wajib as a social institution has its own complex and dynamic norms and rules that shape the way it takes place. Further, it differs from one social occasion to another and is also shaped by the relationship between the people involved. It is observed that mostly women are involved in giving and taking *Wajib* although men also contribute. Sometimes both the male and female (normally husband and wife) who constitute a household contribute together; in other cases, they contribute individually. It depends on the occasion and the person who is in need for help—if he is close or relative to the male or the female.

To show how complex and dynamic *Wajib* is, it is interesting to present an example. On any occasion, people help each other in different ways and at different levels depending on who is this person in need, the financial capabilities of both the giver and receiver, how they are related, and the history of their relationship. Generally, the help is called *Wajib*, but the contributions are classified depending on the type of occasion. Respondents differentiate between the help they pay in sad and happy occasions. In sad occasions, the money contributed is called *Guran* and in happy occasions, it is called *Sewal*. Like in cases of birth giving and weddings, most people come to visit but not all are invited to the celebration. Those who are invited are supposed to contribute individually by paying money on the seventh day of birth giving or bring *Khulud* that is a small vessel filled with crops or sugar or coffee. Women usually write this down to remember who paid and how much was paid. The volume of help in these cases depends on how close the people are. For example, sisters, brothers, close relatives and generally people within the closer networks contribute more than others do and contribute valuable things like a sheep, gold, and clothes for the baby in cases of birth giving. The same applies for weddings: the close relatives buy gifts for the bride like gold or house furniture but contribute money and livestock for the groom, which can help him to complete the celebration that he has to pay for. Especially in the case of weddings, people who are invited for the celebration have to pay money after they eat the main festival meal. Somebody carrying a plate and notebook will be sitting inside the house for women and outdoors for men collecting money and writing down the names and the amount of money. The amount of money differs between individuals and normally people within the closer networks contribute more.

Generally, people contribute money in small amounts varying from S£ 2-25 depending on the relationship and how much the person paid on previous occasions. For example, when Rugaia paid S£ 10 for Aldur in her last birth giving, Aldur should pay back more than the S£ 10 in the case Rugaia gives birth or another event. If Aldur pays back the exact S£ 10 this means the relationship is not improving, so, next time Rugaia will contribute the same and so on. If Aldur would pay back nothing, most of respondents claim, that for one time this will be respected but if the person repeats it again, this relationship of paying on occasions will be discontinued. No one contributes less; it is believed to be shameful and humiliating. Moreover, respondents said that the whole amount increases over time, so in the past they were paying two to five pounds but now this is not acceptable since this is now very little money and, therefore, they pay more.

The main sources of money for *Wajib* contributions are savings of the household as mentioned above. This is reflected in the statement of the majority of respondents who claim that one of the main reasons of savings is the obligation to pay for *Wajib*.

Women and men contribute other non-material resources besides visiting like labor. It is the norm that the people of the household should do nothing. Therefore, other women cook, clean the house and receive and farewell guests while men distribute the food, slaughter the livestock and prepare places for people to sit and eat. At the end of the celebration day, the house should be clean and organized like the way it was when the day started.

On most occasions, the contributions cover a considerable part of the expenses. On funerals it can be generally said, the contributions cover all expenses, but on weddings only a significant portion of the expenses is covered. The money collected for weddings and funerals is used to cover the expenses of the occasion itself, which is not the case in birth giving. In this case the money will be given to the woman and she uses the money the way she wants, normally, to buy livestock, house furniture or gold, but the money is not used for the birth giving event.

How people help each other in cases of death in Al Dagag is unique and interesting, since in these cases every adult person, male or female is obliged to individually pay the same amount of money. Hassan explains why it is obligatory:

> "*In the case of death it is different since all of us we have to pay, because this is a loss of a person and it is a very sad event and many people come and stay in the funeral house. We do not want it to be 'Moot wa kharab dear' (death and household destruction) and also it could happen suddenly and in every household plus it happens regularly*".

In this quotation, the main aim of *Wajib* in case of a funeral is set to cover the whole expenses of the funeral and not allow any resources of the funeral household to be used. People are not invited like in the case of weddings, but all people from inside and outside Al Dagag come. Normally, many people come and stay for some days. Thus, what Hassan means is that they do not want the household of the funeral to take these big expenses at the same time of their loss.

To explain more, in the case of a funeral in Al Dagag, people eat three meals in the funeral house using the money they have contributed for two or maximum three days of the funeral. The equal contribution amounts to S£ 5 paid by each person; the total money is given to a responsible person like an uncle who will be in charge of buying all the needs for the funeral. During this period, all expenses are paid from the money collected, in case it is not enough, additional money will be collected. At the end, men sit together and calculate all the expenses paid. If there is any money left, they give it to the responsible person in the household of the dead person. The important thing is that the people of the village, not the family of the person who died, should pay all expenses. Sometimes the collected money is more than the expenses of the funeral; in this case, the rest will be given to the family of the person who died. Agba Alnoor explains, "*When my husband died after the funeral, they gave me* S£ *60*".

Normally, people get all the necessary things from the shops in Al Dagag. The money collected is given to the shopkeeper in advance who keeps records of what is taken out of the shop until the last day of the funeral.

In other sad emergencies, people contribute differently. In cases of the death of a child or infant, *Wajib* is also done differently. People do not follow the same procedures like explained above, but they contribute individually and normally do not pay money, but women bring *Khulud*. They come every day to visit the mother and help her with the housework for seven days.

On occasions such as severe sicknesses that lead to physical disabilities, in cases of accidents or deaths, the help is judged as obligatory to everyone. Normally, people contribute money in such cases and the amount of money is more than on other occasions. In cases of small accidents and normal sickness, they contribute individually and unevenly; some people contribute more than others depending on the factors I mentioned above; albeit it could happen that some people might collect money in groups. In many cases, they contribute crops or other assets. What is equally important besides collecting money is the visit people pay to a sick person who is hospitalized or in the house. In case of Abdalla, when his wife was injured in an accident, most of the people of Al Dagag visited her in the hospital carrying food or money.

In the many cases of fire, that burn down the complete house, most people contribute with money, crops, clothes, house or kitchen utensils brought from their own houses. Both men and women collect materials for rebuilding and help rebuilding the main components of the house.

Exchange of food is viewed to be significant in Al Dagag as insurance mechanism and as part of the *Wajib* that takes place normally. Customarily, the members of the extended family and household eat together. Food is normally and on a daily basis exchanged between households. I could observe many times when they send some of the prepared food to another household, sometimes neighbours, sometimes not. This also takes place within the concept of reciprocity where others are expected to do the same. Thus, the exchange of small amounts of food or food ingredients with neighbors, keeping a note in the head about the quantity given by either to ensure a fair repayment when needed by the other is believed to be normal happenstance. The exchange of food as insurance mechanism in Al Dagag as I observed necessitates the immediate return of the initial or other goods as stated by Adams (1993). One plate full of cooked food which is given to another household will be returned in a very short time (maybe on the same day) also filled with food, crops, sugar or other goods. In some cases, food is gifted to help someone in need as stated by respondents.

In some occasions, people help each by giving gifts in some events also considered *Wajib*. Gifts can take different forms like cooked food, livestock, clothes, crops and others. In the case of wedding, the groom normally gets livestock as gift for the wedding main meal. This confirms the argumentations of Adams (1993) and Fafchamps (1999) about gifts (cf. chapter 2); however, it is included in the case of Al Dagag as an insurance mechanism more than as a coping strategy. One could argue in the case of Al Dagag that it is not only linked with any religious believes as stated by Adams (1993) but more with social relations, norms and traditions.

Wajib also might sometimes be ambivalent and not a social network without problems. Even if it is considered very significant, it also has some types of moral hazards. These moral hazards take place because emergencies occur regularly and people live in poor and vulnerable conditions. They still need to contribute, or they will be excluded from the social network. They even calculate it in the household expenses (as explained in chapter 7) fearing that some emergencies will happen to someone and they will need to pay.

Alradeea who is destitute, divorced with two children and has nobody to help her financially, explains such types of moral hazards:

> "*I stopped contributing in such cases (of fire) unless the person is a very close relative. It is happening because of carelessness of women, and I do not have anything left to give them, not even time, so I stopped participating in most cases.*"

The case of Alradeea and others illustrates that sometimes paying *Wajib* for the destitute can also be a financial burden and that is why it is described by respondents as an emergency. In this way, there is lack of incentive to participate in *Wajib* since respondents mention that they cannot cover the *Wajib* payment on many occasions that might take place at the same time for different people or that occur regularly like fire.

Going over the main points mentioned above I can summarize that *Wajib* is common in Al Dagag and represents a very important insurance mechanism against emergencies; the financial benefits from such arrangements cannot be ignored. In addition to that, this help they pay to each other is more complex and dynamic than the simple meaning of paying money as contributions.

8.6.2.2 Nafeer

Schultz et al. (2008) focus on *Nafeer,* work groups formed by people to assist each other during agricultural peak times by contributing their labor.

To define *Nafeer* respondents in Al Dagag stated that *Nafeer* is help in form of group work that is provided to a person in order to get him or her out of an emergency concerning either farming or building houses or other aspects. It is an activity done for free for someone in need and it takes either the whole day or one working shift like *Dahwa* or *Sarba*. Most respondents are to some extent involved in *Nafeer* work for agriculture in Al Dagag. Some ask for *Nafeer* every agricultural season, others do it but not that regularly. However, *Nafeer* for cleaning hibiscus has recently been happening so often in Al Dagag, which it is always done as *Sahra* that starts with sunset and normally goes the entire night until they finish the whole quantity. *Sahra* for cleaning hibiscus is done by both males and females but more females do it. Generally, *Nafeer* aims at achieving huge amounts of work that cannot be performed in one day by one person. The person in need calls specific people for *Nafeer* forced by fear to lose crops or in situations of building or rebuilding houses in cases of heavy rains or fire for the fear of not finding a place to live in.

Nafeer also reflects the engagement of people in social networks; calls for *Nafeers* are conducted within close social networks. Generally, when people from a different tribe call for *Nafeer* not many people come. For instance, when Khamesa once called for *Nafeer* for weeding her land, she received the least number of people, i. e., only 17 persons to help her. Khamesa believes that this is the case because she is not from the *Gawama* tribe. However, this can also be explained by the fact that people perceive her and her husband, Hassan as not in an urgent need since they have assets in addition to the cart her husband received as credit from the IFAD project.

The main obligation in *Nafeer* is that if a person calls for *Nafeer*, any of those who helped have the right to also call him or her for *Nafeer.* This reflects the concept of "*helping each other*" and also, the concepts of reciprocity and mutual exchanging of benefits of giving and taking. For example, Abdalla states, "*If you help people they will help you when you need them*". However, for women it is sometimes different since they can call for *Nafeer* without being obliged to go for *Nafeer*. Instead, women can do other types of work like participating on occasions of doing domestic work. Dawa for instance, as she is the midwife in the village, will not take the fees for delivering the woman in case the father or the mother of the child helped her in *Nafeer*. It is acceptable that some people send their sons or daughters to work instead of themselves and everyone should bring his or her own tools.

Therefore, it is not always *Nafeer* for *Nafeer* but people can "payback" by other benefits or resources. However, the only benefit of *Nafeer* mentioned by respondents is helping each other to do heavy work, few respondents explicitly point out that it reduces costs of agriculture production. However, generally, it can be argued that *Nafeer* does in fact reduce the cost of production, for instance the cost of hiring farmers to help in any farming activity like harvesting. Still, the reduction of costs is not calculated or regarded as important as helping someone to deal with an emergency as mentioned by respondents.

The person who calls for *Nafeer* should prepare some food. In the case of *Sarba,* it should be a full lunch meal, which is the main meal of the day. In case of *Dahwa* and *Sahra*, since people finish or start working at sunset, the meal will be traditional cakes called *Zalabeea* and tea. Most respondents call for *Dahwa* and *Sahra* because at this time of the day everybody finishes his or her own work. The preparation of *Zalabeea* and tea is not costly like a full lunch meal.

The frequency of *Nafeer* calls is also affected by the season. For example for the year 2009, there were not many *Nafeer*s for harvesting, since most crops failed to grow; most calls for *Nafeer* were *Sahra* for cleaning hibiscus.

The poor call for *Nafeer* every year, more regularly than the better-off. Still, the better-off people also call for *Nafeer.* It is observable by many respondents that when the person is in real need and he/she is destitute, more people come than in the case of a better-off person. Hassan's wife, Um Mohamed, mentions that she called people to help her to do *Sahra* only once; she is not doing it frequently. Some people are shy to ask for *Nafeer*, in this case their relatives or friends will call people. Alnoor Mohamed said, "*if I see my brother (including neighbors or relatives) in urgent need, I call for Nafeer for him before he will lose the whole crop*".

However, *Nafeer* also has some sorts of moral hazards and it is also ambivalent. People in Al Dagag debate *Nafeer* more than *Wajib*. While few people complain of giving *Wajib*, many complain of the frequency of *Nafeer* calls that take place at the same time in the year because *Nafeer* in some cases is related to help provided for agriculture like during harvest or weeding. Additionally, some respondents ask why the better-off call for *Nafeer* if they can afford to hire laborers who might be the same people who are called for *Nafeer.*

For instance, when some respondents call for *Nafeer* outside their close network of the extended family, they might not get many people to do the work. For example, Aldur mentions that if she is called for *Nafeer* she might not go to all of them. She will go for *Nafeer* only if the person is in real need, like when old or sick, and for close family members. Um Balaina, who is considered destitute, explains that she only calls her relatives and family members, because these are the people she will also help when they are in need. Furthermore, she states that if she calls everyone she will not be able to go to them when they are in need. This was experienced by Alradeea who called for *Nafeer* to build her house and only few people came to help her. She explains this by her attitude of not going to any occasion recently, since she is very poor and needed to work for money all the time; she is the same respondent who complained about paying *Wajib* frequently in case of fire. Alradeea further states that she cannot leave her work to help in *Nafeer* because she lives from day-to-day income.

Thinking over what has been discussed so far regarding *Nafeer*, it is apparent that *Nafeer* is common in Al Dagag and done every year by many people. It is assumed to be done for the poor; however, even the better-off call for *Nafeer* although they are able to hire farmers. The main benefit mentioned is to help each other, few respondents focus on the financial benefits. Generally, *Nafeer* brings more controversy and is less frequent than *Wajib*.

To conclude this chapter, I would like to point out the links between what has been mentioned here and the discussion about the use of credit and why the poor need finance in chapter 3. As it is stated by Heidhues (1994), Helms (2006) and Rutherford (2009), credit should not only be provided for production, but also to smooth consumption. It is clear from what respondents mention that the life-cycle events pointed out by these writers constitute a significant part of the expenditure of the households, as respondents also include it in the calculation of expenses in Al Dagag as explained in chapter 8.

Thus, financing life-cycle events and insurance against risk and shocks represent a significant part of the financial demand of the people in Al Dagag. People are not only in need for credit for production but also for events significant for their wellbeing and security. Living in such a vulnerable situation urges the need for insurance. What I have found in Al Dagag is that social capital plays a significant role in both financing life-cycle events and insurance against shocks and disasters. The role played by social capital in Al Dagag is also supported in the work of Bartkus and Davis (2009) and Baker (2000) mentioned in chapter 3. Resources exchanged within these social networks constitute the benefits each member receives and constitute the measurement of social capital as emphasized by Groot et al. (2007, cf. chapter 2). Additionally, in Al Dagag, social capital is measured not only in resources and benefits from such relations (help or money contribution in *Wajib*) but also in the size of social networks. For example, many respondents compare the numbers of people who helped in *Nafeer*, which Groot et al. (2007) call the extent to which one can call upon people when necessary.

9 Microfinance in Al Dagag

Ali remembers the time when he was indebted to the IFAD village fund "*it was stressful time, every month is a disaster until I pay the installment, I had to explain myself many times till I paid the whole loan back from the crops I produced that season and of course not in time*" (in-depth interview, Al Dagag, 2009).

9.1 Introduction

After giving a brief overview of the main initiatives of microfinance provided in North Kordofan State (NKS); the focus in the main course of the chapter shifts to the discussion of microfinance efforts provided in Al Dagag by the International Fund for Agricultural Development (IFAD). IFAD provided microfinance services through both establishing the Al Dagag informal village fund and a partnership with the Agricultural Bank of Sudan (ABS) Al Rahad branch. A brief evaluation of the project, using IFAD reports or interviews I conducted with the ABS and IFAD officials, is followed by the main arguments develop completely on the basis of the perspectives on the project of the people of Al Dagag themselves.

The rural poor themselves describe their experience with both the village fund and the ABS and compare between procedures, types of loans, cost of transactions, and assess the experience of group formation. This chapter aims to look deeply into the exercise of microfinance for the poor, how microfinance of banks and NGOs is provided, and how people perceive its benefits and problems. Respondents' assessment of outreach and payment as well as the impacts of the IFAD microfinance project in households and generally in the village are discussed. The argument which impacts of microfinance should be studied emerged in both the views of respondents and the literature. Consequently, the question whether it is enough to look at the impact of microfinance as profitability only or whether it is necessary to investigate substantial effects is dealt with in this chapter and also the use of credit for consumption or production.

Regarding microfinance efforts in NKS government and donor sponsored institutions and NGOs are present in the state such as the ABS or IFAD. In addition to that, semi-formal institutions like co-operatives and informal financial arrangements such as money lending and *Shail* contracts, *Sandouqs* and loans from relatives and friends also exist.

Generally, there are 15 commercial banks working in NKS. Among them is the ABS, which has 10 branches scattered throughout the state. The ABS is the most specialized bank in providing microfinance to farmers in the state. All ABS as well as other banks' services are regulated by the Central Bank of Sudan (CBS). However, the main efforts to provide formal finance for the poor are performed by NGOs. Moreover, as I extracted from interviews with microfinance experts, the dominance of the indigenous financial systems like *Shail* over the formal institutions is obvious, however this is discussed in the next chapter.

NGOs engaged in microfinance in NKS encompass the World Health Organization (WHO), the United Nations Children's Fund (UNICEF), the Kordofan Rain-fed Agricultural Project (KORAG) implemented by the CARE Technoserve project, the United Nations Development Project (UNDP) Area Development Scheme (ADS) of El Obeid, and IFAD's North Kordofan Rural Development Project.

The microfinance schemes of these NGOs are scattered in NKS aiming to increase the coverage of their services. Something also to be considered is that these organizations not only provide financial help but also other development assistance for the poor to deal with the chronic poverty in the state. Thus, they are engaged in the provision of basic services like education, health and other developmental efforts. While WHO and UNICEF have only limited interventions in NKS through linkages with the Savings and Rural Development Bank in the Al Semaih area and North of El Obeid, IFAD is fully involved in the provision of microfinance and other developmental efforts in all of NKS.

The KORAG implemented by CARE Technoserve started 1987 to assist both ends of the credit chain, the ABS as well as the farmers of the Sheikan Locality. KORAG technical and financial assistance helped the bank to give loans to agricultural co-operatives with crops used as collateral (IFAD, 1999). KORAG also worked closely with ABS and the El Obeid agricultural research station, to improve farm productivity, as well as farmers' access to credit. In 1989, with the assistance from Technoserve the ABS in El Obeid initiated a mobile saving bank, which served village's market centers in the locality on a weekly basis, and provided savings and current accounts to its rural customers. Technoserve operations in Sudan have been suspended in 1990 due to the cooling of relations between Sudan and the United States of America (IFAD, 1999).

Another microfinance effort started after Technoserve in NKS is the Area Development Scheme of El Obeid (ADS), which was part of the UNDP integral rural development project. Initially, the program was implemented in four rural councils of the Sheikan Locality in NKS. UNDP has adopted a method of channeling credit through a rural financial intermediary termed "Village revolving funds". The revolving funds were established with an uneven resource allocation system; between all the services provided, this consequently meant that most of the project funds were used for the administrative budget, which threatened the provision of credit. The village funds resources were in general depleted over few years due to many factors (IFAD, 1999).

The most recent NGO working in rural development in NKS is IFAD. IFAD works through the North Kordofan Rural Development Project (NKRDP), which is the only NGO microfinance effort present in Al Dagag. Based on the IFAD progress reports 2006 (project overall evaluation report), 2007 (rural finance component evaluation report), 2008 (project overall evaluation report), the completion report 2009 and the vision for restructuring the NKRDP to enhance the project sustainability, recent information about the project is presented in the next sub-chapter. In addition to the individual and group interviews with respondents, interviews were conducted also with the IFAD country program manager in the Khartoum office, the former and the present coordinators of the project in El Obeid, the general manager and the credit officer of ABS in the Al Rahad branch, and the project field coordinator of the IFAD office in Al Rahad. Additionally, the Al Dagag village fund general coordinator and the credit committee coordinator were interviewed.

9.2 Microfinance in Al Dagag

9.2.1 Introducing IFAD North Kordofan Rural Development Project (NKRDP)

In June 1999, the Government of Sudan and IFAD founded the NKRDP with an implementation period of 7 years (2000-2007) and one additional year for assessment and evaluation. Activities started in early 2001. The project operated under an agreement between IFAD and the Ministry of Finance and National Economy (MOF) through the ABS. The project is implemented to initiate linkages between IFAD, the ABS and the self-help groups that were supposed to be established by IFAD during the project period. The link between IFAD and the ABS was performed to realize IFAD best practices that include building on institutional potential, than to create new institutions (Schneider, 1997: 57ff.). Through the establishment of the self-help groups, IFAD aimed at community mobilization and participation; they were supposed to be the informal institutions in Al Dagag. These efforts fall within the process of institution building of downgrading of banks in order to make them suitable for funding the poor and linking financial institutions as described in chapter 2.

The NKRDP leading implementing agency is the project management unit in El Obeid, which was responsible for directing and supervising the day-to-day operations of the project in two localities of Um Rawaba and Bara. From about 500 villages in the two localities, 320 villages were animated and mobilized over five years (260 villages fully received the project services while the remaining 60 villages were partially covered). This target later decreased to only 173 villages; these represent the villages where the full services of the project were available and the village funds functioning in 2007 (IFAD, 2009: 20). The primary target group was estimated at 69,290 households in the 173 villages.

The overall goal of the project was to improve the living standard of the communities within the project area, particularly, to assure food security and enhance the resilience to drought and natural disasters; mainly by mobilizing community savings and providing financial advice integrated in the project. However, other components, mainly community development, natural resources utilization and development, project management and local capacity building and construction of the El Obeid-Bara road also were included.

Once a village was selected, extensive animation and sensitization was to be undertaken to generate awareness among villagers about different project components and to mobilize the community. This step was to be followed by the formation of a village development committee in order to be registered as one of the village rural development organizations called "the village funds". The village funds were registered under the State Village Development Committees Law (VDCL), which was specifically endorsed for providing the legal framework for the IFAD village funds. This law allowed the village funds to undertake financial intermediation through managing savings and credit services (IFAD, 2007: 7). IFAD staff considers the issuing of this law a remarkable effort, since the village funds were established to be self-help groups and informal institutions that generally in Sudan are not allowed to receive savings deposits from the public as mentioned in chapter 6. However, in reality, this was not performed in such a way since the village funds had to keep the funds with the ABS and did not have full authority over the saved funds.

The budget of the project was supposed to be shared between the government of Sudan, IFAD and the community itself. Out of the project budget of SDD (Sudanese currency in 2001) 7.75 million (equivalent to S£ 7,750), SDD 1.17 million (S£ 1,170) were allocated to the rural finance component. Of this amount, SDD 0.65 million were designated as project grants to support rural finance through informal lending in the project villages. The remaining SDD 0.52 million were designated as a credit line to the ABS, to enable it to provide formal financial services in the project villages (IFAD, 2007).

The total project funds directed to the component of microfinance were distributed between the ABS and the village funds. The ABS was supposed to lend this money to the villagers in two ways; group loans and individual loans, which will be explained later in this chapter. The amount of funds given to the village funds should also be kept with the ABS but the village funds' coordinators took the disbursement decisions.

A whole range of activities were financed including sheep raising, sheep fattening, milk and poultry, small industries, services, trade, consumption, improved seeds, irrigated farming, crop production, crop marketing, stoves, and buildings (IFAD, 2006: 25). However, not all these activities were funded in all villages.

Within each village fund, there are three committees, the microfinance, the community development, and the women empowerment committee. The microfinance committee (also called lending committee) consists of four members (chairperson, treasurer, accountant, and loan officer). The members' role is to manage and control the village fund's credit operations and saving mobilization activities and to report and run the day-to-day accounting transactions.

The main constraints the projects faced were migration of some village extension workers and credit committee members. This affected the performance of the village funds in a number of villages. Additionally, the bookkeeping system and the financial procedures were seen by some communities as too complicated and had to be simplified to suit the educational level of the members (IFAD, 2006: 29). Generally, the high illiteracy rate of inhabitants affected the performance of many villages and led to their early withdrawal from the project. I visited Kabaka, a village near Al Dagag, which was among those villages dropped out in the early stages of the project for very low initial credit and savings performance. The main problems presented to me by the credit coordinator were that people were not motivated to join the project, did not participate in the initial meetings, and did not understand the project well. The credit coordinator claimed the high rate of illiteracy as the main reason, since there is no primary school in the village and very few inhabitants ever received any education. As a result, the number of people registered with the village fund and the amount of compulsory savings collected was not enough for IFAD to support the village fund, so the village was dropped out of the project in 2002.

The results of the evaluation of the project are presented in IFAD reports. The 2007 evaluation report of the credit component showed unsatisfactory results due to low repayment rates as mentioned. Meanwhile, in the general evaluation report (IFAD, 2009: xiv, xxi) the overall credit lines were evaluated to be satisfactory[1]. However, this component of the project will not be sustainable, unless major structuring efforts take place (IFAD 2009: xviff.; expert interview 5).

The evaluation results prompted me to conduct interviews with experts to understand the different views and results. They revealed that the overall credit performance declined especially during the last years because of the handover process of the village funds supervision from the IFAD project management unit to the ABS, which took longer than planned. Other constraints with regard to the delegation of authorities from the IFAD management unit to the government units were discussed. The sharp drop of

[1] This is the general evaluation of the project done by IFAD (IFAD, 2009: xv); three levels of rating were provided to evaluate the project components, highly satisfactory, e. g. construction of the Al Obeid-Bara road; moderately satisfactory e. g. natural resources utilization and development; and satisfactory e. g. rural finance services.

market prices especially for livestock due to adverse climatic and macroeconomic conditions resulted in quite low profit margins. Finally, law repayment rates were emphasized as another factor.

The main results of the evaluation showed outreach performance in the household targeting 51 %, membership outreach 29 %, outreach to poor households 45 % and outreach to women-headed households 46 %. (IFAD, 2007: 26). Another main criterion for evaluation was the repayment rate. The consolidated repayment rate of all the village funds ranged between 79 % and 83 % for the last three years (2004-2006). Any repayment rate below the 90 % mark was considered unacceptable under any condition, thus the overall repayment rates were unsatisfactory (IFAD, 2007: 15).

The final evaluation divided the total number of villages served into three categories in order to structure a new project phase dedicated to the issue of sustainability, which is planned to start in 2010[2] (IFAD, 2008). The categories are successful, moderate in performance and villages considered failures (IFAD, 2008). According to this report, the main criteria used for classifying villages are the same criteria used to evaluate the project throughout its performance mentioned above. Villages in the repayment range of 75-100 % are considered successful, villages in the range of 50 %-74 % average or moderate and villages below 50 % repayment performance failure and their program participation to be liquidated. IFAD officials consider the report central since it determines what can be done next to ensure project sustainability (IFAD, 2008).

To give an overview about the number of villages in each of these three categories in the Al Rahad administrative unit where Al Dagag is located, out of 28 villages served by the project, only 3 were considered successful, 14 moderate, and the remaining 11 failures. Al Dagag was evaluated as a moderate performer.[3] One of the main reasons for evaluating the Al Dagag fund as moderate is the declining repayment rates of the years 2003, 2004, 2005 and 2006 with 100 %, 100 %, 86 %, and 77 % respectively (IFAD, 2007a). The repayment rates show a gradual considerable decrease in the last years of the project and no further loans were given from 2007 until 2010 when I visited Al Dagag the last time. This result to a great extent matches what has been theoretically stated by Pischke (1994: 148) about the default problem encountered by many NGO programs.

Specifically in Al Dagag and from the brief report prepared by the Al Dagag village fund committee (IFAD, 2007a), it is stated that 131 households were registered as members in the Al Dagag village fund, and 319 individuals were provided with loans either from Al Dagag village fund or the ABS, 31 % of whom were women. With many problem associated with the bank in providing microfinance in Al Dagag the village fund encountered another set of problems. Results show that several issues were questionable regarding the performance of the village fund in Al Dagag and will be presented throughout this chapter. Most are related to the village fund governance, management and financial discipline and transparency. In the absence of any external monitoring, elites and better-offs capturing funds is an issue and, consequently, the inclusion of poor households is doubtful. In addition to that, the credit demand and supply gap at the village fund level is very large which was clear from the number of people in need for finance compared to the number of loans provided, which covered but a very small percentage of the demand presented in Al Dagag in absent of any assessment of the total demand.

9.2.2 Credit and Savings from the ABS and Al Dagag Village Fund

IFAD is the first and only NGO providing microfinance in Al Dagag; before that, only indigenous financial arrangements were available. The link that IFAD has established with the ABS (Al Rahad branch) was the first opportunity for all respondents to get loans from a bank. This is clear from the fact that most respondents started to take credits from the ABS for the first time when the IFAD project started in 2003, before they had no connections with the bank. After the IFAD project terminated only a few respondents, mainly Asha Alnoor and Basheer, continued taking credits from the

[2] The phase aimed for the project sustainability already started in January 2010. In interview five it is mentioned that this phase started by establishing a central fund that will be the responsible body for other village funds and to replace IFAD. More credit is planned to be provided for villages which have shown satisfactory performances.
[3] To understand better why Al Dagag ranked as moderate I visited two other villages (Rehood Alnabag and Mandoor) and conducted interviews with the credit committees in these villages. The result from the analysis of these interviews and the comparison between them and Al Dagag is presented in appendix 1.

ABS till 2009. This represents the discussion about the availability and the performance of banks in rural poor areas presented in chapters 3, 4 and 6.

While the ABS is a governmental specialized bank managed and regulated by the CBS, a general committee selected among Al Dagag people themselves managed the Al Dagag village fund established by IFAD. The credit committee was responsible for managing the microfinance component. The committee members were trained in the village fund financial rules, regulations and loan policies and procedures. The village fund coordinator was responsible for all activities. The accountant maintained accounts and kept books, the treasurer handled and managed cash and the loan officer was responsible for loan administration functions, including repayment follow-ups. At the end of each year, 30 % of a village fund profits were distributed amongst the village fund committee members as incentives. This was a considerable amount of money for the members of the project committees at the beginning of the project.

All loans from the ABS or the village funds were given within the Islamic finance system implemented in Sudan and all institutions were required to use the Islamic modes of finance as mentioned in chapter 6.

9.2.2.1 Types of Loans

ABS was supposed to provide two types of loan products for the NKRDP communities including Al Dagag; first, group loans provided for clients in villages that show satisfactory performance of repayment. Once the credit committee approved a loan and handed the applications to the ABS, the ABS credit officer accompanied all the borrowers from the village fund to the market where the assets were purchased and handed to the borrowers. This was performed in accordance with the Islamic mode of *Murabaha,* which was the only mode of finance used to provide loans to respondents. Thus, clients were not supposed to receive loans in a form of cash money but instead in kind. Second, individual loans were given; however, only after clients had organized in groups.

The size of loans was different between the ABS and the village fund. The ABS provided bigger amounts of funds that could exceed S£ 500 with no ceiling, unlike the village fund, that provided loans only of less than S£ 500. Any application of funds received by the village fund of more than S£ 500 were transferred to the ABS, this was one of IFAD project terms of loans.

The loans provided through both the village fund and the ABS ranged from loans for enhancing agriculture and raising livestock to loans directed to non-farm activities such as loans for petty trading and transportation. Table 5 illustrates credit provided for all clients in Al Dagag in the 2003-2006 period.

Table 5: Credit provided by IFAD through both ABS and the Al Dagag Village Fund 2003-2006

Year	Type of credit	Source of credit	Budget (S£)	Number of recipient	Women	Men
2003	Improved seeds	ABS	16,250	77	38	39
	Weeding	Village Fund (VF)	2,000	20	11	9
	Livestock	VF	2,150	7	6	1
	Supporting widows	VF	200	6	6	-
	Loan for education	VF	150	1	-	1
	Petty trading	VF	2,000	5	2	3
	Transportation/carts	VF	700	1	-	1
2004	Crop trading	ABS	6,400	8	1	7
	Petty trading	VF	900	2	2	-
	Transportation/carts	VF	1,900	3	-	3
	Livestock	ABS	23,250	36	16	20
	Medicines	VF	100	1	-	1
	Gas stoves	VF	320	4	4	-
	Weeding	VF	600	1	-	1
	Water pumps	ABS	4,200	2	-	2
	Watching club[4]	ABS	2,500	1	-	1
	Generator	ABS	1,500	1	-	1
	Fridge	ABS	1,500	1	1	-
2005	Livestock	VF	2,250	10	3	7
	Gas stoves	VF	160	1	1	-
2006	Petty trading	VF	250	1	-	1
	Livestock	VF	3,100	7	2	5

Source: Table prepared with my own data with the assistance of the general coordinator of the Al Dagag village fund and the coordinator of the credit committee fund in reviewing all books kept for credit provided in Al Dagag.
Note: There were no ready statistical reports counting number, types and years of loans provided.

As shown in table 5, small sized credits were given to both men and women. Generally, the budget for providing loans was very small compared to the total budget of the project in Al Dagag. Much of the total project funds directed toward the enhancement of basic services provision like building the primary school. However, the provision of credit gradually decreased in the last two years and no more loans were provided for clients in 2007. Loans for consumption, education and to support widows were very few and small in their amount and not regularly provided. Loans directed toward enhancing agriculture production was given only once for improved seeds, while funds for weeding and water pumps were provided in a very limited scope. Moreover, loans for raising livestock were provided in all the project stages targeting a considerable number of clients. Very small amounts of money were provided through the village fund while the bank played a very limited role and provided very specific loans and was absent in the last two years.

[4] The watching club is a club for watching satellite TV for a fee.

9.2.2.2 Group Lending

Loans provided through the bank and the village funds were offered under the condition that clients should be divided into solidarity groups of 10-15 members, headed by a group leader. Clients were organized in groups at the beginning of the project; however, the function of these groups was not clear aside from fulfilling the loan prerequisite. While an IFAD report (2007: 16) states that groups should ensure joint liability behavior, in reality, the system of joint liability was not enforced. When a member failed to repay the installments in time, the group did not repay the money on behalf of the delinquent borrower. The loans were not distributed in rotating terms, and the group was not used as guarantee for paying back. The majority of respondents found the group formation not successful and did not understand the purpose of it. This also applied to the ABS, which insisted on forming groups to be used as guarantee but later never used the groups to this end. Groups were only used as guarantee at the beginning of the project and only in the case of loans for improved seeds. Even in the provision of the improved seeds the process performed individually and by the credit committee and not by the group members. Clients applied for loans individually, the amount of seeds needed by each applicant was specified and then the aggregate amount of improved seeds reported to the bank (Interview with the coordinator of the village fund).

Additionally the idea of a rotating fund was completely absent: if one of the group members did not repay the others still could take loans. Most of the respondents did not know if other members received credits and paid back or not. Therefore, the groups never had any function and people stopped meeting after some time.

The composition of the groups was another debatable issue. For forming the groups at the beginning of the project, people had been asked to choose group members, not all of them from one family. However, later many changes took place and at the end many groups consisted only of one family like the group of Isa who was in one group with his father, brothers and uncles. A question was raised here in the course of the discussion with respondents why they were changing groups even if groups were not functioning. Most respondents said that the idea behind the pattern of having family groups was that when they are not able to repay and in case they go to jail, a group of family members will help them to pay the debt, which is why they prefer to be in a group of family members. However, it has not always been family members in the group who pay default loans; also other family members from outside the group have been involved.

Another point is that at the beginning every group had a leader, who should be informed before applying for a loan and was supposed to follow up on the repayment as well as organize meetings. Borrowers were supposed to repay the loans to the group leader during monthly meetings, and the group leader in turn to submit the repayments collected to the village fund's loan officer. However, in Al Dagag the groups were not functioning in that way and group leaders like Hassan were never given the chance to perform such duties.

Theoretically, group loans can play a significant role in reducing the cost of transaction (Moll, 1994: 83); however, in the case of Al Dagag this aim was not realized by the IFAD project.

9.2.2.3 Cost of Transaction

The cost of transaction for loans provided through ABS did not include the cost of funds as theoretically intended, i. e. interest paid to savers and depositors (Moll, 1994: 76) since the original fund comes from the partnership between IFAD and the Government of Sudan. In the case of the IFAD project the cost of transaction consisted of the administrative costs of providing and collecting the loans plus the costs of opening bank accounts for every client. Thus, respondents had to pay S£ 25 for opening a bank account plus other administrative charges. In total, it could reach S£ 60. For respondents who never applied for loans from the ABS the transaction fees are a major reason. Clients further have to pay costs of traveling between Al Rahad town where the ABS branch is located and Al Dagag. Other costs involved after receiving the loan were transport of assets purchased from the loans, for instance when respondents received sorghum as credit from the ABS in Al Rahad market they had to pay for the transport to Al Dagag. Cost of transportation to go every month and pay the installments is calculated by respondents in this category.

For the clients of the village fund, the initial cost of receiving a loan was not as much as the one of the bank. However, they were asked to pay a registration fees and they were asked to save in advance. Respondents, who did not register with the village fund, stated that the payment of the registration fees (S£ 25) and the compulsory initial savings were some of the reasons not to apply. Thus, it is obvious that since some people were unable to pay such costs in one lump sum they were excluded from project benefits. The cost of transaction including bank fees paid to a bank might still be a lot larger than the transaction cost paid for the village fund; people's inability to pay even small amounts of money to the village fund shows their living situation of misery and poverty. The case of Mustafa Mohamed who is considered destitute and has 12 children presents a good example since he could not pay the fees for the village fund, although he was in an urgent need for a credit. Another case is Alnoor Mohamed, who worked on the land of the village fund coordinator to pay the registration fees and compulsory savings; however, later when he wanted to apply he was told that he was not registered because he was not qualified.

The criterion of being in "urgent need" is mentioned by respondents themselves. In fact, it reflects their conception of credit and the fact that credit is linked with their need for cash and not perceived as credit to improve an already existing business or start a new one.

9.2.2.4 Procedures

Since the criteria for getting a loan from the ABS followed the general regulation of the CBS, respondents who applied for credit through the IFAD project needed to provide two types of collaterals. One is a recommendation from the village fund, the other is a check signed by the beneficiary that contains the installments the client has to repay including the profit margins that will be explained below. The bank asked clients to prepare a feasibility study for the project to be funded; however, most clients were illiterate and someone had to prepare it for them. In contrast to this, the village fund did not ask for guarantees other than the trust of the village fund committee, however, this trust tuned out to select those who have other sources of income.

Prerequisites set by IFAD for providing loans through the ABS were the same as the conditions of any commercial bank. However, in order to become eligible for a loan from the village fund, a member should deposit an initial registration fee as mentioned above and save at least S£ 2 per month for three months before the loan disbursement. The initial membership fee is refundable, in case a member wishes to withdraw from a village fund or if the village fund is dissolved. To become eligible, the village fund members fill up loan application forms, which are consolidated by the village fund to generate the total demand for loans. In reality, applicants were asked to write a simple request to present the details of the type, purpose, amount of money, and expected profits and to promise to pay back in time; the committee never evaluated the total demand for loans in Al Dagag. Some respondents like Asha Alnoor never wrote such a request to the village fund and still was given loans. Any application needed to be approved first by the village fund credit officer (also called the coordinator of the credit committee) in agreement with the village fund coordinator. The village fund coordinator and the credit officers processed any application, obtained the approval of the operations manager and sent the application to the financial controller at the controlling unit in Al Rahad. The latter was, after adequate scrutiny and approval of the project director, to arrange transfer of the loan fund to the respective village fund that is from the NKRDP account to the respective village fund's current account, maintained in an ABS.

Depending on funds availability, the time between application and loan disbursement was supposed to range between 1-3 weeks for loans from the ABS and the village fund as stated in IFAD reports. However, it took some respondents three months to get the loans from the ABS. The time between the application and receiving the money was not so long in the case of the village funds where some respondents reported receiving the money after a few days. However the procedures of the bank were so complicated that most respondents had to travel between Al Rahad and Al Dagag several times to open a bank account and submit documents, all of which made the time between loan application and loan disbursement rather long and costly. This aggravated the price volatility problem for loans provided for crop trading. At time of loan application market prices were high, but by the time of loan disbursement prices had often gone quite low. This led to immediate losses incurred by many clients as will be explained later in this chapter.

Regarding the Islamic modes of finance used in IFAD project, all respondents received their loans from the ABS and the village fund through *Murabaha* contracts. All respondents explained that they were directed by the bank or the village fund officers to use *Murabaha*. It means respondents were supposed not to receive cash but be paid in kind with crops, mainly sorghum, livestock or goods like a fridge or generator. Respondents had to pay a *Murabaha* profit margin of 1.5 % to the bank and 3 % to the village fund. The 3 % collected by the village fund was further divided between the bank (1.5 %) and the village fund (1.5 %). Even for consumption loans clients had to pay profit margins.

The village fund was not restricted in using *Murabaha* as in the case of Asha Alnoor who received S£ 120 in cash at her home from the coordinator of the credit committee, although she did not even apply for a loan. She explains that she was trusted by the members of the village fund committee; she recalls that after she received the money she thought about what could be done with it. Such a type of loan or contract shows confusion of procedures of the village fund. Moreover, some people understand what *Murabaha* is, but many do not understand the real meaning of *Murabaha* or cannot explain it or compare it with other modes of finance. They only know *Murabaha* how it has been explained by the village fund or the bank officials. Most understand that they have to pay profit margins and say if *Murabaha* is an Islamic method then it is good.

Generally, although the experiences of respondents show that the procedures of the village fund were sometimes contradicting and confusing, they were much easier than the procedures of the ABS. Moreover, what is provided in Al Dagag was microcredit but not microfinance; for only at the beginning of the project the village fund used the compulsory saving approach to mobilize clients' savings. The bank did not provide any savings or insurance facilities and was not engaged in any efforts to mobilize savings in Al Dagag during the IFAD project, other than the normal free of interest savings generally provided by all banks in NKS. None of the respondents keep savings with the ABS or other banks. However, financial services like savings and insurance are highly needed in such communities where the daily life of people is shaped with great uncertainty and risks affected the performance of the project.

9.2.3 IFAD Credit Project Outreach and Target Group in Al Dagag

Most respondents complain that the criteria for selecting clients were not clear and confusing; they give examples that some people who got loans were not very poor or in urgent need while others were even excluded for being poor. The criterion of being in an urgent need is mentioned by the respondents not by IFAD. Respondents repeatedly list Rugaia as an example of not poor because she is a teacher, and not in an urgent need because she does not have any children.

It is obvious that the bank only targeted well off people, those who are trusted by the village fund that they are able to pay back. There were no clear criteria for selecting clients by the village fund; the term "trust" was misused: and the committee included only those who have other sources of income like a son working in Khartoum or those who have livestock prior to receiving loans. The word trust was not explained by its ethical and moral meaning but by the existence of other sources of income that will enable the client to repay the loan in the future. The village fund did not ask for guarantees, but they used the criterion of having different sources of income in the household. Thus, trust became another word for collateral, however not used as one.

Furthermore, elites capturing resources in the IFAD project in Al Dagag was observed, this concerns people like Rugaia, Zainab, Hassan and others who are and were not poor or in an urgent need for credit like other people but were given loans. In addition to that, some clients were old like Fadil, Agba Alnoor, Kaltoom, and Hafeez and their children were grown up and working and they were still given loans for the reason that their sons can repay for them. Others were young, active and in an urgent need like Um Balaina, Umbelal or Alnoor Mohamed but were not granted any loans even if they applied. In addition to that the loans received by the members of the village fund committee are criticized by respondents. Respondents specifically talk about the loans received by the general coordinator, credit coordinator and the cashier. People also question the uses of the project funds, where and how the village fund committee spent the huge funds.

It was not clear why some respondents were given loans throughout all stages of the project while others were not. For instance Hassan, Asha Alnoor, and Basheer, who were trusted to repay, received loans through all phases of credit provision whereas most destitute only got improved seeds in the first phase 2003 but did not receive any loans in the later phases of providing livestock and small projects. Others who applied were excluded from the whole project by the credit committee for different reasons which feel confusing for most respondents.[5] Some people were rejected by being told that clients are allowed to get only one loan in order to give chances to others. Haloum was told that livestock is given only to men. In the case of Hameed the committee argued that there is no fund available while at the same time other people got loans. Others were told to wait for people to repay. Hassan who received only one loan from the village fund and refrained from applying a second time mentions that he prefers to deal with the bank but not with the "Rugaia fund"[6], and refuses to elaborate why.

Some destitute who did not apply explain they could not pay the contribution fees or the compulsory saving that the village fund asked people to pay before taking credit. Saida mentions that she did not go to ask about loans because she thought that loans would put a burden on her shoulders that she is not able to handle. By this, she means that she will be indebted and might not be able to repay the loans. Abualgaseem and his wife Khadiga did not participate in the project because although they had heard about the project they had been not contacted by the village fund committee and they were shy to request despite being in great need.

In the group interviews, another view is presented, that the main reason for not applying at all is that people did not know about the project. Some questioned the source of the IFAD fund thinking that the source of the IFAD money is illegal because coming from unknown sources, which they believed inacceptable in Islam. Many people were scared to apply after the experiences of relatives, neighbors or friends who could not pay back and went to jail.

As a result, not so many people have participated in the IFAD project in Al Dagag, although many have been in an urgent need for credit as they classify themselves. From this, one can conclude that the project from the people's perspective has had a limited outreach in Al Dagag. This is in addition to that fact that most of the project clients were better off before the project. Thus, the phenomenon of elites capturing funds plays part since the majority of respondents were selected because they have other sources of income that guaranteed their repayment of loans. Control over the distribution of funds rested with the village fund committee who received loans themselves. The question I would like to raise here is whether elites capturing funds reflects the capitalism and commercialization thinking of the new era of microfinance discussed in chapter 3 and 6. Loans did not really reach the destitute but the better-off people in Al Dagag even if this was not intentionally performed by IFAD. Clients, who received loans from the ABS were obviously better-off except in the case of loans for improved seed. None of the respondents who received loans from the ABS was very poor or destitute.

What is generally expected from giving loans to the ones who can bay back is that the repayment rate will be satisfactory. However, in reality this is not realized as will be explained in the next subchapter.

9.2.4 IFAD Credit Project Repayment Performance in Al Dagag

Theoretically, microfinance always followed the idea that credit is used to enhance the productive capacity of the borrower, which will increase his future income and in turn will allow him to pay interest and repay the loan, as stated by Heidhues (1994: 33). This is the logical and theoretical sequence of the use of loans and the repayment performance. The main empirical results show that in Al Dagag this did not happened in reality.

Generally, it is mentioned in most IFAD reports that the credit repayment performance of the ABS loans has been better than of the village funds loans. In Al Dagag, all respondents who received loans from the ABS have paid back their loans, even some people paid late. However, this has often been the case because family members had to pay the money in order to release the client from the jail. Respondents who did not pay until 2010 received loans from the village fund. Most respondents revealed that they do prioritize the repayment of the ABS loans over village fund loans. Because they are aware that, the bank can take

---

[5] This issue was discussed in individual interviews as well in group interviews.

[6] By using this label he links it to Rugaia because Rugaia was the coordinator of the credit committee who decided many issues, particularly selection of clients. Some people accepted her, others did not.

serious actions against default cases. Thus, the repayment rate for the bank was high while for the village fund was low reaching only 60 % in the last years (IFAD, 2007a).

Another result from the analysis of interviews is that only a few respondents could afford repayment from profits out of the businesses the credit was acquired for in the first place, which would have fulfilled the rationale of microfinance as presented above. The majority paid back using other sources like income from agricultural production or from the seasonal migration. The main reasons for this are too short time was to produce profits, people having to sell the assets received as credit, or losing them due to a shock or disaster. Different respondents employed different strategies to repay their loans either to the bank or the village fund. These strategies reflect each case's conditions and the diversified sources of money, which were used to pay back. Hashim who was asked to repay in one sum lump at the end of the loan period could not pay in time. Therefore, he went to Khartoum to work there specifically to repay and sent the installments from there. Alnaeem who got a loan from the village fund to raise livestock was asked to repay in three monthly installments. It took him more than one year to repay the loan to the village fund but and he used different sources, mainly his agriculture production. Other people borrowed or liquidated household assets or asked their relatives to help them repay.

In the interviews when asking why people did not repay at all or not within the allotted time limit, the village leaders including the coordinators of the village fund and the credit committee reply that the agriculture seasons were bad and there were crop failures and drought. As a result, the committee asked IFAD to postpone the payments, so until now many people have not repaid to the village fund. The answer is justifiable since it is clear from respondents' interviews that bad seasons not only affect the agriculture production but also the nonfarm activities because they are to some extent connected to agriculture. For instance, carts provided as credit are mainly used to transport crops or petty trading of crops and livestock. Bad seasons also affect the purchasing power of the income negatively. However, what is clear from this information is that the committee knows that clients will pay from other sources.

With regard to the procedures of repayment, respondents were asked at the beginning to pay back to the village fund and the bank in monthly installments that varied according to the type of the loan. However, later loans directed to agriculture like the improved seeds provided by the ABS are paid back at once after 10 months since they pay back in crops not in cash. In this case, respondents were asked to repay directly to the bank in Al Rahad, which incurred more cost of traveling and transportation in addition to the profit margin and the initial transaction cost. Thus, respondents faced the fact that they do not only have to pay back the loan and profit margin, but in some cases, the transaction cost exceeded even the amount of the loan. The procedures of paying back for the village fund were not consistent, that some respondents paid back in installments, others in one lump sum. Most respondents mentioned that the time given to them to repay was very short; clients were asked to pay in 3, 6, or 10 months; however, it is not clear why they were asked to repay in different periods of time, even if they received loans for the same purpose.

Although the majority of those given loans were selected along their expected ability to repay, still many of them could not repay in time. Thus for not repaying ABS loans on time many respondents went to jail; however, some were released when they promised to pay the money back in a specific and very short time ranging from tomorrow to one week. Others could not pay or promise to pay immediately and had to stay in jail until their families collected and repaid the money. Some respondents possessed livestock or crops saved in the house; they could sell it and repay for others who did not have savings.

Generally, repaying loans was problematic for the majority of respondents including those who later showed successful credit performance like Asha Alnoor. Some cases of respondents like Alnaeem who got a loan to buy a tractor could not repay in time, so he had to borrow and liquidate his savings in order to repay, but later things went better and he could even lease the tractor to other people.

Some women who were arrested they were excused to go home after they promised repaying the whole amount of money in a very short period of time. Kaltoom got a loan to buy livestock and was asked to repay in one lump sum after 6 months. However she could not because most of the livestock died, so she went to jail for two days. She was released because of her age. Her sons who work outside of Al Dagag had to send some of the money and she sold the rest of the livestock to pay the whole loan. Going to jail especially for the female respondents was a shameful experience as Haloum explains: "*During the investigation in the police department I was the only lady there and so many men, I was so embarrassed and felt ashamed, I asked them to release me and promised to repay in a few days and I did*". Not only women felt ashamed but also some male respondents. Hassan was also concerned about his image and reputation in the village after going to jail. However he stresses on his account that he was not the only one who went to jail: "*Not only me but also people like Asha Alnoor, Hamdalla, Kaltoom, Hafeez, Shaikh Ahmed went to jail for not paying back, it was a general condition, then our families had to pay back, then we have been released*".

Respondents who received loans directed to nonfarm activities also experienced difficulties in repaying their loans. For instance, Isa who got a loan from the ABS to buy a generator had to repay his loan from selling his agricultural production. He explains, "*I was so furious since I thought all people will desire to get electricity in their homes, and then only three houses asked for the services, I had to talk to IFAD people to postpone my loan repayment but they refused, I had to pay back from my crops*".

Some people did not repay to the village fund until 2010. Some of them did not pay on purpose like Abdalla who explains: "*Now I'm still left with* S£ *130 that is the last installment but I will not pay it. It is not that I cannot pay* S£ *130 but I do not want to repay since it is money for development, it is nobody's money as the people of the village fund said, it is for us and for our development*". Many other respondents who are confused about the source of IFAD money and its purpose also mention this. Two interrelated arguments are stated by many respondents: *Firstly*, people argue that IFAD money is "*nobody's money*", and it does not belong to a specific person thus, people should not be forced to repay. The *second* argumentation relates to the main objective for which IFAD money is used. Respondents believe that IFAD money is brought for their development—they call it money for development (*mal al tanmeea*) and should be used for this, thus they should not pay it back. This led to a decrease in the repayment rate of the project. Moreover, it reflects confusion of people's perception of microfinance and its purpose, uses and sources of funds and contradicts the rationale of microfinance as stated by Heidhues (1994: 33) and presented above. This discussion is also linked to the respondents' perception of using the loans for production or consumption purposes, an issue that will be discussed next.

9.2.5 Impact of the IFAD Project in Al Dagag: Short-Term Profitability or Substantial Long-Term Impact

Again considering the theoretical rationale of the microfinance mentioned above, I would like to argue here that the objective of microfinance should not only be increasing income, since in the situation of Al Dagag people, their livelihood is threatened by many personal shocks as well as or general or natural disasters. In such a vulnerable environment, increasing income could happen and still erode in a very short time. Thus, the question of profits is not the limit of this study; rather it is investigated further how respondents have used their loans and what profits they got out of them and how and if this provided them with a sustained source of income and/or enhanced their assets, capabilities and capital.

9.2.5.1 Profitability

Considering credit performance of respondents, I grouped them into three categories. *First*, those who made immediate losses or who sold the assets received as loans and used the money for consumption. *Second*, those who made profits at the beginning but were not sustainable or all profits were used for consumption purposes, and consequently capital or businesses were not developed, and they became more vulnerable to risks. *Finally*, those who made profits and used them to develop their businesses that have been able to provide them with a sustainable source of income and/or accumulate assets and capital, and thus help them to get out of poverty and vulnerability.

Some clients made immediate losses because of fluctuating prices, quality of assets provided and shocks and disasters that occurred in Al Dagag. A clear example of how the quality of assets provided and variations of prices generated of losses, are the loans provided by the ABS to clients as sorghum that is supposed to be used in crop trading business. These loans were a failure and respondents suffered huge losses; however, they had to pay for transportation, traveling, taxes and other expenses plus the profit margin for the bank, since in a *Murabaha* contract the bank does not share the loss. The main reason was that the quality of the sorghum provided by the ABS was not good. It was stored for a long time by the bank, but still provided for current market prices. Therefore, most of those who received loans of sorghum generated big losses as in the case of Hashim who received 17 sacks of sorghum, sold to him by the ABS for S£ 40 per sack while in the market the highest price was S£ 37 per sack for new crop and S£ 35 for stored crop. Additionally, after selling all crop immediately he had to pay for all expenses and costs mentioned above. The case of Fadil illustrates the same; he received one sack of beans as improved seeds. Since the quality was not good, he produced only two sacks, and when he wanted to sell them, prices were so low that he had to pay an extra S£ 50 to balance the required amount of repayment.

Many of the respondents who received improved seeds at the beginning of the project mention that the quality of seeds provided by the ABS was not good and they either lost the crop or produced very little. Respondents who immediately lost their capital still had to repay and did so by using other sources of income. In this category, I also grouped several respondents who say that they sold the whole or part of the assets received as loans and used the money for consumption in the household. Among many examples is Haloum who sold the livestock to pay for food and school fees of her children who were studying in Al Rahad. Omima sold the livestock because her son was sick and had to be treated in Khartoum.

The second group includes respondents who made profit at the beginning but later lost their profits and/or the capital. In these cases, the impacts of loans did not last for long considering the vulnerable environment people in Al Dagag live in. Even if they made profits, they were not substantial because of the small amounts of funds received. Those who made profits were faced with a set of problems, for instance loans provided for rising livestock is explained by many respondents as a good experience that has enabled them to generate immediate profit since they breed in the short time. However, they lost their assets or their profits later. Clients who received loans to raise livestock were asked to repay in monthly installments in 10 months. In few months, new-born livestock had grown up and some even multiplied. However, most of respondents either sold or lost their livestock a long time before the 10 moths specified by the bank or the village fund. Kaltoom received S£ 1500 from which she bought livestock for S£ 1100. However, she gave them to a herdsman to take care of near *Khour* Abuhabil. Even if they were grown up and breeded, later she lost most of the sheep in the flooding that year and was left with two, which she sold for only S£ 290. Since she was asked to repay in 10 months, and the agriculture season was bad, she went to jail for not paying back and her family had to pay the money. Hafiz received S£ 1000 from the ABS and he bought 10 goats. Breeding was successfully and in 10 months, they were 28, but he sold most of them to cover household expenses and others died.[7]

What is clear from the cases in these two groups, which include the majority of respondents, is that neither the credit nor the profits could be sustained. Even in the few cases when credit helped respondents to make profit and to increase household assets at the beginning, because of their difficult situations they could keep neither profits nor capital for a long time.

After illustrating the credit performance of the majority of respondents in Al Dagag who were not so successful in making or sustaining profits or capital, I would now like to present some of the few cases that can be considered as successful. The first case of Hassan reflects how loans directed to finance agriculture could be significantly successful and yield considerable profits. The case of Hamdalla presents how loans directed to petty trading also could be significant in providing sustainable income when it is used in the same businesses the client was already doing before receiving the loan. The case of Basheer is important for two points: Firstly, because he got the biggest loan in Al Dagag and secondly because he also used profits for improving his trade. At the end, I will introduce the most successful credit performance in the case of Asha Alnoor and illustrate how she managed not only to

[7] Other examples are Hamdallah and Ali. Also Dawa who took a machine to produce pasta but later could not market her pasta mainly because it is time consuming and people preferred the ready pasta they buy from the shops. Fatima who grew sesame out of the improved seeds she got from the village fund used the earnings from selling the sesame to buy 8 goats, but later the goats died after getting diarrhea. Batoolay was quite successful in her project of petty trading as she placed a *Tableea* (small table that is used to display goods) in front of her house, and it was successful for selling things like oil and sugar in small amounts; but then, after two years of success, she sold too many things for credit to the people who were digging the Hafeer, most of whom were not from Al Dagag. They left without clearing their credit. Alnaeem made profits that were later used to solve the financial problem of his brother.

generate immediate profits but also to diversify, sustain and build up her businesses.[8] These issues are clear only in these few successful cases. The case of Asha Alnoor reflects the traders' dilemma in Al Dagag.

An interesting point to be raised here is the fact that most of the successful IFAD clients used their profits for giving *Shail* to people in Al Dagag, as in the cases of Asha Alnoor, Basheer, Zainab Rugaia and Farhana.

Hassan is considered better-off by others because he is a university graduate and migrated to the Golf area for many years; he however classifies himself as poor. He was one of the only two IFAD clients in Al Dagag who asked for loans for enhancing their agriculture work. These two loans were used for buying water pumps to be used in *Khour* Abuhabil as a complementary irrigation system to rains or the natural floods of the *Khour*. Hassan explains that the credit helped him to increase his production land to a great extent. He further states that instead of producing 10 or 12 sacks sorghum in the years before using the pump, he is now producing an average of 24 sacks; however, he also mentions that the pump needs regular maintenance, for which he may need further loans. In fact, I interviewed Hassan in the three phases of data collection and when I updated his previous interviews in 2010, I found out that he was the only one who produced a reasonable amount of sorghum considering the fact that 2009 was a bad season for multiple reasons. Despite the spread of a crop disease that led to sorghum crop failure, he still produced 20 sacks while other respondents only harvested one or two sacks of sorghum or even lost the whole crop. The main reason mentioned by him is that using the pump allows him to grow earlier than the others; when *Khour* Abuhabil started early in April, Hassan started cultivating his land; thus when the disease spread he had already harvested most of his crop. He also adds that having the pump has helped him because he does not depend on rains only.

Hamdalla has five young children, received three loans, two from the village fund for petty trading to increase his work as butcher that he was already doing before the IFAD project and a third loan from the ABS to buy a donkey cart. Hamdalla used most of the loan fund and profits in developing his business as a butcher. He explains that the loan from the bank was the last because of the very long and complicated procedure. He had to wait for a long time for loan disbursement, and he needed to travel to Al Rahad several times. However, the donkey cart was successful and until 2010, he has considered it as one of the main source of income. His older son Kalas who is 8 years old now works with the cart after school time, while Hamdalla takes care of the butchery and other businesses like crop and livestock trading which he started recently using the profits of the loans he received. Hamdalla mentions that he has been making profits until now and his work as butcher flourishes using money also from the cart and the other businesses; so now he can slaughter more livestock and people in Al Dagag buy from him and not from the Al Semaih or the Al Rahad market anymore. Before taking the loan from IFAD, he used to slaughter once a week, now he does it three times a week. He is now planning to get a loan to buy a refrigerator to keep the meat. He and his wife Um Noor who I also interviewed believe that their life is much better than before, since Hamdalla could upgrade his business and this has resulted in considerable increase in income and savings in livestock that he also trades. For the three years, I visited Al Dagag he was one of the few men who do not need to migrate looking for work outside Al Dagag. Um Noor explains that their situations in the household is much better than before, she points out the new furniture, the extension in the residual and agricultural land that they recently purchased and the fact that her kids are going to school.

Basheer also has continued taking loans from the bank and used all the loans to boost his crop and livestock trading businesses, Even though he started his businesses before the IFAD project, after he got the first loan, his business improved. He said that the credit from the ABS was a turning point in his trade. He said the main reason behind his success is that he received the biggest loan in Al Dagag of S£ 1,900 from the bank in 2004. The loan was directed to livestock trading and he bought sheep. In addition to this loan, he also received two loans from the village fund. Basheer believes that his previous experience in trading helped him to be successful to a great extent, also his commitment, willingness and honesty in dealing with money issues.

With other successful cases like Rugaia, Zainab and Farhana, the cases of Hassan, Hamdalla and Basheer were not destitute before they got loans from IFAD; they had something to build upon. Hassan

[8] Some other successful cases are Rugaia, Zainab and Isa.

had his knowledge and the money he gained from his work in the Gulf area while Hamdalla already had his work as a butcher besides farming and also his father is one of the three shopkeepers in Al Dagag, which has helped him in many cases as he explains. Basheer was a crop trader even before he received loans from IFAD.

The next case is a unique case considering the fact that Asha Alnoor was destitute before getting the loans from IFAD. She and her husband were farming their own land and Asha used to work as a basket house-to-house vendor, which is called *tyjara al sabat* (basket trade). In addition to these, Asha and her husband also used to work as a laborer on other people's land. This explains why she is considered as the most successful credit performance case in the whole village; her experience is documented by IFAD and presented in many reports and presentations.

In 2003, Asha Alnoor asked the ABS for a refrigerator but she was convinced by the people of the village fund to apply for livestock, because having and using a refrigerator was a new idea in Al Dagag. Therefore, the coordinators of the village fund were afraid that it is not going to make a profit. Therefore, Asha applied for a loan to raise livestock in 2003, she received S£ 1000, and bought 10 sheep, but this was not successful because she could not keep the livestock, some were lost and others died so she was only left with two. Therefore, Asha could not repay the money in time, she went to jail and had to repay later from selling the crops she cultivated that year. After that, she and Batoolay applied for a loan (S£ 50 each) from the village fund and this time she used the money to make cakes and powdered juice, Asha narrates:

> "*Me and Batoolay, one of the members of my group, thought to get credit from the village fund to make powdered juice and cakes. We got 50 Pound for each in Ramadan. ... We were working together; we sold a very good quantity. We were selling here in Al Dagag and the near villages too (al heela wa al halal).*[9] *When Ramadan finished we collected all the money we got and divided it between us then we paid back the loan to Rugaia with 3 % profit. ... Yes the profit was good... I used it to buy kitchen utensils big plates and 3 pots ... yes this time I paid from the business itself not like the livestock raising loan when I had to pay form selling my crops.*"

After that she got another loan from the village fund, she recalls:

> "*Then Rugaia came to my house and she gave me S£ 120 she said 'take this money and do any investments with it, then pay it back with 3 % profit margin'; she put the money in my hand and closed it. I took the money and went to El Rahad market and bought powdered juice, powdered okra, soap, crops and one mango box... Wait I'm telling you, I made juice powder, and divided it and the other things in small plastic pages like the normal plastic bags and I collected them in my 'sabat' (basket); I told you before that I used to do this especially in summer when there are no farming activities. I used to go from house to another to sell things I put in my basket. It was hard for me at the beginning but I had to do it for my children, since at that time they were young and needed education we were in difficult situations (halatna saba)... the loan improved to great extent my basket trade ... yes I got good profits.*"

However, all through this time, Asha did not give up the idea of the fridge and insisted in 2004 to apply for a loan to buy one. She got a loan of S£ 1500, was accompanied by the coordinator of the village fund and the bank credit officer to the market, and bought a fridge of 14 inch using the whole amount of money. For the transportation, she had to use her own money. This was the first fridge in the whole village. However, Asha could not repay from the business of the fridge because the idea was new and the amount of ice the fridge produces was not enough to get much profits to cover the loan repayment. However, later she made good profits out of the fridge when she started to make ice cream and sell it in Al Dagag primary school, cold drinks, and cold water.

The small basket trade of Asha soon became a small shop inside her house:

> "*Then so many people used to come to buy things from the house like ice or cold drinks if they have guests and they could not find me in the house. So, I thought it is better to stay at home, and also I'm not young as before. So, I stayed at home but I thought maybe it is better if I stay at home to buy more things so when the ladies come they can find all what they need. I went to Al Rahad market and bought things like onion, sugar and oil, and stayed at home. Then the idea grew up*

[9] *Hila* is the village and *halal* is the plural and means the surrounding villages.

> *and this how the shop started. I needed to bring more things people of the village need and ask for like tea, soap, biscuits, date and sweets that I can sell on a daily basis...*"

The shop has been very successful, what I also observed is that Asha built up good social relationships with many people inside and outside Al Dagag especially women, more than the two other male shopkeepers. In most of the interviews, respondents mention Asha and her shop a lot more than the others. In addition, it is stated very clearly in many interviews that people would prefer to deal with Asha than the other shopkeepers. These relationships have been built through her house-to-house trading and her attitude of giving loans in case of emergencies and selling on credit. In addition, her charisma and strong personality have helped her to a great extent.

Asha also mentions that besides investing in her business she has used the profit for her children's education; something she considers crucial. Later two of her children graduated from universities and others were following their steps. Things then went so fast, after the fridge, she got a loan to buy a generator in 2005 and to do other businesses. By 2010, many houses were buying electricity from Asha. From the profits she got from the shop, she built a water basin, build a bakery, and build a separate room for the shop. She even mentions thinking about applying for a credit from the bank to buy a car that she will use as public transportation.

The case of Asha shows how credit can be successful for starting and improving businesses. Asha's life as well as the life of her family members has changed completely as a result of the loans she received from the IFAD project. She and her family graduated from their miserable and poor situation to be one of the better off households in Al Dagag.

9.2.5.2 Long-Term Impact

Positive long-term impact is considered to be a "sustainable" source of income that allows for more savings and accumulation of assets according to the definition of poverty and vulnerability within the livelihood discussion mentioned in chapter 2, 7 and 8. I asked respondents what benefits they have gained from taking loans from both the ABS and the village fund and how they perceive the impact of the IFAD project on their capabilities, livelihood assets and capital.

For this, I would like to start with Asha Alnoor since she is the only case in Al Dagag who graduated from poverty using IFAD loans. Others had some sort of investment before receiving IFAD loans, which makes it difficult to distinguish between impact of IFAD loans and others. In the case of Asha, it is obvious that she got ahead of the stage of making profits to even get a sustainable source of income; moreover, she ensures this by diversifying her sources of income in varied businesses and trades, which she has introduced gradually since receiving her first loan from IFAD. Now Asha has enough income to cover the household expenses and to keep more savings than other people. She even invests her profits in giving *Shail* and crop trading and this is considered by her more profitable than all her other businesses. I found out that most forms of capital discussed in chapter 2 are positively affected in the case of Asha. Her sustainable income (economic capital) is used for her children's education (human capital). Asha can also get more and bigger loans from the bank and can provide any guarantee (access, financial capital), she is able to give *Shail* (financial capital), she has rebuilt her house of mud and finally she bought a piece of residence land in the nearest town (physical capital). However, it is difficult to understand the effect of microfinance on the social capital in the case of Asha since she is a trader and a shopkeeper and affected to great extent by the trader's dilemma explained in chapter 2. What I have observed is that although Asha helps her community still some people criticize her for doing businesses in the commercial and profit maximizing way because sometimes she has to be tough with them to keep her aim of making profits and not only to help them in passing their emergencies and disasters. However, her social relations are much better than of the other shopkeepers, this might be her way to solve the trader's dilemma and to get more people to buy from her shop.

In addition to the personal impact, Asha thinks that the impact of the loans she received is also extended to be general and affect many people in Al Dagag not only her family. Asha thinks that not only she benefits from the credit she received but the whole village. In this context, she mentions that now she needs workers to help her, so she is providing employment opportunities in the village. Now the people of Al Dagag can drink cold water, use ice from her fridge, buy bread from her bakery, which was the first one in the village. They can charge their mobiles and get electricity from her generator, buy from the shop in cash or credit (as now they have more than two shops), borrow from her in cash, sell their small amounts of crops in her shop, and buy things for happy or sad occasions, sometimes even big quantities on credit. Asha is very proud of introducing these things to the village. In addition, she now feels secure against any emergencies or disaster. All her children are well educated and she is a well-known crop trader in and outside Al Dagag. In her point of view, her desires to be better, and most important her children to be educated, her natural sense of doing businesses and the help she got from her sons were the main reasons behind her success and the sustainability of her businesses.

Other respondents vary in their responses showing diversified uses of loans and profits and how it impacts on their household income and other assets. Most of the respondents have used parts of their profits or the loan for consumption purposes. These include buying food, covering sickness expenses, buying house furniture, and clothes for the Muslim Eid festival, paying school fees, building or maintaining houses, reducing the time spend in seasonal migration. All these are considered to be positive impacts on livelihood capital. The few successful cases used their profits for improving their businesses or starting other or new businesses that help them to earn more stable income as presented in the four cases above.

To conclude this subchapter I would like to present how the villagers themselves differentiate the impact of the credit provided by IFAD. In the interview with the village leaders,[10] including the village fund coordinator and the credit committee coordinator, the impact of credit on the household earnings and financial status were calculated. Clients of the Al Dagag IFAD project were grouped into three categories:

— The *first* group is worse off than before since they generated losses and had to repay from other sources (40 %).
— The *second* group is left just like before since they generated profits but later they lost profits and/or capital for various factors mentioned above (40 %)
— The *third* group is perceived as successful clients who generated profits and could build up sustainable sources of income that positively affected the household savings, assets and livelihood capital (20 %).

A justification of this result is also given in the group interview; that the composition of the loans portfolio was very risky and combined with the low repayment rates, which made the chances of making heavy losses very high. In addition to many cases of drought due to rain shortages and other shocks like crop failures due to crops diseases, insects and others, also livestock diseases, death or loss most people could not repay and that has lessened the impact and threatened the sustainability of the Al Dagag village fund work. When crop fails, the money from selling livestock is used for meeting household consumption needs and not for making loan repayments. This situation has resulted in several defaulters, who later faced the burden of repaying with no assets to be used.

I argue here, using the cases presented above, that microfinance on the one hand can help in getting a sustainable source of income, accumulate savings and thus can enhance people's poor situation and thereby their livelihood. Microfinance can be a tool to fight poverty and to get people safely away from what Ellis (2000) calls the "edge" which represents their vulnerability. However, on the other hand, microfinance can leave people worse off than before or just the same; both show an unfavorable impact. Unfortunately, people and households who are negatively affected or left just like before constitute the far greater majority with 80 % of those who received credit in Al Dagag. Moreover, as it has been revealed that most of the successful cases had some sort of investment or savings before they received the loan, I can thus argue here that microfinance alone has sustained the livelihood of only one person in Al Dagag.

To conclude this chapter, according to what has been presented so far most of those who received loans were those who were trusted by the village fund committee to repay. Most of these cases have other sources of income like remittances or saved assets like crops or livestock. The destitute were only given few loans at the beginning of the project as improved seeds, but the same respondents were not included when livestock or petty trading loans were given. Loans given to support female-

[10] In this focused group interview, it was important to include people having different points of view that support or do not support the IFAD project and the interview ended up by not only collecting information but also sharing of information between respondents.

headed households of widows who are considered destitute were few and also only given in the first phase of the project. The poor with no other sources of income are those who failed to benefit from receiving loans in the long run. Some of them made immediate profits however lost them due to the uncertain and highly vulnerable situations they live in.

Most of the loans were given for production purposes but the capital or the profits were used for consumption. What has been presented here is not meant to make a case against providing consumption loans or using profits for consumption purposes. Nevertheless, I want to argue that in an environment that threats the livelihood of people, the provision of credit has a very short and only immediate impact on household consumption. The number of those who graduated from poverty using loans from the IFAD project in Al Dagag is very low compared to the number of those who are left as before or have been negatively affected. Most of those who made profits lost them later due to shocks and disasters and a considerable number of clients also lost their loans for different factors presented above. Most used the profits or the credit itself for household consumption. Many respondents did not make any profits or just returned the funds back plus paying the profit margins.

I want to argue here using the case of Al Dagag that it is right what has been discussed in the literature about the difficulty of separating consumption from production in poor households (Heidhues, 1994; Helms, 2006; Rutherford, 2009: 38f.; cf. chapter 3). However, this strengthens the theoretical argumentation that the poor need multiple financial services that could smooth consumption, increase and improve production and contribute to insurance. It is obvious from the IFAD project details mentioned above that loans for consumption were very few and limited. Besides, the savings mobilization failed to realize its potential, accompanied by the absence of any insurance mechanisms. I consider these to be the main reasons that have hindered the realization of any substantial and longer impact of microfinance. This also confirms what has been discussed in chapter 3 as Heidhues' (1994) Helms' (2006), Rutherford's (2009) and Robinson's (2009) main argumentation is that the provision of credit only for production for household living in very risky environment where food security is an issue is not helpful.

Another important point to be raised here is that this is not to say that those who used profits for consumption did not benefit; in fact, in some cases, this helped in building up capital like human capital in the case of paying for school fees; but the impact is also affected by poverty and vulnerability. For instance, one could get a loan for education of one child; however, the loan might be very small and only suffice for school fees for a few months. Moreover, this child will be soon be forced by the family's poor situations to leave the school for many other reasons or even die from sickness like in the cases I mentioned in chapter 8. Thus, the impact cannot be sustained for the long term considering the unstable and vulnerable situations they live in. However, in many cases consumption loans lead to enable respondents not to sell their assets but rarely resulted in the accumulation of assets for the same cause of vulnerability to different types of risks.

What is more to this discussion is that the factor that has affected the realization of long-term impact and has been raised by the respondents themselves is the size of loans provided. It is obvious that the loans provided by IFAD reflect the theoretical definion of microfinance that loans for the poor should be small (Abugre, 1994; Heidhues, 1994) as discussed in chapter 3. However, it is clear that when respondents receive such small amounts they cannot utilize them to get substantial or long-term impact considering their vulnerable situation; while in the successful cases the prosperity of businesses increased as the size of the loans increased. Thus, size of the loan was one issue that should be focused on when looking for more effective substantial and longer impact of microfinance.

Coming back to the issue of the mobilization of savings, the performance of the saving component performed by the village funds for mobilizing savings has been evaluated by IFAD (IFAD, 2009) as being relatively weak because the current average savings per household represents less than 1 % of their total saving potential (IFAD, 2009). Savings are regarded as a means for getting the first loan from the village fund. The disbursement of subsequent loans is not linked to the quantity of savings. As a result, savings withdrawals are common after accessing the first loan. There are no other incentives for savings mobilization. Thus, members find it more remunerative to deploy saved up money in additional units of livestock, rather than saving their money with the village fund. In addition to that, the bank does not provide any incentives on savings for individuals or village funds. The funds collected by the village fund at the beginning of the project have not been paid back to clients as it was supposed to or used in any other projects; where these funds actually are is a question raised by many respondents. This might point to the mismanagement and corruption of the village fund executive committees in Al Dagag that have resulted in the deterioration of the village fund performance.

The impacts of IFAD and the ABS discussed above matches to a great extent much of what have been argued theoretically about banks and NGOs providing credit for the poor. NGOs are closer to grass-roots operations than banks and they have been working directly with communities and adopting more flexible methods in trying to use credit as a poverty alleviation tool. However, many dilemmas concerning their work are presented in chapters 3, 4, and 6 and also apply to the case of Al Dagag (cf. Pischke, 1994; Seibel, 1994; Bouman and Hospes, 1994; Abugre, 1994; Shete, 1999; Buchenrieder, 2000; Seibel, 2004; Nagarajan and Meyer, 2005; Elhiraika and Ahmed, 1998; Ibrahim and Arbab, 2006; IFAD, 2006, 2007, 2009). Combining microfinance in an integrated development approach with other elements such as awareness building, training and education goes at the expense of the provision of microfinance in the case of Al Dagag, since most of the funds were used more for community development facilities like building the Al Dagag School. Many issues revealed from the case of Al Dagag and questionable in the literature concerning NGOs provision of finance are also relevant to IFAD, such as the institutional capability to manage money, effective cost recovery and the sustainability of NGOs projects. NGOs also remain reluctant to charging a positive real interest rate, which undermines indigenous financial systems and largely lacks the discipline required for the provision of sustainable financial services (Abugre, 1994: 158). For one thing, NGOs are almost never truly self-reliant which affects the program's sustainability as also has become clear from the case of IFAD in Al Dagag.

Moreover, what respondents in Al Dagag mention about the microfinance efforts of ABS falls in line with the international debate on microfinance provided through banks. Writers like Adams et al. (1984), Pischke (1994: 52), Seibel (1994: 27), Bouman and Hospes (1994: 14), McLeod (1994: 14), Moll (1994: 70), Lapenu, (2002: 302), Nagarajan and Meyer (2005) and Elhiraika (2003) provide theoretical analyses to illustrate evidence of the difficulty of banks to provide financial help to the poor. The performance of banks and the programs, projects and schemes they support, however, have remained below expectations in most developing countries including Sudan for so many reasons explained in chapter 4 and 6. Furthermore, there is a general problem of reaching out to the very poor in rural areas by both banks (ABS) and NGOs (IFAD) in Al Dagag.

Moreover, in spite of poor results of bank performance in microfinance around the world, finance in Sudan using the case of IFAD and the ABS in Al Dagag microfinance still relies almost entirely on governmental banks or NGOs (Elhiraika, 2003: 31, expert interviews 1, 2, 3 and 4). Even acknowledging the recent efforts of the Central Bank of Sudan since 2002 in restructuring and downgrading banks, especially the ABS, they are still far from reaching rural poor as has been revealed in the case of Al Dagag.

10 Indigenous Financial Arrangements in Al Dagag

"*Even if Shail is exploitative but it is the only resort for cash in September, without it our children can die of hunger*" (in-depth interview with Farah Al Obied, Al Dagag, 2010).

"*Sandouq is very good because we use your own money and just like putting it aside to when you need it,... we decide our turns from the beginning when we say that 'I need my turn to be in this month', but in cases of emergencies, we give it immediately to the one who has the emergency*" (in-depth interview with Dawa, Al Dagag, 2010).

10.1 Introduction

This chapter is divided into three subchapters; the first investigates informal finance institutions in Al Dagag, including all indigenous financial arrangements such as Rotating Savings and Credit Associations (ROSCAs) or as they are called in Sudan *Sandouqs*, the money lending system *Shail* and other indigenous financial institutions which are embedded in the society of Al Dagag. Most of these arrangements take place beyond the fringe of formal financial markets where Adams and Fitchett (1992: 1) have also located them. Detailed information about each of these institutions is provided to show both benefits and problems associated. Descriptions how these institutions function, of organizational arrangements, procedures, membership, use of funds and repayments and changes over time are presented.

The second part shows how respondents compared and ranked both formal and informal institutions depending on their availability, outreach, access and size of loans. The ranking reverses the theoretical argumentation and the practice of focusing on the formal institutions ignoring the potentials of the indigenous ones. This is further argued in favour of upgrading or linking informal to formal institutions rather than downgrading banks. The main reason behind the suggestion is the fact that informal institutions have been embedded in the society for a long time; they demonstrate tendencies of consistency and rapid growth. This is also reflected in the many changes, which take place in both cases of *Sandouqs* or *Shail,* which are discussed and their impact presented.

In the third part, the importance of the informal finance for the case of Al Dagag and the possible relationships between the formal and informal institutions are discussed. The main focus of this part is on finding linkages between these institutions. Moreover, this part is devoted to showing how the behavior of formal and informal institutions could be in the case they coexist in rural areas. The case of Al Dagag is compared with the theory with regard to the three forms of coexistence between formal and informal financial institutions competition, co-operation and complementation. The main question is; which form of coexistence is more applicable to the case of Al Dagag and what are the effects. This discussion also serves as conclusion for this chapter.

10.2 *Sandouqs* in Al Dagag: Small but Effective

10.2.1 General Overview

The definition and descriptions of *Sandouqs*[1] provided by respondents in Al Dagag to great extent matches the description of "simple" ROSCAs provided by Geertz (1962), Ardener (1964), Ardener (1996), and Schultz, et al. (2008) presented in detail in chapters 4 and 6. *Sandouqs* in Al Dagag are simply a network of women who contribute the same amount of money in a fixed period of time; the collected fund is given to each one of them in rotation.

Sandouqs are not a new financial arrangement in Al Dagag, since most respondents said that *Sandouqs* were also done by their mothers and grandmothers; however at this time it is no longer the same procedures as will be explained below. The initial idea of the recent *Sandouqs* in Al Dagag came from the

[1] It is also called Sandug in the literature (Schultz, et al., 2008; Rehfisch, 1972).

neighboring village Kabaka[2] where they have had successful *Sandouqs* for a long time.[3] The point stressed by Ardener (1996: 1) in a her critique of Geertz that ROSCAs need not necessarily fade away as more developed financial institutions replace them, is completely true for the case of Al Dagag. *Sandouqs* have existed there since a long time and even with the existence of other financial institutions and the introduction of microfinance efforts to the village, women still prefer to form and join *Sandouqs* for the many advantages they have. Moreover, *Sandouqs* are located between the unsustainable microfinance efforts conducted by NGOs (IFAD) and banks (ABS) on the one hand and the exploitive money lending contract of *Shail* on the other hand.

There are many *Sandouqs* in Al Dagag. I personally heard about six or seven but the ones I chose for study are four *Sandouqs* that were running in 2010 and done for cash money. There is another type of *Sandouq* in Al Dagag, in which members contribute money to buy kitchen utensils for everyone in rotation; however, it is only one *Sandouq* and I decided not to go into detail about it, but I asked about it accidentally when I interviewed some respondents. It is only open to family members, as Kaltoom, the founder of the Sandouq, explains: "*We know each other well and we know that we are going to pay and if one could not pay her sisters can pay for her and she repays later or not, it does not matter we are all one family*". In this case, the members do not meet but only collect the money and buy the utensils since they live so near to each other some of them even live in the same household. However, the woman whose turn it is never gets the money in cash, normally the organizer or someone else assigned by the organizer will accompany her to the market to buy the utensils, and the transportation fees will be paid out of the collected money since they need to travel to Al Semaih or Al Rahad.

Respondents call the cash-based *Sandouqs* I researched by the amount each member has to contribute; thus, they are named "The one pound *Sandouq*", "The five pounds *Sandouq*", "The 10 pounds *Sandouq*" and "The 100 pounds *Sandouq*". I selected these *Sandouqs* for the reason that they show great differences and variations with regard to who can join them and the amount of the fixed contributions. In addition to that, they represent the extreme as well as the normal types of *Sandouqs* in Al Dagag concerning the amount of money paid and collected in what I call the continuum of *Sandouqs* in Al Dagag. At the same time, they share the same attribute that the payments are made in cash.

The one pound *Sandouq* consists of 15 women, every woman has to pay one pound every week that is a total of S£ 15 per week. The money is collected by the organizer and paid to one of them every month; that is S£ 60 in a meeting in the house of the one in turn. Collecting contributions on weekly basis applies also to the S£ 5 *Sandouq* where there are seven members and the S£ 10 *Sandouq* with 10 women. However, the S£ 100 *Sandouq* is different, for it consists of five female teachers of Al Dagag's primary school who share S£ 100 immediately from their monthly salary. One of them receive S£ 500 every month, and the members do not meet.

Generally, in the *Sandouqs* in Al Dagag, the fixed contributions are collected on weekly basis but money is disbursed every month. This is justified in different ways, first much of the money paid for *Sandouqs* is collected by respondents from the expenses of the household that are allotted for every Monday market. Moreover, in summer when men migrate and tend to send money home every week or two weeks, thus, the payment of *Sandouqs* on weekly basis depends on the flows of money in the household. Second, members live in a very risky environment and they might not be able to keep the money for one month. Also, the money collected every week is not that much and it is better for them to accumulate and distribute every month; for then the amount of money will be significant. This system of collecting the money weekly and distributing it monthly is never mentioned in any of the literature about ROSCAs.

Although in the first three *Sandouqs* the contributions are small amounts of money, it was interesting to know why even only one pound since it is a little amount of money. Respondents mention that the one pound is considered easy to be collected from the household expenses considering their difficult circumstances.

---

[2] This village however failed to satisfy the primary requirements of the IFAD project of collecting clients' registration fees and savings.

[3] Some respondents are involved in *Sandouqs* in Kabaka or other near villages or towns.

10.2.2 Membership: Who Can Join *Sandouqs* in Al Dagag?

Generally, *Sandouqs* like other ROSCAs mentioned in literature are considered women's informal arrangements (Ardener, 1964, 1996; Rehfisch, 1980; Schultz et al., 2008), even if some men are allowed to join still through their wives. This attribute make *Sandouqs* to be the most important financial institutions in Al Dagag for women providing them with credit, saving and insurance facilities, since none of the other financial services significantly serve women.

I would like to argue here that the amount of money among other factors determines the membership of each *Sandouq*. This is to say that *Sandouq* membership is determined by the capability to pay the respective amount of money. This is obvious in the fact that different people according to their financial capabilities join different *Sandouqs*. According to the members' attributes, it is obvious that the S£ 1 *Sandouq* and the S£ 100 *Sandouq* represent extreme arrangements, reflecting income situations at the respective ends of the income spectrum. In the middle, the other two *Sandouqs* work with an average amount of money between the two extremes. Accordingly, women have the choice to decide which *Sandouq* suites them. However, they represent a continuum of *Sandouqs* where one extreme is the smallest *Sandouq*, which any women can join because they are contributing only one pound per week. What is obvious is that most of the members are destitute; in fact, this is the only *Sandouq* open to them. The one pound *Sandouq* is followed by the S£ 5 and S£ 10 *Sandouqs* which are joined only by women who are poor but not destitute, can save more money, and show more diversification of income sources. On the other extreme, only the better-off (teachers), those who have a salary, can join the S£ 100 *Sandouq*.

Moreover, respondents who joined the S£ 5 *Sandouqs* live in the eastern part of the village and close to each other. The one pound *Sandouq* is for anybody who is asked by the organizer, Asha Alnoor, but normally the members are people who come to her shop. It is apparent that this is linked to the concept of moral economy as it shows the position of traders in the community and their aim of maximizing their profits collected when dealing with their relatives and friends in the village, who they have strong social relations with.

10.2.3 Organizational Features of *Sandouqs*

No one can join a *Sandouq* in Al Dagag when it has already started unless the woman pays for the turns missed. In order to quit from a *Sandouq* while it is already running, a woman has to return the money in case she already got her turn; if quitting before receiving her turn, the others have to pay back her contributions; however, quitting is not a regular occurrence.

Most *Sandouqs* go for many rounds. The one pound *Sandouq*, for instance, has now continued for three years successfully. The one for S£ 5 is in its second year, and the one for S£ 100 is in its first round but the members express their willingness to continue and have even started to ask other people like Dawa the midwife and Asha Alnoor to join them in the second round.

Doubling usually does not take place and women normally do not join more than one *Sandouq* due to their financial situation, only a few like Rugaia and Dawa who have monthly salaries are members in more than one *Sandouq*. For example, Dawa joined two *Sandouqs*, the S£ 1 and S£ 5 *Sandouq* and now she thinks about joining S£ 100 one. Also Kaltoom who is poor but not destitute is involved in two *Sandouqs*.

The order of rotation is discussed and agreed upon by all members. In the S£ 5, S£ 10 and S£ 100 *Sandouqs* the rotation is fixed from the beginning and well known to all members. However, it may change later when one of the members faces an emergency. Sometimes the rotation is fixed by drawing lots but normally the members select the turns depending on the needs of each member and the events they are expecting like birth giving during the rotation period. For instance, one could say that I would like to have my turn in a specific month when I have specific occasion. However, in the one pound *Sandouq* this is a little bit different. Here the organizer is the one who fixes the rotation, as some of the interviewed women mention. They complain that they might not even know when their turn comes. For instance, Alradeea says that the organizer does not ask her which turn she wants, but she will determine the turn normally to the end, because she might not pay in time. Alradeea said "*I wait without knowing if this is my turn or not*" but she says that if she has an emergency like a sick child she is sure they will give the turn to her. This from one side shows how the organizer, in the case of Asha, controls the rotation as she has many other connections with the members. From the other side this also shows how *Sandouqs* may be a very important insurance mechanism. The flexibility of rotation helps all women to cover urgent expenses and that is why they consider *Sandouqs* one of the most appropriate means to save next to the option of buying livestock. Some female respondents even prefer joining a *Sandouq* over buying livestock for the fact that they might join a *Sandouqs* without telling their husbands, this is related to the system of allocation discussed above in chapters 2 and 7.

In all *Sandouqs* in Al Dagag, one woman is the organizer or the leader. The main attributes of a leader are described as active, honest, and respected in the village. Furthermore, it is stated that the leader should not be in an urgent need for the money she is collecting. For instance, Asha Alnoor who owns a shop in the village, Mansora who is the Shaikh's wife and does not have children, and Rugaia who is a teacher and does not have children are the leaders of the *Sandouqs* I researched. Some respondents also mention that they have joined the one pound *Sandouq* because Asha Alnoor is the organizer and she can pay for those who cannot pay at time. Organizers are not paid for their work, but as mentioned above, the money is collected every week and kept with the organizer for one month. Thus in the case of Asha as it is agreed upon the members she can borrow the money and return it before the turn comes. All this makes it attractive to join a particular *Sandouq*, women members trust the organizer and some of them even save their cash money with the organizer outside the *Sandouq* arrangements.

In all types of ROSCAs mentioned in the literature and *Sandouqs* in Al Dagag, women who face problems of payment still have to pay the money. Defaulting can create problems but people in Al Dagag deal with this in a very good way. If a woman cannot pay at one turn, her situation and excuses are considered and normally it is agreed that she pays later. However, when this is repeated, members will ask her to leave the *Sandouq* immediately if she did not take her turn; and if she already took her turn she needs to borrow and pay the money back otherwise she will never join this *Sandouq* again or any other *Sandouq* in the village. This behavior toward defaulters is considered a guarantee for *Sandouqs* in Al Dagag since every woman is afraid to lose her financial reliability. Asha even explains that when a woman is asked to leave a *Sandouq* she will not be treated the same again and even for other financial transactions like buying from the shop on credit or taking *Shail*. For that, Alradeea said if she has no money she will collect wood and sell it to pay the one pound for the *Sandouq*. Those who are engaged in the one pound *Sandouq* can bring anything from the house like eggs or small amounts of crops to the shop of Asha Alnoor. This also demonstrates that when arrangements are indigenously initiated and members voluntarily and willingly join them, these arrangements show coherence in characteristics and procedures.

10.2.4 Social or Financial Institutions: Functions of *Sandouqs* in Al Dagag

The most important function of *Sandouqs* mentioned by respondents is that women are able to save an amount of money they could not save individually. Specifically because of their poor and vulnerable situation, women are always in need for cash in the household. However, they cannot save individually because of many persistent expenses in the households. Generally, women in Al Dagag do not have access to any savings facilities that help them to collect even small amount of money.

Another important role of *Sandouqs* in Al Dagag is their role as insurance mechanism similar to the role discussed in chapter 4 (Kimuyu, 1999; Klonner, 2003; Gugerty, 2005; Fang and Ke, 2007). This function is obvious because in all these *Sandouqs* in Al Dagag, any woman in need for cash to deal with an emergency is able to take the fund even if it is not her turn. Sometimes they divide the whole amount of money between the two, the one in urgent need for cash and the one in turn. In case more than one woman is in need to take the fund then the seriousness of each case will be considered in the meeting and funds either divided or given to the one in the more urgent need. Agreeing to this rule is one of the main conditions of joining *Sandouqs* in Al Dagag and considered non-negotiable by respondents. If one does not agree from the beginning she cannot join the group, it is openly discussed and agreed upon before starting the rounds. Moreover, since the money is collected on weekly basis and kept for one month with the organizer anyone of the group can borrow the funds and return the money before the turn comes. These specific characteristics of *Sandouqs* in Al Dagag make them very flexible institutions that contribute significantly to the serious vulnerability in the village in addition to their role in saving and credit.

In addition to the saving and insurance functions, *Sandouqs* are important in other ways like the fact that women meet every turn and this facilitates social connections besides the financial aspect. Members of the three *Sandouqs,* except the S£ 100 *Sandouq*, meet every month in the house of the person in turn. They expect all of them to come and if someone is not coming, she needs to excuse herself; otherwise, the one in turn will not visit her in her turn. Normally the members bring coffee and sugar, while the charcoal and the coffee utensils have to be prepared by the woman in turn. These meetings are not something that can be ignored since members consider them important to strengthen the social aspect of *Sandouqs*. However, when asked if respondents consider *Sandouqs* social or financial arrangements, while stressing the importance of both they prioritize the financial benefits. This locates *Sandouqs* in Al Dagag between the pure financial *Sandouqs* found by Schultz, et al. (2008) in urban and semi-urban Khartoum on the one side and Ardener who describes ROSCAs in the horn of Africa where ROSCAs are valued more for their social support than for their financial benefits (Ardener, 1996: 8) on the other side.

Most respondents in Al Dagag mention that *Sandouqs* are financial at first, they stress their need for money to cover urgent expenses and emergencies; however, the members do not ignore the building up of social solidarity and social connections during their meetings. The importance of the social aspect is also different from one group of women to another, reflected in their economic status; the destitute like Alradeea say that the purpose is basically financial since this is what they need. Other respondents like Hadia link the two aspects: "*The money we get is very important but also we sit together, we talk and dance, normally we go back to our houses better than we came*". Hadia's explanation focuses on their need for the money; yet, she does not ignore the social connections that build up by joining *Sandouqs*. Other women who are not really destitute consider both financial and social benefits equally important like Kaltoom who argues that money and other material things will vanish and what is left is the social relations that connect the group of women, the visits, the talk and other social attributes. When the women meet, they know everyone's news, issues, and they tell secrets and discuss problems. Kaltoom also mentions that *Sandouq* meetings strengthen her relationship with other group members. Thus while the money they get is important the social aspect is also important.

Another important function of *Sandouqs* in Al Dagag is that considerable amounts of money gained from *Sandouqs* are used to pay *Wajib*[4] and this reflects another social aspect of *Sandouqs* in Al Dagag. It also reflects how *Sandouqs* contribute to the insurance against emergencies. Women save in *Sandouqs* to use the money to help others when they encounter any emergency.

What I have found in Al Dagag is a little different from what Schultz, et al. (2008: 30) found in urban and semi-urban areas of Sudan, where they conclude that *Sandouqs* mainly address financial needs and not so much mutual aid or social exchange. This is explained by the fact that women in urban and semi-urban areas might not meet to collect the money. However, in Al Dagag meetings that take place every turn are quite important for the members. This could indicate differences between urban and rural areas for village people are still bounded by solidarity and mutual help. However, it seems significant that the S£ 100 *Sandouq* members never meet. This may be because not all teachers live in Al Dagag. Nevertheless it seems that this case is similar to what Schultz et al. (2008) describe for urban and semi-urban areas of Khartoum, and does not to a great extent represent the indigenous or local financial arrangements that have existed in Al Dagag for a long time. It might be something imported from more urbanized areas. Its different attributes also bring a sort of change to the patterns of *Sandouqs* in Al Dagag in that the women do not meet.

10.2.5 Utilization of *Sandouq* Funds

Answering the question how *Sandouq* money is used, most respondents basically list four main purposes: covering urgent household needs, savings in livestock for future needs, paying *Wajib*, and buying female goods. The following diagram shows the utilization of *Sandouq* funds, it has been developed from individual and group interviews.

[4] Mutual system of helping people in cases of occasions explained in chapter (livelihood)

Diagram 3: Utilization of *Sandouq* Funds in Al Dagag

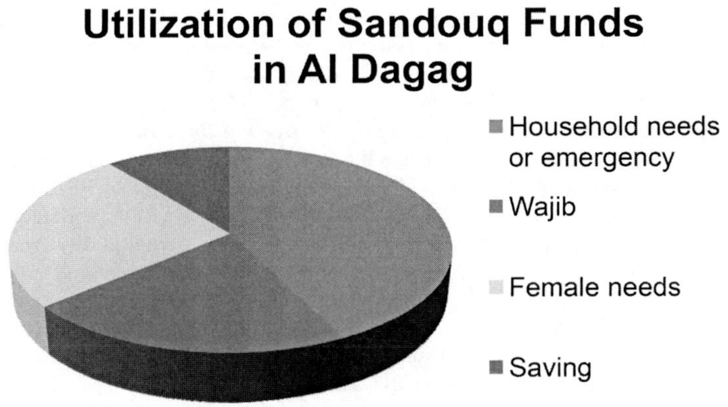

Source: my own diagram developed from individual and group interviews in Al Dagag 2009-2010
Note: The percentages are representing the frequency of mentioning every element

This diagram shows how *Sandouqs* have a significant effect on the welfare not only of the households but also of the community.

In addition, the part of the money received that is used for immediate or future household consumption indicates the important role that *Sandouqs* play in securing livelihood. Examples of household needs and emergencies mentioned by respondents are birth giving expenses, a sick child, a food shortage while the husband is not around, school fees, children clothes, and maintenance of the house. For instance, Umalhasan reports that she used the money of the one pound *Sandouq* to buy sorghum to feed her children. The majority of respondents pay these expenses directly while few have given the money to their husbands to cover a household need. However, in this case it is considered a loan that should be returned eventually. For instance, Amna gave the *Sandouq* money to her husband as a loan; he used the money in the household. Khamesa mentions the same but adds that if he will not repay she will take the money for the *Sandouq* for the next turn from him. The fact that women give *Sandouq* money as a loan to their husbands also strengthens the research finding that women in Al Dagag have separate pockets and they have control over their money.

Generally, who uses money received from *Sandouqs* in Al Dagag is the same as what is mentioned in the literature (Schultz et al., 2008). The contributed money comes from different sources (sometimes household budget or husbands' money); the woman is the only one in the household who decides about how to spend the money. However, from diagram 3 it is obvious that women often use the money to cover parts of the household expenses. Respondents explain that they pay for household needs or emergencies when the husband does not have the money to pay or they pay for things the husband is not willing to pay like female goods, such as Sudanese women's perfumes, clothes, or house utensils like bed sheets, kitchen utensils, chairs, and tables. Using the money for buying female goods is viewed as important by female respondents while men prioritize these goods as less important. The percentage of *Sandouq* money used for household needs supports my argument that women significantly contribute to the welfare of household. Not only that, also the income allocation system in Al Dagag shifts from the view of men as breadwinners to more patterns of shared responsibilities as discussed in chapter 7.

It is stated five times by different respondents that they have used the money for savings, mainly for buying livestock, and in one case, Bakheta bought a golden ring to save her *Sandouq* money. However many respondents mention that when they receive the money they pay for one or two next turns which I also count as savings. In addition to that, some women like Kaltoom who is involved in two *Sandouqs* take only part of the money and leave the rest with the organizer, especially Asha Alnoor who will use the money for her trade, until Kaltoom is in need of it. Asha saves the money and can use it in her business without interest. I find this contradicts the assessment that the *Sandouq* organizer is not paid; at least in the case of Asha Alnoor this is different, for she receives a financial benefit from organizing a *Sandouq* in that she can invest the funds free of interest or charge. In the case of the S£ 100 *Sandouq* two respondents report that they are going to use the money for giving *Shail*.

The contribution of the *Sandouq* fund to household, savings and others makes them significant in bridging shortages in household spending. It is equally important as men's migration when there are no agriculture activities. If money from *Sandouqs* is used for covering the cost of an emergency or dealing with urgent food shortages this helps to enhance the welfare of the household, and provides a certain degree of security. This argument can also be justified by their flexibility of rotations. This is well discussed in the literature (Ardener, 1964; Klonner, 2001); in ROSCAs with a predetermined order the order may be changed in favor of a participant who suffers an unforeseen liquidity crisis.

My results regarding *Sandouqs* in Al Dagag go in line with Krahnen and Schmidt (1994: 47) and Pischke (1992: 326ff.). According to them, ROSCAs have three main functions; firstly the accumulation of saving, secondly the transformation of the size of savings, thirdly the intermediation between depositors and in some cases the insurance against individual hazards. This is also stressed by Geertz (1962) for whom ROSCAs represent one of the basic savings habits of people. For this reason, he supports ROSCAs and highlights their importance for the creation of saving in developing countries. Adams (1992: 13) presents the same argumentation, for according to him ROSCAs help people to pool savings and tie loans to deposits. However, the *Sandouqs* in Al Dagag are only simple arrangements, not like the ones Adams describes where large amounts and many people are involved and the amount of money is sometimes greater than the amount held in banks. Still, the S£ 100 *Sandouq* represents to some extent a type mentioned by Adams (1992: 13f.), which is organized between employees of official institutions, however in Al Dagag joined by few people. Overall, the majority of respondents in Al Dagag consider *Sandouqs* very important because they help people to save a considerable amount of money, which they could not save regularly by themselves. The members get back their own money thus they are not indebted to anyone. Khamesa stresses that *Sandouqs* are voluntary savings arrangements that she joins when she feels she can do it and Alradeea comments: "*Joining a Sandouq makes me feel secure that I have some savings or I'm waiting for something valuable to come*".

Sandouqs have changed over time also in Al Dagag. The original version of *Sandouqs* in Al Dagag matches to great extent the one described by Rehfisch (1980). In the past *Sandouqs* were performed among women who contributed a little saved portion of goods that are normally consumed in the household, mainly sugar. The same applies to *Shail* that was exchanged in the past dealing in the form of crops and is now done by money. However, arrangements where contributions are made in sugar still exist in Al Dagag but not in rotation. This could be the point to introduce *Gameea* in the next sub-chapter.

10.3 *Gameea*: An Indigenous Insurance Mechanism

A *Gameea* has all the attributes of *Sandouqs* mentioned above; only that a *Gameea* is not a rotating arrangement. In Al Dagag *Gameea* is done only once a year to cover the sugar consumption of Ramadan or other types of assets like kitchen utensils. Indeed, there are three types of *Gameea*, one to collect sugar, a second to collect money (one pound) to buy sugar and the third is to collect money to buy utensils that can be used for events like weddings and funerals. With regard to the sugar *Gameea,* women start contributing money or sugar a few months before Ramadan, and near to Ramadan, they meet all together and divide the whole amount of sugar among them. All participants meet once when the organizer distributes the sugar contributed or bought for money, however in the *Gameea* for utensils members never meet.

The *Gameea* for utensils is composed of households instead of individuals. Each household contributes S£ 20 once. From the money, the *Gameea* buys the utensils and stores them in the village storage room built by IFAD. Every one of those households who paid the initial contribution is allowed to borrow the utensils. When anything is lost or broken replacements need to be made. Few respondents have joined this *Gameea*; the main reason being that they cannot pay the initial contribution.

With regard to the *Gameea* for sugar, women contribute one *Ratul*[5] sugar and sometimes one bar of soap every week for three or four months until Ramadan starts. Then they distribute the whole quantity among them. Alternatively, they collect money to buy sugar and other stuff for Ramadan like oil, dates and so on. The participation in a sugar *Gameea* depends on the season. If the season is good, more people participate. Most respondents get more sugar than they need for Ramadan. Thus, they can sell it and use the money for other things. For instance, Khamesa bought one goat from the sugar *Gameea* because the sugar she received was more than what she needed.

The one *Ratul* sugar is not difficult to be collected and many respondents use the rest of the house sugar for *Gameea*. Others sell small amount of crops or other things like eggs to buy one *Ratul* sugar. Only one woman out of my respondents who is destitute did not join a sugar *Gameea*, mainly because she cannot save the amount of sugar requested for contribution. The majority of respondents join one either in Al Dagag or in the nearest village with their relatives.

Gameeas for collecting sugar for Ramadan have been there in Al Dagag for a very long time, Shamom who is old talks about *Gameea* for sugar in the past and mentions that even her mother and grandmother joined such a *Gameea*. From these attributes *Gameea* becomes apparent as an important insurance mechanism against expected or unexpected future household expenses. As well, it represents an indigenous arrangement to finance consumption purposes.

10.4 Money Lending in Al Dagag: The Dilemma of *Shail*

The main argumentation I extracted from the *Shail* experience is that these institutions might reflect the shift in the society from a subsistence peasant society to a more commercialized one. Geertz (1962) in the case of ROSCAs supports this argument; however, I find it more applicable to the case of the *Shail* system in Al Dagag.

10.4.1 Model of *Shail* in Al Dagag

Although usually *Shail*[6] is mentioned in the literature for the case of the Al Gezira Scheme, (Wilmington, 1955; Brausch, 1964, Adam and Apaya, 1973: 104), I can report that *Shail* exists in some parts of Kordofan (Kevane, 1992). However, in the beginning of my research I doubted its existence in Al Dagag. Answers to my initial questions in 2007 confirmed this. However, in an interview[7] in 2008 with Shaikh Ahmed who has a shop in Al Dagag and is not satisfied with the IFAD project mentions that he gives *Shail* although IFAD does not permit it. Thus, I investigated in this confusing issue. By 2009 and the end of the IFAD project[8] I found out that *Shail* never stopped in Al Dagag even though it was reduced during the period of the IFAD project. The main reason against *Shail* stressed by IFAD officials in their training sessions was that *Shail* is not the proper source of finance for the poor because it is exploitative and people should stop dealing with it. Thus, respondents were reluctant to talk of it. In general, the *Shail* system has been found in Sudan for a long time, scholars like Wilmingtom (1955) and Brausch (1964) describe *Shail* in Sudan already in the 1950s and1960s and give evidence that the *Shail* system existed even before that, as presented in chapter 6. In Al Dagag *Shail* is not new either, many respondents mention that it has existed for a very long time. However, it is different from what has been mentioned in the literature and it also has changed from how it was done before. The recent changes are not reflected in the literature yet.

I will first discuss how *Shail* has recently taken place in Al Dagag and then discuss how it has changed over time and how it differs from its description in the literature. Respondents describe *Shail* today as "*receiving small amounts of money when we are in urgent need in September*". People have to

---

[5] One Ratul = 450 gram.

[6] In the literature the spelling Shayl and Sheil, are used; however, in Al Dagag *Shail* is called *Mashal*, using the language of the area, and the trader is called *Mashal* trader.

[7] Who passed away before my visit in 2009.

[8] This is also due to changing of my position and introduction to the villagers as mentioned in the methodology chapter.

repay with crops, mainly sesame[9] in October or not later than November. For instance, when I was in Al Dagag in 2009, interviews with respondents and *Shail* traders revealed that a farmer could borrow S£ 50 in cash from a *Shail* trader in September mainly to cover the cost of an urgent household need like the cost of treating a sick child. The contract is conducted under the condition that he or she has to repay one sack[10] of sesame in October (the market price of one sack Sesame in October 2009 was S£ 105). Why is *Shail* only used in September? Respondents explain that in September, there are no other options to get cash, for all crops are on the way but not yet ready to be harvested, there is no farming work available and men cannot migrate because they are waiting for the crops to be ready. They call September "*mafrag al habatain*" (the small space between two parts of one seed, e. g. groundnuts). In this month relatives or friends cannot give free of interest loans and shopkeepers stop selling on credit, all financial contract are performed in *Shail*.

One of the main conditions of *Shail* contracts is that payments should be made in an amount of crop, which is specified in the initial contract. Normally in Al Dagag, traders prefer to deal with sesame for the main reason that its prices are always high and stable since it is considered as one of the most important cash crops in Sudan.[11] After harvesting time it is well known that sesame prices in the market are high; for example in 2008 (interview with Shaikh Ahmed) the market price of one *Guntar*[12] sesame was over S£ 90 while traders had given *Shail* for S£ 40 in September. Mariam asked in September to get *Shail* for S£ 100 that she will repay with 2.5 *Guntar* sesame after one month. If she could have sold the crop in or after the harvest time in the market, she would have sold it for S£ 225.

Shail prices increase every year; when I returned in 2009 the *Shail* price for one *Guntar* sesame was S£ 50 and the market price after harvest S£ 100-110. That means the interest rate was more than 100 %, thus traders more than doubled their investment. All *Shail* traders say that in case prices in the market are less than the *Shail* price set at the beginning of the contract, they take the loss. However, they report that this has never happened before when dealing with sesame, and it happened only once in the past when *Shail* was given in sorghum. In responding to the question how they determine the price of *Shail*, the three *Shail* traders I interviewed explain that it is not them who determine the prices but the big crops traders in El Obeid or Al Rahad. *Shail* traders also mention that as soon as the prices are fixed no trader would increase or decrease them. One of the *Shail* traders comments that she tried once to raise the price but she thought it is not wise for the fact that the big crop traders will punish her and later she will not be able to sell the crop she collected, and if she reduces the price she thinks nobody will take *Shail* from her.

It is obvious from the definition above that respondents are asked to repay in a very short time, it is common that all recipients should repay in October or at last in November immediately after harvest.

In discussing who takes *Shail* and how regularly, the analysis of interviews and the constant comparison of cases and categories revealed that the classification into better-off, poor and destitute makes the difference. The ones who give *Shail* are the better-off, while the poor and the destitute are the recipients. The difference between the poor and the destitute is that the poor take *Shail* but not regularly, because they have some sort of assets, and only sometimes when they are in an urgent need for cash in September they tend to take *Shail* while all the destitute report resorting to *Shail* contracts every year. From the total number of interviewees only two respondents never took *Shail* before, the majority of respondents took *Shail* even the better-off and also the *Shail* traders like Zainab and Asha Alnoor have taken *Shail* before they belonged to the group of the better-off. Asha explains: "*When we were poor and my children were young and went to school I took Shail*".

Discussing if *Shail* is exploitative or not and why, some respondents express that they ask for *Shail* as the only help they can get in September; however at the same time they think that *Shail* is not Islamic and illegal because of its high interest rates, the significant variations in prices, and the short time of repayment. People also question why it is done for a specific crop and only in a specific month during the year. Contrary to this, *Shail* traders are convinced that *Shail* is Islamic and legal since it does not include payment money for money as Islam prohibits.

---

[9] Recently in Al Dagag *Shail* has only been given only for Sesame and no longer for Sorghum or Hibiscus.
[10] One sack = 105.7 liters based on the U.S. bushel, or 109.1 liters based on the British Imperial bushel.
[11] It is also used for producing oil, thus its price is always high.
[12] One Guntar = 143.8 kilogram.

Explicitly most respondents perceive *Shail* as exploitative. Although they take the cash to solve urgent needs like feeding their children, later they give their crops, which they cultivated the whole season for a very low price. Therefore, they solve their immediate problems by getting bigger and longer-term problems. By taking *Shail* people reduce the agricultural production that is supposed to be used for subsistence, and thus endure not only income shortages but also endangerment of their food security among other problems.

Alradeea, for instance, one of the destitute in Al Dagag with no regular income and no saved assets, produced only two sacks of sesame in the season of 2009. These two sacks she had to pay back to the *Shail* trader. She took S£ 75 as *Shail* from two *Shail* traders in September because she and her two children were in urgent need to buy sorghum for food, and at that time, their own crops were not due for harvest. The two sacks of sesame valued more than S£ 150 in the market after harvest, which could have covered the household food expenses for some times. The *Shail* trader in turn got 100% profit if he or she sold the crop immediately in the market.

The case of Mustafa Mohamed is even more severe, it shows how *Shail* can leave farmers in great indebtedness. Mustafa took *Shail* for five *Guntar* of sesame in 2008 and could not pay due to the bad season in that year. He promised the *Shail* trader to pay in 2009, but 2009 he had to take another *Shail* (five *Guntar*) however, from different *Shail* traders, so he now had to pay back 10 *Guntar* of sesame. In light of the crop failure of 2009, Mustafa now thinks that he will not be able to pay and he is afraid that he will be put in jail. He took the money this year because his wife was sick and he could not cultivate all his land because he was working for others on a daily basis to get daily income.

Amna who took *Shail* to cover a hospital bill describes her experience of taking *Shail*: "*It is so awful that when they came to take my crops I was almost having a heart failure*". Although *Shail* is the only source of credit in September, in most cases I studied, *Shail* left people in miserable and more vulnerable situations. In some cases, recipients were left in great indebtedness to the *Shail* traders. In other words, *Shail* in Al Dagag very much represents the stereotype of money lending that is described by Adams and Fitchett (1992: 7) as exploitative.

10.4.2 *Shail* Transaction Procedures

Shail usually starts when traders announce having money for *Shail*; then needy people will come and ask. Most respondents take from traders inside Al Dagag. No collaterals are required; the whole system is based on mutual trust as mentioned by respondents. Normally *Shail* contracts are not written down in a formal contract manner but the *Shail* trader will write down the names, the amount of money paid, the number of *Guntar*s, the type of crops, and the agreed date of payment. Sometimes witnesses attend the agreement in case more than one person comes to ask for *Shail* but this is not required. Most of the respondents tell the *Shail* trader why they need *Shail*; however, this is not a condition either.

Even if loans are not institutionalized or written in a formal contractual manner, still *Shail* traders could claim their money from defaulters. They resort to the native system in the village and in case this is not successful, they can bring the issue to the police department in Al Rahad. All respondents and *Shail* traders claim that this would happen in case of defaulting however I have not come across any case of *Shail* recipients who went to jail for not paying, even though I did find a few cases who did not pay in time or not at all but still were not taken to jail. Asking every respondent who takes *Shail* regularly why they are keen to pay back, Hukum Al Gadeer explains why people fear to default even if they might not been taken to jail: "*No way, you have to repay otherwise nobody will give you again. Especially in that month when you are looking at your kids crying from hunger, we have to repay to take next time*". Um Balaina is one of the few not allowed to take *Shail* again since two years ago she took *Shail* and she could not pay in time. She states, "*it was a big scandal and the trader was mean he told everyone that I did not repay, since then if I ask for Shail nobody gives me*". The case of Um Balaina brings the discussion to the question of what the criteria for giving *Shail* are.

Generally, the criteria for giving *Shail* to farmers do not depend on whether the farmer's crops are good or not or if he is poor or better-off but only on the moral reputation of the person. It really depends on trust in its pure meaning and not on having other sources of income like with the IFAD village fund credit officials. From what I have experienced, all people asking for *Shail* have been given, whether poor or not. The main criteria listed by *Shail* traders are therefore previous experience and financial reputation. For instance, Asha Alnoor mentions that she would never give *Shail* to someone who did not repay to her once or to the other traders. The reputation of a person is not linked only to *Shail* contracts, but some people are viewed as problematic from Asha's experience as shopkeeper or organizer of a *Sandouq*.

Another important issue in the repayment of *Shail* is that in case of not repaying, defaulters will be dealt with according to their social relationship and connections to the *Shail* traders; for example close relatives are not punished as much as those who are not. Radea who received *Shail* from her husband (who is married to two wives) was worried to repay but interviewing her showed that she is not as much worried like the others who received *Shail* from strangers. Rugaia as a *Shail* trader also mentions that in many cases the *Shail* recipients could not bring back the whole amount of crop that they agreed to repay; however, if they are close relatives and it is a small amount she will not talk about it, but she might not give them *Shail* if they come again.

Another way of distributing risks of giving *Shail* to the poor is that generally limits are put on how many *Guntar* one person can take. These limits depend on the financial capabilities of that person. The *Shail* trader might determine the number of *Guntar* every one can take and they prefer to distribute the whole amount of money they have among as many people as possible. It is clear that by doing so they distribute the risk of defaulting. However, in order to get bigger amounts, people ask for *Shail* from more than one trader.

Giving *Shail* and the way *Shail* traders deal with defaulting is also connected to bad and good seasons of agriculture production. If the season is bad or there are well known individual cases of crop failures the borrowers have to buy the crop from the market and give it to the *Shail* trader. In these cases, borrowers pay additional costs like the cost of transportation. It is very rare that a *Shail* recipient is allowed to repay in money and only happens with very close relatives. In this case he or she will be asked to pay the same money as received and the contract is regarded a free of interest loan. This happened only once during my fieldwork with a close relative of Rugaia. Zainab, a *Shail* trader, explains that in the case of default, she will allow the farmer to pay in installments of crops that he has to buy from the market. However, in this case she might not give them *Shail* money again. Zainab also comments that if the person is a close relative he or she can repay next year. This contradicts the statement of Asha Alnoor that she will give anyone except those with a bad financial reputation, an answer also given by Rugaia who stresses the point that she gives *Shail* to everyone in order to help her relatives and not only to make profits. Rugaia also mentions that she is more flexible with people in Al Dagag concerning repayment of *Shail* because she wants to protect them from dealing with the big *Shail* traders who might not understand the situations of the poor. Additionally, she argues that if the people deal with her then they reduce the cost of transportation and costs they pay when taking the crops outside Al Dagag.

Generally, there is no stereotyped behavior or general pattern concerning delaying or defaulting, the procedures are set by the traders according to the case in present. It also to a great extend linked to the social relationship between the lender and the recipient.

Normally in Al Dagag, the *Shail* trader collects the crop from the farmer and pays the cost of transportation; the traders come with empty sacks to the fields of the farmer and take the crops. However, traders outside Al Dagag wait for the farmers to bring the crops to them, and then the farmers have to pay the transportation costs. Generally, the crops collected by the *Shail* traders are stored until prices are high.

It is obvious from the interviews with *Shail* traders that they give *Shail* mainly for the high profits they can get. The financial benefits of *Shail* are well confirmed by traders, however as expressed by all *Shail* traders it has another social side of helping people when they are in an urgent need. Zainab who has been giving *Shail* for 6 years explains that the main reason besides profit is that people come to her in desperate times when they need to feed or treat their kids and ask for *Shail*, "*I do it for the profits and also to help people when they are in need*".

However, traders' supposed motives behind giving *Shail* and the view of *Shail* recipients who recognize *Shail* as exploitative clearly contradict each other. This contradiction is explained by the moral economy and the trader's dilemma. It is clear that by making excess profits from the people who are in their social networks *Shail* traders feel guilty and try to explain their behavior by stressing that they are helping their people. This reflects the notion of moral economy where traders look to maximize their profits and at the same time depend on the community for their own survival. It expresses the various ways in which community customs and social pressures force economic actors in a society to correspond to traditional norms. Thus, *Shail* traders tend to be more involved in social networks and provide other benefits to the poor.

As sources of *Shail* money, the traders report normally using their own savings. Zainab states, "*I started when I got credit from IFAD in form of a sheep raising loan and I got good profits out of it then I used this profits for giving Shail*". All *Shail* traders agree that they save during the season in order to give *Shail* in September. Not only Zainab started when she got profits out of loans from IFAD project but also Asha Alnoor, Rugaia[13] and Farhana[14]. The *Shail* traders whom I interviewed (Asha, Rugaia and Zainab) report being three out of seven recent *Shail* traders in Al Dagag, and that the number has increased over the past few years; before there were fewer *Shail* traders in the village.

Not surprisingly, *Shail* traders' income has increased significantly by giving *Shail*; however, since people including Rugaia as a *Shail* trader perceive *Shail* as exploitative I was eager to find out how this could affect the *Shail* traders' social image and social connections in the village. Surprisingly, the three *Shail* traders agree that it has improved their position financially and also socially. Many respondents do not accuse the traders but they point the finger at their need or the absence of other options. What is obvious here is that *Shail* traders keep their good image in the village by adopting several coping strategies. For instance, they do not behave aggressively with default cases and forgive in case the amount of crops is less than what was contracted. In other times, they give people more time to pay back and in the case of close family members, they tend to postpone the deal to the next year. Further, I can observe from the case of Rugaia that she gives free of interest loans during the farming season to many people, which I also consider a coping strategy. Rugaia is a teacher in the Al Dagag primary school where she also helps many parents by either exempting them from or postponing the school fees. In few cases she even pays the school fees for the children herself. Asha Alnoor organizes the one pound *Sandouq* that is joined by the poor and destitute women, thus she has the power to select women for this *Sandouq* and the *Gameea* for utensils that can be used for occasions in the village. Moreover, she is the coordinator of the women committee of the IFAD project. She also sells on credit and helps many people by giving them free of interest loans during the farming season and is involved in many other transactions to keep her social image in the village. This is also applied to transactions with shops (like Asha Alnoor's own shop) that will be explained below.

Zainab says that giving Shail has positive effects on her social status since now all people respect her: "*Now I have a voice in the village and people say that Zainab solved our problems by giving us Shail. For example one person said that I rescued his son by giving him Shail otherwise the child could have died if I had not given him money for treatment*".

10.4.3 Transformation of *Shail* Contract

It is interesting to show how *Shail* have changed over time and how *Shail* contracts in Al Dagag are different from what have been mentioned in studies in the Al Gezira State. These changes can be grouped in three points: Cash for sesame contracts, the purpose and time of taking *Shail*, and who receives and who gives *Shail*.

Cash for sesame: According to the literature (Kevane, 1993: 516; Brausch, 1964: 345) *Shail* is given in cash and is returned in crops; however, in the past, *Shail* was not given in cash in Al Dagag. Zainab and other respondents explain that in the past *Shail* was an amount of sorghum received by the farmer who had to return it in sorghum, one old sack for a new sack. Today *Shail* is given in the form of money to the farmer and he is obliged to repay it only in sesame not sorghum or groundnuts as it was in the past (also stated by Kevane, 1992: 520).

Purpose and time of taking Shail: The purpose for receiving *Shail* in Al Dagag today is not inputs or labor or other uses for agriculture how it has been in the past or what is mentioned in the literature but poor farmers use *Shail* for consumption purposes, mainly to cover expenses of an emergency.

---

[13] In my first interview with Rugaia in 2008 she said that there are no *Shail* transactions in Al Dagag because of the awareness raising done by IFAD project. However, in 2009 I interviewed Rugaia as a *Shail* trader.
[14] I did not interview Farhana as a *Shail* trader.

Moreover, according to the literature the *Shail* trader gets involved during the growing season, not only for financial matters but also for social responsibilities, since he supposedly provides other services besides *Shail*, for instance Brausch (1964: 345) recalls from Wilmingtom (1955) that:

> "*Some of the 'services' which the creditor supplies are technical; for instance he will often supervise and advise the cultivator during the crop season and at harvest time so that the work is done with care and efficiency compatible with the lender's stake. Other services are of a nature which transcends the immediate commercial relationship between lender and borrower. By communal tradition the borrower is not merely a 'client' but in* many *ways a social responsibility of the lender. The latter* may *be expected to lend extra money for medical emergencies, weddings, birth ceremonies, etc., regardless of the status of the outstanding loans... the lender must, under pain of communal ostracism, make further loans to a delinquent cultivator—even though he might be ready to write off the debt—if the cultivator's livelihood depends on it. This is but one aspect of the moral obligation which moneylenders by tradition and sometimes also by inclination accept once a steady credit relationship has been established. Thus, Shail had very important social implications, which often outweighed its economic aspects.*"

In the cases of this quotation, *Shail* traders and recipients have a steady and strong relationship that goes beyond *Shail*. This relationship starts when giving *Shail* at the beginning of the season and the trader gets involved during the whole season. However, in Al Dagag, recently this not been the case; traders do not get involved during growing season, *Shail* is given only in September and repaid in short period of time. This makes the relationship between the lender and the borrower a sort of pure financial relations different from the one in the quotation.

Who receives and who gives Shail? In Al Dagag *Shail* is given to anyone including the poor and destitute and not like only to a small number of well-known borrowers as reported by Kevane (1993) and Buckley (1997: 1084) and others. The main outcomes of this study reveal that the main guarantee for repaying is trust and financial reputation backed up by the fact that in cases of default family members are responsible to pay for the defaulter. Thus, at the end the *Shail* trader will get his or her money back. Another point is that even family members can be asked to take *Shail* in September, it is clear that this shows a transformation of *Shail* contract since I have never come across any case of *Shail* between family members in the literature. It also shows contradicting results to what I have found concerning how people help each other in Al Dagag. For instance, Aldur took *Shail* from her father and had to pay it back whereas Radea took *Shail* from her husband. What I have observed is that this behavior is acceptable in Al Dagga since no one complained or perceived it as something unusual.

To conclude the discussion; what Geertz (1962) argues for the case of ROSCAs I find more applicable to the system of *Shail* in Al Dagag. Geertz (1962: 242) describes how institutions can be an intermediate rung from peasant to more commercialized thinking:

> "*... [It is a] means of which traditionalistic forms of social relationship are mobilized so as to fulfill non-traditionalistic economic functions. It will be seen, in fact, to be an 'intermediate' institution growing up within peasant social structures, to harmonize agrarian economic patterns with commercial ones, to act as a bridge between peasant and trader attitudes toward money and its uses*".

I find this applicable to great extent not to the *Sandouqs* in Al Dagag but more to the system of *Shail*. Geertz's (1962: 260) elaborates:

> "*[It is an] 'intermediate' institution which links traditional motivations to modern functions, serving at the same time to transform those motivations toward a more rationalistic basis; it 'facilitates' the learning of new skills, patterns of behavior, and value orientations, and makes possible some changes in the structural principles in the general direction of modernization, without undermining the basic cohesion and solidarity of the group... [It is an] intermediate institution, a product of a shift from a traditionalistic agrarian society to an increasingly fluid commercial one, whether this shift be very slow or very rapid. It, too, mobilizes familiar motivations and applies them to unfamiliar purposes, while serving at the same time to reconstruct those motivations on a more flexible basis*".

In Al Dagag *Shail* is now done by traders in a commercialized and professional way. Moreover, it is revealed that the number of *Shail* traders increases and they aim to make profits rather than any other benefits. They became professional crop traders and most of them are now well known in the trade. In this case, *Shail* is an intermediate institution that reflects shifts in the society from looking for subsistence to more commercialized orientations, especially because *Shail* trading is increasing and could be considered a livelihood pattern as explained in chapter 7. This also reflected in reorienting some of the society values and norms to accept such behavior; mainly because the poor *Shail* clients realize it to be exploitative, however, their demand for *Shail* loans increases rapidly.

From the traders' side, *Shail* also facilitates the learning of new skills of making money, engaged in commercial and trade transactions in not only Al Dagag but even extending to the outside market.

In addition to that, the commercialization of *Shail* transactions is also supported by the fact that it takes place even within one family and among members of the same household. Additionally, the guiding transactions principles, the way of repayment, the penalties or incentives for giving *Shail* and how these affect any future transactions make Geertz's argumentation more applicable to the *Shail* system in Al Dagag than to *Sandouqs*.

10.5 Financial Transactions with Shops in Al Dagag

For all respondents, it is normal to buy on credit or borrow cash from the shops, mostly during summer when men have to migrate looking for jobs. Hameed explains, "*When I'm not here my children can take anything from the shop on credit and I send them money to repay*". Farhana who is a teacher and is also considered one of the better-off in Al Dagag is the only respondent who does not buy on credit or take cash credit from the shops. She explains that she can pay in cash and that her husband has a shop in Sinar in the Blue Nile State and usually sends grocery or money.

It is observable that one household member, normally the head of the household, buys on credit, and in some cases the wife also has a separate account. As Haloum explains: "*My husband used to buy on credit on his name, but sometimes I buy on my name and I pay by myself, my son send to me so I can pay*". This also indicates what has been described in chapter 7 that women have separate purses and income pooling is not common in Al Dagag. Since most people buy on credit, it is clear that they have to repay in a short time normally not more than two weeks. Most respondents prioritize borrowing from shopkeepers over other types of loans; this shows the importance of the transactions with shops in Al Dagag. Most respondents state that when they get some money, the first thing they do is to pay shopkeepers. For instance, Kaltoom explains: "*When I get money I pay the shopkeeper immediately because I will need to take again, we need it all the time*". Hassan admits that he even borrows money from a relative or a friend to repay the shopkeeper since he will be dealing with him all the time. People can repay also in crops or other things like a chicken or eggs that has the same value of the debt by evaluation of the shopkeeper.

Some people set themselves limits for their accounts depending on their financial capability. For example, Bakheta will not exceed S£ 50; others like Amna will not exceed S£ 20 before paying back. However, the shopkeeper also sets limits for people who known to be unable to repay in a short time. Normally the shopkeeper will ask this people to repay first as soon as they reach S£ 10-20.

Some respondents even have special accounts that they should repay in one week or the maximum of two weeks. The shopkeepers call such accounts "closed accounts", while others with diversified sources of income are allowed to have an "open account" which they can balance monthly. Asha Alnoor explains that only people who have a son or a relative working permanently outside Al Dagag can have monthly accounts in her shop. In these cases, they can buy on credit for the whole month whereas others have to pay in a shorter period normally one week. Another common financial transaction with shops in Al Dagag is related to social occasions such as funerals and in a few cases weddings. People as mentioned before collect their contribution to cover the cost of funerals. This money will be given to the shopkeeper, who keeps it in an account for this special occasion.

Generally, cash credit from the shopkeeper is not available to anyone. The shopkeeper will not give credit unless in the case of real emergency or to those he or she knows to repay, which are mostly people who have children or relatives working permanently or seasonally outside Al Dagag. The main problem for the shopkeeper is that people have to repay in a short time since the goods sold on credit are the capital of the shopkeeper, which needs to circulate to generate profits. On the other side, the shopkeepers normally sell most of their goods this way considering the fact that people buy from the shop in Al Dagag and do not go to the nearest markets where things are cheaper only because they can buy on credit in the village. Selling on credit is considered profitable by Asha Alnoor. Asha also is sure that when she helps people they will not go to other shops or to the town for to buy their needs. Still, cases of default can create problems between the shopkeeper and the borrower that might result in mistrust between the two parties; consequently, this will affect future relationships.

The relationships between the shopkeepers and his customers as well as *Shail* trading in Al Dagag and how this is embedded in social relationships can be described by the so called traders' dilemma discussed by Evers and Schrader (1994) and others. Evers and Schrader (1994) describe the situation of a shopkeeper in a moral economy as a dilemma, a situation in which an actor has to choose between two courses of action, both deemed to be equally unfavorable, undesirable or at best neutral. In a community like Al Dagag where solidarity, mutual assistance, and reciprocity shape the relationships between people, traders like Asha Alnoor can find themselves in a dilemma situation where they either serve their own trading interest of maximize profits or help their relatives, friends and the people they live with.

Evers and Schrader (1994: 7) explain a situation just similar to the situation of Asha Alnoor. On the one hand, traders need to buy goods from fellow peasants who are members of their own village community and with whom they have social relations, but sell to others outside the village where prices are determined by big traders. Evers and Schrader explain:

> "*In their own village prices are influenced, if not determined, by a 'moral economy' of fair prices and by a predominance of the use value rather than the exchange value of subsistence crops. Outside the village they are confronted with the anonymous, often 'anarchic', demand of the open market with often widely fluctuating prices. Traders tend to be caught in the middle and are justly called 'middlemen' in this sense, bearing the risk not only of economic loss but also of discrimination and peasant wrath*" (Evers and Schrader, 1994: 7).

On the other hand, traders need to sell their products to their fellow villagers:

> "*Let us consider the case of a woman in a small rural community who sets up a shop to sell kitchen utensils... If she asks for the highest prices from her fellow villagers she will be ostracized for being greedy. If she is generous both in terms of a low price and in extending credit, she will face losses and possibly bankruptcy*" (Evers and Schrader, 1994: 8).

This example explains exactly where Asha finds herself in Al Dagag. She sells to villagers and buys their crops and other goods outside the village on the market. Asha as a petty trader normally sets her prices higher than the market prices; still she considers the ability of people to pay. At the same time, she also knows that if she increases the prices too much then nobody will buy from her. Still she knows most people tend to come to buy from her shop since the other alternatives are either to go to the Al Semaih market once a week or to travel far to the Al Rahad market or to deal with other shopkeepers. Most people prefer to buy from shops in Al Dagag for supplying their daily smaller needs or to bridge a shortage in goods that they already bought from other markets. Besides, shops in Al Dagag play an important role in buying small amounts of crops on cash something villagers cannot find in the other markets.

Diversifying her business to include almost all goods needed by any household in Al Dagag puts her in a monopoly situation in the village. She deals with products ranging from foodstuff, water, and other households' needs to crops. Moreover, in buying from or selling to people in Al Dagag she is the one who set prices and negotiates with villagers. All this makes her shop the shop that people prefer. In addition, she treats those who deal with her shop differently; they are more welcome than at other places to ask for free of interest credit to cover the cost of an emergency. It is clear that this is similar to what have been presented by Adams and Fitchett (1992: 16) as a situation when loans are linked to the marketing of goods. They present cases of merchants in various countries who provide loans to some of their customers to facilitate purchases or sales of goods.

This example not only shows how trading takes place in Al Dagag but also how financial transactions are embedded into a complex networks of social relations and social norms. This is also reflected in the literature about moral economy as explained in chapter 2. Moreover, it shows that economic exchange is a tool to strengthen solidarity and social connections and serves as an insurance mechanism for both the traders and their clients. As well, this provides answer to the question of how trading in such situations may happen without endangering the purpose of maximizing profits. That is to say, what Asha gains from her shop is not considered unfair accumulation of wealth by villagers, something that would endanger her reputation in the village.

10.6 Credit from Relatives and Friends

Loans between relatives or friends in Al Dagag are widespread and constitute free of interest loans given when relatives or friends ask (cf. Adams and Fitchett, 1992: 12). Such a loan does not include any formal procedures and normally encompasses only small amounts of money to be repaid in a short time. In Al Dagag, the amount of money varies between S£ 1 and S£ 20. Sometimes it can even be more depending on the financial capabilities of the lender and the borrower. These credits are mainly granted in emergencies like child sickness, unexpected guests, food shortages, school fees, traveling for emergency, income shortages and sickness disabling labor.

Respondents do not only borrow cash but also other assets like crops for consumption or food to bridge a gap in the household consumption. In such cases, the repayment will be in the same type of assets and the same quantity. It implicitly includes the notion of reciprocity that who gives today might be in need to borrow tomorrow. The promise includes the date of paying back and how they will repay; Batoolay explains, "*if you borrow from a relative or friend you have to say when and how you will repay, I think if you have nothing nobody will lend you and your word is the only guarantee you provide. For example you should say I will repay when my son sends money to me or when I sell my crops*".

Respondents borrow from relatives and friends with no difference whether they are destitute, poor or better-off; however, the poor borrow more regularly. Respondents to great extent consider loans from relatives and friends a way of strengthening social relations and creating closeness and solidarity between people. The main problems are that it can also create problems in cases of default or delay, which can threaten any future relations. Another problem is that it is not always easy to find someone who has cash reserves and also in Al Dagag such types of loans normally do not take place in September when most people are in need. Moreover, people who have some savings to be used for urgent needs are forced to give them away if some of their relatives ask.

Generally, respondents' standpoint about free of interest credit from relatives and friends in Al Dagag corresponds to Steinwand's (1994: 297) and Bouman's (1994: 116) assessment that family loans and different mutual assistance networks can provide opportunities of money lending and constitute a significant portion of the whole credit arrangements in Third World countries (cf. chapter 3).

10.7 Comparison and Ranking of Sources of Microfinance in Al Dagag: Reversing the Theory

Before breaking into the discussion about comparing and ranking financial institutions, it is worth mentioning that many respondents rather hesitate to take credit and believe that it is better to work than to take credit or being indebted to individuals or organizations. Respondents are worried about the humiliation that they might face, when they ask for money or when they cannot repay. They think that if they do take credit it is better to get loans directed to enhance their farming activities.

The main criteria used as a basis for comparing and ranking financial institutions are access and availability, easiness of procedures and outreach and type of target group that each source of microfinance accommodates. These criteria are developed from both literature and consulting with respondents. Impacts compared in terms of which institutions are more helpful in providing security in cases of income shortages and consumption insufficiency.[15] Table 6 summarizes the main results of comparing and ranking financial institutions in Al Dagag.

[15] Impact and outreach adopted from Zeller and Meyer (2002) to investigate microfinance institutions, while access and availability and easiness of procedures are stated by respondents.

Table 6: Comparing and Ranking Microfinance Institutions in Al Dagag

Criteria / Ranked	Access and Availability	Providing larger amounts of money	Easiness of Procedures	Outreach and Target Group
First	Buying from shops on credit	Bank	Buying from shops on credit	Buying from shops on credit
Second	Credit from relatives and friends	IFAD Village fund	Credit from relatives and friends	Credit from relatives and friends
Third	*Shail*	*Sandouqs*	*Shail*	*Shail*
Fourth	*Sandouqs*	*Shail*	*Sandouqs*	IFAD Village fund
Fifth	IFAD Village Fund	Credit from relatives and friends	IFAD Village fund	*Sandouqs*
Sixth	Bank	Buying from shops on credit	Bank	Bank

Source: Table developed in a group interview with respondents in Al Dagag village, NKS (21. 12. 2009)

The discussion will be presented according to how respondents ranked institution starting from the ones better in providing financial services for them. What is obvious is that the sequence is reversed as respondents start with the informal institutions, and banks are located at the end of the list.

10.7.1 Indigenous Money Lending Systems in Al Dagag

10.7.1.1 Financial Transactions with Shops in Al Dagag

Almost all respondents consider financial transactions with shops the most convenient form of financial transaction. Thus buying from shops on credit or taking small cash loans in cases of income shortages is ranked the first financial choice. They regard it as the fastest, easiest, and the most available way of getting small amounts of money, additionally it is a free of interest loan. Thus, they rank it first considering three out of the four criteria set above. However, it is ranked the last when the amount of loan is considered. The shopkeeper knows everybody well and understands the situations of every household in Al Dagag. Thus, he or she can set limits to the amount of money he or she gives or sells on credit. The main problem with this financial relationship is the fact that people have to repay in a short time. In addition, all goods in Al Dagag shops are much more expensive than general market prices. The shopkeeper tries to avoid risky transactions also by considering seasonality in the flow of income, and such loans are not available in September. All respondents agree that even if taking loans from shops or buying on credit helps people it is still considered a debt that has to be repaid sooner or later, which for many respondents leads to more income shortages in the future. Additionally, in cases of default it creates problems between the shopkeeper and the borrower.

10.7.1.2 Credit from Relatives and Friends

Most respondents think it is always better to borrow from relatives and friends in cases of income shortages. However, when loans are needed for investments the IFAD village fund is believed to be better than relatives or friends. As it is obvious from table 6, these types of loans are ranked second in three out four criteria after the loans and other transactions with shops, meanwhile ranked fifth regarding amount of loan. Respondents believe that relatives and friends are more understanding since they know their circumstances well and understand when they are not able to repay. Moreover, respondents even consider loans from relatives and friends a means of strengthening social relations and creating closeness and solidarity between people. The main problem mentioned by respondents is that in the case of default or delay future relations can be threatened. Furthermore, such loans are not available all the time, since most people live in and experience the same situation.

10.7.1.3 Shail

Respondents consider *Shail* one of the worst financial arrangements because of its high interest rate and the fact that they pay back with the crops they have spent a whole season cultivating. They need to repay in a very short time. It is seen as a financial burden because they cultivate their land under very unpredictable conditions. Even with all these problems associated with *Shail,* it is still ranked the third regarding outreach, easiness of procedure and access and availability. *Shail* is also ranked better than *Sandouqs* regarding access and availability because it is accessible by all people, males or females, unlike *Sandouqs*. Generally and surprisingly, it is ranked before the IFAD village fund and ABS in the total ranking. Even if IFAD carried out many efforts to reduce *Shail* in Al Dagag, these efforts were not successful. The outcomes of this study reveal that the most successful beneficiaries of the IFAD project in Al Dagag are now the most well-known *Shail* traders, for example Asha Alnoor. For the *Shail* traders it is considered very profitable which makes them continue providing *Shail*.

However, what makes *Shail* come to third rank after shops and relatives and friends is the fact that almost all respondents take *Shail* regularly. It is regarded as the only option in September and available for everyone, especially the poor. The procedures of *Shail* contracts are viewed as easy and simple; borrowers' transaction costs are low and disbursement is immediate. They all agree that *Shail* solves real and significant problems when no other options are available.

10.7.1.4 Sandouqs

Sandouqs come in rank before the IFAD village fund and after *Shail* when outreach and target group are regarded. It is always a women- association; therefore, it serves a more limited target group than *Shail* and the IFAD village fund. Most women think that *Sandouqs* are the best as it allows both credit and savings of funds that would otherwise have been used for family immediate needs. Furthermore, *Sandouqs* are considered significant in strengthening women's bonds and social connections. Additionally, every woman in Al Dagag can join a *Sandouq* because different *Sandouqs* are available that suite different women's financial capabilities. Female respondents use *Sandouqs* to save their own money (so they are not indebted) in order to be used for future income shortages. Women respondents prefer *Sandouqs* for being flexible in getting the money when they are in urgent need. Most of them agree that it is a voluntary arrangement that they choose to join when they know they are capable of paying. The only negative thing about *Sandouqs* is the fact that they need to wait for a long time to get their turn, especially those who are at the end of the list. The problem of delaying paying the contribution is also mentioned.

10.7.2 Semi-Formal and Formal Financial Institutions

10.7.2.1 Al Dagag Village Fund Established by IFAD

Considerable numbers of respondents think the IFAD village fund was best for providing investment and production loans considering the above mentioned criteria. However, it is ranked worse than all indigenous financial arrangements and it is ranked only better than the bank. Advantages mentioned are no collaterals required and easy procedures. Respondents got the loans quite fast and IFAD seemed to be not strict regarding repayment procedures. Few respondents think that the village fund stimulated savings since saving was compulsory for registration. Altogether, the procedures of the village fund were easier than those of the ABS bank were; however, more complicated than the indigenous money lending systems mentioned above. Respondents ranked the IFAD village fund after *Sandouqs* regarding its accessibility, availability and easiness of procedures while it comes before the *Sandouqs* for including both men and women.

The majority of the respondents stresses the point that community development facilities provided by IFAD like building the school, training the only health assistant and the midwife and helping in building the village *Hafeer* (water basin used by the whole village) are much better than the credit project. On the contrary, the credit program is assessed as weak and ineffective in providing loans to the poor and in collecting the money back, which has threatened its sustainability.

10.7.2.2 Loans from ABS

The ABS is ranked the last institution in providing financial help to rural people counting the above mentioned criteria. Not surprisingly, it is ranked the last when three out of four criteria discussed and the best when the amount of loan is concerned. Expectedly, none of the destitute in Al Dagag has received loans from the bank. The main advantage mentioned is the amount of funds available depending on the type of the project the borrower applies for; there are no limits for the amount of money. While some respondents find that the time of repayment was suitable, others say it is too short to make an investment. The long time between applying and loan disbursement makes many respondents fail to prepare their agriculture land or weeding. Collaterals have to be provided in form of checks promising to pay the whole amount of money including the profit margins. Additionally, a guarantor who knows the applicant well is needed. The majority of the people mention the low prices of crops provided by the bank compared to the current market prices.

The bank is viewed as not accessible or available for everyone, the only chance villagers get to deal with the bank has been through the link with IFAD project. Only two respondents continue taking loans from the ABS after the end of the IFAD project. Other respondents criticize the fact that the bank is far and they need to pay for transportation to reach the nearest bank branch in Al Rahad. The most important critique of the bank is its restricted repayment procedure that is viewed as the most aggressive experience for most respondents since some people went to jail for not paying. Their families had to pay from selling saved crops and other assets. Thus, most of the few respondents who received loans from the bank are left worse than before.

To conclude this discussion, *Sandouqs, Shail* and transactions with the shop, friends and relatives constitute the informal finance in Al Dagag. I would like to argue here that such informal arrangements are more sustainable and effective in dealing with the financial demand of the poor in Al Dagag and thus leave a more positive impact.

For the case of Al Dagag, the definition provided by Adams and Fitchett (1992: 6) of what informal finance means is completely applicable. They constitute informal institutions commonly operated without collateral, typically dealing with short-term transactions and often working in a legally grey or obscure area. Moreover, it holds true what has been argued by Adams and Fitchett (1992: 3) that informal loans and informal deposits are common among and between all economic classes and are dynamic, innovative and flexible arrangements are well adapted to what people actually need. Furthermore, I would like to argue that from what has been mentioned above it is obvious that these indigenous arrangements play a significant role in bridging income as well as food shortages.

The success of the informal finance comes from its creativity in providing different types of loans; in many cases, it is free of interest.[16] On the contrary, loans from the IFAD village fund and the ABS seemed misdirected by capturing by elites, mismanagement, inflexible or confused procedures and the whole project proved to be not sustainable as it vanished by 2006 as described in chapter 9. This makes the informal institutions more adequate for the poor in the village.

The informal arrangements are ubiquitous and thrive in the sense that they have stayed for long time in Al Dagag unlike the formal and semi-formal institutions of ABS and IFAD. Informal loans are common among different people with no regard to their economic or social situations and classification whereas formal and semi-formal institutions serve the better-off and those who have other pros-

[16] Even if *Shail* is described as exploitative in nature of high interest rates and its existence at a specific time of the year when the villagers are in an urgent need for cash and no other sources of funds are available; it still helps people to overcome shortages in food and other basic needs necessary for their survival.

perous sources of income. Thus, various forms of informal finance provide valuable services to many individuals. It is obvious that the bank is not appropriate to deal with the destitute who live not only in poverty but also in vulnerable conditions. The bank does not understand the type of demand of the poor and cannot adjust to their situation. IFAD provided a good chance for credit and saving; however, they have been faced with many problems mentioned in the previous chapter. IFAD has helped some people to accumulate assets that have been used to help other people in terms of informal arrangement like *Shail* in September or free of interest loans during the agricultural season.

10.8 Linkages among Financial Institutions in Al Dagag

At the time when IFAD and the ABS were providing their services in Al Dagag, different formal and informal institutions were available in the village. I find it interesting to understand how these formal, semi-formal and informal institutions have influenced each other when coexisting in Al Dagag. The relationship between formal and informal institutions is also discussed in the literature. Seibel and Parhusip (1992) and Krahnen and Schmidt (1994: 38) suggest three forms of relationship between both formal and informal institutions and I can find some connections to Al Dagag situations.

The first is when these institutions compete with each other, which is supposed to create forms of competitive and liberalized markets in which only demand and supply control market behavior. The existence of such relationships may lead to reduction of the informal sector by reducing the interest rates and the spread of the market interest rates. This is not true in the case of Al Dagag since at the time when all institutions were providing credit the supply of the informal credit reduced, however, never discontinued and the interest rates did not reduce to equal the market interest rates. The reason was that the formal supply was rigid in its procedures and its provision of finance shaped by many types of bias and inefficiency that offset standard behavior of the financial market. The use of loans in production or consumption was another determinant factor. Considering the demand of Al Dagag people, most informal loans were directed to consumption purposes. Loans from the IFAD village fund or the ABS even were given for production activities, but then the assets were sold or profits were used for consumption purposes; still clients were asked to repay the loans, profit margin and other costs.

The second form of coexistence is when the two institutions complement each other; in this case, the formal institutions provide loans to those who are successful and the poor resort to the informal institutions. This to some degree applies to the case of Al Dagag. The ABS started its financial services directed to people who can pay money back and after the termination of the project, only those who were successful in using the loans are still connected to the bank. After the withdrawal of IFAD, the provision of credit was not sustainable and the informal institutions are the only resort for the poor.

The third form is co-operation that I call *direct* cooperation can take place between the formal and informal sector described by Krahnen and Schmidt (1994: 39) as a situation when crop traders who sell and buy in the informal sector are the moneylenders, so their activities are financed by the formal market to finance people in the informal. I find this to great extent applies to Al Dagag. The cases of Asha Alnoor and Basheer are good examples of co-operation, since they are funded by the bank and they buy and sell crops in the informal markets. Another form of indirect co-operation which could also be called non-intentional cooperation is the fact that most people who have generated good profits out of the loans received from the IFAD credit project have used the profit to give *Shail* like in the cases of Asha Alnoor, Rugaia and Zainab. This is despite the efforts of IFAD project officials to reduce *Shail,* which never happened. They are now also able to provide more free of interest loans to help their relatives and friends.

The main argument I support here is that the credit provided from IFAD and the bank fostered informal institutions including *Shail* that people depend on as sources of finance even if this was not planned by IFAD.

What is the concern here is the fact that during the planned phase of enhancing sustainability that IFAD the loyalty of IFAD village fund coordinators has become questionable since some of them are the *Shail* traders in Al Dagag. This creates a confusion of interests that discourage people from dealing with *Shail* and at the same time the interest of making profits as *Shail* traders. The other point of connection is the fact that in September when all respondents are in need for consumption credits other forms of finance, mainly loans from relatives and friends and the transaction with shops are likely to stop and only *Shail* is available.

11 Conclusion

"*Microfinance is not bad it is wonderful but it has bad side. Microfinance can promote dept and it does not encourage savings, we should say save and not take loans, saving is good, dept is bad, it has regrettable social affects in some places and communities*" Malcolm Harper on the conference "Lessons of Microfinance to be Learnt for Sudan", 6th of January 2010 Sudan Friendship Hall when describing microfinance).

"*It is better for us to work than to take credit, and if there is credit it will be good if credit is given for enhancing agriculture like providing pumps and tractors*" (statement by Hassan, describing what poor people need to sustain their livelihood in Al Dagag, in-depth interview, Al Dagag, NKS).

11.1 Introduction and Summary

This chapter aims to conclude the discussions extended throughout the research. I find it worth mentioning that this research started by a vision to portray Sudanese rural livelihoods in villages and followed the question to see whether microfinance is able to sustain rural livelihoods. However, during the research process many new questions arise facilitated by the use of the inductive methodology of the GT.

Throughout the research different categories emerged from the data, which are presented in detail in the empirical chapters. This includes the concept of livelihood within the analysis of poverty and vulnerability. The path to build on the livelihood approach using the constructivist thinking of Grounded Theory went to include the determinants of the rural livelihood such as the composition of households, the decision making and distribution of resources processes and the livelihood strategies of rural people. The analysis of interviews suggests focusing on two forms of capital that are the economic including the financial capital and the social capital that seem to have significant impacts on rural livelihood. It has also emerged from the data to shift the question of the research from the concept of microfinance to the concept of financial relations, which seems to include varied types of financial institutions and practices. These institutions and practices go beyond the concept of microfinance in its institutionalized or formalized way, which is exclusively used within the current microfinance revolution in Sudan. Thus, indigenous financial mechanisms such as *Sandouqs* and transactions with shops are examined in a detailed way as the narratives of the interviewees reveal their importance to the people's livelihoods. This suggests the focus on comparing formal and informal institutions in the provision of finance for the poor. What is more is the linkages I have found between the two forms of capital that is presented in the transformation between the social capital and the financial capital. Social mechanisms like *Wajib* and *Nafeer* are realized to provide great financial help to members of these social networks in Al Dagag.

This chapter is meant to provide a conclusion by presenting the main findings regarding the livelihood approach and how this approach is altered by the incorporation of these findings. Moreover, in this chapter the answer to the question of if financial relations including microfinance can enhance rural livelihood or not is illustrated.

11.2 Constructing the Rural Livelihood Approach

In portraying the livelihood of people in rural areas of Sudan, it has become clear that analyzing the main determinants of livelihood in the Sudanese context is essential. One can argue that the core of these determinants is in the intra-household relations and distribution of resources, keeping in mind the structure of the nuclear and the extended family households that I have found in Al Dagag and presented in chapter 7. These relationships are also extended within the fabric of the social norms of the tribe and the family and social networks that tie up different households. Other determinants of household livelihood strategies in the case of Al Dagag are shaped and affected by these intra-household relations. One illustrative example is the process of seasonal migration, which must be considered a matter of household not an individual decision. It is obvious that most of the decisions made within the household affect and are affected by the livelihood strategies and patterns employed in the household.

These strategies and patterns are a result of the conflicting and cooperating behaviors within the household. Also relevant to the discussion is the way the bargaining power distribution within the households affects the allocation of resources and capital within the specific and special social system of the village, thereby not forgetting the fact that all these take place in the context of chronic poverty and vulnerability. These phenomena are to a great extent found to affect and limit the livelihood of rural people and direct their strategies towards the main aim which is survival not wellbeing and security.

Along the same line of reasoning, one can conclude from the case of Al Dagag that the changes in the intra-household relations are shaped by the bargaining process and result in changing household members' positions and relations within a conflict and cooperation context. To explain more, these changes seem to take the society from the traditional social norms towards giving more space to women. Specifically one can argue that the system of men as breadwinners changes giving room to patterns of shared responsibilities between men and women. The emergence of cases where women step out and take the full responsibility is evidence of this.

In the scope of this discussion, the similarities and differences between livelihoods of men and women are also revealed. This is reflected in the fact that men tend to pursue different livelihood strategies than women. For instance, men can migrate while women cannot. Indeed most livelihood activities or resources are specifically associated with men or women, even in farming, where men tend to have the clay land located near *Khour* Abuhabil while women tend to get the mostly sandy land near to the households and which is not fertile enough to grow different kinds of crops; and indeed some crops are associated with women. These differences add a gender dimension to the concept of livelihood and stress the fact that livelihood can be different for men and women. This also provides details for the general theoretical argumentation of Lont and Hospes (2004: 8), who argue against assuming a singular and stereotypical livelihood strategy, which might in fact include quite fundamental dissimilarities between livelihood strategies of for example women and men or other groups like rich and poor. What is also revealed from this research is the fact that some of these differences between the livelihood of men and women are in the favor of women while others are not. However, generally speaking, women in Al Dagag and seemingly in the region of Kordofan play a significant role in sustaining livelihood; evidence for this is their role in building up and maintaining social capital that seems to be crucial in sustaining livelihood. In addition to that, they also have access to land and access to different financial relations. They do their own farming and dispose over their income; women generally have their own purses. Most of their income is directed to the welfare of the household. Therefore, it can be argued that the differences between men and women reflect on the one site conflict but on the other side cooperation between household members.

Another important factor is the drastically changing environment that leaves major fingerprints on the main patterns of livelihood and leads to the emergence of new livelihood activities and the diminishing of others. Droughts are regular and severe to the extent that they negatively affect agriculture, which is the main source of livelihood in the village and the surrounding areas. Diversification of livelihood patterns is not a choice but a simple requirement for people to survive. The high degree of diversification people are forced to do to fight the chronic poverty and vulnerability represents an addition to the existing livelihood approach literature.

To illustrate, *Shail* is considered as a livelihood pattern, a significant change to existing livelihood descriptions relevant to Al Dagag. Looking at the way *Shail* takes place, how and why it is done, one can argue that it should be regarded as an example how a part of society (or people who are considered as *Shail* traders, whose number is increasing) changes. They alter the way they do business from a traditional way of the past to a more modern, commercial and profit-oriented way. This can be also explained by the change in behavior of better off household from seeking subsistence to engaging in business and other more commercialized activities. However, this economic behavior is still embedded in the strong social system that enhances the concept of helping each other in the rural community. Most of the traders are therefore confronted with what is called the traders' dilemma, as explained in chapter 2 and 9. On the other side, *Shail,* which is an income opportunity for the better-off in the village, at the same time is a major "livelihood dilemma" that urges the poor to decide between two unfavorable scenarios in the month of September. These are to either take *Shail* and pay back from their crops for very low price or to be subjected to different types of life threatening risks like hunger or sickness. Taking *Shail* is considered an unfavorable situation because it is associated with very low prices, differences in prices and their need to pay from their crops used for subsistence as well as their need to pay in short period of time (in many cases no production left in a bad season).

Within this discussion, the effects of the changes in the surrounding environment on the livelihood patterns become evident; the climate is reflected in the agriculture system and practices. Generally, agriculture is done in a very simple and traditional way, which I described as inheritance of not only land but also the farming practices. The dependency on rain-fed agriculture is considered one of the main causes of poverty and vulnerability and one of the problems associated with agriculture. The environment has led to changes in the livelihood patterns, such that *Shail* has been introduced as a new pattern, while rising livestock is no longer considered one as it has been always described in literature of livelihood or peasants households. Livestock is now considered the best savings opportunity that household prefer among others. As I explained above in chapter 7 and supported by the argument of Ashley and Nanyeenya (2005: 243), livestock plays the same role as banks in absence of any savings services provided from any formal institutions. They can even be better than a bank for many reasons, for example they can be liquidated easily to meet an urgent need for cash.

The effects of these changes can be realized in the composition of the livelihood patterns and strategies of the rural households. One can use the changes in the natural or economic capital as examples. The discussion over these changes emerged in the research and intensifies the definition of livelihood provided by Chambers and Conway (1992), Chambers (1995 and 1997), Ellis (2000) and Ellis and Freeman (2005) and adds details to what has been theoretically argued by Chambers (1997) who describes the rural livelihood as complex and dynamic. Generally, this research re-conceptualizes the definition of rural livelihood to include all the above mentioned changes. Livelihood cannot be perceived as static, but as changing over time as it is obvious from the case of Al Dagag where livelihood patterns, strategies and also types of employed capital change rapidly.

An important element in constructing a grounded theory about rural livelihood in Sudan emerged from the data is the significance of the social capital for sustaining rural livelihood. Social networks play a significant role as insurance mechanisms among others. From the case of Al Dagag, one can conclude that the social capital affects the whole life of rural people. Its importance is seen in their day-to-day as well as in life cycle activities and events. This extends the scope of the social capital as described in the literature. In the description of the livelihood approach, an equal weight was put to all types of capital however; it is not obvious that one form of capital could have more weight in the live of people than the others. From the findings of this research, the social capital is significant in sustaining rural livelihood. Within this discussion about rural livelihood capital, is has also been revealed to be connected and transformed from one form to another. The data I collected strongly supports Bourdieu's (1986) notion of conversion of different forms of capital, especially between social and economic or financial. Analyzing networks of social capital as *Wajib* and *Nafeer* in Al Dagag, it has become clear that the main resources exchanged in the social networks are financial.

Another addition to the livelihood concept is the level of deprivation I have found in Al Dagag. Al Dagag people as most of the people in Sudan's rural areas just seek to survive; this is clear from their perspectives on security or wellbeing in chapter 8. This level of poverty and vulnerability significantly shapes and limits the livelihood patterns, forms of capital and strategies and affects to a great extent what people are able and capable to gain.

What is special about the case of Al Dagag and may be in other different other rural areas of Sudan, is the fact that the social capital is based on the tribal structure and norms. Even if not so many tribes live in Al Dagag, still this is clear on both tribal level and sub-clan level. In this situation norms and values of social networks are conducted within the tribal structure of the society. People are compelled by their kinship relations and their closeness to each other. This is considered one reason for the strong and intense social capital found in Al Dagag. However, the role of social capital that proved important for fighting poverty and more so vulnerability is something rarely discussed in the literature on the topic. The focus on the social capital in the livelihood approach allowed in the case of Al Dagag to implicitly include different concepts like reciprocity and trust within the social fabric.

This research has also widened the scope of the concept of livelihood by including different aspects connected to other categories like poverty and vulnerability. While most of the literature treats these concepts separately, the findings of the research show that even if they focus on different aspects the concept of livelihood is to a great extent linked to both vulnerability and poverty. In other words, it is proved to be valid that poverty is not the same as vulnerability but they are linked in the way that the poorer people are the less assets and resources they have and the more vulnerable they become. In the case of Al Dagag, it is obvious in the way that the most vulnerable people are the poorest who lack different types of assets like livestock. This is not to say that the better-off are not vulnerable; but they are less vulnerable since in case of emergencies they can use their saved resources to come out of the stressful time.

Developmental interventions and policies need to decide whether to tackle income alone or to be connected with other forms of livelihood capital. Even if income is considered important for people in Al Dagag, it does not reflect the whole scope of their poverty and vulnerability. Other important factors, chiefly other types of capital, need to be included in dealing with people's situations. The concept of income is enlarged in this research to include income from labour, remittances, gifts, non-cash exchanges, and *Shail* that are all calculated explicitly in the household and resources from *Wajib,* which are implicitly considered.

11.3 Can Microfinance Sustain Rural Livelihood in Sudan?

Considering the definition of livelihood (including the discussion about livelihood capital, strategies, and people's capabilities as well as the changes taking place), it has become apparent that microfinance provided thorough NGOs (IFAD) and banks (ABS) has sustained rural livelihood only in very few cases, but affected the majority of respondents negatively or left them just like before taking a loan. Thus, it is obvious that unfortunately the microfinance impact has been exaggerated. Comparing the impact mentioned in the literature and presented in chapter 3 and the impact extracted from interview analysis in this research it has been revealed that microfinance has had a very limited impact on sustaining rural livelihood in Al Dagag.

This limited impact is clear first from the number of people who benefited from the loans or in the microfinance language of people who graduated out of poverty and misery. What has been discussed in chapter 9 shows that only 20 % of clients are able to generate income that is sustainable, and consequently have received a positive impact on other forms of capital and household assets. Still, within this percentage, most of respondents were better off before receiving loans from IFAD or the ABS, only one person in the village graduated from poverty depending on using only loans from the IFAD and ABS project. The case of Asha Alnoor illustrated in chapter 9 constitutes the only success story to be told about providing institutionalized microfinance in Al Dagag.

Providing microfinance for the better-off and those clients who have other sources of funds was successful and credits led to a positive impact in businesses and the economic stratus of households. In this case, microfinance is no longer a product of finance for the poor as indicated in chapter 3. Expert interviews in Sudan and reports about microfinance presented in chapter 6 support this argument.

In addition to that, the impact of microfinance has been exaggerated because it is revealed from the case of Al Dagag that microfinance can leave the clients just like before (40 %) or even worse off than before (40 %). Comparing these 80 % of cases to the 20 % success stories one can conclude that microfinance can actually be a threat to rural livelihood. This comes along with what has been mentioned by microfinance experts as presented in chapter 6 in their evaluation of the microfinance practice in Sudan and the findings of Lont and Hospes (2004), Bateman (2010), Roy (2010) and others presented in chapter 3, who consider microfinance as poverty capital and a poverty trap. In this case, microfinance is regarded as not sustaining the livelihood of people but placing more threats to their survival like becoming deeply indebted. Since not only the respondents are indebted but due to the strong social system of helping each other in Al Dagag the threats are extended to other households and family members who have to pay the debts on behalf of a defaulted debtor who often enough has gone to jail.

The details of the microfinance project in Al Dagag show other unfavorable aspects of the microfinance design and practice. Inappropriate loan terms like loan size, timing of loan, loan disbursement and repayment period, application procedures, debt collection procedures and confusion in understanding the project aim and implementations have undermined the possible success of credits. Further problems emerged among them capturing of loans by elites, mismanagement and varied problems in implementing the project compared to its planning. It is not as simple as it is always mentioned by the project officers that the main problem is the low repayment rates. What I have observed is that many other problems resulted in the problem of low repayment behavior. In some cases, even when repayments were possible, respondents refused to pay the money because they misunderstood the source of IFAD project funds and the planned purposes for which these funds are supposed to be used for. Thus, these problems have threatened the project's sustainability, outreach and the realization of significant and substantial impact.

I also wish to emphasize two further points; first, the establishment of the village fund to be an informal institution and second the link between the ABS and IFAD. With regard to the first point, I would like to question whether informal institutions can be established through an external body like IFAD. It is well known about informal institutions that they are established by the people themselves as a result of their willingness and voluntarism. This strengthens people commitment toward the institution; even if one considers experiences like the Grameen Bank that started as informal institution but was quickly transformed and registered as a formal institution owned by the poor themselves (Grameen Bank Website). In the case of Al Dagag, the village fund was never accepted and considered an informal institution compared for example to the ROSCAs, which exist successfully and for long time in the village. In the perception of the people, the village fund was always linked to IFAD. This may also explain why the village fund was not successful and sustainable compared to indigenous informal institutions like *Sandouqs* that are based on reciprocity, commitment, voluntarism, willingness and trust. These are found to play a major role in the sustainability of these institutions over such a long time and are not found in the case of the village fund.

The link between IFAD and the ABS, as it was planned to ensure the success of the project but the implementations highlighted exactly why banks fail to serve the poor and should stick to what they are good at, as explained in chapter 9. The link did not result in downgrading the bank procedure to serve the poor and consider their specific situation; for instance, loans were not designed for individual clients considering their repayment capabilities and type of businesses they are doing among other problems mentioned in chapter 9. As a result, the project and the link was a failure except in the few cases reported above.

In relation to the products of finance discussed in chapter 3, it is obvious that what is provided in Al Dagag by IFAD and the ABS is not microfinance but mainly microcredit. It is clear that credit was the main financial product, whereas the mobilization of savings was viewed as weak by project officials and respondents alike. There were no insurance facilities provided at all in the project. All this confirms the discussion about microfinance in Sudan presented in chapter 6. Studying the demand of the poor for finance, which is also repeatedly mentioned in the literature, the poor need more than just credit. Consequently, the provision of credit in the absence of proper savings mobilization and insurance has threatened the sustainability of loans and businesses established by loans considering the very vulnerable environment in rural areas. Here I would like to argue that if microfinance is expected to have a long-term impact on people's livelihood not only rural poverty in its narrow definion of income providing credit is insufficient, the poor may need savings and insurance facilities even more than credit.

Providing loans to alleviate poverty in highly vulnerable conditions with no efforts of savings and insurance exactly matches what Abugre (1994) describes as pouring liquids in a bottomless bottle. According to the results of this research, providing production credits in such an environment leaves little positive impact on the life of only few people. The demand of the poor includes financing consumption and life cycle events besides their need for savings facilities and insurance. Considering the highlighted importance of both savings and insurance revealed in this research as products of the finance for the poor, it might be suitable to establish specialized institutions to provide such services in the way that suit the poverty situation and financial demand in the new phase of microfinance in Sudan. Alternatively, it might also be useful if microfinance institutions start with these two products before providing credit.

Based on the results of this research, one can strongly argue here that if microfinance is successful in increasing the access of the poor to savings, insurance as well as credit, they will be able to invest in physical capital to increase the productivity of existing assets and provide working capital for the purchase of inputs (production). In addition, this will allow for consumption smoothing, enabling major expenses of life cycle events such as health treatment or funeral costs to be met and helping the poor in building and accumulating assets that provide insurance opportunities (savings and insurance), only then it could be successful in sustaining rural livelihood.

In the discussion about microfinance, the concept of Islamic microfinance has been emerging. This research has revealed that the rural poor may not understand the whole concept of the Islamic finance and its modes and techniques, as illustrated in chapter 9. They only conceptualize it as the prohibition of usury or *Riba*. All of my respondents got loans from IFAD or the ABS using *Murabaha*, however few understood the real meaning of the concept, and many could not explain it or compare it to other modes of finance. However, it is preferred by them simply because it is called "Islamic". However, the prohibition of *Riba* is also respected when *Shail* contracts are conducted. What is more to this discussion is the fact that it is normally not discussed by the people and merely accepted for labels what are the modes of finance or what is the difference between them . This has allowed the formal financial institutions to use *Murabaha* more than the partnerships modes like *Musharaka* or other modes of finance that might suit the poor better. It may be time to revise and evaluate the application of Islamic finance and the techniques, which are currently used to deal with the shortcomings in the applications. Financial policies should strengthen the use of the diversified modes of finance.

In the absence of any formal microfinance options or even when inappropriate ones exist, the rural poor resort to indigenous institutions which in the case of Al Dagag are *Sandouqus*, *Shail*, and different types of transactions with moneylenders, shopkeepers, family members and friends. Many of these financial transactions take place within the social networks in Al Dagag. These institutions have been found to be significant for sustaining rural livelihood more than the formalized microfinance in Al Dagag. Even while respondents considered *Shail* exploitative for the problems mentioned above it is still the only source of finance that many poor and destitute can get in the most difficult month of the year, when their survival is threatened. *Shail* helps them not to lose their assets during September, but interest rates are very high and thus, it plays an influential role in the food and water availability in many of the poor and destitute households in September, but also put threats on their future subsistence. *Sandouqs* provide an important savings mechanism and the funds are used in the households to bridge any gaps in consumption or to cover the expenses of life cycle events or emergencies. Connecting this to the advances in the microfinance sector around the world as presented in chapter 3 such institutions have recently been revealed to be more prosperous if linked to formal financial institutions. However, they are totally ignored in the case of Sudan where policy makers view banks and NGOS to be the appropriate providers of microfinance.

Within this discussion about informal finance in Al Dagag, I would like to emphasize repeatedly and explicitly the importance of social networks like *Wajib* and *Nafeer* in providing rural people with saving and insurance opportunities. They have been found to smooth consumption, enhance production (*Nafeer*) and finance life cycle events, which makes them important products of microfinance as described in chapter 3.

Generally, informal finance plays a significant role in the survival, which is considered the main target of household strategies and activities. However, for its limited terms like the size of the loans and terms of transactions as well as the high interest rates of the *Shail* system its impact does not go beyond the role explained above. As the recent advances in the informal sector suggest, also in Sudan they might have a more substantial role in sustaining rural livelihood when focused on, developed or linked to formal or semi-formal institutions.

To conclude, as it has been revealed in this research, microfinance in the way it is provided in rural areas of Sudan does not play any beneficial role in enhancing the livelihood of people or alleviating their poverty as supposed to because of the vulnerable situation of people in rural areas. Thus, people resort to indigenous financial arrangements and social networks in their quest for survival. However, they are still poor, vulnerable and live on the edge; taking into account the changing environment their situation in fact deteriorates rapidly. Finance for the poor in this case needs to be designed in a way to focus on their demand (savings, insurance, and credit); moreover, the informal finance arrangements might have a more effective role when they are upgraded or linked to the formal and semi-formal institutions.

Bibliography

Abu Shouk, Ahmed Ibrahim (1998): Kordofan: From Rribes to Nazirates, in: Stiansen, Endre and Kevane, Michael (eds.): Kordofan Invaded: Peripheral Incorporation and Social Transformation in Islamic Africa, Bril Leiden, Netherlands.

Abugre, Charles (1994): When Credit is Not Due: A Critical Evaluation of Donor NGO Eperiences with Credit, in: Bouman, F.J.A and Hospes,. Otto (eds.) (1994): Financial Landscapes Reconstructed: The Fine Art of Mapping Development. Westview Press Boulder, CO.

Ackerly, B. A. (1995): Testing the Tools of Development: Credit Programmes, Loan Involvement and Women's Empowerment, in: IDS Bulletin. 26 (3), pp. 56-68.

Adam, F. H. and Apaya, W. A. (1973): Agriculture Credit in the Gezira. Sudan Notes and Records. 5A, pp. 104 and 115.

Adams, Alayne (1993): Food Insecurity in Mali: Exploring the Role of the Moral Economy, in: IDS Bulletin 24 (4).

Adams, Alayne M., Cekan, Jindra and Sauerborn, Rainer (1998): Towards a Conceptual Framework of Household Coping: Reflections from Rural West Africa, in: Africa 68 (2).

Adams, Dale W. and Fitchett, Delbert A. (eds.) (1992): Informal Finance in Low Income Countries. Westview Press. Boulder, CO.

Adams, Dale W.; Graham, Douglas H. and von Pischke, J.D. (eds.) (1984): Undermining Rural Development with Cheap Credit. Westview Press Boulder, CO.

Adams, Dale W. (1995): From Agricultural Credit to Rural Finance, in: Quarterly Journal of International Agriculture 34 (2), pp. 109-120.

Adler, P. S. and Kwon, S. W. (2002): Social Capital: Prospects for a New Concept, in: Academy of Management Review 27 (1), pp. 17-40.

African Development Bank Group (ADBG) (2010). Sudan: Country Brief (www.afdb.org/en/countries/east-africa/sudan).

African Development Bank Group (ADBG). (2006). Sudan: Country Dialogue Paper (www.afdb.org/en/countries/east-africa/sudan).

Agarwal, Bina (1997): Bargaining and Gender Relations: Within and Beyond the Household, in: Feminist Economics 3 (1), pp. 1-51. (http://www.binaagarwal.com/downloads/apapers/bagaining_and_gender_relations.pdf.)

Ahmed, Ausaf (1993): Contemporary Practices of Islamic Financing Techniques. Islamic research and training institute, Islamic Development Bank, Research Paper No. 20.

Ardener, Shirley and Burman, Sandra (eds.) (1996): Money-Go-Rounds: The Importance of Rotating Savings and Credit Associations for Women. Berg Oxford and Washington D.C.

Ardener, Shirley (1964): The Comparative Study of Rotating Credit Associations. Journal of the Royal Anthropological Institute XCIV, pp. 201-229.

Ashley, Ateve and Nanyeenya, William (2005): More than Income: Pro Poor Livestock Development Policy in Uganda, in: Ellis, Frank and Freeman, H. Ade (eds.) (2005): Rural Livelihoods and Poverty Policies. Routledge Studies in Development Economics. Routledge London and New York.

Babbie, Earl (2004): The Practice of Social Research. 10th edition. Wadsworth, Thomson Learning Belmont, CA.

Baker, Wayne E. (2000): Achieving Success Through Social Capital: Tapping the Hidden Resources in Your Personal and Business networks. Jossey-BassSan Francisco, CA.

Bartkus, Viva Ona and Davis, James H. (eds.) (2009): Social Capital: Reaching Out. Reaching In. Edward Elgar, Cheltenham, UK.

Bateman, Milford (2010): Why Doesn't Microfinance Work?: The Destructive Rise of Local Neoliberalism. Zed Books New York.

Becker, H. S. et al. (1961): Boys in White. Student Culture in Medical School. University of Chicago Press Chicago, IL.

Berg, Bruce. L. (2007): Qualitative Research Methods for the Social Sciences. 6thedition. Pearson Education Boston, MA.

Bering, Ntee (2002): The Lesotho Agricultural Development Bank, in: Coetzee, Gerhard (ed.): Agricultural Development Banks in Africa: The Way Forward. African Rural and Agricultural Credit Association Nairobi, Kenya.

Bernstein, Henry; Crow, Ben and Hohnson, Hazel (1992): Rural Livelihoods: Crises and Responses. Oxford University Press in association with The Open University, London, UK.
Bhandari, Bishnu (2003): Participatory Rural Appraisal(PRA). Institute for Global Environmental Strategies. IGES (http://www2.hcmuaf.edu.vn/data/ntquyet/PRA.pdf)
Blake, David (ed.) (2000): Finance: A Characteristics Approach. International Studies in Money and Banking. Routledge London and New York.
Bong, Sharon A. (2007): Debunking Myths in CAQDAS Use and Coding in Qualitative Data Analysis. Experiences with and Reflections on Grounded Theory Methodology, in: Mey, G. and Mruck, K. (eds.): Grounded Theory Reader. Center for Historical Social Research. The Official Journal of Quantum and Interquant. Supplement No. 19.
Booth, W. J. (1994): 'On the idea of the moral economy', The American Political Science Review, 88 (3), pp. 653-667. (http://www.workandsociety.com/downloads/theo3.pdf)
Bouman, F. J. A and Hospes, Otto (eds.) (1994): Financial Landscapes Reconstructed: The Fine art of Mapping Development. Westview Press Boulder, CO.
Bouman, F. J. A (1994): Informal Rural Finance: An Aladdin's Lamp of Information, in: Bouman, F. J. A and Hospes, Otto (eds.): Financial Landscapes Reconstructed: The Fine art of Mapping Development. Westview Press Boulder, CO.
Bouman, F. J. A. (1989): Small. Short and Unsecured Informal Rural Finance in India. Oxford University PressOxford, UK.
Bourdieu, Pierre (1986): Forms of Capital, in: Richardson, G. John(ed.): Handbook of Theory and Research for the Sociology of Education. Greenwood Press New York.
Bourdieu, Pierre. and Wacquant, L. J. D. (1992): An Invitation to Reflexive Sociology. University of Chicago Press Chicago, IL.
Bourguignon, Francois (2006): From Income to Endowments: The Difficult Task of Expanding the Income Poverty Paradigm, In: Grusky, B. David and Kanbur, Ravi (eds.): Poverty and Inequality. Stanford University Press Stanford,CA, pp. 76-102.
Brausch, Georges (1964): Changes and Continuity in the Gezira Region of the Sudan. International Social Sciences Journal. Social Aspects of African Resources Development. Paris, pp. 341-357.
Brock, Karen (1999): Implementing a Sustainable Livelihoods Framework for Policy-Directed Research: Reflections from Practice in Mali. Institute of Development Studies. Working Paper No. 90, Sussex, UK.
Bryant, Antony and Charmaz, Kathy (eds.) (2007): The Sage Handbook of Grounded Theory. Sage London.
Buchenrieder, Gertrud and Theesfeld, Insa (2000): Improving Bankability of Small Farmers in Northern Vietnam, in: Savings and Development 24 (3).
Buckley, G. (1997): Microfinance in Africa: Is it either the Problem or the Solution?, in: World Development, 25 (7), pp. 1081-1093.
Cater, Robert (2001): Microfinance and National Policy. Paper presented at the International Conference on NGOs and Poverty Policy. Beijing. China.
CBS website: http://www.cbos.gov.sd/
Central Bank of Sudan (CBS) (2007). Microfinance Unit: Role and Mission Report (November 2007). Khartoum, Sudan.
Central Bank of Sudan and UNDP (2002): Micro Finance Policy for Sudan. Khartoum, Sudan.
Central Bank of Sudan in collaboration with the Ministry of Social Welfare, Women and Children Affairs and the Microfinance Unit (2008): Microfinance: As an Effective Tool for Poverty Alleviation in Sudan. Workshop proceedings, Khartoum, Sudan.
Central Bank of Sudan (2008): 48th Annual Report.
Central Department of Statistics (2008): North Kordofan State Report. Khartoum, Sudan.
Chambers, Robert and Conway, Gordon R. (1992): Sustianbale RuralL: Practical Concept for the 21st Century. Institute of Development Studies Discussion Paper 296, Sussex, UK.
Chambers, Robert (1983): Rural Development: Putting the Last First. Longman London, UK.
Chambers, Robert (1989): Editorial introduction: Vulnerability, Coping and Policy, in: IDS Bulletin, 20 (2).
Chambers, Robert (1995): Poverty and Livelihood: Whose Reality Counts? Institute of Development Studies, Discussion Paper 347, Sussex, UK.

Chambers, Robert (1997): Whose Reality Counts? Putting the First Last. Intermediate Technology Publications London.
Chapra, M. Umer. (2008): The Global Financial Crisis: Can Islamic Finance Help Minimize the Severity and Frequency of Such a Crisis in the Future? A paper prepared for presentation at the Forum on the Global Financial Crisis to be held at the Islamic Development Bank.
Charmaz, Kathy (2006): Constructing Grounded Theory: A Practical Guide through Qualitative Analysis. Sage London. UK.
Cheston, Susy and Kuhn, Lisa (2002): Empowering Women through Microfinance. Paper for the Microcredit Summit New York.
Christen, Peck R. (1992): Formal Credit for Informal Borrowers: Lessons from Informal Lenders, in: Adams, Dale W. and Fitchett, Delbert A. (eds.): Informal Finance in Low Income Countries. Westview Press Boulder, CO.
Coetzee, Gerhard and Graham, Douglas (2002): Restructuring Agricultural Development Banks in South Africa, in: Coetzee, Gerhard (ed.): Agricultural Development Banks in Africa: The Way Forward. African Rural and Agricultural Credit Association Nairobi, Kenya.
Coetzee, Gerhard (2002): Rural Finance. Department of Agricultural Economics Extension and Rural Development Working Paper No. 2002-04. University of Pretoria Pretoria, South Africa.
Coleman, James S. (1988): Social Capital in the Creation of Human Capital, in: The American Journal of Sociology, 94 (Supplement: Organizations and Institutions: Sociological and Economic Approaches to the Analysis of Social Structure), pp. S95-S120.
Compassion Politics (2009): Evaluating the Criticism of Microfinance, Microloans, and Microlending (http://compassioninpolitics.wordpress.com/2009/02/07/evaluating-the-criticism-of-microfinance-microloans-and-microlending/)
Conning, Jonathan and Udry, Christopher (2005): Rural Financial Markets In Developing Countries. Center Discussion Paper No. 914. Prepared for the Handbook of Agricultural Economics. Vol. 3. Agricultural Development: Farmers. Farm Production and Farm Markets, edited by Evenson, R. E. P. Pingali and T. P. Schultz. http://ssrn.com/abstract=756965.
Cross, Catherine; Gelderblom, Derik; Roux, Niel and Mafukidze, Jonathan (2006): Views on Migration in Sub-Saharan Africa: Proceedings of an Africa Migration Alliance Workshop. HARC (Human Sciences Research Council and Development of Social Development) Press Cape Town. South Africa in Association with Department of Social Development Pretoria, South Africa.
Crow, Ben (1994): Finance in Context: Exploring Diverse Exchange Conditions, in: Bouman, F. J. A and Hospes, Otto (eds.): Financial Landscapes Reconstructed: The Fine art of Mapping Development. Westview Press Boulder, CO.
Davies, Susanna (1993): Are Coping Strategies a Cop-Out? IDS Bulletin 24 (4).
Dejong, Jocelyn (2007): Capabilities, Reproductive Health and Wellbeing, in: Hulme, David and Toye, John (2007): Understanding Poverty and Wellbeing: Bridging the Disciplines. Routledge London and New York, NY.
Denzin, Norman K. and Lincoln, Ivonna. S. (eds.) (2005): The Sage Handbook of Qualitative Research, 3rd Edition. Sage London.
Department for International Development (DFID) (1999): Livelihoods Approaches Ccompared: A Brief Comparison of the Livelihoods Approaches. Study prepared by Diana Carney, Michael Drinkwater and Tamara Rusinow (CARE), Koos Neefjes (Oxfam), Samir Wanmali and Naresh Singh (UNDP). DFID London.
Dercon, Stefan and Hoddinott, J. (2005): Health, Shocks and Poverty Persistence, in: Dercon, Stefan (2005): Insurance Against Poverty. Oxford University Press Oxford, UK.
Dercon, Stefan (2005): Insurance Against Poverty. Oxford University Press Oxford, UK.
Deshingkar, Priya and Start, Daniel (2003): Seasonal Migration for Livelihoods in India: Coping, Accumulation and Exclusion. Working Paper 220. Overseas Development Institute London, UK.
Dey, I. (1999):Grounding Grounded Theory. Academoc Press, San Diego, CA.
Dolan, Catherine (2005): Household Composition and Rural Livelihoods in Uganda, in: Ellis, Frank and Freeman, H. Ade (eds.): Rural Livelihoods and Poverty Policies. Routledge Studies in Development Economics. Routledge London and New York.
Doyal, L. and Gough, I. (1991): A Theory of Human Need.Macmillan London.

Drake, P. J. and Robertson, Martin (1980): Money, Finance and Development. Mackenzie Oxford, UK.

Elbashir, Abdalla (2008): The Impact of Formal and Semi-Formal Finance on Performance of Village Sandouq Services: A Case of A North Kordofan Rural Development Project (unpublished master thesis). University of Kordofan El Obied, Sudan.

Elhiraika, Adam B. and Ahmed. Sayed A. (1998): Agricultural Credit Under Economic Liberalization and Islamization in Sudan. AERC Research Paper No. 79. African Economic Research Consortium Nairobi, Kenya.

Elhiraika, Adam B. (2003). On the Experience of Islamic Agricultural Finance in Sudan: Challenges and Sustainability. Islamic Development Bank, Islamic Research and Training Institute Research Paper No. 63.

Ellis, Frank and Freeman, H. Ade (eds.) (2005): Rural Livelihoods and Poverty Policies. Routledge Studies in Development Economics. Routledge London and New York.

Ellis, Frank (2000): Rural Livelihoods and Diversity in Developing Countries. Oxford University Press Oxford, UK.

Eltigani, Mahgoub and Safiidin, Osman (2009): The Sudanese Human Rights Quarterly issue 29. An ad hoc publication issued by Sudan Human Rights Organization Cairo, Egypt.

Eltigani, S. Mohamed and Fadalla, Bashir O. M (1989): Problems Arresting Private Sector Development in Western Sudan. Sudan Economy Research Group. Discussion Paper No. 13. University of Bremen, Germany.

Emery, Douglas. R. and Finnerty, John D. (1991): Principles of Finance: With Corporate Application. Wes Publishing St. Paul, MN.

Evers, Hans-Dieter and Schrader, Heiko (eds.) (1994): The Moral Economy of Ttrade: Ethnicity and DevelopingMmarkets. Routledge London and New York.

Eyben, Rosalind; Kabeer, Naila and Cornwall, Andrea (2008): Conceptualizing Empowerment and the Implications for Pro-Poor Growth, POVNET on empowerment, Institute of Development Studies (IDS) Sussex, UK.

Fafchamps, Marcel and Lund, S. (2000): Risk-Sharing Networks in Rural Philippines. Mimeo Oxford, UK.

Fafchamps, Marcel (1999): Rural Poverty, Risk and Development. Report submitted to FAO. FAO Economic and Social Development Paper No. 144. Food and Agriculture Organization of the United Nations Rome, Italy.

Fang, Hanming and Ke, Rongzhu (2006): The Insurance Role of ROSCAs in the Presence of CreditM: Theory and Evidence (http://www.ssc.wisc.edu/~scholz/Seminar/rosca-wisc.pdf).

Fiebig, Michael; Hannig, Alfred and Wisniwski, Sylvia (1999): Savings in the Context of Microfinance: State of Knowledge. Consultative Group to Assist the Poorest (CGAP) (http://www.gtz.de/en/dokumente/en_savings_in_context_of_MF_Fiebig.pdf and http://www.cgap.org/assets/images/savings.PDF).

Fields, Gary S. (2007): Dual Economy. Working Paper No. 17 ILR Cornell University, Ithaka NY (http://digitalcommons.ilr.cornell.edu/workingpapers/17).

Financial Sector in Sudan. http://www.sol-sd.com/print.php?a=2022.

Findlay, Jeanette and Wright, Robert E. (1994): Gender, Poverty and the Intra-Household Distribution of Resources. Discussion Paper Series No. 913. Center for Economic Policy Research London.

Flick, Uwe (2006): An Introduction to Qualitative Research. 3rd Edition. SAGE New Delhi. India.

Flick, Uwe (ed.) (2007): Designing Qualitative Research. SAGE New Delhi, India.

Fukuyama, F. (1995): Trust: The Social Virtues and the Creation of Prosperity. The Free Press New York.

Geertz, Clifford (1962). The Rotating Credit Association: A Middle Rung, in: Development. Economic Development and Cultural Change 10 (3).

Ghate, Prabhu (1994): Lending to Microenterprises through NGOs in the Philippines, in: Bouman, F. J. A and Hospes, Otto (eds.): Financial Landscapes Reconstructed: The Fine art of Mapping Development. Westview Press Boulder, CO.

Glaeser, Edward L.; Laibson, David and Sacerdote, Bruce (2000): The Economic Approach to Social Capital. Working Paper No. 7728. National Bureau of Economic Research Cambridge, UK.

Glaser, Barney and Strauss, Anselm L. (1967): The Discovery of Grounded Theory: Strategies for Qualitative Research. Aldine Publishing Chicago, IL.
Goldman, M. (2005): Imperial Nature: The World Bank's Struggles for Social Justice in the Age of Globalization. Yale University Press New Haven, CT.
Goldstein, Markus; de Janury, Alain and Sadoulet, Elisabeth (2005): Is a Friend in Need a Friend Indeed? Inclusion and Exclusion in Mutual Insurance Networks in Southern Ghana, in: Dercon, Stefan (2005): Insurance Against Poverty. Oxford University Press Oxford, UK.
Government of Sudan; United Nations Development Programme (UNDP) and United Nations Human Settlements Programme (UN-Habitat) (2002): Microfinance Policy for Sudan. Project Report No. SUD/02/003. Prepared by Anuradha Khati Rajivan and Mustafa Jamaluddeen Abukasawi.
Grameen Bank Website: http://www.grameen-info.org
Granovetter, Mark (1985): Economic Action and Social Structure: The Problem of Embeddedness, in: American Journal of Sociology 91 (3), pp. 481-510.
Grawert, Elke (1998): Making a Living in Rural Sudan: Production of Women Labour, Migration of Men and Policies for Peasants Needs. Macmillan Press London.
Green, Maia (2007): Representing Poverty and Attacking Representations: Perspectives on Poverty from Social Anthropology, in: Hulme, David and Toye, John (2007): Understanding Poverty and Wellbeing: Bridging the Disciplines. Routledge London and New York.
Groot, Wim; Brink, Henriette Maassen van den and Praag, Bernard van (2007): The Compensating Income Variation of Social Capital. Center for Economic Studies and IFO Institute for Economic Research, CESIFO Working PNo. 1889.
Grootaert, Christiaan and Bastelaer, Thierry van (eds.) (2002): The Role of Social Capital in Development. Cambridge University Press Cambridge, UK.
GTZ (Deutsche Gesellschaft für technische Zusammenarbeit) and FAO (Food and Agriculture Organization) (2004): Agriculture Production Lending: A toolkit for local officers and loan portfolio managers. Pact Publications, USA.
GTZ (Deutsche Gesellschaft für technische Zusammenarbeit) (2002): Microfiance in the Context of Financial Systems Development, Eschborn, Germany.
Gugerty, Mary Kay (2005): You Can't Save Alone: Community in Rotating Savings and Credit Associations in Kenya. http://www.sscnet.ucla.edu/polisci/wgape/papers/2_Gugerty.pdf
Guiso. Liugi; Sapienza, Paola and Zingales, Luigi (2000): The Role of Social Capital in Financial Development. Working Paper No. 7563. National Bureau of Economic Research Cambridge, UK.
Haan, Arjan de (2000): Migrants, Livelihoods and Rights: The Relevance of Migration in DevelopmentP. Social Development Department. Social Development Working Paper No. 4.
Haan, H. de and Long, N. (eds.) (1997): Images and Realities of Rural Life. Van Gorcum Assen, Netherlands, pp. 1-20.
Haas, Hein de (2008): Migration and Development: A Theoretical Perspective. International Migration Institute Working Papers No. 9, Oxford UK.
Hanifan, Lyda Judgson (1920): The Community Center. Silver Burdett and Co. Boston, MA.
Hassan, Ashraf and Hamed, Abdalla (2004): Livelihood Characteristics of Sedentary Rrural Farm Household in North Kordofan State (unpublished M.Sc. thesis). University of Kordofan El Obied, Sudan.
Heffernan, Shelagh (2000): A Characteristics Definition of Financial Markets, in: Blake, David (ed.): Finance: A Characteristics Approach. Routledge International Studies in Money and Banking London and New York.
Heidhues, Franz (1994): Consumption Credit in Rural Financial Market Development, in: Bouman, F. J. A and Hospes, Otto (eds.): Financial Landscapes Reconstructed: The Fine art of Mapping Development. Westview Press Boulder, CO.
Helms, Brigit (2006): Access for All: Building Inclusive Financial Systems. Conductive Group to Assist the Poor (CGAP). Capturing 10 years of CGAP experience. The International Bank for Reconstruction and Development. World Bank Washington, DC.
Hendriks, Maaike (1994): Trade Arrangements and Interlinked Credit in the Philippines, in: Bouman, F. J. A and Hospes, Otto (eds.): Financial Landscapes Reconstructed: The Fine art of Mapping Development. Westview Press Boulder, CO.

Hishigsuren, Gaamaa (2006): Transformation of Micro-Finance Operations from NGO to Regulated MFI. Paper sets the agenda for the workshop at Microcredit Summit in 2006 IDEAS. USA.
Hodgson, Goffrey M. (2007): Meanings of Methodological Individualism, in: Journal of Economic Methodology 14 (2), pp. 211-226.
Hopkins, Michael and Hoeven. Rolph ven der (1983): Basic Needs in Development Planning. A study prepared for the ILO office within the framework of the World Employment Programme. Gower Publication Aldershot, England.
Hulme, David and Toye, John (2007): Understanding Poverty and Wellbeing: Bridging the Disciplines. Routledge London and New York, NY.
Ibrahim. Bedr; El Din, A. and Arbab, Faris I. B. (2006): Impacts of Macroeconomic Policies on Microfinance in Sudan. Paper Prepared for UNICONS Consultancy Ltd. Khartoum, as part of the Project "Formulation of a Vision for the Development and Expansion of the Microfinance. Sector in Sudan" sponsored by the Central Bank of Sudan.
IFAD (2007): Rural Poverty in the Sudan. http://www.ruralpovertyportal.org/web/guest/country/home/tags/sudan
IFAD Website: www.ifad.org.
IFAD (2002): IFAD Strategy for Rural Poverty Reduction in Western and Central Africa, IFAD Khartoum, Sudan.
IFAD (2004): Western Sudan Resource Management Programm Appraisal Volume I: Main Report Draft. Near East and North Africa Division. Project Management Department Khartoum, Sudan.
IFAD (2007a): Al Dagag Village Fund Report. IFAD Khartoum, Sudan (in Arabic).
IFAD (2007b): Enabling the Rural Pto Overcome Poverty in Sudan, IFAD Khartoum, Sudan
IFAD (2007c): Evaluation of the Rural Finance Component, prepared by Swandip Sinha. IFAD Supervision Report. IFAD Khartoum, Sudan.
IFAD (2008): North Kordofan Rural Development Project. Al Dagag Report. IFAD Khartoum, Sudan (in Arabic).
IFAD (2009): Gender and Rural Microfinance: Reaching and Empowering Women, A Guide for Practitioners. IFAD Rome.
Ikpeleu, Ike (2002): The Nigerian Agricultural and Cooperative Bank Limited, in: Coetzee, Gerhard (ed.): Agricultural Development Banks in Africa: The Way Forward. African Rural and Agricultural Credit Association Nairobi, Kenya.
Illy, H. F. (1983): How to Build in the Germs of Failure: Credit Cooperatives in French Cameroon, in: Pischke, J. D. von; Adams, D. W. and Donald, G. (eds.): Rural Financial Markets in Developing Countries. Johns Hopkins University Press Baltimore, MD, pp. 296-301.
Imady, Omar and Seibel, Hans-Dieter (2006): Principles and Products of Islamic Finance. University of Cologne, Development Research Center. Köln, Germany. (http://www.uni-koeln.de/ew-fak/aef/06-2006/20061%20Principles%20and%20products%20of%20Islamic%20finance.pdf)
Johnson, Susan and Rogaly, Ben (1997): Microfinance and Poverty Reduction. Oxfam UK and Ireland.
Kabeer, Naila (1994): Reversed Realities: Gender Hierarchies in Development Thought. Verso New York.
Kabeer, Naila (2001): Conflict Over Credit: Re-evaluating the Empowerment Potential of Loans to Women in Rural Bangladesh, in: World Development 29 (1).
Kalajian, Lisa (2007): Thomas Dichter of the Washington DC-based Think Tank the Cato Institute Calls Potential of Microfinance "Grossly Overestimated". Microcapital Monitor 26/02/2007 (http://microcapitalmonitor.com/cblog/index.php?/archives/674-Thomas-Dichter-of-the-Washington-DC-based-Think-Tank-the-Cato-Institute-Calls-Potential-of-Microfinance-Grossly-Overestimated.html)
Kandiyoti, Deniz (1988): Bargaining with Patriarchy, in: Gender and Society 2 (3), pp. 274-290.
Kelle, Udo (2007): "Emergence" vs. "Forcing" of Empirical Data? A Crucial Problem of "Grounded Theory" Reconsidered, in: Mey, G. and Mruck, K. (eds.): Grounded Theory Reader. Center for Historical Social Research. The Official Journal of Quantum and Interquant, Supplement No. 19.
Kevane, Michael (1993): Is the Sheil a Shill? Informal Credit in Rural Sudan, in: The Journal of Developing Areas 27, pp. 515-534.

Khanker, S. and Pitt, M. (1998): The Impact of Group-Based Credit Programs on Poor Households in Bangladesh: Does the Gender of Partcipants Matter?, in: Journal of Political Economy 106 (5), pp. 958-996.

Kimuyu, Peter Kiko (1999): Rotating Savings and Credit Organizations in Rural East Africa World Development. 27 (7), pp. 1299-1308.

Klonner, Stefan (2003): Rotating Savings and Credit Associations when Participants are Risk Averse, in: International Economic Review 44 (3), pp. 979-1005.

Klonner, Stefan (2001): Essays on Rotating Savings and Credit Associations (doctoral dissertation). Department of Economics, Ruprecht-Karls Universität Heidelberg, Germany.

Konseiga, Adama (2005): Household Migration Decisions as Survival Strategy: The Case of Burkina Faso. Forschungsinstitut zur Zukunft der Arbeit (Institute for the Study of Labor). Discussion Paper Series IZA DP No. 1819.

Krahnen, Jan Pieter and Schmidt, Reinhard H. (1994): Development Finance as Institution Building: A New Approach to Poverty-Oriented Banking. Westview Press Boulder, CO.

Krantz, Lasse (2001): The Sustainable Livelihood Approach to Poverty Reduction: An Introduction. Swedish International Development Cooperation Agency Division for Policy and Socio-economic Analysis (http://www.forestry.umn.edu/prod/groups/cfans/@pub/@cfans/@forestry/documents/asset/cfans_asset_202603.pdf).

Lakwo, Alfred and Haan, Leo de (2010): Rethinking the Impacts of Microfinance in Africa: Business Change or Social Emancipation, in: European Journal of Development Research 22, pp. 529-545.

Lapenu, Cecile (2002): The Microfinance Revolution: Implications for the Role of the State, in: Zeller, Manfred and Meyer, Richard (eds.): The Triangle of Microfinance: Financial Sustainability, Outreach and Impact. The International Food Policy Research Institute. John Hopkins University Press Baltimore, MD.

Ledgerwood, Joanna and White, Victoria (2006).: Transforming Microfinance Iinstitutions: Providing Full Financial Services to the Poor. The International Bank for Reconstruction and Development. The World Bank and Microfinance Network. Washington, DC.

Levy, Fred (2002): Apex Institutions in Microfinance. CGAP Occasional Paper No. 6, Washington, DC.

Library of Congress, Federal Research Division (2004): Country Profile Sudan. . http://memory.loc.gov/frd/cs/profiles/Sudan.pdf

Long, Norman (1972): Introduction to the Sociology of Rural Development. Manchester University Press Manchester, UK.

Lont, Hotze and Hospes, Otto (eds.) (2004): Livelihood and Microfinance: Anthropological and Social Perspectives on Saving and Debt. Eburon Academic Publishers Delft, Netherlands.

Loury, Glenn (1992), The Economics of Discrimination: Getting to the Core of the Problem, in: Harvard Journal of African-American Public Policy 1, pp. 91-110.

Mavrotas, George and Kelly, Roger (2001): Savings Mobilization and Financial Sector Development: The Nexus, in: Savings and Development 25 (1).

Mayer, R. L. (2001): Micro-Finance, Poverty Alleviation and Improving Food Security: Implications for India, in: Lal, R. (ed.): Food Security and Environmental Quality. CRC Press Boca Raton, FL.

McLeod, Ross. H. (1994): A Changing Financial Landscape: The Evolution of Finance Policy in Indonesia, in: Bouman, F. J. A and Hospes, Otto (eds.): Financial Landscapes Reconstructed: The Fine art of Mapping Development. Westview Press Boulder, CO.

Mey, G. and Mruck, K. (eds.) (2007): Grounded Theory Reader. Center for Historical Social Research. The Official Journal of Quantum and Interquant, Supplement No. 19.

Meyer, Richard L.; Graham, Douglas H. and Cuevas, Carlos E. (1992): A Review of the Literature on Financial Markets and Agribusiness Development in Sub-Saharan Africa: Lessons Learned and Suggestions for an Analytical Agenda. Economics and Sociology Occasional Paper No. 2008. Rural Finance Program. Department of Agricultural Economics and Rural Sociology, Ohio State University Columbus, OH.

MFU Website: http://www.mfu.gov.sd/

Mills, Albert J.; Durepos, Gabrielle and Wiebe, Elden (2010): Encyclopedia of Case Study Research. Volume 1. SAGE London.
Ministry of Agriculture, North Kordofan State (2009): North Kordfoan Sustainable Rural Development Project Report. Khartoum, Sudan.
Ministry of Finance and National Economy (MOF) (2002): Sudan Economic Potential and Development Prosepects. MOF Khartoum, Sudan.
Moll, Henk. A. J. (1994): The Performance of Banks in Rural Financial Markets, in: Bouman, F. J. A and Hospes, Otto (eds.): Financial Landscapes Reconstructed: The Fine art of Mapping Development. Westview Press Boulder, CO.
Morduch, J. (1995): Income Smoothing and Consumption Smoothing, in: Journal of Economic Perspectives 9 (3), pp. 103-114.
Morduch, J. (1999): The Microfinance Promise, in: Journal of Economic Literature 37, pp. 1569-1614.
Morduch, J. (2000): The Microfinance Schism, in: World Development 28 (4), pp. 617-629.
Moser, Caroline (1993): Gender Planning and Development: Theory, Practice and Training. Routledge London and New York http://awidme.pbworks.com/w/page/36321785/Moser-Gender-Planning
Mutunhu, T. E. (2002): Agribank of Zimbabwe, in: Coetzee, Gerhard (ed.): Agricultural Development Banks in Africa: The Way Forward. African Rural and Agricultural Credit Association Nairobi, Kenya.
Nagarajan, Geetha and Meyer, Richard L. (2005): Rural Finance: Recent Advances and Emerging Lessons, Debates and Opportunities. Working Paper No. AEDE-WP-0041-05. Department of Agricultural. Environmental. and Development Economics. Ohio State University. Columbus OH.
National Bank of Sudan (NBS) (2007): Sudan Economic Report http://www.banqueaudi.com
Naudé, Wim; Santos-Paulino, Amelia U. and McGillivray, Mark (2008): Vulnerability in Developing Countries. United Nations University. Research Brief No. 2. New York.
North Kordofan State (NKS) Government (2008): Report 2008. North Kordofan State Development Plan & Urban Structural Plan.
Nussbaum. Martha C. (2005): Capacities and Fundamental Entitlements: Sen and Social Justice, in: Agarwal, Bina; Humphries, Hane and Robeyns, Ingrid (2005): Amartya Sen's Work and Ideas: A Gender Perspective. Routledge London and New York.
Olubiyo, S. O. and Hill, G. P. (2000): The Operation of Co-operative Savings and Credit Association in Kwara and Kogi States Nigeria, in: Savings and Development24 (2).
Osman, Ahmed Abu Hassan (2002): Rural Poverty Among Family and Male Headed Household in Shikan Province (unpublished M.Sc. thesis). University of Kordofan. El Obied, Sudan.
Ozturk, Ibrahim (2008): Global Financial Crisis Highlights Benefits of Islamic Finance. http://www.todayszaman.com/tz-web/yazarDetay.do?haberno=156567.
PaanLuel Wël: South Sudanese Blogger (2011):The Second Republic's Open Wounds. http://paanluelwel2011.wordpress.com/2011/08/19/sudan-sets-3-years-to-overcome-eco-impact-of-south-sudan-separation/
Pagura, Maria and Kirsten. Marié (2006): Formal—Informal Financial Linkages: Lessons from Developing Countries, in: Small Enterprise Development 17 (1), pp. 16-29.
Pearce, Douglas (2003): Buyer and Supplier Credit to Farmers: Do Donors Have a Role to Play? Paving the Way Forward for Rural Finance. Paper prepared for International Conference Nagarajan & Meyer on Best Practices, Washington, DC, June 2-4 2003 (www.basis.wisc.edu/live/rfc/cs_15b.pdf).
Pischke, J. D. von (1991): Finance at the Frontier: Debt Capacity and the Role of Credit in the Private Economy. World Bank. EDI Seminar Series. Washington, DC.
Pischke, J. D. von (1992): ROSCAs: State of the Art Financial Intermediation, in: Adams, Dale W. and Fitchett, Delbert A. (eds.): Informal Finance in Low Income Countries. Westview Press Boulder, CO.
Pischke, J. D. von; Yaron, Jacob and Zander, Rauno M. (1998): Why Credit Project Repayment Performance Declines, in: Savings and Development 22 (2).
Pischke. J. D. von; Schneider, Hartmut and Zander, Rauno M. (1997). Introductory Interview: Principles and Perspectives, in: Schneider, Helmut (ed.): Microfinance for the Poor? Development Centre Seminars. OECD and IFAD Paris, France.
Polanyi, Karl (1977): The Livelihood of Man, edited by Harry W. Pearson. Academic Press New York.

Punch, Keith (2005): Introduction to Social Research: Qualitative and Quantitative Approaches, 2nd Edition. SAGE London.
Putnam, Robert D. (1993): The Prosperous Community: Social Captial and Public Life, in: American Prospect 13, pp. 35-42.
Putnam, R.; Leonardi, R.; Nanetti, R. Y. (1993): Making Democracy Work. Princeton University Press Princeton, NJ.
Quibria, M. G. (2003). The Puzzle of Social Capital: A Critical Review. ERD Working Paper No. 40. Asian Development Bank Manila, Philippines.
Rabby, Talukder Golam; Azam, Nurul Mohammad; Mahbuba, Yeasmin;Hoque, Mohammad Ziaul (2010). Decision Making Method in Seasonal-Domestic-Migration: A Critical Appraisal, in: International Review of Business Research Papers 6(6).
Rahman, Abdur (1995): Principles of Islamic Banking, in: Nida'ul Islam 10 (http://abdurrahman.org/economics/principlesIslamicBanking.html)
Rahman, Aminur (2004): Microcredit and Poverty Reduction: Trade-off Between Building Institutions and Reaching the Poor, in: Lont, Hotze and Hospes, Otto (eds.): Livelihood and Microfinance: Anthropological and Social Perspectives on Saving and Debt. Eburon Academic Publishers Delft, Netherlands.
Rawls, J. (1971). A Theory of Justice. Harvard University Press Cambridge, MA.
Rehfisch, F. (1980): Rotating Credit Associations in the Three Towns, in: Pons, Valdo (ed.): Urbanization and Urban Life in Sudan. University of Hull, Hull, UK.
Rhyne, Elisabeth and Otero, Maria (1994): The New World of Micro Enterprise Finance: Building Healthy Financial Institutions for the Poor. Kumarian Press West Hartford, CT.
Robinson, Marguerite (2001): The Microfinace Revolution: Sustainable Finance for the Poor. InterAct Washington, DC.
Robinson, Marguerite (2009): Supply and Demand in Microfinance: The Case for Financial System Approach, in: Hulme, David and Toye, John: Understanding Poverty and Wellbeing: Bridging the Disciplines. Routledge London and New York.
Rosenberg, Richard (2006): Aid Effectiveness in Microfinance: Evaluating Microcredit Projects of the World Bank and the United Nations Development Program. Focus Note 35. CG Washington, DC.
Roy, Ananya (2010): Poverty Capital: Microfinance and the Making of Development. Routledge London and New York.
Rutherford, Stuart (1999): The Poor and Their Money: An Easy About Financial Services for the Poor People. The Department of International Development New Delhi, India.
Rutherford, Stuart (2009): The Poor and Their Money. Practical Action Publications Warwickshire, UK.
Rychard, Anderze (2006): Social Capital and Institutions: A Tentative Analysis of the Polish case. Discussion Papers No. P2006-011. Wissenschaftszentrum fur Sozialforschung (WZB) Berlin, Germany.
Saith, Ruhi (2007): Capabilities: The Concept and Its Implementation, in: Stewart, Fances; Saith, Ruhi and Harriss-White, Barbara (eds.): Defining Poverty in the Developing World. Palgrave Macmillan. New York.
Saleem, S. T. (1987): On the Determination of Interest Rates in Rural Credit Markets: A Case Study from the Sudan, in: Cambridge Journal of Economics 11 (165,172).
Sander, Cerstina and Maimbo, Samuel Munzele (2003): Migrant Labor Remittances in Africa: Reducing Obstacles to Developmental Contributions. Africa Region Working Paper Series No. 64.
Sarantakos, S. (1993): Social Research. Palgrave Macmillan New York.
Schmidt, Reinhard H. and Kropp, Erhard (eds.) (1987): Rural Development: Guiding Principles. GTZ Rural Development Series Eschborn, Germany.
Schmidt, Reinhard H. and Zeitinger, C. P. (1994). Critical Issues in Small and Micro Business Finance. IPC Publications. Frankfurt, Germany.
Schneider, Helmut (ed.). (1997): Microfinance for the Poor? Development Centre Seminars, OECD and IFAD Paris, France.

Schreiner, Mark and Nagarajan, Geetha (1997): Predicting Creditworthiness with Publically Observable Characteristics: Evidence from ASCRAs and ROSCAs in Gambi, in:. Savings and Development 22 (4).
Schreiner, M. (2005): Measuring Saving, in: Savings and Development 29 (1), pp. 21-38.
Schultz, Ulrike (2005): Buying Food and Stretching the Money: Changing Gender Roles in Sudanese Households, in: Kracht, Uwe and Schulz, Manfred (eds.): Food and Nutrition Security in the Process of Globalization and Urbanization. LIT Muenster, Germany.
Schultz, Ulrike; Makkawi, Asia and Elfatih, Taysser (2008): Women and Finance in Rural and Urban Sudan: A Case Study in Greater Omdurman and Khartoum. Humboldt University Berlin. Working Paper No. 87/2008. Berlin, Germany.
Scoones, Ian (1998): Sustainable Rural Livelihoods: A Framework for Analysis. Institute of Development Studies IDS Working Paper No. 72. Sussex, UK.
Seebens, Holger (2009): The Economics of Gender and the Household in Developing Countries. Peter Lang. Frankfurt, Germany.
Seibel, Hans Dieter and Parhusip, Uben (1992). Linking formal and informal finance: An Indonesian Example, in: Adams, Dale W. and Fitchett, Delbert A. (eds.): Informal Finance in Low Income Countries. Westview Press Boulder, CO.
Seibel, Hans Dieter (1994). From Cheap Credit to Easy Money: How to Undermine Rural Finance and Development, in: Bouman, F. J. A and Hospes, Otto (eds.): Financial Landscapes Reconstructed: The Fine art of Mapping Development. Westview Press Boulder, CO.
Seibel, Hans Dieter (2000): Agricultural Development Banks: Close Them or Rreform Them? Finance and Development 37 (2).
Sen, Amartya (1980): Famines, in: World Development 8,. pp. 613-621.
Sen, Amartya (1982): Poverty and famines: An Essay on entitlement and deprivation. Oxford University Press. Oxford UK.
Sen, Amartya (1993): Capability and Wellbeing, in: Nussbaum, Martha C. and Sen, Amartya: The Quality of Life. The United Nations University. Oxford University Press Oxford, UK.
Sen, Amartya (2005): Capabilities, Lists and Public Rreason: Continuing the Conversation, in: Agarwal, Bina; Humphries, Hane and Robeyns, Ingrid (2005): Amartya Sen's Work and Ideas: A Gender Perspective. Routledge London and New York.
Sen, Amartya (2006): Conceptualizing and Measuring Poverty, in: Grusky, B. David and Kanbur, Ravi (eds.): Poverty and Inequality. Stanford University Press. Stanford, CA, pp. 30-46.
Shankland, Alex (2000):Analyzing Policy for Sustainable Livelihoods. Institute of Development Studies. Research Report No. 49. Sussex, UK.
Sharma, S. and Chamala, S. (1998): Moneylender and Banker in Rural India: The Images from Below, in: Savings and Development 22 (1).
Shete, N.B. (1999): Alternative Models of Micro-Finance: Experiences of Indian Commercial Banks, in: Savings and Development 23 (4).
Siddig, El Fatih Ali; El-Harizi, Khalid and Parto, Bettina (2007): Managing Conflict Over Natural Resources in Greater Kordofan Sudan: Some Recurrent Patterns and Governance Implications. IFPRI Discussion Paper No. 00711.
Stark, Oded (1991): The Migration of Labour. Basil Blackwell Oxford UK.
Steinwand, Dirk (1994): Moneylending and Modern Times: Informal Credit in Thailand, in: Bouman, F. J. A and Hospes, Otto (eds.): Financial Landscapes Reconstructed: The Fine art of Mapping Development. Westview Press Boulder, CO.
Stewart, Frances (1985): Planning to Meet Basic Meeds. The Macmillan Press London.
Stewart, Frances; Saith, Ruhi and Harriss-White, Barbara (eds.) (2007): Defining Poverty in the Developing World. Plagrave Macmillan. New York. USA.
Stiansen, Endre and Kevane, Michael (eds.) (1998): Kordofan Invaded: Peripheral Incorporation and Social Transformation in Islamic Africa, Bril Leiden, Netherlands.
Strauss, Anselm and Conbin, Juliet (1990): Basics of Qualitative Research: Grounded Theory Procedure and Techniques. SAGE London.
Strauss, Anselm and Corbin, Juliet (1998): Basics of Qualitative Research: Techniques and Procedures for Developing Grounded Theory. SAGE London.
Strauss, Anselm and Corbin, Juliet (1997): Grounded Theory in Practice. SAGE London.

Suleyman, Gaafar Bashier (2002). The Role of Child Friendly Village Initiatives to Achieve Rural Development: A Case Study of North Kordofan State (unpublished M.Sc. thesis). University of Khartoum Khartoum, Sudan.

Swift, Jeremy (1989): Why Are Rural People Vulnerable to Famine? in: IDS Bulletin 20 (2).

Thankom, Arun; Hulme, David; Imran, Matin and Rutherford, Stuart (2009): Finance for the Poor: the Way Forward? In: Hume, David and Thankom, Arun (eds.): Microfinance: A Reader. Routledge London and New York.

Tocqueville, Alexis de (1945): Of the Use Which the Americans Make of Public Associations in Civil Life, of the Relation Bpublic Association and the Newspapers, Relation of Civil to Poitical Association and How the Amercians Combat Individiualisim by Principle of Self-Interest Rightly Understood, in Phillips Bradley (ed.): Democracy in America, Volume 2.

UN (2010): The Rural Poverty Report (http://www.ifad.org/rpr2011/)

UNA GB (2011): Southern Sudan Referendum Announcement: One country or two? http://unagb.wordpress.com/2011/02/08/southern-sudan-referendum-announcement-one-country-or-two/

UNA-GB Website: unagb.word press.com

UNDP (2001): Gender in Development Programme, Learning and information pack, Gender analysis (not published)

UNDP (2001): Learning and Information Pack: Gender Analysis. Gender and Development Program Report. New York.

UNDP (2008): UNDP Country Programme Document for Sudan (http://arabstates.undp.org/contents/file/CPD/Sudan_2009_2012.pdf).

UNDP (2010): Human Development Report, UNDP New York (hdr.undp.org/en/reports/global/hdr2010/).

UNDP-Sudan (2011): Status of MDGs in Sudan 2010. http://www.sd.undp.org/mdg_fact.htm

UNICONS Consultancy (2006): Situational Analysis of the Microfinance Sector in Sudan. Report prepared by Abukasawi, Mustapha, Hassan, G.; Abubaker, I.; Faris Arbab, I. B. and El Din, Ibrahim Badr A.

UNICONS Consultancy (2006): The Vision for the Development and Expansion of the Microfinance Sector in Sudan. Khartoum, Sudan.

UNICONS Consultancy (2007): Microfinance in Sudan: An Assessment of the Current Status of the Industry for the First National Consultative Forum on Microfinance. This technical note has been prepared by Caterina Meloni (World Bank), Maja Bott (UNDP) and Dirk Hansohm (UNDP). Khartoum, Sudan.

USAID and FEWS Net (2011) Sudan Security outlook http://www.fews.net/docs/Publications/Sudan_OL_2011_10_final.pdf

Vaessen, Jos (2001): Accessibility of Rural Credit in Northern Nicaragua: The Importance of Networks of Information and Recommendation, in: Savings and Development 25 (1).

Village Profile Sheets (2008): Ahfad University for Women. School of Rural Extension, Education and Development Omdurman, Sudan.

Vogel, Rober (1984): Savings Mobilization: The Forgotten Half of Rural Finance, in: Adams, Dale W.; Graham, D.H and von Pischke. J. D. (eds.): Undermining Rural Development with Cheap Credit. Westview Press Boulder, CO, pp. 248-265.

Vonderlack, Rebecca M. and Schreiner, Mark (2002): Women, Microfinance and Savings: Lessons and Proposals, in: Development in Practice 121(5).

WCED (1987): Global Policies for Sustainable Agriculture, a Report of the Advisory Panel on Food Security. Agriculture, Forestry and Environment to the World Commission on Environment and Development, Zed Boooks London and New York.

Weerdt, Joachim de (2005): Risk-Sharing and Endogenous Network Formation, in: Dercon, Stefan (2005): Insurance Against Poverty. Oxford University Press Oxford, UK.

Wilmington, Marten W. (1955): Aspects of Moneylending in Northern Sudan, in: Middle East Journal Spring 1955, pp. 139-145.

Wisner, Ben; Blaikie, Piers; Cannon, Terry and Davis, Ian (2004): At Risk: Natural Hazards, People's Vulnerability and Disasters. Routledge London and New York.

Wright, Graham A. N. (2000): Microfinance Systems: Designing Quality Financial Services for the Poor. Zed Books Dhaka, Bangladesh.

Yaron, Jacob Benjamin; McDonald, P. Jr. and Piprek. Gerda L. (1997): Rural Finance: Issues, Design and Best Practices. Environmentally and Socially Sustainable Development Studies and Monographs Series No. 14. World Bank. Washington, DC.

Zander, Rauno (1994): Barriers to Credit Access in Rural Sri Lanka, in: Bouman, F. J. A and Hospes, Otto (eds.): Financial Landscapes Reconstructed: The Fine art of Mapping Development. Westview Press Boulder, CO.

Zander, Rauno (1997): Integrating the Poor Into the Rural Finance Mainstream: Issues and Options, in: Schneider, Helmut (ed.): Microfinance for the Poor? Development Centre Seminars. OECD and IFAD. Paris, France.

Zeller, Manfred and Sharma, M. (1998): Rural Finance and Poverty Alleviation. Food Policy Report, International Food Policy Research Institute. Washington, DC, pp. 5-32.

Zeller, Manfred and Meyer, Richard L. (eds.) (2002): The Triangle of Microfinance: Financial Sustainability, Outreach and Impact. John Hopkins University Press Baltimore, MD and London.

Zhang, Yuan and Wan, Guanghua (2008): Can We Predict Vulnerability to Poverty? United Nations University – WIDER Research Paper No. 2008/82.

Appendix: Picture Album

The Village Al Dagag

Al Dagag Situated Near the Main Road Between Khartoum and El Obied, leading to Darfur

Main Street

Al Dagag Community

Al Dagag Men Gathering

Women Coffee Gathering the Researcher Conducted 2007

Singing and Dancing during a Sandouq Meeting

Al Dagag Households

Simple Furniture Inside Houses

Where Livestock is Kept in the Household

Old Building Technique

New Building Technique

Livelihood in Al Dagag

Traditional Farming

Traditional Crop Processing

Hassan's Water Pump (Loan Provided by the IFAD Project)

Hassan's Production 2009

Cultivation Using the Flooding of Khour Abuhabil

Helping the Wife Clean Hibiscus

The Common Place for Keeping Livestock (Mehjar)

Burned House (Common Shock)

The Khour Abuhabil during Summer

Credit and Social Services Provided by the IFAD Project in Al Dagag

IFAD's Most Successful Client and First Fridge in Al Dagag

Asha Alnoor's Shop (Built with Profits from IFAD Project Loans)

Asha Alnoor's Stove for Making Bread (Built with Profits from IFAD Project Loans)

Asha Alnoor's Water Basin in Al Dagag (Built with Profits from IFAD Project Loans)

Isa's Generator (Loan provided by the IFAD Project)

Al Dagag Hafeer (Main Source of Drinking Water; Built by the Safe the Children and IFAD)

Al Dagag Hafeer

Al Dagag Hafeer

Transporting Water from Al Hafeer

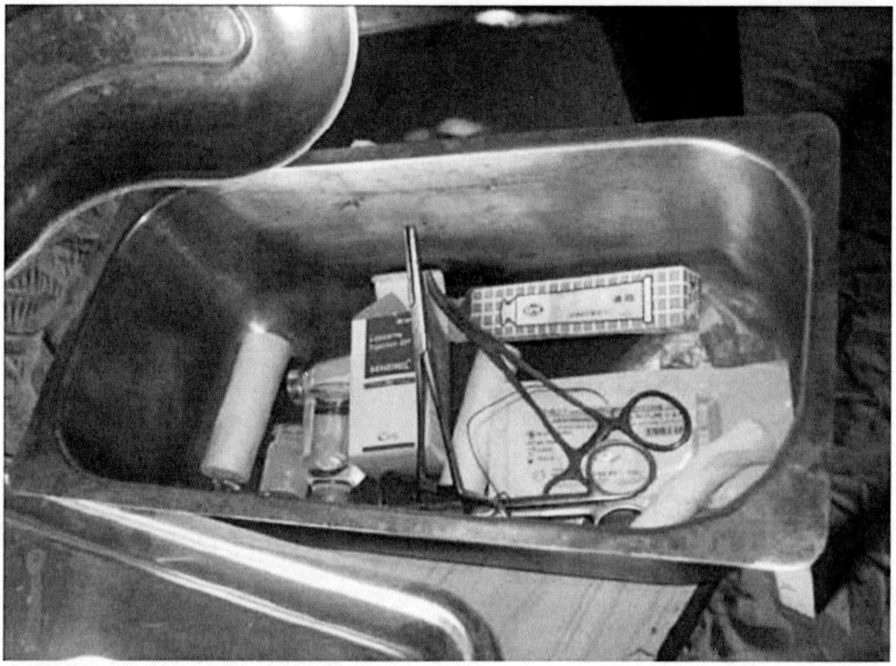

Health Assistant Tools (Provided by the IFAD Project)

Al Dagag Primary School (Built by the IFAD Project)